SOCIETY FOR NEW TESTAMENT STUDIES
MONOGRAPH SERIES

GENERAL EDITOR
G.N. STANTON

2

THE TEMPTATION AND
THE PASSION: THE MARKAN
SOTERIOLOGY

THE TEMPTATION AND THE PASSION:

THE MARKAN SOTERIOLOGY

BY

ERNEST BEST

*Professor Emeritus of Divinity and Biblical Criticism
University of Glasgow*

SECOND EDITION

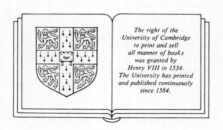

The right of the
University of Cambridge
to print and sell
all manner of books
was granted by
Henry VIII in 1534.
The University has printed
and published continuously
since 1584.

CAMBRIDGE UNIVERSITY PRESS

Cambridge
New York   Port Chester
Melbourne   Sydney

Published by the Press Syndicate of the University of Cambridge
The Pitt Building, Trumpington Street, Cambridge CB2 1RP
40 West 20th Street, New York, NY 10011, USA
10 Stamford Road, Oakleigh, Melbourne 3166, Australia

First published 1965
This edition published 1990

Printed in Great Britain at the University Press, Cambridge

British Library cataloguing in publication data

Best, Ernest, *1917*–
The temptation and the passion – 2nd ed.
1. Bible. N.T. Gospels. Special subjects: Jesus Christ.
Passion
I. Title   II. Series
232.9'6

Library of Congress cataloguing in publication data

Best, Ernest.
The Temptation and the Passion: the Markan soteriology / by
Ernest Best. – 2nd ed.
p.   cm. – (Monograph series / Society for New Testament
Studies: 2)
Includes bibliographical references.
ISBN 0 521 38360 9
1. Bible. N.T. Mark – Criticism, interpretation, etc.
2. Salvation – Biblical teaching. 3. Jesus Christ – Passion.
4. Jesus Christ – Temptation. I. Title. II. Series: Monograph
series (Society for New Testament Studies): 2.
BS2585.6.S25B47 1990
226.3'066 – dc20   90–30941 CIP

ISBN 0 521 38360 9

WG

CONTENTS

PREFACE TO THE FIRST EDITION

OUR primary concern in the following essay is with the soteriology of Mark: What does Mark hold to have been achieved by the life, death and resurrection of Jesus the Christ? Since it is often held that the death and resurrection of Jesus signalled his defeat of Satan, it is necessary to begin with a study of the Markan Temptation narrative; this is followed by an examination of the general place in the Gospel of demonic forces and of Satan. Thereafter we turn to a more direct consideration of our main aim.

Because we are not interested in what Jesus himself thought of the meaning and purpose of his life and death but only with the view that Mark adopts we have to proceed with caution. It is necessary to distinguish in relation to the pericopae of the Markan account the form in which the tradition reached him and the modifications he gave to it. Thus in any particular incident we may have to separate Mark's view of the incident from its original place in the life of Jesus and also from the varying modifications which thereafter it may have received in the early Church. To single out the Markan contribution we need to look at the phrases by which Mark has joined together the incidents he uses; these appear at the beginnings and ends of pericopae: the Markan seams. We also examine the explanatory additions Mark may have made within incidents in order to align them with his main purpose. This by no means exhausts the Markan editing. Since we have no reason to assume that Mark had only at his disposal the incidents he records we must examine his selection of material. Following on that we must consider the order in which he has put together the incidents he chooses, for the relationship of one incident to those which precede and follow it may express Mark's purpose. But since Mark cannot be regarded as being out of touch with the material he uses we must assume that in large part he agrees with it, and where there are within it statements of the function and activity of Jesus we must assume that he accepts these as true statements with which he agrees (we may note how Luke omits Mark x. 45); this is only to say that Mark must have taken a positive and not a negative attitude to what he records; it is incumbent on any alternative view to show actual discrepancy between the material and the editorial work. From that we go on to discuss the titles and names which Mark uses to describe Jesus; all writers and speakers have favourite titles to use of Jesus and in their choice they disclose something of their theology. Finally we look briefly at the Christian community which Mark supposes to have come into existence through the preaching of the Gospel; in what way is that which Jesus has achieved for it reflected in its life?[1]

We may state our problem somewhat differently by saying that we are seeking to determine the Markan kerugma. Within the early Church there would appear to have been a number of different forms of the kerugma.[2] Paul preserves two in I Cor. xv. 3 f. and Phil. ii. 5–11; the first of these would appear to be primarily concerned with human sin, the second with triumph over cosmic forces of evil. In what form did Mark present the kerugma? We are not concerned with the whole of the kerugma, which in some of its forms contained a reference to the eventual return of Jesus. Rather we are setting out to see what the Markan kerugma says about what Jesus has already accomplished. To use a traditional phrase, we are seeking what Mark holds to be 'the benefits of Christ's Passion'. This is not an inaccurate phrase because Mark's Gospel is really a Passion story with a preliminary introduction leading up to the Passion.[3]

We do not view Mark as the last of a series of editors who have worked over the material, introducing new material and modifying what the previous author had put together, nor have we any confidence in elaborate theories of an Ur-Markus. We regard Mark as himself the first to put together the material he uses to make a Gospel, and we assume that he did this in Rome.

---

[1] It will be seen that our methodology differs from that of Schreiber (pp. 154 f.). Justification for any methodology can only lie in the results achieved. It may be noted that Schreiber does not abide by his own chosen course. He considers that where Matthew or Luke changes Mark this is significant for Markan theology. Yet in discussing the significance for Mark of the death of Christ he makes no use of Mark x. 45 which Luke omits!

[2] Cf. p. 128, n. 6.

[3] Cf. M. Kähler's dictum that the Gospels are 'Passionsgeschichten mit ausführlicher Einleitung'.

This is not to say that Mark could treat incidents in an entirely free way; obviously the Passion had to come at the end and the Baptism by John at the beginning, but the Temptation might have been retained until later in the story or spread out through the Gospel. Prior to Mark some of the material may have already existed in collections, for example, ii. i–iii. 6, or the Passion story. In many ways Mark was thus bound by the tradition which came to him, but yet he remained a real author, not just a recorder of tradition. It was his purpose to proclaim the Gospel through the events which he believed, rightly or wrongly, to have happened in the life of Jesus. (We must assume that Mark believes that the incidents he uses actually happened.) His Gospel is itself kerugma. This, of course, does not mean that it was intended only for missionary use; it was intended for use within the community and by the community in its missionary outreach. The strict line which is sometimes drawn between kerugma and didache is not applicable here; every sermon will contain both, and both are contained in Mark. We use kerugma not then in the narrower sense of evangelistic preaching to the outsider but in the wider sense of the essential relevance of Jesus Christ to the world and the Christian community.

All this means that we treat Mark seriously as an author. He has his place in the canon, not because he gives certain historical facts about the life of Jesus, but because, in the same sense as Paul, he preaches Christ. If Paul is viewed as inspired, then in exactly the same way we must so view Mark – though Paul and Mark make their approach to the problem of present-ing Christ in very different ways. This also means that if with any confidence we may take a text or passage of Paul as the inspired Word of God and preach it then we may do the same with Mark, not just seeking to determine the original nature of the incident or the *ipsissima verba* of Jesus, but preaching what we may term Mark's inspired comment.

On the other hand our interest in Mark as author and theologian should not be taken to imply that interest stops there. If we are in any way to seek the historical Jesus then the evidence which we have lies almost entirely in the Gospels. If we are to push back from the Gospels to Jesus then we need to disentangle, not only the influence of the early community on the material as it passed through its hands, but also the distinctive contributions of the evangelists to the material as they put together their Gospels. Any full study of a Gospel involves an examination of three factors: the evangelist's theology, the early Church's modification of the tradition, and the original event. None of these can be taken in isolation, nor can any be neglected, but at times emphasis will lie more on one than on another. If therefore we offer this as an essay in the understanding of the Markan theology we also hope that it will be useful in some small way in the quest of the historical Jesus.

Dr T. A. Burkill's *Mysterious Revelation* (Cornell, 1963) became available just as the MS was completed for the press. The leading themes of his thesis have already appeared in the numerous articles he has published and references to these will be found at relevant points. It has thus not been thought necessary to give page references to the book. The Pelican Gospel Commentary of Professor D. E. Nineham also appeared too late for me to make use of it.

My thanks are due to my wife for her careful typing of my manuscript, to Principal M. Black and Dr R. McL. Wilson, both of St Mary's College, for much useful advice and help in the preparation of the manuscript for the press; to the Rev. J. L. Bailey and the Rev. J. Roberts-Thomson for assistance in the reading of the proofs and the compilation of the indices; to the editors and printers of the Cambridge University Press for their exact work and to the congregations of Minterburn and Caledon who while I was their minister left me sufficient time to write the greater part of what is offered here.

E. B.

PREFACE TO THE SECOND EDITION

THE first edition of this book was divided into two unequal parts. Since its writing very much more attention has been paid by scholars to the second area, the Passion, than to the first, the Temptation, and so the same unequal division has been continued in this additional preface. At the time of the first edition Mark's Gospel was sometimes explained as a continual conflict or encounter between Christ and the Devil. I therefore began then by examining the place of the Devil in the Gospel, and since I concluded that views which understood the Gospel in terms of conflict accorded the Devil too prominent a position, it was necessary to go on and see if Mark presented another understanding of the death of Christ; this led to the writing of the second part of the original work.

Just prior to the first edition a new method of examining the Gospel had been evolved. Redaction criticism, or redaction composition, as it is more properly termed, was becoming the principal tool in Gospel study and being widely used to discover the particular contribution of each of the Evangelists. Today the central concern of those working on the Gospels has again changed, and the reading of each Gospel as a whole is stressed rather than the examination of the details of editing. In view of this new concern I have not attempted to go through what I previously wrote and either defend or change it in respect of the editing of individual verses; indeed so much has been written in this area that a re-examination would require the writing of a second volume longer than the original edition rather than the simple addition of a new preface. I have therefore directed my attention to the new light which is thrown on my central thesis when the Gospel of Mark is read as a whole. Even in this new area there is so much writing that it is impossible to keep fully abreast of it; if it were documented in full together with the other redactional work which has been carried out since the first edition, the footnotes would take over from the body of the text. I have sought to avoid what I now add to the original being reduced to little more than a set of lengthy footnotes or a bibliographical list of relevant literature. I trust that those whose work is not referred to, or not given the consideration they would think necessary, will forgive me. On the whole also I have tried to restrict myself, with a few essential exceptions, to what has appeared since I wrote earlier. Since I have also written elsewhere on a number of the issues which are relevant to this book, I have referred to these writings and repeated neither their argument nor their references.

As in the first edition I have made no attempt to use the results of my examination of Mark to seek the historical Jesus, though some of what I and others have done may be useful in that quest. Work on Mark's theology has paid much more attention to his christology than to his soteriology. This is probably inevitable both because of the way in which the menu for modern study of the Gospel was set by Wrede with his theory of the Messianic secret and because so much of Church discussion has centred on the person rather than the work of Christ. I have not entered into the christological field in this new preface even though some of what I earlier wrote in relation to the titles of Jesus would need revision, but have stuck closely to my soteriological brief. First-century Christians were probably more worried about the benefits of Christ's Passion than the correct title they should use to describe him. At best Mark was trying to explain to his hearers the meaning of the sonship of Jesus, which they all accepted, rather than to assert that he was God's Son; this would naturally lead to a greater concentration on his 'activity' than on his nature.

My views on the Gospel have developed during the twenty-five years since the first edition, and they will be found in detail in *Story*. In brief, I do not take Mark to have been writing to polemicise against false christological or other views, but to sustain and deepen the Christian faith of his community. Its members will already have known most, if not all, the incidents which are in the Gospel. New to them was the way in which Mark strung them together. Since the most connected section of his book is the Passion account, and since that is also our central concern, we shall later look in more detail at the relevant issues in respect of that account. However it is perhaps important to add here that I regard the Gospel as a part of early Christianity and therefore to be inexplicable without paying heed to that background. Thus when the continuity of the narrative is considered, this does not mean its continuity as a piece of literature set in a vacuum. If we wish to understand the Gospel we have to take account of more than the Gospel itself. Writer and hearers, probably a better term than 'readers', which tends to suggest the solitary reader in his own room, shared a common Christian existence which did not always need to be spelt out but which affected all their writing and listening.

THE TESTING

Most of the discussion of the temptation of Jesus has concentrated on the double tradition and the psychological nature of the temptations it depicts,[1] but attention is increasingly being given to the place which each temptation account occupies within its own Gospel. Thus while the relationship of the double tradition to Mark is still discussed as part of the wider synoptic problem, those who examine Mark's account of the Temptation are less and less inclined to see it in the light of the double tradition and explain it thereby.[2] Although there are still some who defend the view that Mark knew the double tradition, most accept his ignorance of it. If this is so, the Markan account can be viewed both as an independent account and at the same time as part of the Markan narrative.[3] Unfortunately those who treat the three accounts together and at the same time seek the special place of each in its Gospel normally give much less attention to Mark than to Matthew and Luke.

Although, when I originally wrote, the continuity of Mark's narrative was not stressed as it is today, what I then wrote was not out of line with that stress since I attempted to seek an understanding of the significance of the Temptation through what followed it in the Gospel. That Mark intended the separate

---

[1] E.g. J. Dupont, *Die Versuchungen Jesu in der Wüste* (Stuttgart, 1969); F. Neugebaur, *Jesu Versuchung: Wegentscheidung am Anfang* (Tübingen, 1986).
[2] Cf. H. Mahnke, *Die Versuchungsgeschichte im Rahmen des synoptischen Evangelien* (Frankfurt on Main), p. 23.
[3] E.g. P. Pokorný, 'The Temptation Stories and their Intention', *N.T.S.* XX (1973/4), 115–27, and most commentators on Mark.

sections of the Prologue, usually taken to be i. 1–15[1] with *vv.* 14 f. perhaps being understood as transitional, to be read as a unit is now more clearly recognised, and this is true whether it is believed Mark united the Baptism and Temptation accounts[2] or, as is more generally accepted, found them already united in the tradition. The Spirit came to Jesus at his baptism, and drove him into the wilderness and conflict with Satan;[3] then as victor he went on to proclaim the rule of God.

The root πειράζειν is used in Scripture with two basic meanings: to test and to seduce.[4] English translators of i. 12 f. have tended to give it the second sense under the influence of the Matthean and Lucan narratives. With the new willingness to view i. 12 f. as an account in its own right, an increasing number of interpreters have come to accept the first sense as at least a possible rendering and thus to see Mark as envisaging a conflict rather than an attempted seduction. In turn this has led to a greater readiness to write of a victory won by Jesus in his encounter with Satan.[5]

The biblical background to i. 12 f. is generally taken to be the picture of Jesus as the second Adam.[6] *Urzeit* and *Endzeit* should have the same pattern, and so the pre-Fall condition of Paradise has influenced the shape of the story.[7] For Mahnke the baptism

---

[1] See in particular L. E. Keck, 'The Introduction to Mark's Gospel', *N.T.S.* XII (1965/6), 352–70; R. Pesch, 'Anfang des Evangeliums Jesu Christi', *Das Markus-Evangelium* (ed. R. Pesch), pp. 311–55. W. Feneborg, *Das Markusprolog* (Munich, 1974), is an exception to this widely accepted view.

[2] This view is espoused by R. F. Collins, 'The Temptation of Jesus', *Melita Theologica* XXVI (1974), 32–45.

[3] On Satan see O. Böcher, *Christus Exorcista* (Stuttgart, 1972), in his index under 'Teufel'.

[4] E.g. Anderson; A. Feuillet, 'L'épisode de la Tentation d'après l'Evangile selon Saint Marc (1, 12–13)', *Est. Bib.* XIX (1960), 49–73.

[5] E.g. A. Vargas-Machua, 'La tentación de Jesús según Mc. 1, 12–13. Hecho real o relato de tipo haggádico?', *Estudios Eclesiásticos* XLVIII (1973), 163–90.

[6] This is strongly disputed by H.-G. Leder, 'Sünderfallerzählung und Versuchungsgeschichte: Zur Interpretation von Mc 1.12 f.', *Z.N.T.W.* LIV (1963), 185–216.

[7] E.g. Pokorný, *art. cit.*; Vargas-Machua, *art. cit.*; Pesch, p. 95 and *art. cit.*; Ernst; Gnilka; Schweizer; Lührmann; Standaert, p. 565; Kingsbury, p. 68; G. Baumbach, *Das Verständnis des Bösen in den synoptischen Evangelien* (Berlin, 1963), pp. 29 ff.; Mahnke, *op. cit.* pp. 28 ff.

is the commissioning of Jesus which gives him a unique position as Son of God; the Temptation then shows that he did not lose this position as Adam once did.[1] Others have seen the account as influenced in part or in whole by the forty years in the wilderness of the Exodus story;[2] in this way the number forty is explained as cannot be done in terms of the Paradise background. The testing of Abraham by God (Gen. xxii)[3] and Isa. lxiii–lxiv[4] have also been held to have influenced the account. Schmithals is unusual in taking the 'forty' as an indication of the totality of Jesus' work.[5] Most commentators simply regard it as a 'holy' number. If the background is Paradise, then the 'beasts' are generally regarded as friendly to Jesus,[6] but it is allowed that this in itself may be a sign of victory,[7] for they would have been 'fierce' prior to their encounter with him. While there was no eschatological expectation that Satan would be at peace with the Messiah (or God) in the End-time, it must be assumed that he was quelled only at the end of the forty days, even if the beasts can be regarded as subdued throughout that period. All this implies a certain inherent inconsistency. If Satan is present throughout the forty days as the use of the imperfect tenses suggests, then the conditions of Paradise do not truly exist; this conflicts with the idea of the beasts as peaceful throughout the

---

[1] Mahnke, *op. cit.* pp. 4 ff.

[2] Some argue for the wilderness as an unfriendly area, e.g. Derrett; R. A. Cole, *The Gospel according to St Mark* (Tyndale New Testament Commentaries; London, 1961), *ad loc.*; Lane; R. Trevijano, *Comienzo del Evangelio. Estudio sobre el prologo de san Marcos* (Burgos, 1971), pp. 181 ff. Haenchen, p. 64, argues that the wilderness is an unfriendly place.

[3] H. A. Kelly, 'The Devil in the Desert', *C.B.Q.* XXVI (1964), 190–220; Pesch, p. 96.

[4] A. Feuillet, *art. cit.*   [5] P. 93.

[6] It is argued (e.g. Mahnke, *op. cit.* p. 25) that Mark uses εἶναι μέτα with the genitive to indicate the friendly association of people with one another, but the total number of occurrences (ii. 19; iii. 14; v. 18; xiv. 67) is too small to enable a firm conclusion to be drawn in respect of Mark when there is no reason to suppose that this was a general rule in Greek. It is Mark's context which supplies the 'friendly' meaning in the other instances. The preposition signifies association without implying either friendliness or hostility; it is the context alone which indicates what meaning is intended.

[7] 'Wild beasts' can indicate either ferocious or large non-agricultural animals (Mahnke, *op. cit.* p. 214, n. 112).

period. In any case the conditions of Paradise are present by the end of the period, if we allow that Mark intended to see the Temptation in these terms. The 'wilderness' is generally taken to be symbolic rather than 'real'.[1] Mahnke[2] rejects the idea of it as an area specifically associated with demons and argues that in Mark it is rather a place of solitude and nearness to God, an eschatological location of the peace of Paradise; whether the wilderness generally indicates nearness to God in Mark or not, at i. 13 it is Satan who is mentioned as present, and not God.

Mark does not state explicitly in i. 12 f. the result of the contest;[3] this must be sought in the continuity of the narrative: either in i. 14 f., for Jesus would not have been able to proclaim the Gospel if he had not first overcome the rule of Satan,[4] or in the exorcisms, where Jesus displays his power over evil,[5] or in iii. 27, where, as was argued in the first edition, Satan is held to have been bound, thus enabling the exorcisms to take place.[6] It can also be held, in conjunction with any of these, and indeed apart from them, that Mark did not need to state a result, since all his readers knew that Jesus was stronger than Satan and the remainder of the story would have been meaningless had Jesus not conquered Satan at its beginning.

This raises the question of the activity of Satan in the remainder of Mark's account. He is often arbitrarily introduced into it because we are accustomed to think of him as the sole cause of sin and temptation (a legacy of Milton?). Now that Mark is treated on its own and not explained through the other Evangelists (in Luke Satan remains active up to and including the Cross), scholars are less and less inclined to view Satan as active throughout the whole Gospel. He is not mentioned in relation to the 'temptations' of viii. 11; x. 2;

[1] E.g. Feuillet, *art. cit.*; Gnilka.
[2] *Op. cit.* pp. 34–7.
[3] Mahnke, *op. cit.* p. 33, is exceptional in viewing the result as given by the peacefulness of the beasts.
[4] This appears to be the view of Keck, *art. cit.*, who sees the word 'Gospel' as itself expressing victory. See also Pesch, p. 98.
[5] Feuillet, *art. cit.*; Schmithals.
[6] See n. 6 p. xxii below.

xii. 15.[1] In his study of evil in the Synoptic Gospels Baumbach points out that 'the unforgivable' sin of iii. 28 f. is not traced back to Satan, and this though Satan appears in the context. Sin begins in the human heart.[2] Though Satan appears in the interpretation of the Parable of the Sower (iv. 15), it is not as the opponent of Jesus.[3] His appearance there is no more inconsistent than when he is said to be defeated in the Cross and Resurrection but is also said to continue to perplex Christians (cf. Eph. i. 21 – 3 and vi. 10 ff.). In Gethsemane Jesus is tested by God and not by Satan.[4]

[1] Pesch, *art. cit.* pp. 340 f.; Gnilka, p. 59; D. Rhoads and D. Michie, *Mark as Story: An Introduction to the Narrative of a Gospel* (Philadelphia, 1982), p. 77. G. H. Twelftree, 'EI ΔE ...ΕΓΩ ΕΚΒΑΛΛΩ ΤΑ ΔΑΙΜΟΝΙΑ' in *Gospel Perspectives*, VI (ed. D. Wenham and C. Blomberg; Sheffield, 1986), pp. 361–400, assumes that because temptation continues Satan must be seen as active therein, but Twelftree is discussing the historical life of Jesus and not the course of the Markan narrative. F. W. Danker, 'The Demonic Secret in Mark, a Reexamination of the Cry of Dereliction (15.34)', *Z.N.T.W.* XLI (1970), 45–69, is one of the few who continue to view the references to testing or tempting in these verses as induced by Satan, but he offers no precise evidence for this opinion other than that Satan's influence may be supposed even if it is not mentioned. This is to accept a view of Satan which only came into wide acceptance after the period of the N.T. He argues in more detail that since the attitude of the scribes is described as blasphemous in iii. 22 ff. this indicates that wherever blasphemy is mentioned it must be satanically motivated. He also argues that Jesus is accused in xiv. 58 of magic and so Satan is to be traced here. Since also the crucifixion is the great *peirasmos*, it must be viewed as a contest between Jesus and Satan (this assumes what needs to be proved). Against all this we need to ask why if Mark wished Satan's influence to be seen in the Passion he did not introduce him explicitly as Luke did (xxii. 3); why should an allegedly principal character be written out of the total story after once being introduced unless it is intended that he should have no further part in the story? For further criticism of Danker see G. Schneider, *Die Passion Jesu nach der drei älteren Evangelien* (Munich, 1973), p. 127. Danker's view is accepted by M. de Burgos Nuñez, 'La communión de Dios con el crucificado. Christología de Marcos 15, 22–39', *Est. Bib.* XXXVII (1978), 243–66. There are also some, e.g. L. Williamson, *Mark* (Atlanta, Georgia, 1983), p. 37, who without giving any reasons still continue to see a cosmic struggle underlying the whole Gospel, and a few others (e.g. Schenk, pp. 57 f.; Harrington, *Mark* (Wilmington, Delaware, 1979), p. 8) who simply introduce Satan into the Passion without saying why.

[2] Baumbach, *op. cit.* pp. 26, 36.

[3] *Ibid.* p. 38. The interpretation is of course pre-Markan and is another instance of the preservation by Mark of pre-Markan material; see *Disciples*, pp. 31–48.

[4] Pesch, *art. cit.* p. 341.

This leaves only viii. 33.[1] It is increasingly accepted that Satan is here only a figure of speech, for Peter is said to think *human* thoughts and not those of Satan. In the Jewish literature of the period Satan is never identified with individual people, though he may control or inhabit particular people (Apoc. Sed. v. 5; T. Naph. viii. 6; T. Asher i. 8; Asc. Isa. iii. 11).[2] In Mark demons inhabiting people are not depicted as the cause of their sin, though this is true sometimes elsewhere (T. Reub. ii – iii; T. Dan. ii – iv; I Enoch xv. 11 f.; xvi. 1; xix. 1; 1QS iv. 9 ff.), and those possessed are not exhorted to fight against demons as they would be against sin; demons are regarded purely from a soteriological angle.[3] The dualism of viii. 33 is not then between God and Satan, but between God and man. This implies that after i. 11 and iii. 27 (he is not actually present here but is discussed) Satan disappears[4] from the narrative in so far as the narrative treats Christ (he is still an opponent of believers in iv. 15), unless he can be found to be present in some way in the Passion account. Whilst this may be so for Luke (e.g. xxii. 3), it is impossible to discover his presence in Mark; when the Passion narrative is examined using the methods of literary analysis which draw out the characters involved, he does not appear among the 'adversaries' named in it.[5] This is not surprising, since he was a comparatively recent entrant into Jewish theology and had no proper equivalent in the Greco-Roman world. He could indeed be described as an opponent of the Passion kerugma (viii. 31) of suffering in that

[1] The only detailed discussion of this verse appears to be that of B. A. E. Osborne, 'Peter: Stumbling Block and Satan', *N.T.* XV (1973), 187–90, who argues that Peter is called Satan because he has identified himself with Satan, who is himself to be identified with the evil *yezer*. Gnilka comments that the reference to human thoughts is a late addition, possibly due to Mark. He notes that in early Christianity heretics were termed tools of the Devil (Rom. xvi. 17–20; II Cor. xi. 13–14; Acts xiii. 10; *Ign. Philad.*; vi. 1 f.) and that the rejection of Christ as crucified may fall in this area. W. B. Müller, 'Die christologische Absicht des Markusevangeliums und die Verklärungsgeschichte', *Z.N.T.W.* LXIV (1973), 157–93, takes this idea to indicate that the human thought of Peter is satanic.

[2] Baumbach, *op. cit.* p. 38.

[3] *Ibid.*, pp. 43–5.

[4] Lane, pp. 60 f., is exceptional in viewing the encounter with Satan as continuing throughout the remainder of the Gospel.

[5] Cf. van Iersel, pp. 174–6.

he seeks to prevent the sufferings of Jesus rather than to cause them.[1]

If Satan effectively disappears from the Gospel after i. 12 f. and if those verses are viewed as depicting conflict and victory, what is the nature of that victory? So long as the encounter with Satan in i. 12 f. was viewed as psychological temptation as in Matthew and Luke this question did not arise, because Satanic seduction could be expected to continue throughout the life of Jesus; once psychological temptation is no longer the key issue, the nature of the victory needs to be considered. Unfortunately most of those who accept i. 12 f. as representing victory fail to spell out in what they believe this consists. While it may be described as eschatological (i.e. as belonging to the End-time), this does not illuminate its nature except in so far as it implies a total victory. Attempts to state clearly the nature of the victory are not helped by Mark's failure to indicate precisely the outcome of Jesus' encounter with Satan.

An analysis of iii. 20–35 shows vv. 22–30 as the centre of a Markan sandwich. In iii. 22 the scribes criticise Jesus and in the following verses he responds with two illustrations (24 f.) and a general conclusion (26) followed by another conclusion (27). There is however a stutter in the argument at this point. While the final illustration (27) appears to take up 'house' from the preceding verses it uses it with a different sense, no longer as indicating the 'family' living in the house, but the house as 'building'. Moreover v. 27 is no longer a response to the original question of the scribes.[2] This suggests that it is an addition to the original discussion, a conclusion reinforced by its appearance in the Gospel of Thomas (logion 35) without any connection with anything similar to the preceding discussion in Mark.[3] It also appears in

---

[1] Baumbach, op. cit. pp. 29, 50.

[2] Cf. Haenchen, p. 146; A. Fuchs, Die Entwicklung der Beelzebulkontroverse bei den Synoptikern: traditionsgeschichtliche und redaktionsgeschichtliche Untersuchung von Mk 3, 22–27 und Parallelen verbunden mit der Rückfrage nach Jesus (Linz, Studien zum Neuen Testament und seiner Umwelt), pp. 103 f.

[3] The determination of its meaning in the Gospel of Thomas is difficult since it stands in isolation; equally difficult is its original meaning. Most of those who discuss the latter appear to accept its Markan context as original and so deduce the meaning from Mark. But if it did not originally belong in the present Markan context the field is wide open; it may even have been a kind of exhortation to disciples: 'Hold on to what you have; do not let your hands be tied.'

a slightly variant form in Luke xi. 19 f., though Luke may well here depend on Mark.[1] If iii. 27 existed originally as a separate logion, was it Mark who united it to vv. 22–6? As there is nothing to suggest this,[2] we may take the present connection as pre-Markan. The saying may have been created under the influence of the Old Testament (Isa. xlix. 24 f.; liii. 12; Ps. Sol. v. 3³); basic to the Old Testament imagery is the attack by Yahweh on his enemies; however in Mark the sequence of thought implies that the strong man is not God but Jesus.[4] This entails a certain amount of allegorisation, and though this may be abhorrent to modern susceptibilities, it would not have been to Mark (cf. iv. 14–20). Rhetorical analysis, if taken into account, shows v. 27 as the rhetorical centre of iii. 20–35,[5] and this would again emphasise its importance for Mark.

All interpreters seem to be agreed that iii. 27 must be related in Mark's thinking to Jesus' exorcisms, for it emerges as they are being discussed. The σκεύη must then be either the expelled demons or the people who as demon-possessed are in thrall to Satan, and the image points to the victory of Christ over the demonic world. But does it present that as a victory over Satan himself? Although I argued strongly for this in the first edition, not many exegetes have accepted that conclusion;[6] most tend to be

[1] Fuchs, *op. cit.* pp. 95 ff.

[2] Pryke, p. 155; D.-A. Koch, *Die Bedeutung der Wundererzählungen für die Christologie des Markusevangeliums* (Berlin, 1975), pp. 140–7; E. F. Kirschner, 'The Price of the Exorcism Motif in Mark's Christology with Special Reference to Mark 3.22–30', Ph.D. thesis, London Bible College, 1988, p. 46. My hesitant suggestion (p. 150) in the first edition of this book that Mark himself may have formed iii. 27 was clearly wrong.

[3] Derrett, pp. 81 f., less probably relates it to the Exodus.

[4] Cf. Kirschner, *op. cit.* pp. 64–6, for a discussion of the influence of the Old Testament.

[5] Cf. R. Meynet, 'Qui donc est "le plus fort"? Analyse rhétorique de Mc 3, 22–30; Mt 12, 22–37; Luc 11, 14–26', *R.B.* XC (1983), 334–50; J. Lambrecht, *Tandis qu'Il nous parlait: introduction aux paraboles* (Paris, 1980), pp. 150 f.

[6] Those who have moved towards the adoption of this view include P. S. Minear, *Saint Mark* (Layman's Bible Commentaries; London, 1963), p. 66 (but contrast p. 131); Standaert, pp. 89, 567 f.; Kingsbury, 69 f., 144; Trevijano, *op. cit.* p. 181; W. Foerster, *T.W.N.T.* VII, 157 f.; R. Grob, *Einführung in das Markus-Evangelium* (Zurich and Stuttgart, 1965), pp. 15, 45; H. E. Turlington, *Mark* (Broadman Bible Commentary; Nashville, Tennessee, 1969), p. 271; Matera, *Passion*, pp. 53 f. Pesch, *art. cit.*, is more hesitant. Fuchs, *op. cit.* pp. 98 f. n. 183, sees the possibility of iii. 27 reflecting an early Christology. Jeremias, I, pp. 72 f.,

indefinite over the nature of Christ's victory. The more we emphasise the connectivity of the Gospel, the more reasonable it appears to be to relate i. 12 f. and iii. 27 and therefore to see in the former the basis of the latter. The change from Beelzebul in *v.* 22[1] to Satan serves to confirm this. Few commentators today, on the other hand, see Mark as governed by the idea of Jesus' life as a continuous struggle against Satan reaching its conclusion in the Passion. Satan has disappeared from the story, and the Passion must be seen in some other light. Whenever a seemingly important character, Satan, is written out of a story, we need to find a reason. We need also to remember that it is probably only to our latter-day eyes that he is important; Mark's hearers would not have seen him as the sole explanation of evil and therefore as Jesus' continual opponent. In essence what Mark has done is to transfer to the Temptation the defeat of Satan and the cosmic powers presented by some of the other New Testament writers as taking place in the Passion. In doing this it must be allowed that he has no more solved the problem of the continuance of Satan's activity in the lives of believers than they have. Both for them and for him there must be a final victory in the End-time when all things are subject to God.

THE PASSION NARRATIVE: STRUCTURE

If, then, Mark does not understand the death of Jesus as a victorious contest with Satan, how does he understand it? A crucified man, and Mark makes no attempt to play down the demeaning and horrible manner of Jesus' death since he refers repeatedly to the Cross and crucifixion, would not be thought worthy of worship unless he was held to be of supreme importance and/or those who worshipped him received some benefit from his death. In narrating the Passion however Mark does not set out to prove Jesus was a person of importance. This is already accepted by his hearers, and in case they may have forgotten precisely who Jesus was, Mark reminded them at the very outset

considers that the suggested interpretation of iii. 27 went back to Jesus. G. R. Beasley-Murray, *Jesus and the Kingdom of God* (Exeter, 1986), pp. 108–11, while allowing the possibility of the interpretation, prefers to see Jesus' whole ministry as 'characterised by triumph over Satan', but he is treating the life of Jesus rather than the Gospel account of it.

[1] The appearance of the name Beelzebul, whatever its spelling or etymology, is another instance of Mark's preservation of received tradition (cf. *Disciples*, pp. 31–48).

that Jesus is both Christ and Son of God (i. 1, 11) and later that he is Son of Man. The contrast between the true nature of Jesus and his humiliating death is continually brought out, e.g. by the title Son of Man which Mark[1] uses both in relation to his suffering (e.g. viii. 31) and to his coming again in power and glory (xiii. 26; xiv. 62). He is anointed both as king and for his burial at the moment his arrest is being plotted (xiv. 1–11); he confesses his true identity at his trials (xiv. 61 f.; xv. 2); he is executed as King of the Jews (xv. 26). It is in fact the very high value Mark's hearers give to Jesus that has made the Cross into a problem (cf. I Cor. i. 18 ff.). Yet within the total story the Cross is nullified by the Resurrection, which serves as vindication. There is no doubt that Mark believes in the Resurrection and relates it to the death (viii. 31; ix. 31; x. 33 f.). His narrative moves on directly from the Cross to the empty tomb (xvi. 8; I take this to be Mark's intended ending).[2] The Cross cannot then be isolated from the Resurrection.[3] This does not however answer the problem set by Jesus' shameful death. God might have taken him up into heaven in a chariot of fire as he did Elijah; that he did not do so leaves the offence of the Cross.

A number of approaches were possible; an offence can to some extent be neutralised if placed in a defined category or explained as part of a wider process. Jesus might be seen as the fulfilment of God's plan as revealed in the Old Testament. Without directly isolating particular promises which Jesus had fulfilled, for the category of promise and fulfilment does not appear to have been important for Mark, the early believers (we are not concerned with what Jesus may have thought about his own death) might

[1] On Mark's use of the Son of Man title see M. D. Hooker, *The Son of Man in Mark* (London, 1967); Kingsbury, pp. 157 ff.

[2] See *Story*, pp. 72 ff.

[3] Cf. G. Schille, *Offen für alle Menschen: Religionsgeschichtliche Beobachtungen zur Theologie des Markus-Evangeliums* (Stuttgart, 1974), p. 78.

[4] On Mark's use of the Old Testament see A. Suhl, *Die Funktion der alttestamentliche Zitate und Anspielungen im Markusevangelium* (Gütersloh, 1965); D. J. Moo, *The Old Testament in the Gospel Passion Narratives* (Sheffield, 1983); H. C. Kee, 'The Function of Scriptural Quotations in Mark 11–16', *Jesus und Paulus. Festschrift für Werner Georg Kümmel* (ed. E. E. Ellis and E. Grässer; Göttingen, 1975), pp. 165–88; H. Anderson, 'The Old Testament in Mark's Gospel', *The Use of the Old Testament in the New and Other Essays: Studies in Honor of William Franklin Stinespring* (ed. J. M. Efrid; Durham, N.C., 1972), pp. 280–306.

have looked for 'patterns' within the Old Testament and Jewish thought and literature, and perhaps even in the wider Hellenistic world, which would have provided a background against which to view the sufferings of Jesus. This might have led them to see him as the innocent martyr who laid down his life for a good cause,[1] or as the Righteous Sufferer depicted in some of the Psalms,[2] or as the humiliated and exalted Son of God of the Book of Wisdom,[3] or as the Servant of Yahweh of Second Isaiah,[4] or as the paschal lamb (I Cor. v. 7; since Mark depicts Jesus as dying on the day after the slaughtering of that lamb, this was not a possible view for him[5]), or as the murdered prophet (Matt. xxiii. 29–36,[6] a view which again was not one acceptable to Mark since he clearly distinguishes between the role of Jesus and that of the prophets in viii. 28 f.; xii. 1–12). Many if not all of these ideas have parallels in the Greco-Roman world,[7] and Mark's Hellenistic hearers could have begun to appreciate them even though the way in which Mark makes Jesus' death a universal event was foreign to Hellenism. It has also been argued that Mark used or, more correctly, opposed a more purely hellenistic concept in which Jesus was regarded as a 'divine man' and his Passion seen as an attempt to play down that view which

---

[1] E.g. G. W. E. Nickelsburg, 'The Genre and Function of the Markan Passion Narrative', *H. T. R.* LXXIII (1980), 153–84; J. Pobee, 'The Cry of the Centurion – a Cry of Defeat', *The Trial of Jesus* (S.B.T., 2nd series, 13, ed. E. Bammel; London, 1970), pp. 91–102; Rau, pp. 2209–14.

[2] E.g. L. Ruppert, *Jesus als die leidende Gerechte? Der Weg Jesus im Lichte eines alt- und zwischentestamentliches Motivs* (S.B.S. 59; Stuttgart, 1972); H.-J. Steichele, *Der leidende Sohn Gottes. Eine Untersuchung einiger alttestamentlicher Motive in der Christologie des Markusevangeliums* (Regensburg, 1980); K. D. Kleinknecht, *Der leidende Gerechtfertigte* (W.U.N.T. 2. Reihe 13; Tübingen, 1984), pp. 17–192.

[3] E.g. E. Schweizer, *Erniedrigung und Erhöhung bei Jesus und seine Nachfolgern* (A.T.A.N.T. 28; 2nd edn, Zurich, 1962).

[4] E.g. Jeremias, pp. 276 ff.

[5] *Pace* J. Navonne, 'Mark's Story of the Death of Jesus', *New Blackfriars* LXV (1984), 123–35.

[6] Dormeyer, pp. 13 f., 262–4, finds this understanding in the pre-Markan tradition; cf. G. Richter, 'Zu den Tauferzählungen Mk 1.9–11 und John 1.32–34', *Z.N.T.W.* LXV (1974), 43–56.

[7] See for references Hengel, pp. 1 ff.; S. K. Williams, *Jesus' Death as Saving Event. The Background and Origin of a Concept* (Missoula, Montana, 1975), pp. 137–63; G. Friedrich, *Die Verkündigung des Todes Jesu im Neuen Testament* (Neukirchen-Vluyn, 1982), pp. 37 ff.

had been deduced from his miracles.[1] Probably most, if not all, these interpretations came into the minds of the first Christians at some stage and have left their marks on the material of the tradition. In a sense many of them are attempts to defend the fact of the crucifixion rather than attempts to penetrate deeply into its meaning. Were there also attempts to do the latter, and did they influence Mark? Before we go on to examine that, it is possible to say at this point that from the way Mark uses the titles of Jesus it is clear he was not arguing that Jesus became Son of God, Christ or Son of Man through his death.

In what is essentially a re-examination of Mark's understanding of the death of Jesus the present approach will be made through the one area which was not adequately treated in the first edition, i.e. the continuity of the narrative, in particular that of the Passion; a consideration of the continuity of the whole Gospel of which the Passion is only a part naturally cannot be excluded. The Markan Passion narrative has been intensively examined in recent years in an attempt to uncover the tradition received and developed by Mark. Unfortunately no consensus has appeared.[2] Clues enabling differentiation between the Markan and pre-Markan material have been sought in doublets, in Markan vocabulary and stylistic features, in improbabilities in relation to the Jewish legal system, in references to the Old Testament introduced in a non-Markan manner, in the presence of particular theological themes (e.g. apocalypticism). If there is no agreement on the content of the pre-Markan Passion narrative, there is none either on

---

[1] E.g. T. J. Weeden, *Mark: Traditions in Conflict* (Philadelphia, 1971). For a discussion and full references see J. D. Kingsbury, 'The "Divine Man" as the Key to Mark's Christology – The End of an Era', *Int* XXXIV (1981), 243–57 and Kingsbury, pp. 25–45. It is possible to accept the view that Mark offers a suffering Christology in the Passion without supposing that he is fighting against a 'divine man' Christology.

[2] For discussions of the various views see Juel, pp. 1–39; Donahue, pp. 5–51; G. Schneider, 'Das Problem einer vorkanonischen Passionserzählung', *B.Z.* XVI (1972), 222–42; Mohr, pp. 11–43; J. Schreiber, B.Z.N.W., pp. 275–365; Linnemann, pp. 54–69; B. L. Mack, *A Myth of Innocence* (Philadelphia, 1988), pp. 249–68; J. Ernst, 'Der Passionserzählung des Markus', *Theologie und Glaube* LXX (1980), 160–80; W. Schenk, 'Der derzeitige Stand der Auslegung der Passionsgeschichte', *Der evangelische Erzieher* XXXVI (1984), 527–43.

where it begins. Pesch[1] places this as early as viii. 27, while Ernst[2] selects xv. 21*b*; most however set the beginning at either xi. 1 or xiv. 1. The variety of answers to these problems is an indication of the difficulty of the task. There was probably more than one oral narrative of the Passion, for a different narrative seems to underlie the Johannine account, and Luke may have been influenced by yet another.[3] Apart from this we cannot exclude the possibility that several narratives may have been simultaneously in use in any one Christian community for different purposes.

Jesus' death and Resurrection would have had to be presented differently when used in evangelisation from in the context of a Eucharistic service. Even if used in evangelisation different presentations would be required in the market place and in the Jewish synagogue. (Much more attention has been devoted to the detection of the form of the narrative than to the use to which it may have been put.) The 'market place' itself could be ordinary people or on occasions, e.g. in Athens, the 'intellectuals'. The synagogue could be more or less highly influenced by Hellenism. In each case the approach would be varied. There would also be different situations within the Christian community arising out of the time available for worship and the place where it was held (the small group in a house church or the larger group when a number of house churches came together). A different approach might again be needed in a charismatic service from one where the Eucharist was the centre. It is probably best then to suppose there existed a pool of pre-Markan traditions about the Passion from which preachers and evangelists selected the material appropriate to their particular audience. Consequently it is wrong to speak of *a* or *the* pre-Markan narrative, and equally wrong to think of Mark as joining together two disparate narratives,[4] or of a narrative

---

[1] II, pp. 1–27. For detailed criticism of his view see F. Neirynck, *Evangelica. Collected Essays* (B.E.T.L. LX; Louvain, 1982), pp. 527–50; Pesch has responded to criticisms in 'Das Evangelium in Jerusalem: Mk 14, 12–26 als ältestes Überlieferungsgut der Urgemeinde' in *Das Evangelium und die Evangelien* (W.U.N.T. 28, ed. P. Stuhlmacher; Tübingen, 1983), pp. 113–55.

[2] Pp. 395 f.

[3] Cf. V. Taylor, *The Passion Narrative of St Luke* (S.N.T.S.M.S. 19; Cambridge, 1972); T. Schramm, *Der Markus-Stoff bei Lukas* (S.N.T.S.M.S. 14; Cambridge, 1971), pp. 50 f.

[4] So Schreiber, *Theologie* and B.Z.N.W.; Schenk.

which went through a number of editions of which Mark's was the final.[1] It is also most improbable that he was the first to put together a consistent narrative out of pre-existing fragments,[2] though he was probably the first to write such a narrative down.

The various pericopae which were used on each occasion to create a continuous account would have been individually imprinted with different understandings of the death of Jesus, as hero, prophet, suffering servant, etc., and these understandings would have been carried into any connected account which put them together. Equally the separate pericopae would have carried wider theological leanings, e.g. apocalyptic, Gnostic, into the account. It is necessary to determine whether these understandings and wider leanings continued to be of importance for Mark; he may not have rejected them, but equally he may not have stressed them. He may have extended some of them or added an entirely new interpretation of his own. Any such emendations would appear both in the way he strung the pericopae together and in his internal editing of them.

It is highly probable that the particular Passion narrative which Mark constructed for his Gospel was intended for use in the Christian community and not in the 'market place' or synagogue.[3] Naturally the death of Jesus featured regularly in the worship and instruction of the community, and Mark will have had available not only a pool of pericopae relating in various ways to it but also an accustomed way, or ways, of stringing some of the pericopae together for use within or outside the community. As he compiled his narrative he may have rejected some pericopae which he regarded as of primary importance for evangelisation and only hinted at others which he could assume the members of his community would know so well that only a hint was necessary. If he did this, we today are unable to detect the content of these pericopae. Nor have we other similar narrative compilations from his hand to show us by what principles he would have been guided in stringing pericopae together. On the other hand we can have some idea of the ways in which he would have edited individual pericopae because a sufficient number of these

[1] So Schenke, *Christus*; Dormeyer; Mohr.
[2] So Linnemann.   [3] See *Story*, pp. 93–9.

covering a variety of topics still exists.[1] What this means can be best illustrated with an example. It is almost universally agreed that the basic form of xiv. 58 and xv. 29 was pre-Markan and that Mark has created two variants of that basic form which he has inserted in two different contexts. How did such a saying exist prior to Mark's use of it? It does not appear to be of the type which would survive long in isolation. If Mark transferred it from another pericope into its present contexts, we have lost that pericope.[2] However its new position and the non-use of the pericope in which it was originally present would have been at once obvious to the community. Children complain if the details in stories to which they are accustomed are changed, and we are all aware when someone telling a familiar story varies it, and begin to wonder what the variations mean. Mark has preserved many of the details in the pericopae he uses though these details do not quite fit with his own ideas, e.g. in the exorcism of i. 23 – 7 the demon describes Jesus as 'the Holy One of God' though when Mark writes freely about demonic confessions (iii. 11) he uses 'Son of God', a term more appropriate to his Christology. By this preservation of unnecessary, even contradictory, detail[3] Mark shows himself aware that his hearers know the stories he uses. Both variations in the detail of stories and the shape of the new continuous narrative will therefore be important in attempting to deduce the significance Mark, or indeed any author, attaches to the events he records. In what I am writing now I intend to concentrate much more on the continuity of the narrative than on the details of Markan internal editing of pericopae. To a large

---

[1] Since the first edition of this book a great deal of attention has been paid to Mark's editing of individual pericopae; see e.g. Pryke; D. B. Peabody, *Mark as Composer* (Macon, Georgia, 1987); F. Neirynck, *Duality in Mark: Contributions to the Study of the Markan Redaction* (B.E.T.L. 31; Louvain, 1972), and 'The Redactional Text of Mark', *E.T.L.* LVII (1981), 144 – 62; L. Gaston, *Horae Synopticae Electronicae: Word Statistics of the Synoptic Gospels* (Missoula, Montana, 1973); P. Dschulnigg, *Sprache, Redaktion und Intention des Markus-Evangeliums. Eigentümlickkeiten der Sprache des Markus-Evangeliums und ihre Bedeutung für die Redaktionskritik*, 2nd edn (Stuttgart, 1986); M. Reiser, *Syntax und Stil des Markusevangeliums* (W.U.N.T. 2. Reihe 11; Tübingen, 1984).

[2] Our argument is even stronger if we accept the point of view of Donahue, pp. 103 ff., that the two halves of the saying were originally separate and brought together by Mark.

[3] For further examples see *Disciples*, pp. 31 – 48.

degree the latter were examined in the first edition and have been extensively treated in recent literature on the Passion.[1] But it is always important to remember that if Mark added explanatory comments, as say xiv. 27*b*, 28, these will be significant and must be treated as such.

If we focus attention on the continuity of Mark's narrative we do not do so from the point of view which asserts that we must learn everything from the internal structure of the narrative itself, that the narrative can only be understood properly from within the narrative.[2] All words carry with them certain associations, and so when Christians hear a narrative they inevitably import meaning into what they hear. Equally when Mark wrote, the words he used carried meaning with them, a meaning which he would normally have shared with his hearers. Our understanding of the contemporary wider Christian significance of Mark's words will then help us to see into the meaning of his story. To deny that a story can only be understood from within itself is not to say that we do not learn from one part of a story about another. What we hear in earlier parts determines how we listen to later sections. Insights once gained are reused, e.g. the beginnings of opposition in ch. ii predispose us to accept the Cross as the inevitable end. But learning about the end from the beginning can only be at best a partial approach. For Mark, in writing to instruct his community and deepen its faith, also knew he had much in common with it and so could leave many things unsaid.[3] Unfortunately we do not know in detail what knowledge Mark could assume his readers possessed. Probably they knew

---

[1] Again authors differ over Markan editing: many hold that he created completely new pericopae, while others, e.g. Pesch, take a much more conservative position in respect of his interventions in the tradition.

[2] See, for example, L. Marin, *The Semiotics of the Passion Narrative: Topics and Figures* (Pittsburgh, 1980); J. Radermakers, 'L'évangile de Marc. Structure et théologie', and P. Mourlon Beernaert, 'Structure littéraire et lecture théologique de Marc 14, 17–52', both in M. Sabbe, *L'Évangile selon Marc* (B.E.T.L. XXXIV: 2nd edn, Louvain, 1988), pp. 221–39 and 241–68. On the relation of theology, narrative and semiotics with special reference to the Passion there is a set of papers by P. Beauchamp, P. Corset, J. Delorme, J. Calloud, F. Genuyt, J.-N. Aletti, C. Turiot, A. Delzant and E. Haulotte in *R.S.R.* LXXIII (1985), 1–228.

[3] Cf. *Story*, pp. 116 f.

little of Palestinian geography but accepted the general Christian theological beliefs of that period. In addition he and they will also have shared beliefs peculiar to their own small community. This implies that Mark's hearers already possessed some understanding of much of the material he used. In particular they knew the outcome of the story, and therefore when they heard it much of it would carry a note of irony. The provision, moreover, of a connected sequence of pericopae meant that each pericope would in effect be a comment both on the total sequence and on each of the other pericopae. In essence then, what Mark offered to his hearers was a commentary on what they already knew. This is seen at its simplest in his translation of Aramaic words and in his explanatory γάρ clauses. By his positioning of material he also high-lighted some of it over against other portions. If only we knew what he omitted, we would have a better grasp of why he included what he has included. It will be seen that this represents a modification of the position adopted in the first edition (pp. 90 ff.) where I assumed that Mark used and worked over a pre-existing Passion narrative.

Like other Christians Mark's hearers would have already been thinking about the death of Jesus, a stumbling-block to Jews and foolishness to Greeks (I Cor. i. 23). How did others explain and understand it? I have already referred to the possible categories into which believers may have fitted Jesus in order to account for the fact of the Cross. A number of theological interpretations also existed in the primitive community: it was in accordance with Scripture (I Cor. xv. 3); it was for sin (I Cor. xv. 3); it would give deliverance from the wrath to come at the time of the Parousia (I Thess. i. 9 f.); it initiated the downfall of hostile supernatural powers (Phil. ii. 6–11); it was an example of true behaviour (I Pet. ii. 18–25).[1] Mark may have understood the Cross in some or all of these ways, but also in others; since he presents the disciples as failing to grasp the meaning of Christ's mission as a whole and in particular of the Passion, it became all the more necessary to explain the latter.

[1] There is little evidence for the view that the Passion was interpreted gnostically prior to Mark; W. Schenk, 'Der gnostisierende Deutung des Todes Jesu und ihre kritische Interpretation durch den Evangelisten Markus', *Gnosis und Neues Testament* (ed. K.-W. Tröger; Berlin, 1973), pp. 231–43, argues for such an interpretation but acknowledges that Mark eliminated it from the tradition he used.

Before going on to re-examine Mark's understanding of the Passion we need first to look at the continuity of his narrative as a whole,[1] on which students today are laying increasing emphasis.[2] While it is difficult to be sure where to place many of the minor divisions in the story, there is general agreement on the main divisions.[3] After the prologue i. 1–13 (15),[4] which is not a summary but introduces and identifies the main character, there are three major sections, i. 16–viii. 26, viii. 27–x. 52, xi. 1–xv. 47, and an epilogue, xvi. 1–8,[5] assuming Mark intended xvi. 8 as his final verse[6] and that his conclusion has not been lost. Three reasons may be advanced in support of these major divisions:

1. Content. In i. 16–viii. 26 Jesus is seen as a great healer and teacher, victorious in controversy, overcoming demons and sickness, calling disciples who fail to understand what he is about, encountering opposition; the summaries of his activity serve to increase the pressure and speed with which everything happens. In viii. 27–x. 52 a different picture of Jesus emerges as one who is

[1] See *Story*, pp. 129 ff. See also now, Ernest Best, 'Mark's Narrative Technique', *J.S.N.T.* 37 (1989), 43–58.

[2] The continuity of the narrative has been emphasised among others by W. H. Kelber, *Mark's Story of Jesus* (Philadelphia, 1979); Rhoads and Michie, *op. cit.*; Stock; R. M. Fowler, *Loaves and Fishes* (Chico, Calif., 1981); L. Schenke, *Das Markus-evangelium* (Stuttgart, 1988); V. K. Robbins, *Jesus the Teacher: A Socio-Rhetorical Interpretation of Mark* (Philadelphia, 1984).

[3] For a listing of possible approaches see, among others, R. Pesch, *Naherwartungen: Tradition und Redaktion in Mk* 13 (Düsseldorf, 1968), pp. 50–3; Baarlink, pp. 68–107; C. Breytenbach, 'Der Markusevangelium als episodische Erzählung. Mit Überlegungen zum "Aufbau" des zweiten Evangelium', *Der Erzähler des Evangelium: Methodische Neuansätze in der Markusforschung* (S.B.S. 118/119, ed. F. Hahn; Stuttgart, 1985), pp. 137–69; F. G. Lang, 'Kompositionsanalyse des Markusevangeliums', *Z.T.K.* LXX (1977), 1–24; D. A. Koch, 'Inhaltiche Gliederung und geographischer Aufriss im Markusevangelium', *N.T.S.* XXIX (1983), 145–66.

[4] There is a disagreement as to the extent of the prologue; i. 14 f. is in fact a transition section, as are viii. 22–6; x. 46–52; xv. 40–7. On the prologue see most recently F. J. Matera, 'The Prologue as the Interpretative Key to Mark's Gospel', *J.S.N.T.* 34 (1988), 3–20.

[5] These three major sections are accepted by most scholars. Standaert, pp. 44 f., following the rules of ancient rhetoric, sets the end of his first major section at vi.14; Stock, pp. 47–9, follows him in this, though earlier (p. 15) he argued against finding interpretative keys outside the Gospel.

[6] See *Following*, pp. 199 f.; *Story*, pp. 72 f.

about to suffer and whose followers will also have to suffer, something they find impossible to accept. xi. 1 – xv.47 narrates what happened after Jesus reached Jerusalem and reaches its climax in the crucifixion and burial.

2.   Each of the three main sections is held together by different kinds of 'markers', the 'markers' incidentally being those which hearers would easily grasp, for the Gospel was originally compiled to be heard rather than read in solitariness. In the first main section the 'markers' are normally either 'and' or 'and immediately' and create the impression of great haste and activity; though Jesus is constantly on the move throughout this section, the precise details of his journeys are difficult to decipher. The second section in contrast consists of a carefully constructed journey in which the 'markers' are geographical; this journey brings Jesus and his disciples gradually closer to Jerusalem.[1] In the final section the 'markers' are temporal,[2] first expressed in terms of days and then during the final (Jewish) day of crucifixion in terms of hours (xiv. 72, the end of the Roman watch, xv. 1,25,33,34). Though some of these time data may come from the tradition, some at least are due to Mark;[3] those that may be traditional are expressed in Markan language showing his conscious use of them.[4]

3.   The distinction in the way Mark uses Galilee and Jerusalem has often been noted. In the first major section Jesus is active mainly in and around Galilee, but never in Jerusalem; in the second he is on the move from outside Galilee through it to Jerusalem; the third section is set entirely in Jerusalem.

While we may discern these major divisions in the unity of the Gospel,[5] it must be realised that they may not have been as

---

[1]   I have explored the details of this journey in *Following*.

[2]   I differ here entirely from E. Manicardi, *Il cammino di Gesù nel Vangelo di Marco* (An.Bib. 96; Rome, 1981), and Marin, *op. cit.*, who base their understanding of the Passion on the movements of Jesus from place to place and ignore the temporal data.

[3]   E.g. Dormeyer, pp. 67 ff.

[4]   On the careful marking out of the time in this section so that it forms a 'sacred' week and the redaction involved see Schenk, p. 140; Dormeyer, pp. 66 f., 270; Schenke, *Studien*, pp. 27 - 36.

[5]   We see no reason for accepting the view of E. Trocmé, *The Formation of the Gospel according to Mark* (London, 1975), that the Gospel consisted originally of chapters i – xiii. For a detailed examination of his views see T. A. Burkill, *New Light on the Earliest Gospel* (Cornell and London, 1972), pp.160 – 264. See also Standaert, pp. 336 – 67, who contends that chapters xi – xiv form a unity.

obvious and clear-cut to Mark or his hearers. The material flows much more easily than the divisions suggest. i. 14 f. on the one hand brings the prologue to a close and on the other is the essential preliminary to i. 16–20; disciples cannot be called prior to the proclamation of the message to which they are to respond. viii. 22–6, the healing of a blind man in two stages, ties back both to viii. 14–21, in which eyes that do not see are featured, and forward to viii. 27–33, where we meet the semi-blindness of Peter.[1] x. 45–52, the healing of another blind man, by showing someone who responds to the teaching of viii. 27–x. 45 and goes forward with Jesus into Jerusalem, serves to tie together the second and third major sections.[2] The whole Gospel thus flows steadily onward. Since Mark's hearers unlike the original participants know the end of the story, they will not be looking for a successful and happy conclusion but for an understanding of what the story, and in particular the Passion, meant.

A word of warning is necessary here. If Mark presents his thinking about the Passion by means of a story and if he is a good story-teller (the success of actors like Alec McCowen in presenting Mark's story indicates he was a good story-teller), then we need to realise that some of its details may be intended for dramatic effect rather than to make profound soteriological or christological statements, and we should not necessarily see deep theological significance in everything Mark records. The silence of Jesus before his accusers (xiv. 61; xv. 5), broken only by his acknowledgement of his true identity (xiv. 61 f.), is more probably dramatic than an attempt to express a fulfilment of Isa. liii. 7, for it is not a total silence as the biblical passage would require,[3] and Jesus' solemn acknowledgement of his identity adds to the drama. The choice of Barabbas instead of Jesus is equally dramatic, especially so if the original text read 'Jesus Barabbas' or if 'Barabbas' is understood as 'son of the father'. Jesus is judged by the Sanhedrin and by Pilate, but Mark's hearers know that he will eventually judge his judges (xiv. 62). There are times when it may be better to listen to the story than to analyse it in the study.

If the narrative flows onward toward the Cross and Resurrection

Themes (see below) which run right through the Gospel also argue strongly against the view of Trocmé.

[1] See *Story*, pp. 134–9.   [2] *Ibid.* pp. 139–45.

[3] It is not true, as Schneider suggests, *art. cit.*, that martyrs invariably keep silent.

(we cannot exclude the latter because Mark continually looks forward to it: viii. 31; ix. 9,31; x. 34; xiv. 28), then we may expect that a number of issues will appear and be developed in its course. An understanding of Christology might appear a suitable candidate in this connection, but since we have been told from the outset that Jesus is Christ and Son of God (i, 1, 11), the Gospel cannot be an attempt either to work out who Jesus was or to convince hearers of his identity. The difficulty does not lie in understanding what these titles mean but in accepting their meaning, a point made vividly by the frequent references to the blindness, fear and hardness of heart of the disciples. The two titles, Christ and Son of God, together with Son of Man, are brought together in the High Priest's question at the trial and in Jesus' answer (xiv. 61 f.). What requires explanation is not the Christology but the soteriology.

If then we look at the death of Jesus, we see that as Mark tells his story it comes increasingly to occupy the centre of the stage, first in relation to the fact of its occurrence and then in relation to its meaning. Though the study of the second is our main objective, we temporarily lay it aside and concentrate on the first. We are not left long in doubt as to the end that faces Jesus. If the words of the divine voice at his baptism refer either to the servant of Yahweh or to the *Akedah* and not just to Psalm 2,[1] there are already overtones of death, and a hint that the death will benefit others. The first undoubted reference to the death comes at iii. 6, a verse which Mark may well have added to an existing complex, yet careful hearers will have spotted the reference in ii. 19 f. From iii. 6 onwards the first major section (1.16 – viii. 22) contains frequent signs of Jesus' rejection (iii. 21, 22 – 7; v. 17; vi. 1 – 6a). Another pointer to Jesus' death is the death of John the Baptist, a minor passion; if John's life ends in execution, how can Jesus avoid a similar fate? To believers the absurdity of all this is driven home by the way Jesus is presented at the same time as one who cares for people in teaching, healing and feeding them.

In the second major section (viii. 27 – x. 52) Jesus' future death becomes explicit with the predictions of viii. 31; ix. 12, 31; x. 33 f., and it is after this that meaning begins to be attached to the death.

---

[1] So e.g. Matera, *Kingship*, pp. 74 – 9.

Jesus' care for others is now seen in his attempt to instruct the disciples in what is to happen to him and on how they are to live. He is there to serve them (x. 42 – 4*a*), and this service requires the giving of his life for them and for all (x. 45*b*). Thus at the end of this section we encounter for the first time an undisputed statement about the meaning of Jesus' death.

The final major section not only recounts the story of his death but gradually attributes to it more and more significance. To seek this significance we shall follow out a number of the themes which run through this section, but which may also have been partially present earlier. We commence with the theme of the Temple.

THE TEMPLE THEME

The Temple[1] enters Mark's story line as soon as Jesus reaches Jerusalem (xi. 11), and most of his activity takes place in or in relation to it. There are significant incidents in which it features or in which direct reference is made to it. Depending on the date of the Gospel Mark's hearers know that the Temple has already been destroyed by the Romans or that it shortly will be since Jerusalem is besieged by Roman armies. The first significant incident is the so-called 'cleansing' (xi. 15 – 19).[2] Mark has made his account of it the inner portion of one of his sandwiches,[3] of which the two outer layers are the cursing of the fig-tree and the discovery on the following day that it had withered and died (we do not need to inquire into the origin or morality of this story). In this way Mark implies that the cleansing which might otherwise appear only to be a prophetic act carries with it the overtone

[1] Extended studies of the Temple theme or parts of it are to be found in Juel, pp. 117 – 215; Donahue, pp. 53 – 84, 103 – 38, 201 – 3; A. Vögtle, 'Das markinische Verständnis der Tempelworte', *Die Mitte des Neuens Testaments* (Festschrift für Eduard Schweizer, ed. U. Luz und H. Weder; Göttingen, 1983), pp. 362 – 83; D. Lührmann, 'Markus 14.53 – 64: Christologie und Zerstörung des Tempels im Markusevangelium', *N.T.S.* XXVII (1980/1), 457 – 75; W. R. Telford, *The Barren Temple and the Withered Tree* (J.S.N.T. Supplement Series 1; Sheffield, 1980); Kim Seyoon, 'Jesus and the Temple', *ACTS Theological Journal* III (1988), 87 – 131; I have discussed the cleansing from another angle in *Following*, pp. 213 – 22.
[2] On the distinction of 'cleansing' and destruction see Kelber, *Kingdom*, pp. 102 – 4; Kato, pp. 105 – 18.
[3] Pesch, II, p. 190, regards the sandwich as pre-Markan; Ernst, pp. 324 f., allows this as a possibility.

that there is no further use for ever for the Temple,[1] just as there can be none for a dead fig-tree.[2] It may be that the cursing and subsequent withering of the fig-tree is in itself an indication of God's judgement on Israel, for the prosperity of nature and of Israel are linked.[3] If this is so, its understanding depends on a detailed knowledge of Old Testament references to figs which would hardly have been appreciated by Mark's hearers, though it may have led Mark to associate the cursing of the fig-tree with the Temple. In any case the sandwich Mark has created clearly shows that the Temple has failed because it has not been a house of prayer for Gentiles (xi. 17; the verse is probably Markan[4]) as well as Jews. The Jewish leaders have appropriated to themselves God's vineyard (xii. 1–12),[5] and in doing so have caused Israel to cease to play its role as God's people.[6] This in turn suggests that there will be a situation yet to come in which the Gentiles will be at home in God's house, and Mark's hearers would understand by 'my house' their community.[7]

The theme of the Temple is probably encountered also in the Parable of the Vineyard (xii. 1–12). Jesus tells this parable in the Temple, and it may be that in the Markan context the priests and the other Jewish leaders referred to in xi. 27 are still in mind and under attack.[8] This would be so if in particular the question of the authority of Jesus raised in xi. 27–33 related to his cleansing of the Temple. There is in any case an ambiguity in the parable[9]

---

[1] Cf. J. Schreiber, *Theologie*, pp. 134–40; Mohr, pp. 72–7.

[2] Cf. Anderson, p. 264. It is possible, as Schnackenburg suggests, *ad loc.*, that Mark has Jer. vii. 20 in mind since at xi. 17 he plays on Jer. vii. 11; the whole passage in Jeremiah condemns reliance on the Temple; cf. Juel, pp. 132–4.

[3] So Telford, *op. cit.* pp. 134–7, 162 f.

[4] E.g. Mohr, pp. 82–6; Pryke, p. 168.   [5] Cf. Mohr, p. 85.

[6] Cf. Gnilka, II, p. 125; Ernst, p. 326.

[7] On the community as 'house' see *Following*, pp. 226–9, and on the passage as a whole, G. Münderlein, 'Die Verfluchung des Feigenbaumes', *N.T.S.* X (1963/4), 89–104; H. Giesen, 'Der verdorrte Feigenbaum – Eine symbolische Aussage? Zu Mk 11, 12–14, 20 f.', *B.Z.* XX (1976), 95–111. Lührmann, p. 192, limits this understanding of the incident to an underlining of Jesus' authority.

[8] So Juel, pp. 136 f.; Donahue, pp. 124–7; Kato, pp. 118–29; Gnilka, II, pp. 148 f.; Trocmé, pp. 205–7. I have discussed this in *Following*, pp. 218–20. On the parable as a whole see in particular K. Snodgrass, *The Parable of the Wicked Tenants* (W.U.N.T. 27; Tübingen, 1983); Bayer, pp. 89–109; P.C. Böttger, *Der König der Juden – das Heil für die Völker* (Neukirchen-Vluyn, 1981), pp. 27–32.

[9] Cf. Bayer, pp. 99 f.

in relation to the tenants, probably arising from its present christological orientation. The story, given its Old Testament background and inner logic, demands that the original tenants of the vineyard should be the Jews as a people, and the early Christians almost certainly regarded themselves as those who replaced the Jews as tenants of the vineyard;[1] yet *v.* 12, which is probably Markan, seems to level the attack on the leaders, among whom will be numbered the priests. The crowd,[2] i.e. the Jews minus their leaders, can be for or against Jesus; generally they applaud what he does, but in the end they call for his crucifixion (xv. 11 ff.); an ambivalence in respect of where blame should be laid in Judaism is thus not surprising. If the priests[3] are in mind, then they have authority in the vineyard and their authority, which is centred in the Temple, is now to be taken from them. Jesus is continually at odds with the Jewish leaders throughout chapters xi and xiii, implying their rejection as authorities. If in the parable the tenants are taken as the whole people of Israel, then we should understand the significance of their removal as the end of Judaism, though that should not be taken to imply that there would be no Jews in the new community to whom the vineyard is given, since the disciples, themselves Jews, formed its core.

The Temple is explicitly referred to in xiii. 1 f. at the point where Jesus finally leaves it and prophesies its destruction. He does not however say he himself will destroy it, nor does he say who will. Mark's hearers know that it will be, or has been, the Romans, though they will also naturally draw the conclusion that the effective destroyer is God, since throughout the apocalyptic drama of ch. xiii it is he who initiates all the action that brings the end. Less direct references to the Temple are probably also present in xiii. 14[4] and in xiii. 28 f. if in the latter we see a connection between its parable and the fig-tree of xi.12 ff., for 'these things' which are taking place would

---

[1] Pesch, II, pp. 220 f.; Gnilka, II, p. 149. Lührmann, pp. 199 f., argues that the parable means that God has given Jerusalem and the land into the power of the Romans.

[2] On the crowd in Mark see *Following*, pp. 28 f.; *Disciples*, pp. 116–19.

[3] Bayer, p. 102, points out that Jewish leaders are sometimes described as 'builders'.

[4] So Donahue, pp. 128–38; Matera, *Passion*, pp. 65–72; Schweizer, p. 156.

include the destruction of the Temple.[1] In both cases an anti-Temple view is detectable.

The Temple theme is continued in the two accusations of xiv. 58 and xv. 29, in which it is said that Jesus intended to destroy the Temple and rebuild it or another. There has been considerable discussion as to the presence of one or both of these verses in the pre-Markan form of the pericopae in which they now occur. Was only one present, and if so, which? Or did Mark receive one of them in another part of the tradition, insert it in its present position and compose and insert the other, or, possibly, did he compose both? If Mark took at least one of them from the tradition, the nature of the way he may have modified it has also been examined in detail.[2] Whatever conclusions are drawn in regard to the redaction, the repetition of essentially the same statement would draw hearers' attention to its importance. This would be reinforced in that on both occasions it appears at significant moments in the story. If moreover hearers recognised it as an insertion into an accustomed story, they would naturally give it very great attention. In xiv. 58 it is put on the lips of false witnesses during the trial of Jesus, but this does not mean Mark regarded the statement as false;[3] in xv. 29 it is used by those who mock him while he hangs on the Cross. On each occasion the statement differs from that of xiii. 1 f. in that Jesus, not God, is said to be the author of the destruction and there is rebuilding as well as destruction. Though the former change causes difficulties for exegetes,[4] it would probably not have broken the continuity of the theme for Mark's hearers. Already in xi. 12–21 Jesus' cleansing of the Temple had been linked to his 'destruction' of the fig-tree; cleansing the court of the Gentiles was the symbolic beginning of the Temple's

[1] Telford, *op. cit.* pp. 217 f.
[2] See *Following*, pp. 213 ff. for discussion; also Dormeyer, pp. 159–62; Mohr, 253 f.; Schenke, *Christus*, pp. 32–6; D. Lührmann, 'Markus 13.55–64: Christologie und Zerstörung des Tempels im Markusevangelium', *N.T.S.* XXVII (1981), 459–74; J.R. Donahue, 'Temple, Trial, and Royal Christology (Mark 14:53–65)', Kelber, *Passion*, pp. 66–71; see also the reference in n. 1, p. xxxvi.
[3] *Pace* T.J. Weeden, 'The Cross as Power in Weakness (Mark 20b–41)', Kelber, *Passion*, pp. 115–34. Cf. H.M. Jackson, 'The Death of Jesus in Mark and the Miracle from the Cross', *N.T.S.* XXXIII (1987), 16–37; *Following*, p. 214.
[4] See Juel's discussion, pp. 172–207. Jackson, *art. cit.*, suggests that the 'falseness' of the witnesses may lie in their statement that Jesus and not God would destroy the Temple.

destruction. Jesus did not of course destroy the physical Temple, and Mark's hearers know this. The variation which implies the rebuilding of a spiritual Temple is possible without loss of theme, for it is this and not the physical Temple which is important for Mark and his hearers.

The two texts differ in one important respect. Only in xiv. 58 does Mark distinguish between a temple made with hands and one made without. Just as he does not repeat at viii. 28 the fuller description of vi. 14 f. but assumes it, so at xv. 29. The intended distinction is presumably that between a physical building and a non-material or spiritual one,[1] though 'spiritual' should not be understood as suggesting something made by the Holy Spirit. The Temple made without hands is the Christian community, the 'house' of xi. 17. In Judaism, especially at Qumran, and in early Christianity (I Cor. iii. 16 f.; Eph. ii. 20–2; II Cor. vi. 16; I Pet. ii. 4 f.) the community was often regarded as a building.[2] Mark's hearers would then see themselves as the Temple not made with hands.[3] One factor, however, might be thought to disrupt the flow of the Temple theme. In both xi. 15–19 and xiii. 1 f. the Temple is termed τὸ ἱερόν, i.e. the whole complex of Temple buildings, and not ὁ ναός, i.e. the sanctuary proper, the term used in xiv. 58; xv. 29, 38. The distinction is natural; the court of the Gentiles (xi. 15–19) was in the Temple complex but not in the sanctuary, and it is the whole complex (xiii. 1 f.) which has been or will be destroyed. Mark was however bound by the terms[4] he received in the tradition and so retained them on each occasion; elsewhere when the image of the Temple appears he again uses ὁ ναός, the term in the tradition. It is very doubtful if Mark's hearers would have been put off by the change in the term and thus have failed to see the continuity in the theme of the Temple.

The theme appears for the last time at xv. 38,[5] where it is

---

[1] Senior, p. 92.

[2] Linnemann, pp. 121 ff., rejects the idea that the metaphor of the Temple was common in the early Church; for criticism of her position see Juel, pp. 145–68 and *Following*, pp. 215 f.

[3] So, for example, Gnilka, Ernst.   [4] See *Disciples*, pp. 31–48.

[5] H. Sahlin, 'Zum Verständnis der christologische Anschauung des Markusevangeliums', *Studia Theologica* XXXI (1977), 1–19, in seeking to solve some of the difficulties associated with xv. 37–9 assumes, incorrectly, that xv. 38 was later added from Matthew. Much has been written about the rending of the veil and its symbolism and about what the centurion saw which led him

neither the whole complex of Temple buildings nor the sanctuary itself which is destroyed but one of its essential parts, namely the curtain. It is impossible to determine with any certainty whether this curtain was the one separating the Holy Place from the Holy of Holies or the one cutting off the Holy Place itself.[1] In either case what was intended was the end of Jewish worship in so far as that worship centred on the Temple, and perhaps also the opening up of the Temple as a house of prayer for all nations. The idea of destruction enters since the curtain was torn and not pulled aside,[2] and since the tearing can be seen as the Temple's profanation.[3] The rending of the curtain has been taken either as a sign of judgement on Israel or on Israel's religion,[4] or as a sign of the opening up of access to God for all,[5] or, less probably, as an indication that God is no longer in the Temple.[6] Much that has preceded (xi. 12–14, 19 f.; xiii. 1 f.) would suggest the idea of judgement, but what follows, the confession of the centurion, suggests access to God for those who did not previously have it. It may well be that both ideas are present as they were in xi. 12–21, where there was judgement in relation to Judaism and hope opened up for the Gentiles, and in xiv. 58; xv. 29, where the old Temple is judged and a new appears.[7] Yet if access alone were all that was intended, the curtain would not need to have been torn and destroyed; it would have been sufficient for it to be pulled aside.

The Temple theme thus carries with it two ideas which, as we shall see later, appear at other points in the Passion narrative and which spell out at least part of the significance of the death of Jesus. That the Temple theme relates to the Passion is evident from the

to make his confession; for surveys of views etc. see P. Lamarche, 'La Mort du Christ et le voile du temple selon Marc', *N.R.T.* CVI (1974), 583–99; S. Légasse, 'Les Voiles du temple de Jérusalem. Essai de parcours historique', *R.B.* LXXXVII (1980), 560–89; Jackson, *art. cit.*; Schreiber, B.Z.N.W., pp. 160–9.

[1] For full discussion see Donahue, pp. 201 ff. and Juel, pp. 140–2.
[2] Senior, p. 127.　　　[3] So Lührmann, p. 264.
[4] E.g. Schenke, *Christus*, p. 100.
[5] E.g. Haenchen, p. 538; Schweizer, p. 205; Gnilka, II, p. 324; Rau, pp. 2205 f.
[6] Dormeyer, p. 205; J. Schreiber, *Theologie*, p. 37.
[7] Linnemann, pp. 162 f., rejecting all the above views, holds that at the moment of Jesus' greatest weakness the majesty of God is revealed.

'three days' of xiv. 58 and xv. 29, which imply the Resurrection, and from the rending of the Temple veil, which follows directly on the death.[1] The first idea which the Temple theme indicates is the end of some aspect or aspects of Judaism.[2] The Temple, the centre of Jewish faith, has been destroyed, if not yet physically, certainly spiritually. The death of Jesus has brought to an end its worship and it can no longer be the place of atonement. Why Mark should stress the end of Jewish ways of worship is not clear; it may be that he has an anti-cultic bias[3] or, more probably, is aware of Jewish Christians who have not wholly cut themselves off from Jewish ways. In a sense it is not Jews but Jewish ways which are condemned.[4] The second idea which the Temple theme carries is the creation of a new people of God to include both Jews and Gentiles (xi. 17; xiv. 58; xv. 29; and xii. 1–12 if, as is probable, the new tenants are Christian believers). This second idea is not linked to the death alone but to the death and Resurrection, as the 'three days' indicates. Possibly II Sam. vii. 4–17 has influenced this aspect of rebuilding;[5] David is not permitted to build the Temple but it is said his offspring will, and Jesus is the son of David (x. 46–52).

We now follow up these two ideas which have emerged from the Temple theme, commencing with the first and later returning to the second.

From almost the beginning of the Gospel Jesus encounters criticism and opposition from various Jewish authorities in respect of his actions and teaching, although he continues until near the end to be popular with the crowd. From xi. 1 onwards the opposition intensifies. Prior to xi. 1 Jesus' principal opponents

[1] Cf. H. L. Chronis, 'The Torn Veil: Cultus and Christology in Mark 15:37–39', *J.B.L.* CI (1982), 97–114; Schenke, *Christus*, p. 100; Schenke regards xv. 38 as a secondary addition by Mark.

[2] For Donahue, p. 205, this seems to be the total significance of Jesus' death: 'In 15:38–39 he [Mark] portrays the significance of the death of Jesus. The temple has lost its meaning, and the present time is the time for proper confession.' Donahue's scriptural index contains no references to either x. 45 or xiv. 24; if he thought them irrelevant to an understanding of the death of Jesus one would have expected at the very least that he would have argued their irrelevance.

[3] Cf. E. Lohmeyer, *Lord of the Temple* (Edinburgh, 1961), p. 47.

[4] Cf. below, p. 98, n. 3.

[5] Cf. A. Vanhoye, 'Structure et théologie des récits de la Passion dans les évangiles synoptiques', *N.R.T.* XCIX (1967), 135–63.

were the scribes; now the other religious leaders unite with them against him (xi. 18, 27; xii. 13, 18; xiv. 1, 10 f., 43, 53,[1] 55, 65; xv. 1, 10, 31). He had indeed prophesied such opposition (viii. 31; x. 33). Even his popularity with the crowd eventually changed (xv. 8 – 15, 29; a hint of this can be seen in x. 48). At the same time as he depicts the growth of opposition Mark also sets the opposition in an unfavourable light. They prefer a notorious insurrectionist, Barabbas, to Jesus (xv. 6 – 15); he is found guilty even though those who witness against him do so falsely and their witness does not agree (xiv. 56,59); the true spirit of Jesus' opponents is seen in the sharp contrast drawn between their conduct and that of the woman who anoints him (xiv. 1 – 11); they mock him cynically while he hangs on the Cross (xv. 29 – 32; probably a Markan insertion).[2]

The mocking of xv. 29 – 32 is only one of a series of mockings. Almost invariably the content of the mockery is true,[3] but at a deeper level than the mockers realise or intend. The Jewish leaders call on the blindfolded Jesus to prophesy who is about to hit him (xiv. 65); yet though he does not do so at their behest, there is no doubt he can prophesy, for he has prophesied his own death (viii. 31, etc.) and xvi. 7 is a fulfilment of his prophecy of xiv. 58. In xv. 16 – 20 the soldiers mock him as King of the Jews, and this is what he is. In xv. 29 those who pass by deride him as claiming to destroy the Temple and build another, and this in fact is what is actually happening when 'destroy' and 'build' are understood as Mark's hearers would understand them. In xv. 31 the priests and scribes laugh at him as one who saved others but cannot save himself; it is true that he does not save himself, yet what he does saves others.[4] xv. 35 f. may also be another instance of mocking;[5] the bystanders wait to see if Elijah will come to help Jesus, but to the hearers of the Gospel this is ironical, for they know that Elijah is already dead, as is John the Baptist if he is to be

---

[1] G. Schneider, *Die Passion Jesu nach der drei älteren Evangelien* (Munich, 1973), p. 61; Trocmé, pp. 94 ff. For a detailed discussion of the opponents of Jesus see M. J. Cook, *Mark's Treatment of the Jewish Leaders* (N.T.Sup. 51; Leiden, 1978); for our purposes it is unnecessary to follow him in his search for sources based on the way he identifies the leaders; see my review in *T.L.Z.* CVI (1981), 188 f.

[2] So Schenk, pp. 63 f.; Pryke, p. 175.   [3] Cf. *Following*, p. 214.

[4] See pp. 97, 109 f. and lvii below.

[5] So Pesch, *ad loc.*; Matera, *Passion*, pp. 29 – 32; *Kingship*, pp. 122 – 5.

understood as Elijah. In a sense then each mocking viewed ironically is true; together they form a subtle continuation of a trend found throughout the Gospel in which the 'enemies' of Jesus speak the truth: the demons confess him as Son of God (iii. 11 f., etc.); the scribes say he forgives sins (ii. 7); the High Priest and Pilate announce his real identity (xiv. 61; xv. 2). Given all this opposition expressed through mockery and scorn, Mark's attitude to Judaism cannot come as a surprise, and it serves to balance the rejection of Jesus seen throughout the entire Gospel.

How then are we to understand Mark's seeming rejection of Judaism?[1] Is it a rejection of Israel's leaders, as xii.1–12 in its context appears to suggest? Though the leaders are regularly attacked, there is no suggestion that the remedy lies in the appointment of new leaders. Is it the rejection of the sacrificial system of the Temple, which some of the leaders represent? Although there are no sustained direct attacks on the cultus in the manner of some of the prophets, there is an implied attack in xii. 33.[2] Yet since so little is said about the cultus and since also, if Mark dates from around A.D. 70, the destruction of the Temple has already taken place or is imminent, and an attack on its cultus would be unnecessary, we may assume that it is not just the cultus and the priests who are rejected. The priests moreover were hardly mentioned in the earlier part of the Gospel where the main opposition came from the scribes. Is it then the Law which is rejected? While Jesus bids a leper whom he has healed obey the law (i. 44) and himself attends the synagogue (i. 21–8), he is presented as teaching in a new way (cf. ii. 21 f.) with an authority greater than the scribes and as criticising both an over-rigid adherence to the Law (ii. 23–iii. 5; vii. 9–13) and its outward observance instead of a search for inner purity (vii. 20–3). Jesus disagrees with contemporary Jewish teaching on divorce (x. 1–10) and seeks from a rich man more than obedience to the commandments (x. 17–22). He is shown as above the Law (ii. 28; iii. 4) and even as breaking it (ii. 15–17).[3]

[1] For a discussion and rejection of possible anti-Semitism in Mark see H. Baarlink, 'Zur Frage nach dem Antijudaismus im Markusevangelium', Z.N.T.W. LXX (1979), 164–93.

[2] See J.-G. Mudiso Mba Mundla, *Jesus und die Führer Israels* (Münster, 1984), pp. 228–33.

[3] S. Schulz, *Die Stunde der Botschaft* (Zurich, 1970), pp. 52, 83.

Yet this cannot mean a total rejection of the Law or Judaism for Mark repeatedly makes use of the Old Testament both by allusion and direct quotation. The two great commandments (xii. 29 – 31) are drawn from it. In the dispute about divorce Jesus appeals to the Law (x. 1 – 10). Jewish terms are employed to describe Jesus: Messiah, Son of Man, King of Israel. Mark thus relates the new community, which as we have seen is also a part of the Temple theme, to a Jewish past. There is then no total rejection of Judaism. Jews were never excluded from the new community; all its first members were Jews. Perhaps it is best to say that in so far as the cultus and the Law are no longer central to what Jesus does and teaches, Mark may be understood as rejecting a future role for Israel as God's people through whom God will accomplish his purposes. But if Israel has lost this position, has it been given to any other group? Here we return to the second idea in the Temple theme – the creation of another group, the community of Christians – and we now pick this up.

Since the new community comes into existence after the Resurrection of Jesus and because of his death, we may assume that its members will be those who perceive special significance in the death, and rejoice in the Resurrection. From the beginning Mark shows Jesus at work to create such a new community. He calls disciples (i. 16 – 20; ii. 14), even if they do not always follow (x. 17 – 22). He gives a special position to twelve of them (iii. 13 – 19), suggestive of a new Israel, and sends them out to heal and teach (vi. 7 – 13). They are given detailed and comparatively lengthy instruction on the nature of discipleship, especially during the journey of viii. 27 – x. 45.[1]

Yet despite the attention Jesus gives them, they increasingly show their fear of what may happen to them and their lack of understanding of him and what he is about. They grasp neither the significance of his mighty works (iv. 38; vi. 50, 52), nor the purpose of his mission and the need for his death (viii. 31 – 3; ix. 31 f.; x. 32, 35 – 40). Their failure is intensified during the Passion: they sleep when they ought to be awake (xiv. 27, 50), their fault made worse by their protest that they would never do so (xiv. 29 – 31). One of them denies him, again contrary to his protests (xiv. 29 – 31, 66 – 72), one turns to violence (xiv. 47) and yet another

---

[1] On the nature of discipleship see *Following, passim.*

betrays him (xiv. 10 f., 43–6). They are missing while he is crucified. We expect them then to be rejected, yet in xvi.7 they are given a message that they are to be restored, and Peter, who failed most spectacularly, receives special mention in the message. Their restoration means they themselves now have a mission.[1] Both this restoration and mission are known to Mark's hearers. What was it then that enabled them to be restored and to set out on their mission, a mission which in the end led, even if only indirectly (none of the original disciples may have been involved in the mission), to the founding of Mark's community? Why should the disciples be restored when the Old Testament people as a whole are deprived of their position in God's work? It can only be the Passion and their response to it that makes the difference. Here we need to take account of the double role played by the disciples in the Gospel: they are both historical personages and representatives of the continuing Christian community.[2] Since the historical disciples were restored after their failure this can then always be a possibility for the members of Mark's community when they fail.

ATONEMENT

Since restoration is related to the Passion we need now to move on to examine more closely the Passion within the continuity of the Gospel.

The simple answer to the question of the difference between the ultimate fate of the disciples and the Jews generally might appear to be the Resurrection. It is explicitly referred to in viii. 31; ix. 9, 31; x. 34; xiv. 58; xv. 29, and the Gospel ends with the account of the empty tomb. Yet the Resurrection is never introduced without at least implicit reference to the death, and Mark allots much more space to the narration of the death than to the Resurrection. His account of the latter also ends on the same note of fear which has run through the Gospel in relation to the disciples. The Resurrection cannot be set aside, but there must also have been a contribution from the death which helped to firm up the faith of the original disciples so that they were restored

[1] See *Following*, pp. 199–203.
[2] See *Disciples*, pp. 98–130; *Story*, pp. 44–50.

and went on their mission. It is this contribution which Mark hopes will firm up the faith of his own community. But what is it?

We have already seen how the death of Jesus dominates the Gospel from the beginning. As we draw nearer the death we can immediately detect two (there are more) strands in the way in which it is presented. First, it is seen as Jesus' voluntary giving of himself: he determines the journey which takes him to Jerusalem and his death, and during it he predicts his death (viii. 31; ix. 31; x. 32–4); he avers that the Son of Man came to give himself (x. 45); at the end he cries aloud and 'breathes out' (ἐξέπνευσεν) his life. Secondly his death is seen as necessary (viii. 31) and determined by God; this is expressed both directly and by means of the Old Testament (ix. 12; xiv. 27b); Jesus is handed up to his death by God (ix. 31; x. 33; xiv. 41), though Judas may be the human instrument (xiv. 10,21). The two strands of Jesus' willingness and of divine necessity come together in viii. 31; xiv. 21 and are in tension with one another above all in xiv. 35 f. Yet though Jesus' death may have been determined by God as part of his plan and though it may have been a willing and obedient act on his own part, and it can be argued that this takes away some of its scandal, this does not give actual significance to the death in such a way as to make it creative of a new community. So far as the scandal of the Cross goes, it might have been possible to lessen or remove it by stressing the innocence of Jesus as in the Passion narratives of Luke and John; but Mark does not adopt this idea.

Turning now more directly to the way in which Mark sees the death as contributing to the restoration of the disciples and as sustaining his own community, it may be said Mark views Jesus as the typical martyr who will inspire believers with a like determination and love when they face death. Without taking away from Jesus' exemplary death and while acknowledging that there may have been pericopae in the tradition which at some stage stressed Jesus as martyr (e.g. xv. 39, the conversion of torturers), or even that a pre-Markan form did so,[1] it is difficult to see this as the total meaning of the death for Mark. When we compare Jesus' death with those of Jewish martyrs, e.g. those of Maccabean times, we see that Jesus did not die for the Law as they did.

[1] So Dormeyer, *passim.*

More generally most, though not all, martyrs die courageously to preserve a cause which is all-important for the group to which they belong, but Jesus died as a religious revolutionary,[1] and he died alone and in despair (xv. 34) without any supporting group, for the disciples as Mark describes them could hardly be so termed.[2] Perhaps, even more importantly, though some in Mark's community may have suffered martyrdom and others may be about to do so, most of the instruction Jesus gives on discipleship is largely unrelated to martyrdom (e.g. viii. 27–x. 45); Jesus as martyr is therefore far from the centre of Mark's thought. If alternatively his emphasis is considered to lie on imitation as providing the inspiration for the change in the conduct of the original disciples and therefore for the way in which his community is to live, then this will be related not just to Jesus' death but to his whole ministry.[3]

This same argument makes difficult the theory that Mark presents Jesus throughout the Passion as the Righteous Sufferer.[4] The evidence here is certainly much stronger, for a great proportion of the material bears the stamp of this figure; its characteristics are seen especially in the use, a use which Mark may have extended, of the Lament Psalms (e.g. Ps. 22) in a sense other than that of promise and fulfilment,[5] in the reference to false witnesses (xiv. 56), in Jesus' prayer in Gethsemane,[6] in the behaviour of Jesus' disciples which resembles that of the friends of the Righteous Sufferer.[7] Yet again, as in the case of Jesus the martyr, both the original disciples and Mark's community required more than an example of dying, rather an example which would carry them through the whole course of their daily lives. Moreover there are items in Mark's account which are not found in the picture presented in the Psalms of the Righteous Sufferer (this applies also to the picture of the wise Son of God in Wisdom).

[1] Cf. Derrett, pp. 297 f.

[2] See below, pp. lx–lxi for the loneliness of Jesus.

[3] For criticism of the view that Mark presents Jesus primarily as a martyr see Steichele, *op. cit.* pp. 268–71.

[4] On the Righteous Sufferer in general see n. 2, p. xxv above; on the presence of the Righteous Sufferer in Mark see Lührmann; Ruppert, *op. cit.* pp. 48–56; Dormeyer, pp. 98, 212; Matera, *Passion*, p. 44.

[5] See Suhl, *op. cit.* pp. 46 f., 65 f.   [6] So Senior, pp. 70–2.

[7] J.-N. Aletti, 'Mort de Jésus et théorie du récit', *R.S.R.* LXXIII (1985), pp. 147–60.

The Righteous Sufferer does not give his life as a ransom (x. 45) or pour out his blood for many (xiv. 24); at his death no temple veil is rent (xv. 38); he is not expected to return in judgement (xiv. 62); though in despair for a time he dies trusting in God (contrast xv. 34). The deaths of disciples are never eschatological events, nor is the Righteous Sufferer ever presented as bringing salvation to others.[1] The latter point may suggest that Mark sees Jesus as the servant of Yahweh who suffers for others in the terms of Isa. liii. But as was indicated in the first edition, there is little in Mark which can be linked directly to the Isaianic Servant.[2] It would however be wrong to deny that parts of the tradition received by Mark may not have been heavily imprinted with the characteristics of the martyr, the Righteous Sufferer, the wise Son of God or the Servant of Yahweh, and it is certainly possible that Jesus may have seen himself in one or more or these roles.

It may then be that in a much more general way Mark believes his community will be inspired by the example of the whole life of Jesus and not simply by his death alone. It is also true that 'one function of narrative is to so engage the reader or hearer that he experiences himself an experience similar to the one narrated and that he identifies with the character'.[3] It cannot be denied that Mark saw Jesus as a model for the way Christians should live and die. The main discipleship section (viii. 27 – x. 45) shows that believers are expected to follow him in humility and service, in willingness to suffer and in carrying out acts of healing; they are expected to leave home and family as he did (x. 29 f.). Within the Passion account itself Gethsemane provides an example of the way to pray, and the Jewish and Roman trials of how to be patient and courageous when falsely accused.[4] Yet there are striking differences. The believer can hardly expect that his death will result in the veil of the local temple being rent and a new race of

[1] Cf. Gubler, pp. 126, 200–2; Hengel, p. 42.

[2] Cf. Baarlink, pp. 224–42. It is true that the Cross depicts the powerlessness of Jesus (so D. A. Lee-Pollard, 'Powerlessness as Power: A Key Emphasis in the Gospel of Mark', *S.J.Th.* XL (1987), 173–88), but this of itself is not enough to change fearful people into fervent missionaries.

[3] Donahue, p. 231; cf. R. C. Tannehill, 'The Disciples in Mark: The Function of a Narrative Role', *J.R.* LVII (1977), 386–405.

[4] On the way Jesus bore his trial and execution as an example to believers, see Donahue, pp. 210 ff.

humanity brought into the People of God. These things have happened once for all in the death of Jesus. Thus his death is different from anything theirs can be. Even in the narrative preceding the Passion we find Mark emphasising things about Jesus that would not apply to his followers. No one will ask who they are (viii. 27 – 9); no one who loses his or her life for their sake will be saved (viii. 35; if Mark thought imitation was all-important he could have omitted the reference to Jesus from this saying); while Jesus is certainly set out as an example of service in x. 42 – 5*a* he is given a unique position in *v*. 45*b*.[1] Jesus calls disciples to follow him; his disciples do not summon new disciples to follow them, but to follow him. No disciple ever presents his own death as Jesus does in xiv. 22 – 5. There is so much then that differentiates between Jesus and the disciples, not least their total failure when with him to satisfy him, that it is impossible to see Jesus set out only as a model to inspire followers and create them into a new community.

Although Jewish beliefs concerning what would happen to the Temple at the End were not uniform, some kind of change was expected.[2] Since Mark shows Jesus as making statements about the Temple and a new community which is to come into existence through his death and Resurrection, it is then possible that he regards the Passion as an eschatological event. When the Temptation is regarded as a contest between Christ and Satan, it can also be considered an eschatological event[3] in that in it an event takes place which was expected only at the End. Similarly the Cross may have been regarded at some stages of the tradition as an End event. There is evidence to support such a view. The darkness of xv. 33 is nature neither mourning at the passing of a great man nor sympathising with Jesus,[4] but could be an apocalyptic sign.[5] The 'hour' is an eschatological term, and

[1] Cf. *Following*, p. 127; K.-G. Reploh, *Markus – Lehrer der Gemeinde* (Stuttgart, 1969), p. 167.

[2] Cf. Juel, pp. 169 – 209; L. Gaston, *No Stone on Another* (N.T. Sup.; Leiden, 1970), pp. 102 – 12.

[3] Cf. Kingsbury, p. 144.

[4] Cf. C. Burchard, 'Markus 15.34', *Z.N.T.W.* LXXIV (1983), 1 – 11.

[5] Below, p. 98; cf. Schenk, pp. 41 f. The darkness might also be interpreted as indicating the presence of God in Exod. xix. 9; xx. 21; Ps. xviii. 9 – 11; xcvii. 1 – 2; Mark ix. 7; cf. E. Manicardi, 'Gesù e la sua morte secondo Marco 15, 33 – 37', in *Gesù e la sua morte. Atti della XXVII settimana biblica* (ed. P. G. Danieli; Brescia, 1984), pp. 9 – 28.

1

while in xiv. 35 it refers only to the time of Jesus' death, in xiv. 41 it may have apocalyptic overtones (cf. xiii. 32; Matt. xxiv. 44; John v. 25; Rom. xiii. 11; Rev. iii. 10; xiv. 15).[1] The final 'great wordless cry' of xv. 37 has also been interpreted in the same way,[2] and the cup of xiv. 24 been given an apocalyptic overtone in view of its use in that way in Rev. xiv. 10; xvi. 19; xviii. 6.[3] Yet all this is not sufficient to sustain an eschatological interpretation of the Passion,[4] and most of those who accept this kind of interpretation see it as expressed more clearly in an underlying pre-Markan source than in the Markan Passion itself.[5] If it was present in the earlier tradition, it has been toned down by Mark.[6] He distinguishes between the Parousia and the Passion, and the former lies not only in Jesus' future but also in his own (viii. 38; xiii. 26; xiv. 62). There must still be a period during which the Gospel will be preached in all the world (xiii. 10; xiv. 9). Mark of course has many passages outside the Passion narrative with eschatological overtones (e.g. i. 14 f.; x. 29 f.; xiii. 1 ff.). The Passion can be termed eschatological in so far as with it a change takes place that ensures that there will eventually be a Parousia.

References to the Kingdom run through the Gospel and have an undoubted eschatological ring, but generally speaking the Kingdom is not regarded as already present but as still to come.[7] The Kingdom is rarely mentioned in the Passion

---

[1] Schenke, *Studien*, pp. 504–6, 554, takes its use to be Markan. On 'hour' as indicating judgement see Feldmeier, pp. 185–8.

[2] Cf. Schreiber, *Theologie*, pp. 83–9; Schenk, *op. cit.* pp. 38–48.

[3] Cf. T. Lescow, 'Jesus in Gethsemane', *Ev. Th.* XXVI (1966), 161–77.

[4] For a criticism of Mark as an apocalyptic writing see D. O. Via, 'The Ethics of Mark's Gospel', *The Middle of Time* (Philadelphia, 1985), pp. 78–90.

[5] E.g. Schreiber, *Theologie*, pp. 33–40; H. W. Bartsch, 'Historische Erwägungen zur Leidensgeschichte', *Ev. Th.* XXII (1962), 449–59, and 'Der ursprüngliche Schluss der Leidensgeschichte. Ueberlieferungsgeschichtliche Studien zum Markus-Schluss', in Sabbe *op. cit.* pp. 411–33; Schneider, *op. cit.* p. 26. Paul sometimes construes the Cross and Resurrection eschatologically in relation to the Parousia, e.g. 1 Thess. iv. 14; 1 Cor. xi. 26; xv. 20.

[6] So Schenk, pp. 63, 273.

[7] Cf. below, pp. 64–8; Kelber, *Kingdom*; A. M. Ambrozic, *The Hidden Kingdom* (C.B.Q. Monograph Series 2; Washington, 1972); J. Marcus, *The Mystery of the Kingdom of God* (S.B.L.D.S. 90; Atlanta, Georgia, 1986); T. Söding, *Glaube bei Markus: Glaube an das Evangelium, Gebetsglaube und Wünderglaube im Kontext der markinischen Basileiatheologie und Christologie* (Stuttgart, 1985), pp. 150–97.

itself, and only xiv. 25 connects it to the death of Jesus.[1] It is true that the Passion refers on many occasions to Jesus as King, but since when the word Kingdom is used it is the Kingdom of God and not that of Jesus which is intended, these references are irrelevant. Occasionally the Kingdom may be regarded as already present (x. 14 f.; xii. 34; survivals perhaps of the teaching of Jesus?), but for Mark its true coming will coincide with the Parousia. In so far then as the Passion possesses eschatological significance, it is important for believers as a turning-point in the way in which God deals with them. This however does not exhaust its significance. We must therefore look further.

The Passion narrative sets out Jesus as King.[2] The woman in the house of Simon anoints his head in royal fashion (xiv. 3). The inscribed accusation as set out by Pilate affirms his crime as that of claiming to be the King of the Jews (xv. 26), and at the time of the trial before Pilate he is repeatedly so entitled. On the Cross Jews mock him as King of Israel (xv. 32). The royal theme may indeed have entered the story as early as the baptism if Ps. ii is there taken to be the controlling Old Testament text. Sonship and kingship can be associated in Judaism, and these two concepts may then provide one of the themes of the Passion beginning with Jesus' entry into Jerusalem, but it goes too far to speak of kingship as governing the account.[3] If it were, the Cross might then be termed the throne of Jesus and the theme of x. 42b–45a, that the true exercise of authority does not lie in physical or military power but in humble service, be seen as its theme. True strength would then lie in the weakness of the Cross.[4] Such an approach however would only set out the Cross as an example to believers and would not account for the addition of x. 45b to the preceding logia or the prominent place accorded to it by Mark (see below). The Passion is much more than an example of the way power should be exercised.

For believers the death and Resurrection of Jesus entailed the end of the Temple and its cultus. That cultus no longer exists to bring atonement. Is atonement then to be found in the Passion?

---

[1] Cf. Schenk, p. 193; Ambrozic, *op. cit.* p. 199. The reference in xv. 43 hardly contributes much to Mark's understanding of the Kingdom: cf. Ambrozic, *op. cit.* p. 243.

[2] On the kingship of Jesus see especially Matera, *Kingship*.

[3] So *ibid.* p. 61.   [4] So Lee-Pollard, *art. cit.*

To consider this we need to trace again the story of Jesus from the beginning of the Gospel. Throughout he is seen as someone who is concerned to help others; as their shepherd he cares for them by healing and teaching.[1] His service for others in that way is summarised, and in a sense brought to an end in x. 42b – 45a. Yet as x. 45b goes on to indicate, his care for them is now offered in a fresh way in his death. Two passages clearly express his Passion as an action to benefit others, in particular by offering atonement for them (x. 45; xiv. 24). It has been argued that these two references by themselves are insufficient to establish such a view since the idea is missing from the Passion narrative proper.[2] but that is to ignore the sequence of the story. It is only possible to supply an understanding of Jesus' death after its necessity has been established, e.g. by the three formal predictions in viii. 27 – x. 45. It is moreover appropriate to do so as the story moves from prediction to fulfilment. We shall in fact see that there are more than these two references to the death in the Passion story which present it as possessing atoning value.

x. 45b (we are not concerned to discuss whether Jesus spoke

---

[1] I have traced Jesus' caring role in detail in *Story*, pp. 55 – 65.

[2] P. Vielhauer, 'Erwägungen zur Christologie des Markusevangelium' in his *Aufsätze zum Neuen Testament* (Munich, 1965), pp. 199 – 214. Vielhauer's own theory that Mark presents Jesus as undergoing a three-stage (adopted at Baptism, announced at Transfiguration, acclaimed at crucifixion) process of enthronement has been widely criticised (cf. Schreiber, *Theologie*, pp. 218 – 28; Feneborg, *op. cit.* pp. 154 f.; Schenk, pp. 59 f.; Dormeyer, pp. 214 f.; Burkill, *op. cit.* p. 262, n. 115). Others have played down the significance of x. 45 and xiv. 24 for varying reasons: Schmithals, pp. 469 – 71, denies that x. 45 is basic to Mark's understanding of the Passion, and this despite his belief that it was not an independent logion taken up by Mark but his own composition. E. Lemcio, 'The Intention of the Evangelist, Mark', *N.T.S.* XXXII (1986), 187 – 206, appears to regard x. 45 as relatively unimportant because it does not form part of Jesus' public teaching; in that case a great proportion of his teaching as given in Mark must be taken as unimportant. Schreiber rejects any interpretation of the Passion which stresses x. 45 and xiv. 24. His original dissertation has now been published, *Der Kreuzigungsbericht des Markusevangeliums* (B.Z.N.W. 48; Berlin, 1986). Its publication has not led me to modify my rejection of his view (below, pp. 125 – 33); see my review in *J.T.S.* XXXVIII (1987), 495 – 7. See also Linnemann, pp. 139 – 46, 163 – 8.

the logion or not[1]) occupies a strategic position within the Gospel.[2] It was probably already linked to *vv*. 42*b* – 45*a* before Mark united those verses with what now precedes them.[3] If his only purpose had been to stress the general idea of service he could have placed x. 42*b* – 45*a* with equal effect after the prediction of ix. 31. That he has chosen to make Jesus' final logion before he enters the city where he is to die and immediately prior to the actual narrative of the Passion a logion explaining his death shows that he regards the logion as important and as suggestive of the way in which the death is to be interpreted.[4] x. 42*b*–45*a* summed up the 'caring' aspect of Jesus' ministry and 45*b* then gives the rubric under which his death is to be understood.

xiv. 24 is part of the account of the Last Supper,[5] and it is highly probable that it reproduces words used in the form of the Eucharist observed in Mark's community; Mark however has not inserted xiv. 22 – 5 to instruct his community on the way to

[1] Much of the examination of x. 45 has focussed on this point; e.g. H. J. B. Combrink, *Die Diens van Jesus. 'N Eksegetiese Beskouing oor Markus 10:45* (Groningen, 1968); E. Arens, *The* ΗΛΘΟΝ *Sayings in the Synoptic Tradition* (Göttingen, 1976), pp. 117 – 61; G. Dautenzenberg, *Sein Leben Bewahren* (Munich, 1966), pp. 98 – 107; Williams, *op. cit.* pp. 203 – 54.

[2] Cf. E. Lohse, *History of the Suffering and Death of Jesus Christ* (Philadelphia, 1967), p. 19. A. Feuillet, 'Le Logion sur la rançon', *Rev. Sci. Phil. Theol.* LI (1967), 365 – 402, suggests a possible link between viii. 35 f. and x. 45 via Ps. xlix.

[3] See *Following*, p. 123; *Disciples*, pp. 80 – 6. Even if x. 2 – 12, 17 – 31, 35 – 40, 42*b* – 45 had formed a pre-Markan complex as argued by H. W. Kuhn, *Ältere Sammlungen in Markusevangelium* (Göttingen, 1971), pp. 146 – 91 (cf. R. Busemann, *Die Jüngergemeinde nach Markus. Eine redaktionsgeschichtliche Untersuchung des 10. Kapitals im Markusevangelium* (Bonn, 1983), pp. 129 – 45), Mark's insertion of the prediction of x. 32 – 4 emphasises Jesus' death, as does x. 38 f. It is not otherwise mentioned until x. 45*b*. A few scholars hold that Mark himself introduced 45*b* to what preceded, e.g. Trocmé, pp. 157 f.

[4] This still holds true if Mark is editing a pre-Markan complex containing x. 45 composed backwards from x. 45, as is suggested by C. Breytenbach, *Nachfolge und Zukunftserwartung nach Markus: eine methodenkritische Studie* (Zurich, 1984), p. 277. The argument of G. Strecker, 'The Passion- and Resurrection Predictions in Mark's Gospel', *Int.* XXII (1968), 421 – 42 (at pp. 439 f.), that x. 45*b* can be ignored because it belongs to the tradition and not to Mark's redaction is erroneous on two grounds: the placement of the passage is redactional and Mark must be held to agree with the material he has used unless positive evidence to the contrary can be produced.

[5] Dormeyer, pp. 102 – 10, contrary to most commentators, takes xiv. 24*b* to be from the tradition but to have been inserted in its present position by Mark; his grounds seem inadequate.

observe that service (contrast I Cor. xi. 23 – 6; we have no need to discuss which of the two accounts more truly represents what happened) but in order to help them interpret the Passion; it is so placed as to control its understanding.[1] Not only does the saying possess this important position in the Gospel, but it is also a saying which would be heard every time the community celebrated the Eucharist. Mark therefore did not need to drive home the understanding of Jesus' death provided by it. Hence it was sufficient to announce the atoning nature of the death in x. 45 and to remind hearers of it with words they know so well in xiv. 24.

But if Mark did not need to enlighten his community on the meaning of these two sayings there has been no lack of discussion today, in particular of x. 45 and the interpretation of λύτρον.[2] It is the presence of this word which prevents x. 45*b* being taken as merely exemplary.[3] It has been explained both through the idea of payment, either to emancipate a slave or to release a prisoner of war, and through the idea of the freeing by God of his people from captivity. It is not necessary for our purposes to choose between these two; it is sufficient to note that both imply some kind of liberation and that neither defines from what those liberated are set free. In the preceding story Jesus has set men and women free from sickness including blindness, spiritual as well as physical, and from demonic possession, and he has also attempted to set his disciples free from fear, lack of understanding and hardness of heart. Liberation will then be not merely from physical deprivation but, and more importantly, from spiritual failure. Since Mark makes no reference to the 'powers' from which in some New Testament writings believers are liberated, we must

---

[1] Cf. Senior, p. 54; Schmithals, p. 619; G. Schille, *Offen für alle Menschen. Redaktionsgeschichtliche Beobachtungen zum Theologie des Markus-Evangeliums* (Stuttgart, 1974), pp. 73 f.

[2] Almost all the authors referred to in the preceding notes discuss the verse, though often in relation to its possible significance if spoken by Jesus; see also D. Hill, *Greek Words and Hebrew Meanings* (S.N.T.S.M.S. 5; Cambridge, 1967), pp. 49 – 81; M. D. Hooker, *The Son of Man in Mark* (London, 1967), pp. 140 – 7; Feuillet, *art. cit.*; E. Lohse, *Märtyrer und Gottesknecht. Untersuchungen zur urchristlichen Verkündigung vom Sühntod Jesu Christi* (F.R.L.A.N.T. 64), pp. 116 – 22; P. Stuhlmacher, 'Existenzstellvertretung für die Vielen', in his *Versöhnung, Gesetz und Gerechtigkeit* (Göttingen, 1981), pp. 27 – 42.

[3] It is taken in this way by Schenke, *Studien*, pp. 248 f.

assume that he thinks of the freedom as one from sin. In so far as xiv. 24 depends on ideas drawn from the Old Testament cultus it will carry the same idea. There is nothing in x. 45 to suggest that the death of Jesus was regarded as a sacrifice; if this is present anywhere it can only be in xiv. 24, with its reference to covenant.[1] That freedom in relation to sin is the proper explanation here will be confirmed as we see how it features in other ways in the story.

Another, though general, factor is relevant: the conception of Jesus' death as atoning was part of the accepted theological understanding of his death from a period much earlier than Mark and can be assumed to have been part of the theological outlook of most believers. The idea that God gave up Christ for us, in particular for our atonement, is embodied in pre-Pauline fragments (Rom. iii. 24 f.; iv. 25a; v. 6 – 8; viii. 32; Gal. i. 4; ii. 20; I Cor. xv. 3 – 5),[2] and Paul continued this understanding of the Cross (e.g. Rom. xiv. 15; I Cor. viii. 11; II Cor. v. 14 f.; I Thess. v. 10).[3] There are other passages containing the same idea which probably pre-date the writings in which they are found, but because the writings themselves may be later than Mark there is no certainty that the fragments are pre-Markan (I John ii. 2; iv. 10; I Pet. iii. 18). Whether the origin of the idea is to be found in Isa. liii[4] or in the deaths of the Maccabean martyrs[5] is irrelevant to its existence. Dying so that others, e.g. a city or a state, may be benefited and dying as atoning sacrifice were both well-known conceptions in the Greek world, and Mark's readers would thus have at least a partial framework in which to place

[1] Cf. F. Hahn, 'Die alttestamentliche Motive in der urchristliche Abendmahlsüberlieferung', *Ev. Th.* XXVII (1967), 337–74.

[2] For a recent discussion see Gubler, pp. 206 ff.; cf. G. Delling, *Der Kreuzestod Jesu in der urchristliche Verkündigung* (Göttingen, 1972), pp. 9–16.

[3] Cf. Delling, *op. cit.* pp. 17–26.

[4] When Donahue, p. 46, n. 2, suggests that to see Mark within the framework of the Isaianic servant forces an extrinsic pattern on the material he simply indicates his unwillingness to realise that a writer and readers of a particular book may prior to anything being written already possess a framework within which the story will be told, and which does not need to be expressed.

[5] See, most recently, M. de Jonge, 'Jesus' Death for Others and the Death of the Maccabean Martyrs', *Text and Testimony: Essays in Honour of A. F. J. Klijn* (ed. T. Baarda, A. Hilhorst, G. P. Luttikhuizen and A. S. van der Woude; Kampen, 1988), pp. 142–51, and the references there.

the death of Jesus.[1] The discussion whether these Hellenistic parallels imply that the origin of the view of Jesus' death as atoning lay in the early Hellenistic Church rather than in the Palestinian is again irrelevant to its existence. What is important is that Mark and his readers will have been able to understand Jesus' death as one that atoned, i.e. dealt with sin.[2] Both x. 45 and xiv. 24 speak of the death as for 'many'; whatever this meant at an earlier stage, e.g. as indicating all Israel, it probably refers in the Gospel to all people, no distinction being made between Jew and Gentile. That the second person plural is used in xiv. 25 implies that Mark has in mind the whole of his community, which included many Gentiles.

The idea of atonement is normally linked to sin, and the earlier part of the Gospel displays Mark's concern with sin.[3] Repentance is mentioned in the summary of i. 14 f., which is as much a summary of the message of the Church as it is of Jesus. The cleansing of the leper (i. 40 – 5) is probably a symbolic indication of the forgiveness of sin.[4] In ii. 1 – 12 Jesus pardons sin,[5] and he does so as Son of Man; Mark's hearers would recognise this title as the one which is regularly used when his death is referred to, as in x. 45. In ii. 17 Jesus says that he came to call sinners. iii. 28 f. says there is one sin which cannot be forgiven and thereby implies all others can be pardoned. In vi. 12 the Twelve are sent to preach repentance.[6] In xi. 25 Jesus advises how to behave so that God may forgive sin. All this can be taken further. On a number of occasions Mark writes of Jesus as 'saving', using the verb σώζειν.[7] Salvation may be from the judgement to come as in

---

[1] Cf. Hengel, 9 ff.; Williams, *op. cit.* pp. 153 – 61.

[2] Cf. Senior, pp. 61 f.

[3] *Pace* H.-J. Klauck, 'Die Frage der Sündenvergebung in der Perikope von der Heilung des Gelämtes (Mk 2, 1 – 12 parr)', *B.Z.* XXV (1981), 223 – 48.

[4] Below, pp. 106 f.

[5] Donahue, pp. 81 f., argues that ii. 7, 8a, 10 are examples of Mark's insertion technique (cf. pp. 77 – 84, 241 – 3); if so this would indicate that forgiveness was important for Mark; others have taken ii. 10a as a logion inserted by Mark and addressed to his hearers, e.g. Cranfield, *ad loc.*; N. Perrin, 'The Christology of Mark: A Study in Methodology', *J.R.* LI (1971), 173 – 87, at n. 24.

[6] On the place of sin and its forgiveness in Mark see Manicardi, *op. cit.* pp. 163 – 6.

[7] Cf. J. Delorme, 'Le Salut dans l'évangile de Marc', *Laval Théologique et Philosophique* XLI (1985), 79 – 108.

xiii. 13, 20 or from the 'powers', but there is no trace of the latter in Mark and the former fits happily with the idea of salvation from sin since it is sin which will be tested in the day of judgement (in xiii. 13 the person who does not apostatise in persecution, i.e. does not sin, is saved). There are however other occasions when Mark speaks of Jesus as 'saving' (God may also be said to save, x. 26). An ambiguity appears when the verb is used in relation to the healing of the sick (v. 23, 28, 34; vi. 56; x. 52; cf. Acts iv. 12). For Mark the miracles are real, but he often also sees them as symbolic: the death of the fig-tree (xi. 12 – 14) is a symbol of the destruction of the Temple, the giving of sight to the blind (viii. 22 – 6; x. 46 – 52) of the opening up of the mind to truth, the rent veil of the Temple of the cessation of its cultus as a way to God (xv. 38).[1] Thus Jesus' healing of the sick symbolises his saving of humanity. The theme of salvation is carried on into the Passion. Jesus is mocked because he is able to save others but not himself (xv. 31).[2] Through his death he thus becomes the Saviour of all. We can then say that the theme of atonement runs through the whole Gospel[3] and forms at least one key to the understanding of the Passion. Finally the absence of the theme from the predictions (viii. 31, etc.) is not surprising since in essence these pre-date Mark.[4] The necessity of the death has first to be established before it can be interpreted.

Since the first edition the Jewish concept of the *Akedah* has been examined more closely.[5] There is no doubt that the sacrifice of

---

[1] See discussion of the miracles in *Disciples*, pp. 177–96 and below p. 109.

[2] Below, pp. 109 f.; cf. Schenk, pp. 52 f.; Minear, *op. cit.* p. 130; Pesch, II, p. 490; Ernst; Schreiber, *Theologie*, p. 43. Some regard this verse as redactional, e.g. Schenk, pp. 24 f.

[3] Hengel, p. 42, finds it also at xv. 38.

[4] See *Following*, pp. 24, 70, 120, and *Disciples*, pp. 38 f.

[5] Previous work is exhaustively discussed in J. Swetnam, *Jesus and Isaac: A Study in the Epistle to the Hebrews in the Light of the Aquedah* (An. Bib. 94; Rome, 1981), pp. 4–22. For examinations of the biblical and post-biblical material, see *ibid.* pp. 23–85; R. J. Daly, 'The Soteriological Significance of the Sacrifice of Isaac', *C.B.Q.* XXXIX (1977), 45–75; P. R. Davies and B. D. Chilton, 'The Aqedah: A Revised Tradition History', *C.B.Q.* XL (1978), 514–46; Gubler, pp. 345–62; N. A. Dahl, 'The Atonement–An Adequate Reward for the Akedah? (Ro 8:32)', *Neotestamentica et Semitica* (Essays for Matthew Black, ed. E. E. Ellis and M. Wilcox; Edinburgh, 1969), pp. 15–29; J. E. Wood, 'Isaac Typology in the New Testament', *N.T.S.* XIV (1967–8), 583–9; F. Cocchini, 'Il figlio unigenito sacrificato e amato', *Studi Storico Religiosi* I (1977), 301–23; R.A. Rosenberg, 'Jesus, Isaac, and the "Suffering Servant"', *J.B.L.* LXXXIV (1965), 381–8.

Isaac began to occupy an important place in Jewish thought around the time of the writing of Mark's Gospel and that traces of it are to be found in the New Testament (e.g. Rom. viii. 32; James ii. 21 – 3; Heb. xi. 17 – 19); it is less certain how the *Akedah* was understood. Was it regarded in this period as a sacrifice, and, if so, was this sacrifice understood as atoning? It remains probable that Mark was influenced by Gen. xxii in the accounts of the Baptism and the Transfiguration and in the parable of xii. 1 – 12.[1] This is suggested both by the use of ἀγαπητός, a word not too common in the LXX apart from Gen. xxii, and by the difficulty of seeing the influence of Isa. xlii in these passages. We have to assume either that it appeared in the pre-Markan forms of the three pericopae (it is found in II Pet. i. 17) or that appearing in none, Mark inserted it in all three, or that if it appeared in at least one, Mark inserted it in the others; there seems little doubt that he introduced it into the parable.[2] A reference to Gen. xxii however does not of itself imply atoning significance. We can only suggest that if elsewhere in Mark atoning significance is given to Jesus' death, as we have argued it is, and if the *Akedah* concept lies behind Rom. viii. 32,[3] it may also therefore be implied in the accounts of the Baptism and Transfiguration. That Mark deliberately added the word 'beloved' on at least one occasion (xii. 6), so making the parallel of Jesus with Isaac, would be pointless unless some special significance were seen in the 'sacrifice' of Isaac. Were the phrase 'beloved son' more common (Jer. vi. 26; 'beloved daughter' is found in Judg. xi. 34; Tob. iii. 10 and 'beloved child' in Zech. xii. 10; in each case it means 'only'), it would be possible to say that Mark was using a normal phrase to indicate someone with a unique relation to God. The reference to Isaac in the use of the word cannot be denied on the grounds that the paralleling of Isaac with Jesus entails the impossible

---

[1] For a discussion of the Markan material see A. Gaboury, 'Deux fils uniques: Isaac et Jésus, Connexions veterotestamentaires de Mc I, II (et parallèles)', *Studia Evangelica* IV = *T.U.*, CII, pp. 198 – 204; E. Ruckstuhl, 'Jesus als Gottessohn im Spiegel des markinischen Taufberichts Mk I, 9 – II', *Die Mitte des Neuen Testaments* (Festschrift E. Schweizer, ed. U. Luz and H. Weder; Göttingen, 1983), pp. 193 – 220; C. R. Kazmierski, *Jesus, the Son of God: A Study of the Markan Tradition and its Redaction by the Evangelist* (Würzburg, 1979), pp. 27 – 31.

[2] So Kato, p. 122; Gnilka, II, p. 14.   [3] Dahl, *art. cit.*

paralleling of Abraham and God[1] and makes Abraham act out of obedience to God rather than love; typology by its nature is never exact and concentrates on one item while ignoring the imperfections of other details. Perhaps the most we can say is that the parallel with Isaac is suggestive of atonement but that in the light of present evidence of the way the *Akedah* was understood in the first century, firm proof is lacking.

The *Akedah* theme would fit not inappropriately with the cry of dereliction (xv. 34) if it could be supposed that Mark thought of Jesus as expecting some substitution for himself at the moment of death as happened in the case of Isaac. Whether this is so or not, the theme of abandonment is slowly built up throughout the Gospel. It is in keeping with the idea of the Righteous Sufferer whose friends turn against him (Pss. xxxi. 11; xxxviii. 11; lxxxviii. 8),[2] and is therefore a not unexpected theme in the Passion. Throughout the Gospel we see Jesus being steadily abandoned by those from whom he might have looked for help. His relatives think him out of his mind (iii. 21) and cease to be his true family (iii. 31–5). The people of his own village are offended at him (vi. 1–6a). The crowd, comprised of members of God's People and of his own race, though often apparently on his side, finally turns against him (xv. 11–14). The civil authorities, to whom he might have looked for assistance in view of his innocence, hand him over to execution (xv. 2–5). The leaders of his own people from whom basic support could have been expected constantly dispute what he is about; from the beginning they argue with him (ii. 1–12), and in the end after condemning him to death they hand him over to those who will crucify him. He chose his disciples so that they should be with him (iii. 14), and up to his arrest never seems to have carried out any activity in their absence; the óne period of their absence when he sent them to heal and preach Mark fills with an account of the death of John the Baptist (vi. 7–30), and Jesus is not mentioned. Yet again and again his disciples did not understand him. In the final spiritual struggle of Gethsemane those who were with him went to sleep and Mark emphasises their sleep (xiv. 32–42);[3] when he is arrested (xiv. 50) they run away despite their previous professions of loyalty (xiv. 31); Peter goes

[1] So Gubler, pp. 364, 371 f.   [2] Cf. Matera, *Passion*, p. 28.
[3] See *Following*, pp. 146–51.

further in denying (xiv. 66–72) and Judas in betraying him (xiv. 10 f., 43–6). In his last hours all mock him, soldiers, leaders, crowd, even those crucified with him (xiv. 65; xv. 16–20, 29–32). Only the women, and they were of no importance in contemporary eyes, stand by him, and even then not close by him but afar off (xv. 40). Despite all this it is still wholly unexpected when he cries out that God has abandoned him; Righteous Sufferers are never abandoned by God.

That final cry of dereliction aside, there was nothing to surprise Mark's hearers; most of them at some time would have found themselves deserted by friends and relatives, probably at the moment they became Christians, and they would have seen fellow Christians who had committed no crimes put to death by the authorities. Yet they cannot but have been surprised by the final cry which Mark, and probably the tradition prior to him,[1] puts on the lips of Jesus; in their own experience they will always have known God with them in their deepest need. The cry surprises also because there was nothing in the preceding story line to suggest anything other than the continuance of a perfect relation between Jesus and God. In Gethsemane Jesus prayed to be delivered from his death; God was silent then, but surely when the time came to suffer God would have answered affirmatively and not allowed him to suffer. God does nothing. He does not simply leave Jesus to die; he deserts him. The cry of xv. 34 is then a, if not the, high point in the Gospel, stressing the total isolation of Jesus and raising an immense 'Why?'[2] It stands out even more starkly because in it we have the final words of Jesus.

It is possible to make another approach to the cry of dereliction

---

[1] Schenk, p. 55, and Dormeyer, p. 200, represent the minority who believe Mark inserted it into the Passion story. More probably it was already in some forms of the story and led to the allusions from the Psalm elsewhere in the narrative. There is no need for us to enter into the question of its historicity or discuss whether Mark has provided the correct Aramaic; see, for example, X. Léon-Dufour, 'Le dernier cri de Jésus', *Études* 348 (1978), pp. 666–82, and the commentaries *ad loc.*; the existence of the Aramaic together with the translations implies Mark did not create the saying. We should also note that Mark's hearers already knowing that the story will end with this surprising twist would not be stopped from wishing to hear it again. People love rehearing that type of story.

[2] Cf. F. Belo, *A Materialist Reading of the Gospel of Mark* (New York, 1981), p. 229.

and the Cross through the story line.[1] At his baptism God described Jesus as his beloved Son with whom he was well pleased (cf. ix. 7); with the preaching of Jesus the Kingdom of God had in some way arrived (i. 14 f.); he had come to call sinners to God (ii. 17); in the storm he had rebuked the fear and lack of faith of his disciples (iv.40); he had told the father of the epileptic whom the disciples had failed to heal that all things were possible if only there was faith (ix. 23); he had said to those who were amazed at the withering of the fig-tree that if they prayed for anything without doubt in their hearts they would receive it (xi. 23 f.). Would God then have deserted his Son, and could he have so lacked faith that his prayer to escape the Cross would have been ineffective? The story tells us that the Cross was God's intended fate for him. Did God lure him into willingly accepting that fate only to abandon him at its worst moment? If he whose life should be an example to all finds himself forsaken, will others be encouraged? Has the prayer of Gethsemane that the cup should pass from him now been answered with a resounding 'No!'? Whatever the path we take through Mark's story this cry is not the ending we expect. Jesus ought to be courageous and trusting right to the last moment. The cry demands understanding.

The understanding we seek must be one lying within the story line and not one which attempts to discover if the historical Jesus spoke the words, still less one discussing his mental state if he did.[2] It is often argued that when Mark, or the prior tradition, placed the first verse of Ps. xxii[3] on the lips of Jesus it was intended that hearers should realise that he went on to quote the whole Psalm; though the Psalm begins with despair it ends with confident praise of God; we ought therefore to assume that there was no real or lasting despair on the part of Jesus, but perfect

[1] Cf. Alec McCowen, *Personal Mark* (London, 1984), pp. 230 f.

[2] It is of no help in understanding the cry of Jesus to assert that it is the same cry as that of all those who live their lives in misery; cf. Lee-Pollard, *art. cit.*

[3] On the use of Ps. xxii in the Passion narrative see H. Gese, 'Psalm 22 und das Neue Testament', *Z.T.K.* LXV (1968), 1–22; L. R. Fisher, 'Betrayed by Friends: An Expository Study of Psalm 22', *Int.* XVIII (1964), 20–38; J. H. Reumann, 'Psalm 22 at the Cross', *Int.* XXVIII (1974), 39–58; J. Oswald, 'Die Beziehungen zwischen Psalm 22 und dem vormarkinischen Passionsbericht', *Z.K.T.* CI (1979), 53–66; F. Stolz, 'Psalm 22: Alttestamentliches Reden vom Menschen und neutestamentliches Reden von Jesus', *Z.T.K.* CXXVII (1980), 129–48; Moo, *op. cit.* pp. 252–75; Steichele, *op. cit.* pp. 193–279.

confidence in his Father.[1] If this is so we would have to imagine
that the hearers of the Passion narrative given the first verse of
the Psalm had instant recall on the way it ended and realised
without further indication that all of it was to be taken into account
when the first verse was quoted. The minds of scholars, or readers
with plenty of time on their hands, may operate in this way, but
the minds of those listening to a story do not, especially if they
have not been explicitly told that Scripture is being quoted. The
narrative is moving rapidly at this point, and nothing suggests
the need to take time out to meditate on a lengthy Psalm. If Mark
had wished his hearers to envisage Jesus as remaining confident
as he died he could easily have quoted another passage from the
same Psalm which would have expressed this confidence, for the
narrative already carries a number of allusions to it (all of them
incidentally drawn from its 'lament' portions). That Mark quotes
the Aramaic implies he intends us to understand that he is
reproducing the actual words of Jesus and that therefore this is
all that Jesus says and also that it is important.[2] The period of
darkness goes appropriately with the idea of abandonment by
God, for God is a God of light.[3] It is true that Jesus says '*My*
God': God is still his God. Though God desert him he will not
give God up;[4] yet the term Jesus uses, howbeit in accordance
with the Psalm, is God, and not Abba as in Gethsemane. That
he says 'My God' intensifies the sense of abandonment; it is not
some other God but Jesus' own God who has abandoned him.
At the great moments of Baptism and Transfiguration God spoke
to Jesus from heaven; now he is silent.[5]

The cry of dereliction is the moment of supreme dramatic
tension in the Gospel. It comes at the end of the temporal build-
up through days and hours and is only the third time Jesus has
spoken since his arrest. On the first two occasions he acknowledged
his identity (he does not die in 'disguise' but as the one he really
is) and announced his return (xiv. 62; xv. 2). But how could God's
Son and Messiah, the one who is to come in God's name to

[1] E.g. Pesch, II, pp. 494 f.; Matera, *Kingship*, pp. 127 ff.; Schenk, p. 56.
[2] On all this see Léon-Dufour, *art. cit.*
[3] Cf. Mohr, p. 322. If the darkness had been a sign of the presence of
God (see n. 5 p. l) then its ending (xv. 33) leads appropriately to the cry of
dereliction.
[4] Gnilka, II, p. 322.   [5] Cf. van Iersel, p. 189.

judge all, be abandoned by that God? The cry is again highlighted by its only immediate response (xv. 35 f.), a 'crude joke'[1] about Elijah whom everyone knows is dead, whether they are thinking of the historical Elijah or of John the Baptist. The cry is not only a moment of drama but one also of great irony, for Mark's readers know that Jesus was not finally abandoned by God but that God raised him from the dead. To speak of drama and irony however does nothing to indicate the meaning of the cry. It is an astounding ending to the story of Jesus. Since Mark does not normally open up to us the emotions and thought processes of Jesus, we cannot suppose that he is doing that here.[2] No more can we suppose that he records it simply because it is a genuine saying of Jesus, though we may assume that he did believe it was such. It would be highly inappropriate in any form of the Passion story which was used for apologetic, evangelistic or liturgical purposes. It interferes with any presentation of Jesus as the Righteous Sufferer, the martyr, or the true model for Christian living. Luke excludes it as he does some of Mark's other soteriological statements (e.g. x. 45).

Why then has Mark included it? It can only be because he saw in it some theological significance, and since it forms part of the actual crucifixion account that significance will be soteriological. In the earlier story Mark has several times said that Jesus is to be given up into the hands of others, men (ix. 31), Gentiles (x. 33), sinners (xiv. 41), implying not simply their rejection of him but his being handed over by God.[3] Jewish use of the phrase about God delivering people into the hands of others regularly carries with it the idea that God is judging them (e.g. Jer. xxi. 10; Ezek. xi. 9).[4] When God abandons Jesus, is he then judging him? The darkness, if it is a sign of judgement rather than of the presence of God, would not by itself indicate who was being judged. In the story we have encountered already both the judgement of Jesus by the Jewish leaders and Pilate and also

---

[1] N. A. Dahl, 'The Purpose of Mark's Gospel', in his *Jesus in the Memory of the Early Church* (Minneapolis, 1976), p. 57; cf. K. Brower, 'Elijah in the Markan Passion Narrative', *J.S.N.T.* 18 (1983), 85–101.

[2] Cf. *Story*, pp. 118 f.

[3] Cf. W. Popkes, *Christus Traditus. Eine Untersuchung zum Begriff der Dahingabe im Neuen Testament* (A.T.A.N.T. 49; Zurich, 1967), p. 272.

[4] See Feldmeier, pp. 216 ff.

God's judgement of Israel; since neither of these would occasion the abandonment of Jesus by God, they cannot be in mind. The only other possible idea is that God is judging Jesus.[1] We cannot reject such an interpretation because it causes difficulties for a doctrine of the Trinity: that would be a modern objection; Mark had no doctrine of the Trinity, and we cannot suppose he would realise the difficulties he was creating for later theology.

Before we consider the possible meaning of the cry we must follow the lead of those who associate xv. 34 with the prayer of Jesus in Gethsemane.[2] There Jesus prayed (xiv. 35 f.) to escape what God had decreed for him and what up to now he had apparently accepted willingly and unhesitatingly, as we see from his predictions of his death. Yet as the sequel shows, the prayer of Gethsemane was not granted. That prayer is expressed in two forms, in $v.35$ in indirect speech and in $v.$ 36 in direct; there has been considerable discussion as to which is the original, but this does not concern us.[3] The double impact of the supplication however implies its importance. It is introduced by a reference to Jesus' distress and trouble of soul. He had challenged the disciples to drink the cup (x. 38 f.), yet now he himself finds it difficult to drink.[4] His distress can hardly be a simple fear of the manner of his death, for this would mean nothing to Mark's hearers, who will have known many who suffered as painfully, if not more so, without apparent fear; it must then be a fear of death itself as something which might break a relationship with

---

[1] Cf. Lane, pp. 572 f.; L. Goppelt, *Theology of the New Testament* (Grand Rapids, 1981), pp. 189, 197 f., 227; R. P. Martin, *Mark: Evangelist and Theologian* (Exeter, 1972), p. 120; L. Morris, *The Cross in the New Testament* (Exeter, 1976), pp. 42–9; G. R. Osborne, 'Redactional Trajectories in the Crucifixion Narrative', *Evangelical Quarterly* LI (1979), 80–96.

[2] E.g. Schnackenburg, II, p. 154; Lane, pp. 592 f.; Delling, *op. cit.*, p. 70; Bayer, p. 82.

[3] I have discussed the Gethsemane passage as a whole in *Following*, pp. 147–52, but without particular reference to these two verses. On the problems relating to their redaction see Schenk, pp. 193 ff.; Dormeyer, pp. 124–37; Schenke, *Studien*, pp. 495–501; T. Söding, 'Gebet und Gebetsmahnung Jesu in Gethsemani', *B.Z.* XXXI (1987), 76–100; W. Mohn, 'Gethsemane (Mk 14.32–42)', *Z.N.T.W.* LXIV (1973), 194–208; M. Ruhland, *Die Markuspassion aus der Sicht der Verleugnung* (Eilsbrunn, 1987), pp. 23–8; Feldmeier, pp. 84–93.

[4] Cf. Senior, p. 70.

PREFACE TO THE SECOND EDITION

God.[1] In *v.* 36 Jesus prays that the cup should be removed from him. In the first edition Old Testament evidence was supplied to show that this denoted God's judgement on those to whom he reached the cup to drink. Though in later Judaism it also came to signify in a weakened sense a person's fate or destiny where suffering was involved[2] the earlier sense continued and was the more frequent.[3] Within the context of the Gethsemane pericope this earlier sense seems the better interpretation. At the conclusion of the incident Jesus speaks of himself as given over into the hands of sinners, and as we have already seen, this suggests being given out of God's care. Finally the very difficult ἀπέχει could carry a similar significance indicating 'distance' from God.[4] Thus in this pericope we already encounter Jesus praying to God to escape his destiny and not being heard. God's silence leads on to the cry of dereliction, and both imply that Jesus bears God's judgement.

That this is a correct reading of Gethsemane and the cry of dereliction is indicated in two further ways: (1) there are other passages (x. 38 f.; xiv. 27 f.) which can carry the same idea; since we drew attention to most of these in the first edition (pp. 152 – 9 below), it is only necessary now to discuss some fresh points that have arisen; (2) there are passages in Paul with the same significance.

1. Because of the apparent parallel in x. 38 f. between what is happening to Jesus and what is prophesied will happen to James and John it is frequently argued[5] that there can be no judgement involved in the cup which Jesus has to drink; it is not the cup

[1] Feldmeier, pp. 146 – 56, analyses both this fear and its particular expression when the phrase ἕως θανάτου is associated with it as in *v.* 34.

[2] See the evidence in S. Légasse, 'Approche de l'Episode préévangélique des Fils de Zébédée (Marc x. 35 – 40 par.)', *N. T. S.* XX (1973/4), 161 – 77; V. Howard, 'Did Jesus Speak about His Own Death?', *C.B.Q.* XXXIX (1977), 515 – 27.

[3] See Feldmeier, pp. 174 – 185.

[4] *Ibid.* pp. 209 – 15. Bayer, p. 88, sees the 'hour' in xiv. 41 as possibly indicating the time of eschatological judgement; God's wrath is now poured out on Jesus.

[5] E.g. Schenke, *Studien*, pp. 502 – 3; H. Patsch, *Abendmahl und historisches Jesus* (Stuttgart, 1972), pp. 205 – 11; V. Howard, *Das Ego Jesu in den synoptischen Evangelien. Untersuchungen der Sprachgebrauch Jesu* (Marburg, 1975), pp. 97 – 107; Böttger, *op. cit.* p. 98. Reploh, *op. cit.* p. 161, argues that the emphasis does not lie on the fate of Jesus but on that of the disciples; however the proximity of *vv.* 33 f. to *v.* 45 means that Jesus' death cannot be excluded.

of God's judgement or wrath, but only that of suffering, which
need not even entail death. Since the first edition I have discussed
these verses in detail again elsewhere,[1] and see no reason to
modify my original opinion. There is moreover no parallel of
possible suffering on the part of disciples in the Gethsemane
reference to the cup. Paraenetic statements are often linked to
soteriological statements in places other than x. 38 f. (cf. I Pet.
ii. 18–25; Rom. vi. 6; I Cor. v. 7; vi. 19 f.; II Cor. v. 14 f.; Phil.
ii. 1–11).[2] As was argued in the first edition, xiv. 27b[3] is best also
understood soteriologically.[4] It is certainly true that the main
emphasis in xiv. 26–31 falls on the behaviour of the disciples[5]
rather than on the death of Jesus, yet there was no need for Mark
to use and *change* the first part of Zech. xiii. 7 ('I will strike the
shepherd') if he was only interested in the disciples; he does not
say that the shepherd is struck *so that* the disciples may be scattered,
i.e. the purpose of the striking is not simply the scattering of the
disciples.[6] If Mark had been only concerned with the disciples
it would have been sufficient for him to have presented Jesus as
saying 'You will all fall away, for it is written that when the
shepherd dies "the sheep will be scattered"', but Mark draws
out the fact that it is God who strikes the shepherd.[7] 'Striking'
appears to involve more positive action than abandonment (xv.
34), a positive action which is also involved in the cup metaphor
where God reaches it to those who are to drink from it. Finally
it is possible also to see in the Barabbas incident a soteriological

[1] *Following*, pp. 123–5; cf. Schmithals, pp. 467 f.; Feldmeier, pp. 182–4;
Lane, p. 380; Schnackenburg, II, p. 54; Gnilka; Moo, *op. cit.* pp. 116–18;
Harrington, *op. cit.* p. 164; M. Limbech, *Markus-Evangelium* (Stuttgart, 1984),
p. 147; R. Grob, *Einführung in das Markus-Evangelium* (Zurich and Stuttgart, 1965),
p. 167; Combrink, *op. cit.* 145; Goppelt, *op. cit.* I, 189, 227. Bayer, pp. 55–77,
sees judgement involved in the drinking of the cup, but appears to regard the
bearing of judgement as extending also to the disciples. Such a view might be
supported with some interpretations of Col. i. 24 and with the idea of James
and John as undergoing the Messianic Woes.
[2] Cf. Delling, *op. cit.* p. 63.
[3] xiv. 27b is widely recognised as a Markan addition: cf. Schenk, pp. 225 f.;
Dormeyer, pp. 111 f.; Ruhland, *op. cit.* pp. 14 f. Schenke, *Studien*, pp. 388 f.,
regards the whole of xiv. 27–31 as a Markan formulation; cf. Pryke, 172.
[4] Jeremias, pp. 297 f., sees here a representative atonement.
[5] See for example Schenke, *Studien*, pp. 384 f.
[6] Cf. Senior, p. 64.
[7] Cf. Schmithals, p. 632; Feldmeier, p. 184.

significance; Barabbas is the actual guilty person, but it is Jesus who in effect takes his place and dies instead of him.[1] There is thus a sequence of sayings in which it is suggested that the dying Jesus bore God's judgement, and this sequence may be extended if the ἀντὶ πολλῶν of the ransom saying (x. 45) carries the concept of 'exchange'. Mark however does not explain what it means that Jesus should bear God's judgement.

2. In a number of passages Paul expresses thoughts similar to those of Mark, and these passages may provide a clue as to the way this idea was conceived in the early Church. In Gal. iii. 13, which may reflect pre-Pauline ideas,[2] the crucified Jesus bears the curse, presumably that of God. In II Cor. v. 21, which again may be pre-Pauline,[3] he who was sinless is made sin. In Rom. viii. 3 God condemns sin in the person of his Son.[4] When therefore Mark took up the idea of Jesus as bearing God's judgement he was moving in territory which others in the Church had already explored and which he could expect his hearers to understand. The idea clearly bears also some relationship to the idea of representative dying which is found not only in Judaism but also in Hellenism.[5]

THE NEW COMMUNITY

We turn now to the other side of the Temple motif, namely the creation of a new community. The disciples were given a message of hope at the empty tomb, and since Peter's failure had been

---

[1] Cf. Schweizer, *ad loc.*; this would be even more likely to be true if Barabbas (son of a father) is to be understood as 'every man': cf. van Iersel, pp. 180 f.

[2] H. D. Betz, *Galatians* (Hermeneia; Philadelphia, 1979), *ad loc.*

[3] So R. P. Martin, *2 Corinthians* (Word Biblical Commentary; Waco, Texas, 1986), *ad loc.* V. P. Furnish, *II Corinthians* (Anchor Bible), *ad loc.*, regards it as a reworking of Jewish Christian material.

[4] This holds true whether περὶ ἁμαρτίας is a reference to the sin offering or not.

[5] See Gubler, pp. 327–35; Hengel, pp. 19 ff.; P. Stuhlmacher, 'Sühne oder Versöhnung? Randbemerkungen zu Gerhard Friedrichs Studie: "Die Verkündigung des Todes Jesu im Neuen Testament"', *Die Mitte des Neuens Testaments: Festschrift für Eduard Schweizer* (ed. U. Luz and H. Weder; Göttingen, 1983), pp. 291–316; U. Wilckens, *Der Brief an die Römer* (E.K.K.; Zurich and Cologne, 1978), I, pp. 233–43.

particularly striking he was mentioned by name (xvi. 7). This hope exists since and because of the Cross and implies that the failures of the disciples are now forgiven. The new community does not consist of the historical disciples alone. Some of the evidence for it which came to light in the discussion of the Temple motif emphasised the position of Gentiles within it (xi. 17; xii. 9), and the historical disciples were not Gentiles. On the other hand, since the historical disciples are included, it cannot consist of Gentiles alone; the Gentiles have not replaced the Jews as God's People; the new community, the Church, contains both Jews and Gentiles. It is however the presence of Gentiles in it which is one of the main reasons why it may be described as *new*. We need now to go back through the Gospel to discern its interest in the Gentiles.

While from almost the beginning of the story people came to Jesus from Gentile areas and he taught and healed them (iii. 7–12), it cannot be proved that any of them were Gentiles, and Mark's hearers may not have been well enough acquainted with the areas concerned to realise that many of their inhabitants would have been Gentiles. Jesus healed a deaf and dumb man in the Gentile area of Decapolis (vii. 31–7) and fed the four thousand (viii. 1–10) apparently in the same area; in this case the Greek name of the area would probably have alerted hearers to realise that Jesus was dealing with Gentiles. They would have been the more likely to pick this up because immediately prior to it (vii. 24–30) Jesus had healed a Gentile, and Mark points this out emphatically. The story tells how Jesus has just moved on from a dispute with scribes over the Law (vii. 1–23) when a Gentile mother comes to him seeking help for the healing of her daughter. At first Jesus demurs, but she argues with him and he is won over. Since in no other story in the Gospel is Jesus presented as losing an argument, we can only assume that Mark is deliberately drawing our attention to the fact that it is a Gentile who is healed. Mark's concern for the Gentiles appears in a more formal way in xiii. 10, where it is prophesied that the Gospel must be preached to all nations before the End comes (cf. xiv. 9). That concern is probably also present in the 'many' of xiv. 24 and x. 45, which though it may originally have denoted 'all Israel' became for Christians 'all people', and in the twice-repeated logion of xiv. 28; xvi. 7, where Jesus is said to go at the head of his disciples in Galilee, if Galilee is to be understood as Galilee of the Gentiles.[1] The Gentile theme reaches its climax in the confession of the centurion at the Cross (xv. 39);[2] the first human to confess Jesus in an adequate manner is a Gentile.[3] What led the centurion to his utterance has been much discussed; was it the manner of the death of Jesus, or a response to all that he had observed in the crucifixion, or his seeing the rending of the Temple veil (xv. 38), whether physical sight is understood by this or 'insight', or his hearing Jesus' final great cry (xv. 37)?[4] Whichever of these be true, we have in the confession of the centurion the final human word about Jesus in the story prior to his burial, and because of its position it must be taken to carry significance.

It would be incorrect however to over-stress the position of Gentiles as if the new community consisted of them alone. Clearly all those passages which imply a comprehensiveness, e.g. all nations (xiii. 10)[5] and the whole world (xiv. 9),[6] permit the inclusion of Jews within the new community, as does the recognition,

---

[1] Most commentators accept one or other of xiv. 28 and xvi. 7, if not both, as Markan insertions; Pesch, II, p. 377, is unusual in seeing it as part of the pre-Markan Passion narrative. More important is the question whether Galilee is to be understood as Galilee of the Gentiles; for this see discussions below, pp. 157 f., 173–7, in *Following*, pp. 199–203, and the references given in the latter; see now also Kato, pp. 4–8, 23; Manicardi, *op. cit.* pp. 51–72, 171–82; Söding, *op. cit.* pp. 113–20; Schreiber, *Theologie*, pp. 173 ff.

[2] See Kato, pp. 102 ff., for a discussion with references as to the possible Markan nature of the verse.

[3] Pobee, *art. cit.*, sees in this confession the centurion's recognition that Jesus was a hero and his 'conversion'. The absence of the definite article with 'Son of God' occasions difficulty: cf. P. B. Harner, 'Qualitative Anarthous Predicate Nouns in Mark 15:39 and John 1:1', *J.B.L.* XCII (1973), 75–87; E. S. Johnson, 'Is Mark 15.39 the Key to Mark's Christology?', *J.S.N.T.* 31 (1987), 3–22. Whatever the significance of the anarthous words, they indicate some kind of recognition of the importance of Jesus on the part of the centurion.

[4] Cf. Chronis, *art. cit.*; K. Stock, 'Das Bekenntnis des Centurio. Mk 15, 39 im Rahmen des Markusevangeliums', *Z.K.T.* C (1978), 289–301; Jackson, *art. cit.*

[5] xiii. 10 is probably a Markan insertion if not a Markan composition; cf. Kato, p. 138; Söding, *op. cit.* pp. 201 f. The exclusion of the wide reference here by G. D. Kilpatrick, 'The Gentile Mission in Mark and Mark 13.9–11', *Studies in the Gospels: Essays in Memory of R. H. Lightfoot* (Oxford, 1955), pp. 145–58, is unacceptable.

[6] Kato, p. 155 and Gnilka, II, p. 222, argue that the ὅπου clause is Markan.

which must have been obvious to Mark's hearers, that all its first members were Jews. It is however natural that Mark should draw out the positive side of the presence of Gentiles within the community and that after a verse (xv. 38) which could be regarded negatively as emphasising the rejection of Israel he should continue in the next verse with the centurion's confession and its implication of the wideness of the new community.

Mark and Paul approach the problem of the acceptance of the Gentiles from different angles. Leaving aside the statements of Acts which imply Paul was given a commission to evangelise the Gentiles at the time of his conversion, Paul in his own letters argues theologically for their presence in the community; they are there as a direct result of God's intention (Rom. ix–xi), as a consequence of his righteousness, for as sinners all are equal before him and all stand in need of his grace (Rom. iii. 21 ff.); all are one in Christ, since all have been baptised into him (Gal. iii. 27 f.). In Mark however the acceptance of Gentiles begins within the period of Christ's mission on earth and is a part of his teaching. Mark is able to give this position to the acceptance of the Gentiles because his theology, unlike Paul's, has an important place for the life and teaching of Jesus prior to his death. Mark's position again differs from those of Matthew and Luke, both of whom present the risen Jesus as commanding that the Gospel be taken to all people (Matt. xxviii. 18–20; Luke xxiv. 47; Acts i. 8).[1]

The centurion's confession draws out another important point: it is only through the Passion that the new community comes into existence. Whatever prompted the centurion to make his confession it can, if not directly, be traced back to the death of Jesus: e.g. if it was the rending of the Temple veil which moved him, this rending was itself a consequence of the Passion. In the Parable of the Vineyard (xii. 1–9), whether it is the old community or its leaders which are replaced, this only takes place after the owner's son has been put to death. For Mark the Gospel culminates in the death and Resurrection of Christ, and so the preaching of the Gospel (xiii. 10; xiv. 9),

[1] Cf. Best, 'The Revelation to Evangelize the Gentiles', *J.T.S.* XXXV (1984), 1–30.

which is the task of the new community, rests on the Passion. The connection of xiv. 9 to the Passion is especially clear in that here the logion of Jesus is a response to a woman's anointing him for burial.

CONCLUSIONS

If we now attempt to assess the significance of the Passion for Mark, we may conclude in the first instance that he sees it as the climax of his story and that within the Passion itself the climax is first xv. 33–9 and then xvi. 6–8. The most surprising verse is the cry of dereliction (xv. 34), for which nothing has prepared us throughout the whole story apart from Jesus' unheard prayer at Gethsemane. Immediately after the cry the story takes off again with a reference in the rending of the Temple veil to a changed attitude to Judaism followed by a reference to the widening of God's community in the centurion's confession; these in turn are followed by the announcement of Christ's Resurrection, which had already been predicted and associated with the new community. Thus many of the lines of thought that we detected earlier in the story come together in these verses, and they are both climax and summary.

One of these lines was the creation of the new community for one group of which Mark wrote. Both Mark and his readers know that the first members of that community were the disciples, who had signally failed in their endeavours to follow Jesus prior to his Passion. What in Mark's view brought about their changed conduct, and how could what changed them help Mark's hearers? There is nothing in Mark to suggest that the historical disciples suddenly took to heart the teaching of Jesus, which they had consistently refused to do throughout his ministry; everything suggests that the members of Mark's own community had equal difficulty in accepting that teaching, otherwise Mark would not have needed to present it so emphatically. The change in the historical disciples cannot have come from their awareness of the courageous manner of Jesus' death, for they had not been present to observe it and so could not have been impressed by it as the centurion may have been; in the light of the cry of dereliction there was little to impress Mark's hearers with Jesus' courage. Again unlike the centurion it does not seem that the historical disciples

suddenly became aware at the Cross of the true nature of Jesus' sonship so as to appreciate the meaning of his life which they had persistently resisted all the time they had been with him; as for Mark's hearers, they have known that Jesus was God's Son from the beginning of the Gospel and did not need to discover it in his death. Was it then the Resurrection which produced the change in the historical disciples? This cannot be excluded, for from the empty tomb they were sent a message of reassurance (xvi. 7), though by mentioning the women's failure to deliver it Mark may be suggesting that the historical disciples never received it; as for •
Mark's hearers, they already know that Jesus has risen from the dead. But would the historical disciples in any case have been reassured simply to learn of the Resurrection? It did not reassure the women, but made them afraid. To meet again someone whom you have failed, and failed dramatically at a crucial moment, will not bring hope but fear.

In the end then it must be something to do with the death of Jesus which Mark regarded as changing the disciples and hopes will help his own community. Mark has presented the death in different ways, some of which he has clearly adopted from the tradition he received. The life of Jesus, and therefore his dying, was used in the tradition as a model for the life of the disciples, e.g. in the bearing of the Cross, but since the disciples were not very good at copying Jesus' behaviour while he was with him, it is unlikely that his actual death would change their attitude. •
Negatively there are understandings of the death which came to Mark in the tradition but which he does not stress: e.g. Jesus does not die as an innocent victim, and there are understandings which may have been in the tradition but are wholly missing in Mark, e.g. Jesus does not die to establish the Kingdom in its fullness, and his death is not a victory over the cosmic powers of evil, though ch. xiii refuses to allow a narrow understanding of the death lacking all cosmic implications.[1] Mark indeed does not present the Passion as a victory; it is not cast in terms of conflict, as we would expect if victory were a main theme. Though a new community is created, there is no gloating over the end of the old. Because it has been customary in Christian thought to speak

---

[1] R. H. Smith, 'Darkness at Noon: Mark's Passion Narrative', *Concordia Theological Monthly* XLIV (1973), 325–38.

of the victory of the Passion, some scholars have read this into the second great cry of xv. 37,[1] yet there is nothing in that cry by itself to suggest such a theme. It is described as a strong cry; Mark's hearers were well aware that those who were crucified did not die like that but slowly lost strength until they expired; the presence of Simon of Cyrene has already suggested Jesus' physical weakness. The strong cry is then more probably intended to indicate that Jesus did not slip away unobserved into death.[2] In any case whatever victory Mark sees as won was won in the Temptation. More positively in drawing on the tradition we can see that Mark has presented Jesus in various guises, e.g. as the Righteous Sufferer of the Psalms and the suffering Son of Wisdom, as the true Servant of Yahweh, as the Maccabean martyr, without emphasising any of these.[3] But principally Mark has set out his death as a death for others (e.g. 'for many'). Jesus has borne the judgement of God and atoned for the sin of all. He has atoned for the sin of Peter, who denied him but who showed repentance (xiv. 72). Peter, and the others, were re-established. Those who hear Mark's story can then also be restored although they may have failed in their discipleship and service. Not then victory but restoration, restoration after failure in discipleship, and creation, the coming into existence of the new community, are for Mark the central themes of the Passion.

[1] See below, pp. 100 f.   [2] Cf. Gnilka.
[3] Cf. Baarlink, pp. 235–8, 242.

REFERENCES

Anderson = H. Anderson, *The Gospel of Mark* (New Century Bible). London, 1976.

Baarlink = H. Baarlink, *Anfängliches Evangelium: Ein Beitrag zum näheren Bestimmung des theologische Motiv im Markusevangelium*. Kampen, 1977.

Bayer = H. F. Bayer, *Jesus' Predictions of Vindication and Resurrection* (W.U.N.T. 2, Reihe 20). Tübingen, 1986.

Derrett = J. D. M. Derrett, *The Making of Mark*, 2 vols. Shipston-on-Stour, 1985.

Disciples = E. Best, *Disciples and Discipleship: Studies in the Gospel according to Mark*. Edinburgh, 1986.

Donahue = J. R. Donahue, *Are You the Christ?* (S.B.L.D.S. 10). Missoula, Montana, 1973.

Dormeyer = D. Dormeyer, *Die Passion Jesu als Verhaltensmodell*. Münster, 1974.

Ernst = J. Ernst, *Das Evangelium nach Markus* (Regensburger Neues Testament). Regensburg, 1981.

Feldmeier = R. Feldmeier, *Die Krisis des Gottessohnes* (W.U.N.T. 2, Reihe 21). Tübingen, 1987.

Following = E. Best, *Following Jesus: Discipleship in the Gospel of Mark*. Sheffield, 1981.

Gnilka = *Das Evangelium nach Markus* (Evangelisch-katholischer Kommentar zum Neuen Testament), 2 vols. Zurich, 1978 and 1979.

Gubler = M.-L. Gubler, *Die frühesten Deutungen des Todes Jesu*. Göttingen, 1977.

Haenchen = E. Haenchen, *Der Weg Jesu*. Berlin, 1968.

Hengel = M. Hengel, *The Atonement. The Origin of the Doctrine in the New Testament*. London, 1981.

Juel = D. Juel, *Messiah and Temple* (S.B.L.D.S. 31). Missoula, Montana, 1977.

Kato = Z. Kato, *Die Völkermission im Markusevangelium. Eine redaktionsgeschichtliche Untersuchung*. Bern, 1986.

Kelber, *Kingdom* = W. H. Kelber, *The Kingdom in Mark*. Philadelphia, 1974.

Kelber, *Passion* = *The Passion in Mark* (ed. W. H. Kelber). Philadelphia, 1976.

Jeremias = J. Jeremias, *New Testament Theology* I. London, 1971.

Kingsbury = J. D. Kingsbury, *The Christology of Mark's Gospel*. Philadelphia, 1983.

Lane = W. L. Lane, *The Gospel according to Mark*. London, 1974.

Linnemann = E. Linnemann, *Studien zur Passionsgeschichte* (F.R.L.A.N.T. 102). Göttingen, 1970.

Lührmann = D. Lührmann, *Das Markusevangelium* (Handbuch zum Neuen Testament 3). Tübingen, 1987.

Matera, *Kingship* = F. J. Matera, *The Kingship of Jesus* (S.B.L.D.S. 66). Chico, Calif. 1982.

Matera, *Passion* = F. J. Matera, *Passion Narratives and Gospel Theologies. Interpreting the Synoptics through their Passion Stories*. New York, 1986.

Mohr = T. A. Mohr, *Markus-Johannespassion. Redaktions- und traditionsgeschichtliche Untersuchung der Markinischen und Johanneischen Passionstradition*. Zurich, 1982.

Pesch = R. Pesch, *Das Markusevangelium* (Herders Theologischer Kommentar zum NT). 2 vols. Freiburg, 1976 and 1977.

Pryke = E. J. Pryke, *Redactional Style in the Markan Gospel* (S.N.T.S.M.S. 33). Cambridge, 1978.

Rau = G. Rau, 'Das Markus-Evangelium. Komposition und Intention der ersten Darstellung christlicher Mission'. *Aufstieg und Niedergang der Römischen Welt* (ed. H. Temporini und W. Haase). Stuttgart, 1984. II.25.3, pp. 2036–2257.

Schenk = W. Schenk, *Der Passionsbericht nach Markus*. Berlin, 1974.

Schenke, *Christus* = L. Schenke, *Der gekreuzigte Christus* (S.B.S. 69). Stuttgart, 1974.

Schenke, *Studien* = L. Schenke, *Studien zur Passionsgeschichte nach Markus*. Wurzburg, 1971.

Schmithals = W. Schmithals, *Das Evangelium nach Markus* (Ökumenischer Taschenbuchkommentar zum Neuen Testament) [2] Gütersloh, 1986.

Schreiber, *B.Z.N.W.* = J. Schreiber, *Der Kreuzigungsbericht des Markusevangeliums* (B.Z.N.W. 48). Berlin, 1986.

Schreiber, *Theologie* = J. Schreiber, *Theologie des Vertrauens: eine redaktionsgeschichtliche Untersuchung des Markusevangeliums*. Hamburg, 1967.

Schweizer = E. Schweizer, *Das Evangelium nach Markus* (Das Neue Testament Deutsch). Göttingen, 1968.

Senior = D. Senior, *The Passion of Jesus in the Gospel of Mark*. Wilmington, Delaware, 1984.

Standaert = B. H. M. G. M. Standaert, *L'Evangile selon Marc: composition et genre litteraire*. Brugge, 1978.

Stock = A. Stock, *Call to Discipleship. A Literary Study of Mark's Gospel*. Wilmington, Delaware, 1982.

Story = E. Best, *Mark: The Gospel as Story*. Edinburgh, 1983.

Trocmé = E. Trocmé, *The Formation of the Gospel Tradition according to Mark*. London, 1975.

Van Iersel = B. van Iersel, *Reading Mark*. Edinburgh, 1989.

LIST OF ABBREVIATIONS

An. Bib. = Analecta Biblica.

A.T.A.N.T. = Abhandlungen zur Theologie des Alten und Neuen Testaments.

B.E.T.L. = Bibliotheca ephemerimidum theologicarum lovaniensium.

Branscomb = B. H. Branscomb, *The Gospel of Mark* (Moffatt Commentaries). London, 1937.

Bultmann = R. Bultmann, *The History of the Synoptic Tradition* (Eng. trans. J. Marsh). Oxford, 1963.

Bundy = W. E. Bundy, *Jesus and the First Three Gospels*. Cambridge, Mass., 1955.

Bussmann = W. Bussmann, *Synoptische Studien* I-III. Halle, 1925 – 31.

B.Z. = *Biblische Zeitschrift*.

B.Z.N.W. = Beihefte zur *Z.N.W.*.

C.B.Q. = *Catholic Biblical Quarterly*.

Conzelmann = H. Conzelmann, *The Theology of Saint Luke* (Eng. trans. G. Buswell). London, 1960.

Cranfield = C. E. B. Cranfield, *St Mark*. Cambridge, 1959.

Dehn = G. Dehn, *Der Gottessohn*⁶. Hamburg, 1953.

Dibelius = M. Dibelius, *From Tradition to Gospel* (Eng. trans. B. E. Woolf). London, 1934.

Est. Bib. = *Estudios Biblicos*.

E.T. = *The Expository Times*.

E.T.L. = *Ephemerides theologicae lovanienses*.

Ev. Th. = *Evangelische Theologie*.

F.R.L.A.N.T. = Forschungen zur Religion und Literatur des Alten und Neuen Testaments.

Hauck = F. Hauck, *Das Evangelium des Markus* (Theologischer Handkommentar zum N.T.). Leipzig, 1931.

H.T.R. = *Harvard Theological Review*.

Int. = *Interpretation*.

J.B.L. = *Journal of Biblical Literature*.

Johnson = S. E. Johnson, *The Gospel According to St Mark*. London, 1960.

J.R. = *Journal of Religion*.

J.S.N.T. = *Journal for the Study of the New Testament.*

J.T.S. = *Journal of Theological Studies.*

Klostermann = E. Klostermann, *Das Markusevangelium*[2]. Tübingen, 1926.

Knox = W. L. Knox, *The Sources of the Synoptic Gospels*, vol. I. Cambridge, 1953.

Lagrange = M.-J. Lagrange, *Évangile selon Saint Marc.* Paris, 1947.

Lightfoot, *Gospel* = R. H. Lightfoot, *The Gospel Message of St. Mark.* Oxford, 1950.

Lightfoot, *History* = R. H. Lightfoot, *History and Interpretation in the Gospels.* London, 1935.

Lightfoot, *Locality* = R. H. Lightfoot, *Locality and Doctrine in the Gospels.* London, 1938.

Lindars = B. Lindars, *New Testament Apologetic.* London, 1961.

Lohmeyer = E. Lohmeyer, *Das Evangelium des Markus*[11]. Göttingen, 1951.

Marxsen = W. Marxsen, *Der Evangelist Markus*[2]. Göttingen, 1959.

Mauser = U. W. Mauser, *Christ in the Wilderness* (Studies in Biblical Theology 39). London, 1963.

Menzies = A. Menzies, *The Earliest Gospel.* London, 1901.

Moore = G. F. Moore, *Judaism.* 3 vols. Cambridge, Mass., 1927–30.

N.R.T. = *La Nouvelle Revue théologique.*

N.T. = *Novum Testamentum.*

N.T.S. = *New Testament Studies.*

N.T.Sup. = Novum Testamentum Supplements.

Rawlinson = A. E. J. Rawlinson, *The Gospel According to St Mark* (Westminster Commentaries). London, 1925.

R.B. = *Revue biblique.*

Robinson = J. M. Robinson, *The Problem of History in Mark* (Studies in Biblical Theology 21). London, 1957.

R.S.P.T. = *Revue des sciences philosophiques et théologiques.*

R.S.R. = *Recherches de science religieuse.*

S.B.L.D.S. = Society for Biblical Literature Dissertation Series.

S.B.S. = Stuttgarter Bibelstudien.

S.B.T. = Studies in Biblical Theology.

Schmidt = K. L. Schmidt, *Die Rahmen der Geschichte Jesu.* Berlin, 1919.

Schnackenburg = R. Schnackenburg, *Das Evangelium nach Markus*. 2 vols. Düsseldorf, 1966, 1970.

Schniewind = J. Schniewind, *Das Evangelium nach Markus*[6]. Göttingen, 1952.

Schreiber = J. Schreiber, 'Die Christologie des Markusevangeliums', *Z.T.K.* LVIII (1961), 154–83.

S.J.Th. = *Scottish Journal of Theology*.

S.N.T.S.M.S. = Society for New Testament Studies Monograph Series.

Strack-Billerbeck = H. L. Strack and P. Billerbeck, *Kommentar zum Neuen Testament aus Talmud und Midrasch*. 5 vols.

Swete = H. B. Swete, *The Gospel According to St Mark*. London, 1908.

Taylor = V. Taylor, *The Gospel According to St Mark*. London, 1952.

Turner = C. H. Turner, A series of articles in *J.T.S.* 1924–9.

T.W.N.T. = *Theologisches Wörterbuch zum Neuen Testament* (ed. G. Kittel and G. Friedrich), 1932– .

Weiss = J. Weiss, *Älteste Evangelium*. Göttingen, 1903.

Wellhausen = J. Wellhausen, *Das Evangelium Marci*. Berlin, 1903.

Wohlenberg = G. Wohlenberg, *Das Evangelium des Markus*. Leipzig, 1910.

W.U.N.T. = Wissenschaftliche Monographien zum Alten und Neuen Testament.

Z.K.T. = *Zeitschrift für katholische Theologie*.

Z.N.T.W. = *Zeitschrift für die neutestamentliche Wissenschaft*.

Z.T.K. = *Zeitschrift für Theologie und Kirche*.

PART I

THE TEMPTATION

CHAPTER I

THE TEMPTATION NARRATIVE

WE are concerned here neither with the origin of Mark i. 12 f.
nor with an estimate of its historical reliability; rather it is our
purpose to discuss its place in the Gospel and seek its meaning
for Mark. In so doing we make the normal assumption that the
Markan narrative at this point contains no knowledge of the
tradition common to Matthew and Luke (Q). That is not
merely to say that Mark did not know Matthew or Luke, nor
that he did know Q, but also that he did not know the tradition
of the content of the temptations of Jesus. If this assumption is
incorrect and Mark did have some knowledge of the Q tradition,[1] even in a rudimentary form, it will be seen that our
conclusions would be reinforced; for we would then be able to
argue that Mark has deliberately omitted certain elements in
the Q tradition and chosen to emphasise a few details, which
thereby receive a new importance: for example, Mark is not
interested in the nature of the temptations, only in the fact that
a struggle took place. The assumption that Mark did not know
Q means that we must banish from our minds our knowledge of
Q in discussing Mark. Whereas when we come to read Matthew
and Luke it is of great importance to know Mark so that we
may see exactly how they have modified his narrative, our very
knowledge of Matthew and Luke can form a hindrance to our
understanding of Mark because we tend to see him through the
eyes of Matthew and Luke. Neither he nor his first readers knew
the other Gospels and they were not background material for
him as they tend to be for us. With particular reference to the
Temptation narrative, Luke (iv. 13; xxii. 28) is often taken to
suggest that the three temptations were only the beginning of
temptations which continued throughout the earthly life of
Jesus with greater or less intensity.[2] It is not however correct to
read this back into Mark and assume that he is giving us the

[1] So Bacon, *The Gospel of Mark* (New Haven, 1925), pp. 156 f.
[2] This is not necessarily the meaning of these verses in Luke; cf. Conzelmann, pp. 27 f.

beginning of temptations. Indeed we shall see that such a view is untrue to Mark's purpose.

The account of the Temptation in Mark is bare of details. Not only are we not told in what way Jesus was tempted but we are not even told the outcome of the Temptation. The nature of the Temptation must be read from the context; it follows the baptism and precedes the ministry. The result of the Temptation must likewise be gathered from the wider context, though it is possible that Mark intends to convey to us a hint of the issue from some of the details, but this is not certain; it is much more probable that the result must be learnt elsewhere in the Gospel. We shall see that Mark does make explicit elsewhere the outcome of the struggle.

We must now examine the somewhat scanty details of the account itself. The two verses i. 12 f. were not necessarily always united to the baptismal account. They are introduced by Mark's much-loved καὶ εὐθύς. Certain internal evidence suggests different strands of tradition.[1] But Mark, if not earlier tradition, has welded baptism and temptation together. Thus the initial statement of the Temptation narrative, the expulsion by the Spirit into the desert, has had its necessary preliminary in the coming to Jesus of the Spirit in baptism. To describe the action of the Spirit in initiating the Temptation Mark adopts the word ἐκβάλλειν. The element of violence cannot be excluded from the word since he uses it repeatedly in connection with the expulsion of demons (i. 34, 39, 43; iii. 15, 22; vi. 13; vii. 26; ix. 18, 28), and as we shall see there is a strong connection between this present passage and the demonic exorcisms. We must then take it that Mark views Jesus as 'driven out' by the Spirit into the desert. It is not however necessary to equate this with the concept of transportation by the Spirit (I Kings xviii. 12; II Kings ii. 16; Ezek. iii. 12, 14; viii. 3; Acts viii. 39).[2] Jesus is not violently taken up and carried to another place (indeed there is no other instance where the Spirit is said to transport towards evil), but compelled to go. The nature of the compulsion is not made clear, but there is nothing to suggest that Jesus was in an ecstatic condition. The compulsion may have been moral,[3] or it may have been deterministic as in

[1] Cf. Lohmeyer.
[2] Cf. Volz, *Der Geist Gottes* (Tübingen, 1910), pp. 17, 196.   [3] So Cranfield.

I QS iii. 13 ff. where the member of the Qumran community is under the control of the Spirit of Truth. In the Temptation narrative nothing more is said about the activity of the Spirit. He drives out Jesus to the place of temptation, the desert, but he is neither said to tempt Jesus (in the Old Testament God tests or tempts men to train them) nor is he said to help Jesus in his temptation by Satan.[1] This is surprising since it was the experience of the early Church to enjoy the Spirit's assistance in trial and temptation.[2]

It is to the desert that the Spirit leads Jesus. The 'desert' is emphasised. It is both said that Jesus is led to it and that he continues in it forty days. 'Desert' may signify either loneliness and remoteness or the abode of demons. In the former sense it is in Mark the place where Jesus withdraws from the crowds (i. 35, 45; vi. 31, 32, 35). But also according to Jewish demonology the desert is one among other places which demons are specially supposed to inhabit.[3] Probably both ideas are to some extent present in our passage.

In the desert he spent forty days. This is a traditional phrase in Judaism for a lengthy period of time. Some commentators see in this a link with the forty years spent by Israel in the desert after the Exodus,[4] and so picture Jesus here as himself embodying Israel. But Israel was forty years, not forty days, in the wilderness. Moreover they put God to the test rather than were tested by God; certainly they were not tested by Satan. The period of forty days occurs in the lives of both Moses and Elijah (Exod. xxiv. 18; xxxiv. 28; Deut. ix. 9; x. 10; I Kings xix. 8). It is associated in these instances with fasting. Are we so to associate it here? If we are certain that the forty

[1] In the Lukan account Jesus is said to be 'full of the Spirit' (iv. 1) and from this it may be inferred that he had the help of the Spirit in his Temptation.

[2] This may suggest that the Markan form of the tradition did not arise out of the experience of the early Church. That experience would not have shown the Spirit leading to Temptation but delivering from it.

[3] Cf. Strack-Billerbeck, IV, 515 f. Marxsen (pp. 26–8) argues that ἔρημος is not here a geographical designation but represents the abode of Satan; it is thus to be understood theologically rather than spatially. On the desert as evil, cf. Mauser, pp. 36 ff. He emphasises the mythological connections in the Psalms and II Isaiah, pp. 42–4, 51 f.

[4] E.g. Hauck; Lightfoot, *History*, pp. 65 f.

days Jesus spent in the desert is deliberately modelled on the forty days in the lives of Moses and Elijah we must draw that conclusion; but there is nothing to suggest that what happened to Moses and Elijah in their forty days is in any way comparable to what happened to Jesus; for them it was a time with God, not with Satan. The forty days is rather a general period of time; the idea that he fasted during this period will then probably have grown up as a secondary tradition through reflection on the forty-day incidents in the life of Moses and Elijah and also through backward reference from the first temptation in Q. There is thus no need to find in Mark any implicit reference to fasting. In any case Mark has just told us that John the Baptist was able to exist on locusts and wild honey in the desert and therefore was not compelled to starve because he was in desert country; 'desert' does not therefore imply being without food. (Cf. vi. 31 which seems to imply the possibility of eating in the desert.) In Mark, unlike Q, there is no suggestion that the time of temptation fell at the end of the forty-day period. The Temptation rather took place within the period of the forty days and may indeed, so far as Mark is concerned, have lasted throughout that period.

Jesus is here said to be tempted by Satan. In the Old Testament and in Judaism the root πειράξειν and its Hebrew equivalent, the pi'el of נסה, is used religiously of the way in which man tempts God and in which God tests man in order to train him;[1] the great example for Judaism was that of Abraham (Gen. xxii). While the root is not used in the story of the Fall of Adam the conception of temptation is obviously present and in a form closer to our present narrative since in Gen. iii it is the serpent who tempts as it is Satan in Mark i. 12 f. This conception of the testing of man by the powers of evil in order to turn him aside from the ways of God is inevitably present where the powers of evil are given a personal form and a measure of dualism appears, as in the Qumran writings. Thus an element in the Markan form of the temptation narrative may be the Fall of Adam; as we know Christ was represented as the Second Adam in much early Christian literature. This is not to

[1] Cf. Seesemann, *T.W.N.T.* VI, 23–37; Strack-Billerbeck, I, 135 f.; M. H. Sykes, 'And do not bring us to the test', *E.T.* LXXIII (1961/2), 189 f.

be taken as suggesting that Mark i. 12 f. is in origin an explicit reversal of Gen. iii.[1]

There are three other occasions on which πειράζειν is used by Mark in reference to Jesus – namely viii. 11; x. 2; xii. 15. Each time it is the Pharisees (in xii. 15 in association with the Herodians) who attempt to test Jesus. Whereas x. 2 and xii. 15 may be regarded as attempts to test Jesus as to his opinion in regard to certain matters, in viii. 11 the Pharisees tempt him by asking for a sign, one of the ways in which according to the Q tradition the Devil tempted Jesus. Although the word πειράζειν is not used either in the account of Peter's confession at Caesarea Philippi (viii. 32 f.) or in the Gethsemane account (xiv. 32–42) with reference to Jesus, the conception of temptation is definitely present on these two occasions. We shall have occasion to return to this.[2]

Jesus is said to be tempted by Satan, which is obviously used here as a personal name. It is unnecessary to discuss the origin or meaning of this name since by the time of the Gospels its original sense as 'accuser', while not lost, had been swallowed up in the general belief in spiritual powers of evil.[3] The Devil, Mastema, Satan, etc., were names in use to describe the chief among these powers. This is obviously the meaning which Satan has for Mark or his tradition (cf. iii. 22–30). The temptation story is thus seen as a conflict between the Son of God, for so he has been described in the immediately preceding pericope, and the Prince of evil.

There were present with Jesus not only the Tempter, Satan, but also the wild beasts and the angels. Different interpretations have been given of the presence of the beasts. They have been thought to emphasise the loneliness of the desert,[4] but the suggestion of loneliness is immediately contradicted by the

---

[1] The relationship of Mark i. 12 f. to Gen. iii has been thoroughly examined by H.-G. Leder, 'Sündenfallerzählung und Versuchungsgeschichte: zur Interpretation von Mc i. 12 f.', Z. N. T. W. LIV (1963), 188–216, who finds against the interpretation of Christ as the Second Adam. Cf. J. Jeremias, 'Nachwort zum Artikel von H.-G. Leder', Z. N. T. W. LIV (1963), 278 f.

[2] Pp. 28 f.

[3] Cf. Foerster and von Rad, T. W.N. T. II 69–80; Foerster, T. W.N. T. II, 1–21; VII, 151 ff.; Strack-Billerbeck, I, 136–49.

[4] E.g. Cranfield.

reference to the presence of the angels who minister to him. Moreover it is unlikely that Mark would have wished to emphasise human loneliness at this stage of the story, and in his conflict with Satan the Son of God could hardly have expected to find assistance from men. The beasts have been taken as another trait indicating Christ as the Second Adam; as in the days before the Fall Adam lived peacefully with the beasts, so does Christ in the desert.[1] But the parallelism is not very exact in that Christ was in the desert whereas Adam was in the Garden of Eden; nor is great emphasis put in Jewish tradition on the presence of the wild beasts with Adam. A variant of this view sees in the presence of the wild beasts the sign of victory; as in the Messianic times harmony was expected to be recreated between man and the world of nature (Isa. xi. 6 – 9; lxv. 25, etc.), so this is seen to take place in the presence of the Messiah.[2] But we would expect this to be more clearly indicated; wild beasts normally suggest evil rather than good. That they signify evil is the more probable interpretation; the beasts are congruent with Satan and the desert, all of them suggesting the evil with which Jesus must contend.[3] The theme appears in the Old Testament, namely, Ps. xxii. 13 – 22; xci. 13;[4] Isa. xiii. 21 f.; Ezek. xxxiv. 5, 8, 25. Isa. xxxiv. 14 should be compared in its Hebrew and Greek forms (M.T. 'wild beasts', צִיִּים,[5] LXX δαιμόνια). The very fact that in the Messianic kingdom the beasts are at peace with man implies their normal fierceness and opposition, a fact which would have been much more obvious to those living in the Palestine of the first century than to citizens of the western world today. The Roman reader of Mark would also immediately think of their fierceness because of their association with the arena, where at any moment he might have to face their enmity.[6] When we trace this theme of the wild beasts further in Jewish thought we find that they are

---

[1] Cf. Jeremias, *T.W.N.T.* I, 141; Dehn; Taylor; W. A. Schulze, 'Der Heilige und die wilden Tiere', *Z.N.T.W.* XLVI (1955), 280 – 3.

[2] Cf. Schniewind.

[3] Cf. Lohmeyer *ad loc.*; Mauser, pp. 100 f.

[4] In ancient mythology the gods are sometimes depicted as conquerors of evil, standing in a triumphant pose over slain beasts; cf. H. J. Kraus, *Psalmen, ad loc.*

[5] Cf. Langton, *Essentials of Demonology*, p. 42.

[6] F. C. Grant, *The Earliest Gospel* (New York and Nashville, 1943), p. 77.

also associated with the demons and with the angels, though naturally they are not on the side of the angels. The beasts and angels are set in opposition in Ps. xci. 11–13. The beasts and the demons are associated in Test. Issach. vii. 7; Test. Benj. v. 2. Angels, beasts and demons are all associated in Test. Naph. viii. 4.[1]

This then brings us to the ministry of the angels. With Lohmeyer[2] we take it that they and the beasts stand over against one another. But what is their ministry? The obvious answer is that they feed Jesus. This accords with the Q tradition in which the first temptation concerns hunger, and Jesus is said to hunger, and it accords with the basic meaning of διακονεῖν.[3] While it must be agreed that this word retains its basic meaning in the New Testament, including Mark (i. 31), the word also underwent considerable development and was given an important theological overtone. Moreover if we did not have the Q tradition there is nothing in the Markan story other than this reference which would necessarily suggest hunger. Indeed even within the Q form of the tradition the angels are mentioned in another way: Satan tempts Jesus to throw himself from the pinnacle of the Temple saying that the angels will guard him (Matt. iv. 6 = Luke iv. 10, 11 = Ps. xci. 11 f.); now, though it is Satan who says this to Jesus, it surely represents the point of view of the time that in this way angels might minister to the Messiah. It is indeed well known that they minister to men in many different ways.[4] They act as their guardian angels, they intercede for them before God, they mediate visions to them. For our purpose it is important to note that in Heb. i. 14 the word **διακονία is connected with their activity. The angels minister to the Son of Man in maintaining intercourse between** himself and the Father (John i. 51). Angels are also associated with the Son of Man in Matt. xvi. 27, 28 par. In the War Scroll the angels form an army fighting on the side of God against the hosts of evil (i. 10 f.; xiii. 10; xii. 8, 9; xvii. 6; cf. I QS iii. 24 f.; I QH v. 21). In the light of this it is impossible

---

[1] Quoted below, p. 10. [2] *Ad loc.*

[3] Cf. Lohmeyer; Klostermann. On διακονεῖν, see Beyer, *T.W.N.T.* II, 81–93.

[4] Cf. von Rad and Kittel, *T.W.N.T.* I, 75–87; Moore, I, 401–13; Bousset-Gressmann, *Die Religion des Judentums*[3], pp. 320–31.

to restrict the ministry of the angels in the Markan account to the supply of food and drink. Rather they ministered to Jesus in his contest with Satan. Most striking testimony is the connection of angels, wild beasts and the Devil in Test. Naph. viii.4.

> If ye work that which is good, my children,
> Both men and angels shall bless you:
> And God shall be glorified among the Gentiles through you,
> And the devil shall flee from you,
> And the wild beasts shall fear you,
> And the Lord shall love you,
> (And the angels shall cleave to you).[1]

We have now examined the details of the account, but these taken together do not reveal any overwhelmingly convincing theme. We cannot regard Jesus as the new Israel in the desert. Some evidence points to him as the Second Adam engaged in a second duel with the Devil. The Spirit plays a surprising role: it drives Jesus towards Satan but does not assist him in his contest with Satan. Finally none of the evidence indicates in any clear way the result of the Temptation. If we possessed the Markan account only as an isolated pericope and did not know the Q narrative we should be entirely ignorant of the outcome. Information about this must be looked for elsewhere in Mark. It is remarkable that commentators do not seem to mention this surprising lack of conclusion to the account. Lohmeyer alone draws attention to it, but states weakly that the result does not need to be set down because for a divine being it is obvious what it must be.[2] However, Mark does state the result quite clearly in another passage and it is to this we must now turn.

Mark iii. 19b – 35 is a section which hangs together under the theme of the possession of Jesus by a spirit. His family, or

---

[1] Translation as Charles, *Apocrypha and Pseudepigrapha*, II. Charles brackets the last line as a Christian addition. If this is so then it confirms our view that at an early period the ministry of the angels was not regarded as restricted to the supply of food.

It may be noted that Test. Naph. is one of the oldest parts of Test. XII Patriarchs; traces of it have been found among the Qumran material, though not in its present form; cf. F. M. Cross, *The Ancient Library of Qumran*, pp. 34, 149 n. 6; J. T. Milik, *Ten Years of Discovery in the Wilderness of Judah*, pp. 34 f.

[2] *Ad loc.* Cf. Mauser, p. 100; Bundy, p. 61.

friends (οἱ παρ' αὐτοῦ), come to him saying that he is possessed; the scribes from Jerusalem name the devil, Beelzebul, by whom he is possessed; but he argues that what he does, he does by the Holy Spirit. It is not necessary for us to explore whether these separate pericopae represent one incident or the joining of a number of separate incidents under one theme; in certain cases, for example the unforgivable sin, the Q tradition shows significant variation. It is possible that these pericopae were already welded together before Mark received them,[1] but since they reflect one of his favourite editorial tricks in sandwiching incidents together, their conjunction may well be due to Mark.

For our particular purpose the important verse is 27. In the preceding verses Jesus, in a half-humorous argument, accepts the premise of the Scribes that he has an evil spirit and shows that this leads to the conclusion that the downfall of Satan is assured; the premise must therefore be incorrect. In *v.* 27 'The true account of the matter is now given: the positive conclusion to which Jesus himself has been led'.[2] The scribes begin by saying that Jesus is possessed by Beelzebul, a demon of whom little is known.[3] But Jesus at once changes the terminology by referring to Satan. Beelzebul may have been a named subordinate demon or he may have been Satan under another guise; the latter would appear to be the opinion of Mark who says 'by the ruler[4] of the devils he casts out devils'. Thus we have the picture of Satan as ruler of the devils, who are subordinate to him. This is a new feature in Jewish demonology; Satan has not previously appeared as the head of a host of demons.[5] But Satan would also appear to be used not merely as the name of the chief devil but also in a corporate way to denote the whole assemblage of devils: this seems to be the meaning of *vv.* 24, 26 where reference is made to Satan casting out Sstan, and to Satan as divided. The personal aspect reappears in *v.* 27 where the strong man is undoubtedly Satan.

---

[1] Taylor, pp. 92 f.   [2] Menzies, *ad loc.*

[3] Even the spelling of the word is uncertain. The most probable meaning appears to be 'Lord of the House'; cf. the commentaries and Langton, *Essentials of Demonology*, pp. 166 f.; Foerster, *T.W.N.T.* I, 605 f.

[4] ἄρχων equivalent to βεελ equivalent to בַּעַל.

[5] So Foerster, *T.W.N.T.* VII, 159.

The stronger man who enters the house is also undoubtedly Jesus. It would seem wrong to connect this with i. 7 where Jesus is called 'the stronger'.[1] For at i. 7 ὁ ἰσχυρότερος is set in contrast to John the Baptist and not to Satan. Menzies[2] points out an apparent difficulty in the identification of Jesus with the one who enters the strong man's house in that in the only previous encounter between Jesus and Satan, the Temptation, Satan is the attacking power and not the attacked. But is this correct? One of the difficulties of the Temptation story is just the fact that the Spirit is said to drive Jesus out to be tempted, or tested. Jesus thus goes to the desert, the abode of demons, to encounter Satan. The implication of the Q narrative may be that Satan comes to tempt Jesus, but this is not true of the Markan account. Thus we find a link here between the Markan Temptation narrative and iii. 27, in that one of the difficulties of iii. 27 is explained by the reference to the Spirit as driving Jesus to the conflict, just as this peculiar reference in i. 12, contrary to all the experience of the early Christians who found the Spirit defending them from temptation, gives the backing to iii. 27. Thus it was in the Temptation that the strong man met the stronger.

But what happened to the strong man whose house was entered? He is bound and his goods are plundered. The conception of the binding of evil spirits is common in the apocalyptic writings. It presumably takes its Jewish origin[3] in Isa. xxiv. 21 f. and becomes more explicit in Tob. viii. 3; I Enoch x. 4 f., 11 f.; xviii. 12–xix. 2; xxi. 1–6; liv. 4 f.; Test. Levi xviii. 12; Jub. xlviii. 15. It reappears in the New Testament in Rev. xx. 2, where it is explicitly said that it is Satan who is bound. A consideration of these texts will reveal at once that to bind means to render powerless. Satan bound is not a Satan who can still carry on his activities, tempting and deceiving man within limits, but Satan out of the way. Charles notes that in respect of most of the references to the binding of evil spirits, their binding is only temporary and their final punishment comes

---

[1] Cf. Lohmeyer, Cranfield *ad* i. 7. On ὁ ἰσχυρός see Grundmann, *T.W.N.T.* III, 402–5.

[2] *Ad loc.*

[3] The idea existed also in Persian circles; cf. Charles, *Revelation* (I.C.C.), II, 142.

later and is distinct from their binding; for example, cf. I Enoch
x. 4 f. with x. 6, also x. 11 with x. 12 and Rev. xx. 2 with Rev.
xx. 3. Christ has already bound Satan according to Mark
iii. 27; δήσῃ, aorist subjunctive, would suggest one definite act,[1]
and this must be the trial of strength which he had with Satan
in the desert – the Temptation.[2] Test. Levi xviii. 12 is particularly interesting. Of the new priest whom God raises up it is
said 'And Beliar shall be bound by him, and he shall give
power to his children to tread upon the evil spirits'.[3] In Mark,
Satan is bound by Jesus and Jesus gives his disciples authority
over unclean spirits (vi. 7, cf. iii. 15). The argument in Test.
Levi and in Mark is precisely the same. Test. Levi xviii may
either be pre-Christian, in which case it may be the origin of
Mark's argument, or it may have been edited by a Christian
who has appreciated the argument of Mark, or some similar
explanation in the early Church. In either case it is confirmatory evidence for the view we take of Mark's theology of Satan
and his conquest.[4]

Having bound Satan, the Stronger has also plundered his
possessions – τὰ σκεύη. Are we to give a meaning to this, in
effect to allegorise the story, or are we to regard it as picturesque
detail without intended meaning?[5] Since Jesus is making reference to the defeat of underlings of Satan it is probably better to
take τὰ σκεύη as having some definite reference thereto. But
what are they? Men set free from the power of Satan[6] or lesser
devils pillaged and made the possession of Christ?[7] The former
seems the more probable in view of the biblical and non-

---

[1] Leivestad argues that it 'seems a natural assumption ... that the
decisive victory must have taken place on a previous occasion' (*Christ the
Conqueror*, p. 46), yet he rejects this assumption as improbable; his rejection,
however, is based on a consideration of the Q form of the Temptation
narrative, which Mark does not use. Cf. Grundmann, *T.W.N.T.* III, 404.

[2] The objection of F. C. Grant (*Interpreter's Bible ad* iii. 27) that the
Scribes would not have known the Temptation is hardly relevant; Jesus is
stating what has happened, and in any case, Mark's readers do know of the
Temptation, and it is they who are reading the Gospel.

[3] Translation as Charles, *Apocrypha and Pseudepigrapha*.

[4] Cf. pp. 187–9.

[5] Taylor *ad loc.*

[6] Grundmann, *T.W.N.T.* III, 404; Robinson, p. 31; Cranfield, Lagrange,
etc.

[7] Klostermann.

biblical parallels: for example, Isa. xlix. 25; Jub. x. 5 – 8; Luke xiii. 16.[1]

iii. 28, 29 in their reference to the sin against the Holy Spirit obviously imply that the activity of Jesus in the casting out of demons is also an activity of the Holy Spirit. References to the Holy Spirit in Mark (and Matthew) are surprisingly few when we consider the great prominence given to the Spirit in the early Church. Jesus once attributed an Old Testament saying to the Holy Spirit in accordance with the general Jewish view of the Spirit as the inspirer of prophecy (xii. 36). Three times the activity of the Spirit in the community is described: **i. 8, baptism with the Spirit being a reference to the permanent** endowment of the Church with the Spirit at Pentecost;[2] xiii. 11, the Spirit as inspiring the speech of the Christian when on trial; xiv. 38, the Spirit as giving courage in temptation.[3] There are four references to the activity of the Spirit in the life of Jesus: i. 8, he is able to baptise with the Spirit, it being at his disposal; i. 9 – 11, he is permanently endowed with the Spirit at his baptism; i. 12, the Spirit drives him to the contest with Satan; iii. 28 – 30, by the power of the Spirit he casts out Satan's under-lings. It is really only in the last two instances that we can say that we see the Spirit active in the ministry of Jesus and both refer to the same subject – his warfare with Satan. While in the early Church almost all the activities of Christians are ascribed to gifts of the Spirit, here Christ's warfare with Satan is alone so ascribed. Thus we find again that the temptation narrative and our present passage are closely linked.[4] Moreover what we found surprising in the Temptation story, namely, that it is never said that Jesus was helped by the Spirit in the defeat of Satan, is made clear at this point, since it is with the help of the Spirit that Satan's underlings are defeated, and so we may understand the same to have happened in the Temptation itself, the Spirit assisting Jesus against Satan.

[1] Cf. *Gospel of Truth*, xxv. 25 ff.; this appears, however, to depend on Rom. ix. 20 – 4 rather than on our present passage.

[2] Best, 'Spirit-Baptism', *N. T.* IV (1961), 236 – 43.

[3] Cf. below, p. 30. We take πνεῦμα in xiv. 38 to refer to the Divine Spirit rather than to the human; cf. E. Schweizer, *T. W. N. T.* VI, 394; F. Büchsel, *Der Geist Gottes im Neuen Testament*, pp. 180 ff.

[4] Cf. J. E. Yates, *The Spirit and the Kingdom* (London, 1963), pp. 29 ff.

Considering together these two passages, i. 12 f. and iii. 22 –
30, we see that they supplement one another. i. 12 f. has no
conclusion; the conclusion is supplied by iii. 27. They are the
only incidents in which the Spirit is seen as active in the
ministry of Jesus and both concern his warfare with the spiritual
powers. We are thus justified in taking them together and seeing
in the Temptation in Mark not a psychological process but a
contest between Jesus and Satan.[1] For Mark, Satan was thus
defeated and rendered powerless at the very beginning of the
ministry of Jesus and he proclaims his own victory in iii. 27:
'Man höre den Siegesklang, der durch diese Worte geht.'[2] The
Temptation is not then a preliminary to the ministry of Jesus in
which he settles for himself the broad outlines along which his
ministry will run. The Temptation lies within the ministry as
its decisive first act: Satan is overcome; the demonic exorcisms
of the remainder of the ministry represent the making real of a
victory already accomplished. The exorcisms are mopping-up
operations of isolated units of Satan's hosts and are certain to be
successful because the Captain of the hosts of evil is already
bound and immobilised. The defeat of Satan is thus attached
to the Temptation rather than to the Passion.

If this is the Markan interpretation of the Temptation certain
questions at once raise themselves. (1) Does Jesus suffer temptation again after the initial encounter with Satan, and, if so,
from what source does it come? (2) If Satan has been defeated
at the beginning of the ministry what is the meaning of the
Cross for Mark? (3) The early Christians undoubtedly found
Satan very active; how could this be if he is already bound?

Before we turn to an examination of these questions we must
look at the various incidents in which Jesus expels demons from
men and see if these confirm our interpretation of iii. 27. Since
Wrede the importance of these incidents in the thought structure
of Mark has been increasingly emphasised. He drew attention
to the knowledge that the demons had of the nature of Jesus and
of Jesus' attempts to keep them silent so that that knowledge

[1] Leivestad (*Christ the Conqueror*, p. 53), who reaches the conclusion that
the Temptation is a testing rather than a contest, bases his argument on the
Q form of the Temptation story.
[2] Dehn, p. 87.

was not spread abroad.[1] We are not at present concerned with this latter aspect but rather with the status which the demons accorded to Jesus. In i. 24 the demon terms Jesus 'The Holy One of God', whereas in iii. 11 they call him 'The Son of God' and in v. 7 'Son of the Most High God'.[2] We may note that it was as Son of God that Jesus encountered Satan, for at the baptism immediately preceding the Temptation in the Markan narrative Jesus had been termed 'Son of God' by the heavenly voice. The demons thus recognise him under the same category, Son of God, as he defeated their master, the strong one. The title 'The Holy One of God' is much more difficult to explain. '... (it) does not appear to have been an accepted Messianic title. It describes a man set apart and consecrated to the service of God. In some early Christian communities it may have been used for a time as a Messianic name, but the New Testament examples are few and uncertain.'[3] In our present context it presumably refers to someone who stands in a particular relationship to God. The suggestion of Procksch[4] that ἅγιος refers here to the Holy Spirit, if it could be sustained, would be very interesting; as bearer of the Spirit in whose power he encountered Satan, Jesus now encounters Satan's underlings and is so recognised by them. Much more probably the explanation lies in the contrast between ἀκάθαρτος and ἅγιος. 'St Mark's special designation for a demon is "unclean spirit".'[5] Although he uses δαιμόνιον the term 'unclean spirit' crops up again and again as if explanatory of the other word. Matthew and Luke often omit it where Mark has it and only introduce it once each where it is not in Mark.[6] The usage of 'holy' in the cry of the demoniac once again emphasises the irreconcilable difference between Jesus and the demonic powers.

Passing from this to the meaning of the demonic acknowledgement, this can be taken as like recognising like: the demons

[1] Wrede, *Das Messiasgeheimnis in den Evangelien*², pp. 22–32.

[2] The stories in vii. 24–30 and ix. 14–29 are not told primarily to show Jesus in conflict with the demonic world, and do not contain demonic 'confessions'.

[3] Taylor, *The Names of Jesus*, p. 80.   [4] *T.W.N.T.* I, 102.

[5] Ling, *The Significance of Satan*, p. 14.

[6] The Markan phrase 'unclean spirit' in i. 26; v. 2, 13; vi. 7; vii. 25; ix. 25 is altered by either Matthew or Luke or both in their parallels. They introduce the phrase in Luke xi. 24 = Matt. xii. 43.

being supernatural know supernaturally the supernatural nature of the prophet of Nazareth.[1] That the demons should have more than human insight is undoubtedly true, but this in itself does not seem to exhaust the meaning of their recognition of Jesus. In exorcism it was important for the exorcist to know the name of the devil which he was attempting to expel; the demons may then be using the true name of Jesus in an attempt to obtain control over him. Bauernfeind[2] has shown that parallels exist in the magical papyri to the words of the demons in i. 24, iii. 11 and v. 7. While this may again be a factor it does not provide a full explanation. A title is used as the acknowledgement of superiority, not as an attempt to gain control. For Mark the title Son of God is obviously the highest title that can be given; it is the title by which he would have his readers recognise Jesus as their Lord; it is unlikely then that he would have regarded its use by the demons as an attempt to overpower him; rather as a recognition of his overlordship.[3] Equally their description of him as ἅγιος signifies the gulf that lies between them and himself and implies his vast superiority. It is obvious from the stories that the demons wish to have nothing to do with Jesus, τί ἡμῖν καὶ σοί (i. 24; cf. v. 7); whenever they see him they prostrate themselves before him (iii. 11; cf. v. 6, though it is not clear in this latter case whether it is the man or the demon who worships Jesus); they are obviously thrown into confusion at the presence of Jesus, convulsing their 'hosts' (i. 26; cf. ix. 20); at the approach of Jesus the demon cries out (i. 23). The whole implication of these accounts is then the recognition by the demons that Jesus is their master.

Moreover, Jesus behaves throughout as their master. He rebukes and commands them (i. 25; iii. 12; ix. 25). There are no signs of a struggle between Jesus and the demons similar to his struggle with Satan. From the beginning of the encounter with each demon Jesus is in control of the situation.

---

[1] Cf. Lightfoot, *History*, p. 68; Wrede, *Das Messiasgeheimnis in den Evangelien*[2], pp. 28 ff.; Dibelius, pp. 54 f.

[2] *Die Worte der Dämonen im Markusevangelium*. Unfortunately I have not been able to obtain access to a copy of this book and depend on references to it in other writers.

[3] Cf. Ebeling, *Das Messiasgeheimnis und die Botschaft des Marcus-Evangelisten*, pp. 127 f.

The mastery assumed by Jesus over the demons is seen also in the strange phrase which Mark uses when Jesus gives his disciples their commission. He does not send them to exorcise but he gives them authority (ἐξουσία) over the demons (iii. 15; vi. 7). He could not give what he did not already himself possess. All this is so because Jesus has already defeated their master, Satan. With him took place the real contest. It ended victoriously for Jesus, and so when he meets one of Satan's underlings the latter recognises his overlordship from the beginning; at best all he can do is bargain for good terms for himself (v. 10); defeat is certain. Thus a study of the particular demonic exorcisms confirms the conclusion we drew from iii. 27. Satan has been decisively defeated and his kingdom is being reduced.

Since the point of view we have expressed in respect of the Temptation narrative and the demonic exorcisms is so entirely different from that of J. M. Robinson in his book *The Problem of History in Mark*, which itself represents a current trend in the discussion of Mark's Gospel in finding the key to its understanding in the demoniacal,[1] it is necessary that we examine his contentions and endeavour to show their inadequacy.

Robinson begins by noting that in Mark the Baptism and the Temptation are cosmic events. These events signify 'for Mark a decisive occurrence in the realization of the eschatological hope' (p. 27).[2] 'An essential part of the eschatological hope is the overthrow of the devil' (p. 28). The Temptation story and exorcism debate (iii. 22–30) are closely linked and indicate that the struggle between the Spirit and Satan which began in the Temptation continues in every exorcism, 'and the single event of the temptation becomes in the exorcisms an extended history of redemptive significance.... For once the saving action of Jesus over Satan is divided into a series of stories, it has lost its single-event character and is already on the way to becoming a history open to potential continuation within the Church' (p. 30). 'The exorcisms are interpreted in iii. 22–30 in terms of the cosmic struggle between the Spirit and Satan begun in the

---

[1] Cf. J. Kallas, *The Significance of the Synoptic Miracles*; G. Hebert, *The Christ of Faith and the Jesus of History*; H. Sawyerr, 'The Marcan Framework', *S.J.Th.* XIV (1961), 279–94.   [2] Page references refer to Robinson.

temptation' (p. 35). 'The exorcisms ... are the points in a historical narrative where the transcendent meaning of that history is most clearly evident' (p. 33). Robinson examines the various exorcism accounts and finds in them evidence of the continuing struggle between the Spirit and Satan (pp. 36–8). Though less evident the same struggle is present in the other miracle stories of the Gospel, and he finds traces of exorcism language in three Markan miracle stories (i. 43; iv. 39; vii. 35; cf. p. 40). Furthermore, following on the struggle in the exorcism there comes a period of peace, it being made 'evident that violence and death itself have been cast out' (p. 39). He points in particular to ix. 27 where Jesus is said to 'raise' the epileptic boy. Thus he is able to make the step from the exorcism narratives to the Passion and the Resurrection itself: 'The sudden reversal of the situation as the passion narrative is replaced by the Easter story is already anticipated in the exorcism stories, and here the shift is identified as due to the victory over the demon, i.e. Satan' (p. 39).

Robinson then seeks to show that the remainder of the historical narrative must be understood in terms of the cosmic struggle and he proceeds to discuss the debates between Jesus and his opponents.[1] 'For Mark, the nearest parallel to Jesus' debates is not the rabbinic debate, but rather the exorcism' (p. 44). Both debates and exorcism begin in hostility on the part of the opponents of Jesus, whether the opponents be demons or Pharisees: the word πειράζειν is used 'thus making their diabolic instigation clear' (p. 45). The disciples in their debates with Jesus about the Passion are equally instigated by Satan (viii. 33; cf. p. 52). In the debates there is a 'breakthrough to the truth of history and its eschatological basis' (p. 46). Thus Robinson can conclude,

The history which Mark selects to record is presented in its unity as the eschatological action of God, prepared by John the Baptist, inaugurated at the baptism and temptation, carried on through the struggles with various forms of evil, until in his death Jesus has experienced the ultimate of historical involvement and of diabolic antagonism. In the resurrection the force of evil is conclusively broken and the power of God's reign is established in history (p. 53).

[1] Cf. J. C. Fenton, 'Paul and Mark', *Studies in the Gospels* (ed. D. E. Nineham), pp. 89–112, at pp. 102 ff.

As we have done, Robinson connects the debate of iii. 22–30 with the Temptation, but because he fails to understand the metaphor of 'binding', Satan is still active for him in the exorcisms which are a continuation of the struggle of the Temptation. The Temptation has, in effect, been only the first round in the contest and apparently lacks a decisive conclusion. To us the exorcisms represent the plundering of the strong man's house, only possible because the strong man has been bound. We would further hold that in his actual discussion of the exorcism narratives Robinson lays too much stress on the element of struggle; we have sought alternatively to show that on each occasion Jesus is from beginning to end the master, though the demon may attempt to struggle, and he is master because he has defeated already the demon's own master, Satan. Now it is true that many of the other miracles resemble in varying ways the exorcism narratives and that among the Jews sickness was sometimes ascribed to demonic possession. In particular, as pointed out by Ling,[1] the uncleanness of leprosy may be related to the uncleanness of demons:[2] now while this demonic element is present in some of the Markan miracle stories it cannot be easily traced in all of them and it is a big step to take to argue that it must be so discerned. It is only natural that in the healing miracles the cure is emphasised and the period of 'peace' after the miracle stressed. To suggest that for this reason the miracles are to be understood in the same way as the exorcisms because in both the end of the story is 'peace' is surely to draw deep meaning out of a similarity that is inherent in the very nature of healing stories; it is impossible to relate them without mentioning the cured state and the difference between 'before' and 'after'. The attempt moreover to move from the exorcism stories to the resurrection is inadequately based. This movement is made to rest on two features: (a) The violence of the demoniac before cure suggests the violence of the Passion and the peace afterwards suggests the Resurrection; this is again too great a step to take unless there is some deliberate indication in the text that it is intended. (b) Robinson finds such a deliberate indication in the words to the cured epileptic boy when Jesus takes him by the hand and 'raises' him; but

[1] *The Significance of Satan*, pp. 14 ff.
[2] But it may also be related to sin; cf. pp. 106 f. below.

the word 'raise' here is perfectly natural; the demon has already thrown the boy to the ground! There is not in Mark any clear indication that Satan was active in the Passion; Luke by some additions to the Passion narrative does suggest the activity of Satan at the time (xxii. 3, Satan enters Judas; xxii. 31, Satan desires Simon), but such indications are wholly absent in Mark.[1]

Equally to be rejected is Robinson's attempt to find Satan present in the debates that Jesus has with his disciples and with his opponents. It is undoubtedly true, as he stresses, that the actions and the words of Jesus cannot be separated, but since he has failed to show that opposition to Satan governs all the actions of Jesus this in itself is not a reason for expecting to find opposition to the demoniac in the words of Jesus. In making the assumption that the nearest parallel to the debates is the exorcisms, Robinson ignores the fact that in the exorcisms there really are no debates; there are words of command by Jesus but no attempts to prove by argument or use of Scripture the inadequacy of the position of the demon; the demon acknowledges from the beginning the true position of Jesus as Son of God or as Holy One, the opponents in the debates do not; the demons behave utterly differently from the human opponents of Jesus; it is only necessary to quote Robinson himself on this:

We do not find calm conversations, but shouts and orders. The demons 'shout' at Jesus: i. 23; iii. 11; (v. 5); v. 7; ix. 26. In v. 7 the demon 'adjures' Jesus. Jesus 'orders' the demons (i. 27 (*sic*); ix. 25), or 'reproaches' them with an order (i. 25; iii. 12; ix. 25). The only passage approaching normal conversation is in v. 9–13, after the struggle is over and the authoritative word of exorcism had been uttered (*v.* 8) (p. 36).

Robinson points out also the similarity of the hostility of opponents and demons to Jesus; this does not seem exceptional; it is only in the nature of the case that opponents should be hostile; this does not imply they are demonically inspired.[2] Robinson would appear to have more of a point when he draws attention to instances where the opponents of Jesus are said to 'tempt' him (viii. 11; x. 2; xii. 15). We will examine this in our next chapter and see that these temptations come from men

---

[1] Cf. Leivestad, *Christ the Conqueror*, pp. 63 ff.
[2] Cf. also pp. 38 ff below.

and not Satan;[1] in the LXX there is no connection between the root πειράζειν and evil spiritual powers. Robinson also finds a connection with the Cross in Jesus' debate with the disciples about the Passion when Peter is called Satan (viii. 31 ff.); we will see also in our next chapter that this does not imply that Peter is a tool of Satan, rather that he behaves as Satan would behave, were Satan free so to behave.[2] Thus the debates cannot be regarded as extensions of the demonic exorcisms and consequently any argument from the debates as demonic to the Passion as Satanic cannot be made.

When we examine the certain instances of demonic influence in Mark we see that it is confined to the Temptation story itself plus the exorcisms and certain of the miracle stories. In the Temptation story temptation is definitely present, that is, Satan tempts to moral evil, though Mark stresses the conflict rather than the actual tempting. But when we consider the other events we see that in them it is impersonal forms of evil that are involved, for example, madness, leprosy, storm (cf. i. 25 and iv. 39 where Jesus in similar words commands the demon and the storm to be silent). Thus Satan being defeated Jesus encounters his underlings and has to deal with powers that disturb the life of men on the physical plane but do not drive them to moral evil. This is not to deny that there is a unity in evil, but it is to suggest that the demonic powers were not concerned with those aspects of evil which essentially separate a man from God and the removal of which, as we shall see, was at least one of the purposes of the Passion and Resurrection. In actual fact the demonic slowly fades out of Mark; highly concentrated at the beginning it gradually disappears so that in the Passion story it escapes mention altogether. Robinson would take its high concentration at the commencement of the Gospel as indicating it as a main theme for the whole and signifying the true interpretation. It is *a priori* equally probable that it disappears because Mark does not consider it of supreme importance. We have sought to show negatively that Robinson's interpretation is not tenable. We have yet to show positively that an interpretation other than the demonic is what Mark would have us see. But indicative of that other interpretation is the disappearance of the demonic from the Gospel while moral

[1] Pp. 30 f..   [2] Pp. 28 ff.

evil still remains and comes at Jesus from his opponents, his disciples, and finally from within himself in Gethsemane.

Kallas[1] has enunciated views somewhat similar to Robinson concerning the significance of the demonic in the life of Jesus. While his main concern lies with the miracles of Jesus which he views as evidence of the activity of Jesus against Satan and the demonic powers which now rule the world, he also sees the death of Jesus as the final defeat of Satan.

It was in death that Satan's rule became vindicated and perpetuated. Death made his victory final. If Jesus came to fight the strong man, if Jesus intended to break the reign of Satan, then he would have to fight Satan in this, the place where Satan was strongest; in the valley of the shadow of death (pp. 98 f.).

Unlike Robinson, Kallas seeks to set out the significance of the Synoptic miracles, and therefore of the demonic element, for Jesus himself, and is not concerned with the theology of the evangelists, least of all of Mark. But this does not mean that Kallas has nothing to say relevant to our theme. He works throughout with an uncritical view of the Gospels. Whatever he finds in them he assumes to be true of Jesus. This is particularly true of his examination of the self-consciousness of Jesus (pp. 24 ff.), where he makes no attempt to estimate the genuineness of sayings of our Lord. On the basis of the Gospels as they are he quickly reaches the conclusion that Jesus regarded himself as divine (p. 31). This uncritical use of the Gospel also means that what he finds to be true of Jesus and of the demonic element in his life is necessarily also true of all three evangelists, and in particular of Mark, and it permits him to regard the evangelists as possessing a common mind in these matters.

We can go a considerable part of the way with Kallas when he argues that not only in the exorcisms is Jesus waging war against demonic forces but also in the healing miracles. Here he instances Luke xiii. 16; iv. 39 as evidence that this was Jesus' own understanding of what he was doing. The weakness of his method is apparent at this very point. In the latter of these Luke says that Jesus 'rebuked' the disease, just as he is said to rebuke demons (Mark i. 25; ix. 25). But Luke's use of ἐπιτιμᾶν is here an alteration of the Markan account. Moreover, Luke

---

[1] *The Significance of the Synoptic Miracles.*

xiii. 16 belongs to Luke's special material. It is thus impossible to argue from the Lukan view here either that Mark held the same view and that all his healing miracles should be interpreted in this way, or that Jesus himself held this view. Indeed the very fact that one of these cases is definitely editorial on Luke's part and the other comes from this special material would rather suggest that this view belongs either to Luke the editor, which is the more probable, or that it belongs to his special material. This in turn suggests that the entrance of the demonic interpretation into the material came during its transmission and was not original. Just as Luke has a special interest in the Holy Spirit and introduces many references to him, so he may equally have a special interest in the Evil Spirit; the two would go together. It is not our concern here to argue about the view of Jesus himself, but what we have said would suggest that the demonic-cosmic element may have played less part in his viewpoint than is sometimes held. In any case we cannot simply transfer the Lukan view to Mark. In order to find this in Mark, Kallas draws attention to Mark's use of μάστιξ when referring to disease (iii. 10; v. 29, 34). 'In other words, for Jesus and the gospel writers, these ordinary "diseases" were not ordinary at all. They were, instead, scourges, or whips; they were curses, sources of affliction by the evil one. Satan was persecuting these people' (p. 79). But μάστιξ was already used metaphorically of disease without reference to Satan;[1] and so it is not necessary to introduce him at this point. Kallas would have us also see the fight against the demons as continued in the nature miracles; it is easier to agree with him here, especially in the light of the rebuking of the storm (iv. 37–41).

Finally, Kallas considers the Resurrection, the final miracle, as the ultimate contest with Satan. He fails to provide here the necessary evidence from the Gospels themselves that Satan is the angel of death; he fails to show adequately the place of Satan in the Passion story; his attempt to show its cosmic dimension from Matt. xxvii. 51–3 is to make use of very secondary material; his claim to see in Passion and Resurrection the final contest with Satan in which the stronger one wins (cf. pp. 98 f.) ignores Mark's clear statement that at iii. 27 this contest is already over.

[1] Cf. C. Schneider, *T.W.N.T.* IV, 524; Liddell and Scott; Bauer, etc., on the word.

THE TEMPTATION NARRATIVE

The extent to which the demonic background permeates Mark will appear as we proceed: we thus give no direct rebuttal of Kallas's view that it is present and dominant in the Passion and Resurrection.

The approach of Mauser is somewhat different though he arrives at a similar conclusion to Robinson and Kallas. He considers that Mark views the life and passion of Jesus as spent in the 'wilderness'. The 'wilderness' is not a place but a theological theme; in the Old Testament it is the place of evil, of the judgement of God, of repentance, renewal and deliverance. Mark depicts Jesus as continually going into the wilderness and so as constantly in contact with evil, demonic evil. The forty days of the Temptation in the wilderness are typical in this respect; they are not decisive moments in a conflict with Satan but at the beginning set out the whole tenor of the life of Jesus as one of incessant temptation.

But it is not the power of Jesus to overcome evil which is stressed by Mark in i. 13, otherwise a victory over Satan would certainly have been told. In the prologue, the Evangelist simply sets the stage – Jesus and Satan are going to be the main actors in the commencing drama and their encounter alone is the fact emphasised in i. 13. Now, at the end of the drama, the main characters are still engaged in battle, and temptation is still the name of their clash. But the word has assumed a decidedly sinister tone; it is clear that in this last encounter the devil's power is going to carry the day – the hour when the Son of Man is delivered into the hands of sinners is Satan's hour, because the sinners are his instruments.[1]

The final conflict with Satan is thus, as in Robinson and Kallas, the Cross.

We must admit at the outset that the 'wilderness' plays a large part in the Old Testament and that a great many ideas are connected with it. Mauser has shown in the first part of his study how important and widespread is this conception. But many of the ideas connected with the wilderness exist also without this connection. For David the place of evil and temptation was not the wilderness but a built-up area of Jerusalem where he espied Bathsheba; and in the same area he learnt and suffered the judgement of God, repented and was renewed. For Isaiah the temple was the place of revelation;

[1] Mauser, p. 130.

25

there he met Got and responded to him. Mark speaks of the judgement of God borne by Christ, of temptation as coming to Christ, and of deliverance through Christ; the fact that these themes appear does not mean that they can be seen only against the background of the 'wilderness'. If Mark is to be viewed as dominated in them by the 'wilderness' theme then we would expect to see this much more clearly. But Mark's references to the 'wilderness' are not sufficiently clear and precise to enable us to draw the conclusions to which Mauser would lead us.

We may begin with the word 'wilderness'. On p. 78 Mauser tells us that 'the "wilderness" theme is repeatedly used by the Evangelist in editorial remarks' and refers us to pp. 104 f.; but at pp. 104 f. he only indicates three places (i. 35; i. 45; vi. 31–3) where it is used editorially. Not only is it used only occasionally editorially but the phrase so used is different from that which came to Mark in the tradition. In the editorial passages Mark used ἔρημος τόπος (or the plural), whereas the phrase in the tradition is ἡ ἔρημος (γῆ) (i. 3, 4, 12, 13); ἡ ἐρημία (viii. 4) also appears in the tradition.[1] The normal LXX phrase for the wilderness is ἡ ἔρημος (γῆ). Mark's editorial phrase ὁ ἔρημος τόπος is only found once (Dan. LXX iv. 25; Jer. xl. 12 is not a true parallel) in five columns of Hatch and Redpath's LXX concordance. Mauser fails to consider why in giving an Old Testament concept Mark fails to use the universal Old Testament word. The simplest solution is that Mark is not conscious of the Old Testament idea and is using ἔρημος in a different way. And when we examine i. 35, 45; vi. 31–3 we see that the translation 'lonely' (cf. R.S.V. at i. 35) fits the context. At i. 35; vi. 31[2] Jesus wants solitude for himself or his disciples; at i. 45 the phrase is in natural opposition to πόλις. On each occasion it would have been simple enough for Mark to use the normal phrase and so connect what he is saying to i. 4, 12, but he does not do so. Perhaps Mark's change indicates that for him the wilderness period ended with i. 13: thereafter he avoids the normal phrase for the wilderness! There is also too easy an identification of the 'mountain' and the 'sea' with the 'wilderness'. Mauser draws a strong parallel

[1] 'It is reasonable to suppose that in vi. 35 Mark also found ἔρημος or ἐρημία in his tradition ...' (Mauser, p. 105).

[2] Note κατ' ἰδίαν at vi. 31, 32.

between the Transfiguration and the events of Exod. xxiv. There are difficulties in this parallel, but even supposing that we allow it holds, this of itself does not bring us to the wilderness theme. Admittedly the 'mountain' of Exod. xxiv is in the 'wilderness', but that does not mean that therefore the 'mountain' of Mark ix. 2 – 8 is part of the 'wilderness' theme, and that every other reference to mountains in Mark should be taken as a reference to the 'wilderness'. If the background of ix. 2 – 8 is Exod. xxiv, then Mark is only making a connection between the Transfiguration and the law-giving of Sinai, and not necessarily drawing in a whole background of ideas in relation to the wilderness. The 'sea' is certainly demonic in Mark (cf. iv. 35 – 41) and that associates it with the 'wilderness', but it does not mean that every reference to the sea, and there are many, is to be taken as suggesting the wilderness theme. We are thus unable to view the 'wilderness' as a dominant theme in Mark.

Turning more directly to i. 12 f. we are also unable to accept Mauser's contention[1] that the forty days were not a decisive period. The connection which we have attempted to make with iii. 22 – 30, if correct, obviously refutes such a view. Finally we are unable to view the Passion of Jesus as taking place in the 'wilderness'. As Mauser himself shows, the 'wilderness' theme tends to disappear after viii. 27.[2] Since Jerusalem was hardly the wilderness the recurrence of the theme at this point would need to have been made expressly clear. Mauser's proof seems to lie in the argument that in Gethsemane temptation recurs and therefore we are back in the wilderness; this depends on the assumptions: (a) that temptation must be due to the devil; this is doubtful in the case of Mark;[3] Mauser draws here on the work of Robinson, which we have been questioning, 'that Mark understands Jesus' whole mission as an encounter with Satanic forces';[4] (b) that the 'wilderness' is the only place where the Devil operates; this assumption rather begs the question. Even if Robinson's view is correct this second assumption is wrong because the conflict of Jesus with demonic forces takes place not in the wilderness but in crowds and in public places (i. 21 – 8; i. 33 f.; iii. 9 – 12). However, the wilderness theme and the views of Robinson do not necessarily go together; Robinson's ideas could still stand, though the former were untrue.

[1] Cf. pp. 97 – 100, 129 f.   [2] P. 128.   [3] Cf. ch. ii.   [4] Mauser, p. 130, n. 1.

CHAPTER II

THE ORIGIN OF TEMPTATION

IT would appear that we have left little place for Satan in the remainder of the Gospel and so we must examine those places in which he appears and those in which Jesus is said to be tempted, to discover his role therein. This will lead us to a general discussions of evil and its origin in Mark, which will in turn lead to a similar discussion of the same question in the whole of the biblical and post-biblical material.

There are two passages other than i. 12 f. in which Satan is mentioned in the Gospel. He appears first in the interpretation of the Parable of the Sower at iv. 15. It might be thought that we could evade this occurrence by arguing that the interpretation is not original; we however are concerned with the Gospel as it stands, not with what we would put in it if we were writing a life of Jesus. We must point out though that the activity of Satan in the interpretation of the parable is an activity among men; he is not seen as active in the life of our Lord. The interpretation represents for Mark an attempt to place the parable in the life of the early Church, and therefore Satan is here viewed as active in the lives of men. We are at the moment dealing with Satan as active in the life of Jesus and therefore may leave this reference in iv. 15 until later.[1]

The one place where Satan explicitly reappears in the life of Jesus is viii. 33 where, following on Peter's confession of Jesus as Christ and Jesus' own prediction of his sufferings, Peter rebuked him and Jesus in reply says, 'Get thee behind me, Satan'. Cullmann links the phrase closely to Matt. iv. 10 where we have the similar phrase ὕπαγε, Σατανᾶ and continues, 'The devil is now making use of Jesus' own disciple, Peter; that is his greatest trick. ... He who tries to force upon Jesus another Messianic task than the one he has received from God, he who thereby seeks to turn him from this task he has received from God, is a tool of Satan.'[2] In so describing Peter as the tool of Satan, the implication is that Satan is no longer

---

[1] Cf. p. 182. [2] *Peter: Disciple, Apostle, Martyr*, p. 174.

bound, or else Peter must be regarded as possessed by a demon. We must however note that Cullmann is interpreting the phrase as both it and the story appear in the Gospel of Matthew, and not as in Mark. For us it is illegitimate to introduce Matt. iv. 10 into our discussion since Mark, not knowing the story of the three temptations, cannot here be making a veiled allusion to them. Without this direct link the conclusion that Peter is a tool of Satan is not so obvious.

The phrase ὕπαγε ὀπίσω μου is difficult to interpret. From the time of Origen[1] attempts have been made to take the words in a light as favourable as possible to Peter. Thus some commentators have taken it as a plea to Peter to return behind Jesus again as his disciple.[2] ὀπίσω μου is definitely associated with discipleship in *v.* 34 (cf. i. 17, 20) but the verb used is ἐλθεῖν and not ὑπάγειν.[3] An Aramaic or Syriac idiom has been suspected behind the phrase, based on an original σου rather than μου, but this seems unlikely.[4] It is very probable that it must be given the general sense: 'Away from me so as to be out of my sight.'[5] Jesus dismisses Peter because of his Satanic suggestion. But does he mean by this that Peter has taken up the role of Satan or that Satan is making use of Peter as his tool? This is a real distinction. The normal English rendering, 'Get thee behind me, Satan', can be interpreted in either way, but Moffatt's translation, 'Get behind me, You Satan', definitely suggests the former alternative. When in the Matthean account Jesus calls Simon 'Peter', he means that he is to perform the role of a rock in steadying his fellows; when he calls the sons of Zebedee 'Boanerges', he means that they behaved in the tempestuous manner of a storm. Thus it seems better to see Peter behaving after the manner of Satan than as either indwelt by Satan or as his tool. This interpretation is confirmed by the immediately succeeding words where Peter is accused to thinking not the thoughts of God but those of men (cf. viii. 27: Peter is no further on than the crowd). What he puts before Jesus is a

[1] *Commentary on Matt. ad* xvi 22 f.
[2] Schlatter, *Der Evangelist Matthäus, ad* xvi. 23.   [3] Cf. Swete *ad loc.*
[4] See M. Black, *An Aramaic Approach to the Gospels and Acts*[2], pp. 263 f.
[5] C. H. Turner, *J.T.S.* xxix (1928), 287 f., shows that in Mark the fundamental meaning of ὕπαγε is movement away from ('go' as distinct from 'come') the speaker.

pattern of all too human behaviour and not of divine.[1] In putting this temptation before Jesus he is playing the role of Satan, one of whose activities is to tempt men, but he is not Satan; nor may the temptation even be described as Satanic: it is human.

Consequently there is no reason to believe that Mark at this point sees Satan as set free from his binding and as coming again to tempt Jesus. Nor is there any need to accuse Mark of inconsistency at this point in relation to Satan. Satan has been bound, but temptation does not cease: it comes now from man, and from a man who stands in a close personal relationship to Jesus – for those reasons it is perhaps all the more deadly.

Jesus also undergoes temptation in the Garden of Gethsemane (xiv. 32–42). Here we are moving in the same circle of ideas, those of the Old Testament. Jesus sees opposed two wills, his own and God's. Satan is not even mentioned. The temptation now definitely comes from within Jesus himself. There is here no cosmic conflict (the strengthening angel of the Lukan account might imply such) but the simple struggle of human will against divine will. And we may note at this point that this is also the experience of the disciples, with a very different result. They entered into temptation and fell because though the Spirit was ready the flesh was weak (xiv. 38). The dualism of flesh and spirit here is not an inner dualism in man between his upper and his lower natures but the dualism of opposition between God and man; $\sigma\acute{\alpha}\rho\xi$ is man's whole being in weakness and opposition to God; $\pi\nu\epsilon\hat{\upsilon}\mu\alpha$ is God's Spirit ready to help man.[2] Verse 38a may represent the experience of Jesus himself, out of which he gives his counsel to the disciples. It is however unlikely that Mark took it in that way; he does not attribute it to Jesus' own experience and he nowhere shows much interest in the inner consciousness of Jesus.

There are three passages in which the root $\pi\epsilon\iota\rho\acute{\alpha}\zeta\epsilon\iota\nu$ appears, viii. 11; x. 2; xii. 15, and we must now look at these to see if in them it carries the meaning of 'tempt'.

---

[1] The thought is similar to Rom. viii. 5 ff., which if Mark wrote the Gospel in Rome he will have known. Men, not Satan, and God are also in opposition at x. 27; xi. 30–2; cf. vii. 7; ix. 31 for 'men' used in a bad sense.

[2] Cf. Schweizer, *T.W.N.T.* VI, 394 (= *The Spirit of God*, pp. 24 f.); Büchsel, *Der Geist Gottes im Neuen Testament*, pp. 180 ff.

We examine first viii. 11 in which the Pharisees seek a sign from Jesus. Their request comes directly after the feeding of the four thousand and immediately before the discussion of the leaven of the Pharisees and the Herodians, which is itself occasioned by the almost total absence of bread in the ship in which they were crossing the lake. Whether this is the original place of the tradition is unimportant for us; this is where Mark puts it. Whether also Jesus in his historical existence was conscious of himself as Messiah or not is again irrelevant for us; Mark undoubtedly took him to be. All that the Pharisees originally asked may have been a sign that he was a prophet come from heaven, and this may be all that Jesus may have refused them,[1] but Mark sees Jesus as refusing to confirm his Messianic office by a sign from Heaven. Heaven may be taken literally and the Pharisees considered as seeking a sign out of the heavens, as in xiii. 24, 25, that is, a sign of the consummation of the Messianic kingdom;[2] or it may be taken as a Jewish circumlocution for God, and the sign be another miraculous feeding:[3] as Moses fed the Israelites in the desert, so should the Messiah feed his people now (cf. John vi. 30 f.).[4] If the former interpretation is taken then there is a resemblance here to the second temptation in the Matthean form, and if the second interpretation, then a resemblance to the first temptation. This very resemblance suggests at once that πειράζειν cannot be taken here in the simple sense of 'test'.[5] The Pharisees would undoubtedly try out Jesus to see if he was divinely sent, but this very trial was a temptation for Jesus that he should seek to convince men of his Messiahship through a mighty work – something other than the healings and exorcisms which both he and others performed (Matt. xii. 27; Luke xi. 19). We must therefore take this to be a temptation of Jesus. This temptation comes to him from men; explicitly it originates with the Pharisees, but Jesus widens it out to include all men – 'this generation seeks a sign'. 'This generation' is apparently used in a bad sense; it denotes men in their opposition to God (cf. viii. 38; ix. 19; xiii. 30).[6]

[1] Cf. Branscomb.   [2] Cf. Lohmeyer, Menzies, etc.
[3] Cf. Schniewind, etc.
[4] Cf. Bultmann, Hoskyns and Davey, etc., on John vi. 31.
[5] Seesemann, *T.W.N.T.* VI, 28, takes it in the secular sense of 'test'.
[6] Cf. Büchsel, *T.W.N.T.*, I, 661.

There is thus here no trace of Satan.[1] The Pharisees and this generation think the thoughts of men and not of God (cf. viii. 33). An interesting sidelight would be thrown on this if we could take the reference to the spirit of Jesus in viii. 12 as a reference to the Holy Spirit:[2] then we would have the reappearance of the Spirit of God at a moment of temptation. It is however unlikely that πνεῦμα should be taken here of the Holy Spirit.

The two remaining passages do not need detailed discussion. At x. 2 Jesus is asked concerning divorce; there was already considerable divergence of opinion in Judaism, and probably also in early Christianity, on this matter; an attempt is made to trap him into coming down on one or other side. πειράζειν thus has probably the sense of testing someone as to his opinion, hostile intent being present.[3] At xii. 15 it is Jesus himself who uses the word, describing the Pharisees and Herodians who ask him the question about tribute money as 'testing' him. They are again seeking to find out his opinion in the hope that he will commit himself to a view whereby he will either lose the support of the people, if he advises to pay, or will run into conflict with the Roman authorities, and so destroy himself, if he advises to refuse to pay. We come much nearer the meaning of 'tempt' in this passage; a straightforward statement by Jesus that the tax should not be paid might be regarded as a raising of the Messianic standard of revolt; here was an opportunity to win the crowds to himself; there are thus resemblances between this and the third Matthean temptation in that Jesus is here involved in a temptation to obtain power by a political slogan. It should also be noted that on any occasion when Jesus is asked a question

[1] The Lukan parallel is xi. 16. If we accept the view of Conzelmann, pp. 27–9, that, for Luke, Satan left Jesus alone between iv. 13 and xxii. 3 then Luke also can use πειράζειν without any reference to Satan but only to men.

[2] So Schniewind. It may be pointed out that (ἀνα)στενάζειν and πνεῦμα are connected both here and in Rom. viii. 23.

[3] Hebert, *The Christ of Faith and the Jesus of History*, p. 89, considers that Mark has carefully placed this incident and that for him its reference is not to the marriage and divorce of individuals but to the marriage of the Messiah to Israel. 'The answer comes clear and strong, "What God has joined together, let not man separate". The union stands; he is one with his bride, and therefore he must bear her sins.' The Temptation is then a temptation to Jesus to forsake his mission towards Israel.

which involves him in a statement either about his ministry or concerning how men should behave there is the temptation not to speak the truth but to say what men would like to hear. We cannot thus exclude from either x. 2 or xii. 15 the meaning of 'tempt'. Temptations continue to come to Jesus, but they come, not from Satan, or demonic powers, but from men, who are not in any way regarded as satanically possessed.

Having seen that it is not necessary to introduce the figure of Satan into the passages in which Jesus is said to be tempted and that Peter is not regarded as motivated by Satan, we must go on to examine the role of Satan in temptation. In actual day-to-day sin, as distinct from the cosmic origin of sin and evil, what part does Satan play? We are accustomed to think of him as responsible for all temptation. Did Mark hold this view? Is it found in the biblical and post-biblical material? By an examination of his Gospel and of the other material we shall seek to show that neither Mark nor contemporary Judaism attributed the origin of all temptation to Satan.

According to the Markan story Jesus first encountered evil in his conflict with Satan (i. 12 f.) . We are not told the content of the tempting or testing and it would be wrong for us to read into this short narrative the meaning given by Q, where the testing takes quite definitely the form of an attack on the purpose of his ministry. From Mark all we know is that he was divinely led to a clash with Satan in which he was victorious, and victorious to such a degree that he was afterwards able to spoil Satan's house and kingdom.

Closely linked to this encounter with evil in Satan is Jesus' encounter with evil in demon-possessed men, as iii. 27 makes clear. At no point does Mark attribute moral evil, that is sin, to demon possession. Much modern popular preaching, at a loss what to make of the exorcism stories, takes them as analogies of what Jesus can do in the casting out of a grave sin or evil habit; the person is cleansed. Such an approach would have been foreign to Mark. Nor would he have regarded the demonic as in need of psychiatric treatment in a mental home. The demoniac is one in whom a spiritual power of evil has replaced either permanently or temporarily the normal rational, conative and emotional faculties of man; treatment will not cure him; only the presence of a greater spiritual power. In all this Mark is in line with the prevailing thought of his day.

But the demonic is also present for Mark both in the world of nature and in ordinary sickness (i. 43; iv. 39; vii. 35).[1] The presence of this evil in the world around is seen most clearly in the way in which Jesus stills the storm (iv. 37 ff.).[2] Here there can be no question of moral evil; the universe cannot be accused of sinning. Sickness may also be due to demon possession; this, as Ling has shown, may be true of leprosy.[3] However the analysis of Ling at this point is not sufficiently accurate. He is correct in emphasising that Mark calls the demons who possess men 'unclean spirits', that the leper is 'cleansed' (i. 40–5) and that there are examples in Mark of the two other classes denoted in Num. v. 2 ff. as unclean, namely the woman with the issue of blood and those in contact with the dead (v. 21–43).[4] In the exorcism it is not the man who is unclean, but the demon; in leprosy it is the man who is unclean because of his leprosy and who because he is unclean is put out of the camp; again in Mark i. 40 it is the leper who desires to be cleansed and he is made clean by Jesus; the woman with the issue of blood is healed and so made clean; the unclean corpse of Jairus' daughter is brought back to life and so to cleanness. Those who because of uncleanness would have been put outside the camp are accepted by Jesus and in every case are touched by him (i. 41; v. 30, 41); the uncleanness has disappeared altogether. In the case of the demoniacs the unclean spirits are driven out but remain unclean; they still exist; but the leprosy and the issue of blood disappear. The unclean spirit is driven out but the unclean person is made whole. Because leprosy and an issue of blood lead to exclusion from the worship of God they resemble sin, and as the sick person is healed so the sinful person is forgiven; nothing is driven away. Furthermore, much Jewish

[1] Cf. Robinson, p. 40.

[2] The attempt of Kallas, *The Significance of the Synoptic Miracles*, pp. 88 f., to see in every nature miracle an attack on a demonically-possessed universe stretches the evidence beyond breaking point.

[3] *The Significance of Satan*, pp. 14 ff.

[4] The corpse, though instanced by Ling, is not strictly a parallel; it would have been Jairus and his wife, not their dead daughter, who would have been defiled by contact with the corpse; but it was the daughter who was healed.

thought linked leprosy to sin, regarding it as a punishment for sin.[1] Thus we cannot link leprosy too closely to demonic possession; it might equally be related to sin.

Exorcism and the healing of sickness are often set side by side in statements about the activity of Jesus and his disciples (i. 32, 34; vi. 7, 13). But may not sickness be linked with sin? This is certainly the attitude of much modern psychology, which regards sickness as brought on by sin, for example, an ulcer by worry, which is lack of trust in God and consequently sin. Support for this point of view has been drawn from Mark ii. 1–12,[2] where sickness and sin are clearly related. It is very doubtful if we can accept the modern psychological theory that before the man in this story could be healed a guilt complex had to be removed by forgiveness. It is a modern theory: Swete in his commentary of 1898 does not not mention it. It would hardly therefore have been a solution possible in the first century. It may be that Mark falls back here on the old view that sickness is a punishment of God; the man has sinned, God has chastised him with sickness, therefore he must first be forgiven and then healed. This is more probable than the view that the sickness is due to demonic powers, who would hardly have sent the sickness as a chastisement for sin. Where elsewhere these powers appear in the Gospel Jesus deals with them directly, speaking to them and ordering them to depart: here he speaks to the man himself and deals with him. If all sickness is to be traced to Satan, then this thought is not at all apparent at this point, and certainly we cannot draw the conclusion that the man's sin was due to Satan. How then must we interpret the incident? With Mark the argument is surely: since Jesus can heal the sick therefore he can forgive sins. He does the latter first; his power to do so is doubted; he performs the former to prove his power. It is an argument *a minori ad majus*. The power of Jesus is manifested in both actions; if the healings are a sign of the inbreaking of the Kingdom so also is forgiveness; healing and forgiveness are both expected in the Messianic time; they are present now in the life

[1] Cf. below, pp. 106 f.

[2] Whatever the earlier tradition Mark took ii. 1–12 as one incident. In what follows I have drawn largely on an earlier article, 'Mark ii. 1–12', *Biblical Theology*, III (1953), 41–6. Cf. also R. T. Mead, 'The Healing of the Paralytic – A Unit', *J.B.L.* LXXX (1961), 348–54.

THE TEMPTATION AND THE PASSION

of Jesus. Looked at thus the incident as it appears in Mark obviously fits in with the early Church situation. A Christian evangelist begins to preach the forgiveness of sins; men ask him how he can be sure that God forgives sins now, so as proof of the power of God working through himself he heals the sick; if God can deal with the sickness of men, he can deal also with their sin. Since sin and sickness are related, in that both are forms of evil, this argument could be effective; sin would be the greater evil to the Christian but not necessarily to the bystander watching the miracle performed, for whom then it would not be an argument *a minori ad majus*. Thus we cannot conclude that when Jesus heals sickness he defeats demoniacal powers. Rather he may be dealing with sin.

Jesus also encounters evil in the hearts and minds of men as well as in their bodies. Their evil ways are attributed to hardness of heart (vi. 52, the disciples in relation to the miracle of the loaves and fishes, cf. viii. 17; x. 5, the Pharisees in relation to the relaxation of the law of marriage in regard to divorce by Moses, cf. iii. 5).[1] When Peter counsels Jesus to take some other way than thst of the Cross his thoughts are described as 'human' (viii. 33). When the disciples are unable to stay awake and pray in the Garden of Gethsemane their failure is attributed to a weakness of the flesh, that is, as we have seen, a weakness not of the purely physical, but of the whole man (xiv. 38).[2] Men are described by Jesus as unbelieving and faithless (vi. 6; ix. 19). Sin originates from within man and not from outside; it is from within a man that evil thoughts go out (vii. 21–3). The disciples are commanded to beware of the leaven of the Pharisees and Herodians (viii. 15) and, while the precise reference of leaven at this point is not clear, it must imply thinking and acting as the Pharisees and Herodians do. One man can make another stumble and do evil (ix. 42). Likewise a man's own hand or eye or foot may lead him to sin (ix. 43–7). And while Mark quite clearly indicates by his use of Old Testament

[1] Mark uses two words, the root πωροῦν and σκληροκαρδία (x. 5). The former may mean 'blindness' rather than 'hardness'; cf. J. A. Robinson, *Ephesians*, pp. 264 ff. In either case blame attaches to the person; even if it is held that God has blinded or hardened the heart (cf. John xii. 40) the moral responsibility remains; cf. K. L. and M. A. Schmidt, *T.W.N.T.* v. 1024 ff.
[2] Cf. above, p. 30.

quotations that the supreme evil of the Cross was ordained of God, he also clearly traces it to the sin of men. This evil intent of the heart is seen as early in his narrative as iii. 1–6; it appears again in the hostile way in which the Jewish leaders seek to entrap Jesus with their questions so that he will stumble and put himself in their power to destroy him (xii. 13 ff.); the sin of the traitor in xiv. 17–21 may be also linked to the fulfilment of the divine purpose, but not in such a way that the human sin is excused. And throughout the Passion itself the evil of men's hearts is depicted in the way in which they ill-treat and abuse and mock Jesus. Thus he encountered the evil in the hearts of men.

At no point is this evil traced to the work of Satan or to demonic forces. The only apparent exception is viii. 33,[1] and this as we have already seen does not imply that Peter is the tool of Satan or that Satan is active at this point. In contrast Luke quite clearly makes the act of Judas in betraying Jesus an action inspired by Satan (xxii. 3), but this represents his general tendency to intensify the work of spiritual forces both good and evil; thus the denial by Peter is also traced to Satan (xxii. 31–4); this would again warn us against reading these forces back into the historical life of Jesus; they may rather represent interpretative elements of the early Church. In Mark the evil in men whereby they are led to oppose Jesus is consistently led back to the evil intent of their own hearts; it is from within man that evil comes and goes out from him both to render himself unclean and to injure others. The fact that men's culpable spiritual blindness (iv. 10–12) is traced to God shows how far Mark is removed from a Satanic explanation of evil – and from our ideas.

It might however be argued that Mark is simply repeating the tradition as he received it and that the common way of expressing the origin of evil was to trace it to men; Mark, while

---

[1] iv. 15 in the interpretation to the Parable of the Sower might also be regarded as an exception; but whatever the original meaning of the parable Mark clearly sees the attack of Satan in the interpretation as an attack on the followers of Jesus and not on Jesus himself. It is moreover interesting that only one of the three classes of failure is said to be attributed to Satan; the **failure of the other two classes is attributed to tribulation and covetous-**ness; it is unjustified to carry over the attribution to Satan in the first instance to the other two. This is just another example of the fact that Mark sees temptation coming from different sources of which Satan is one, but not the only one.

holding to another theory, the Satanic origin of temptation, does not vary the tradition. This is rendered most unlikely by two factors. (*a*) The attribution of evil to Satan is precisely the kind of matter which an editor could vary in the tradition without seriously affecting the main message of a pericope. That he would be likely to do so is evidenced by the fact that Luke did exactly this with the tradition in making Satan the author of Judas' betrayal and Peter's denials. Mark does not so vary the tradition. (*b*) Some of the passages to which we have drawn attention as evidence that for Mark evil begins in the heart of man are probably his own editorial insertions (iii. 6;[1] vi. 6; vi. 52, cf. viii. 17) and not derived from the tradition. Thus when Mark had an absolutely free hand he did not introduce the Devil as the origin of temptation.

Confirmation of this may be seen in the very different attitude which Jesus takes up to sin in men and to sickness or demonic possession. Sickness and demons are regarded as invading man from outside and must be driven out of him. Sin is too much a part of man to be dealt with in that way. We may begin by noting that when Jesus deals with a demoniac he addresses the demon and not the man who is possessed by it. Until the demon has been expelled the victim is passive in the interview. The sick many times come to Jesus requesting healing for themselves (i. 40; x. 47); Jesus himself speaks to the sick directly (ii. 5, 11; iii. 3; x. 51); he seeks their co-operation in their healing through their faith (v. 34; x. 52; cf. vi. 5, 6); sometimes it is the co-operation of others that leads to their healing (vii. 26–9; ix. 23, 24). This in itself then brings out a difference in the way in which Jesus deals with the sick from that in which he deals with the demoniac, suggesting that for Mark sickness cannot always be seen under the rubric of possession. In sickness the sick person is still a responsible agent able to take part in the healing. Jesus' approach to the sick is different from his approach to the demoniac.

When now we turn to consider how Jesus deals with the evil in the heart of men we see that this distinction is carried further; he is now concerned always to talk with the person himself and

[1] Dibelius, pp. 44 ff.; Bultmann, p. 63, hold that it is Markan. Taylor; Knox, i, 9, ii f.; Lohmeyer; Schmidt, p. 100 consider it part of the traditional material.

induce his co-operation. We may examine his early encounters with opponents as Mark groups them together in ii. 1–iii. 6. Their opposition to Jesus is not necessarily outwardly spoken, but in each case Jesus deals with it by way of argument. On one occasion (ii. 25 f.) the argument is based on Scripture, but on each of the other occasions it reaches down to the true understanding of the relationship of man to God; in iii. 1–6 Jesus penetrates to the true meaning of the Sabbath; in ii. 15–17 he shows the full outreach of the love of God, which cannot be confined to the righteous; in ii. 1–12 he appeals to his opponents to realise the might of God in dealing with sickness and sin. In each case he is concerned, not to show them up in the eyes of bystanders, but to lead them to a fuller comprehension of the ways of God with men. He puts forward a genuine argument in which he attempts to win them over to his own position. The same is true where he encounters his opponents over clean and unclean foods (vii. 1 ff.) and over divorce (x. 2 ff.). It may seem in the series of debates beginning in xii. 13–40, concerning the payment of tribute to Caesar, the resurrection from the dead,[1] the nature of the greatest commandment, and David's Son, that Jesus is a little more abrupt with some of his opponents, seeking rather to show that they are in the wrong than to convince them of their errors. We would note first that these four incidents appear to form a stylised pattern based in part on the questions asked in the Passover Haggadah;[2] thus the main pattern with its rejection of the questioners is motivated by this underlying structure rather than by any sense that opponents are silenced like demons. Secondly, we must remember that the actual form of such a pericope as xii. 13–17, where Jesus seems to silence the Pharisees with a clever retort, lies in the nature of what is happening; stories told of great men always show them silencing their opponents with astute answers. Thirdly, in the passage Mark xii. 13–40 Jesus' somewhat

[1] Matt. xxii. 34 might provide an argument for a demonic understanding of these debates since here it is said that Jesus 'muzzled' (ἐφίμωσεν) the Sadducees; this verb is used of Jesus' exorcism of demons in Mark i. 25 (cf. iv. 39). If so this would be a Matthean heightening of the demonic; unfortunately for such a view Matthew does not use φιμοῦν in describing Jesus' exorcisms.
[2] Cf. D. Daube, *The New Testament and Rabbinic Judaism*, pp. 158 ff.

sharper tone may be accounted for by the fact that his opponents, with the exception of the scribe of *v.* 28, are out to trip
him in order to have an accusation against him, rather than
that they are genuinely seeking information. The same is true
of viii. 11–13. Thus nothing more than the normal sin of men
can be seen in xii. 13–40; Jesus does not treat his opponents as
he treats demons.

Now if it can be argued that the Markan Jesus seeks to enlighten his opponents with truth by his answers it must also be
said at the same time that he intends to puzzle them. This is
Mark's well-known secrecy motif. Jesus muzzles the demons
who would say who he is (i. 25; i. 34, etc.); he forbids the
healed to go round talking about him (i. 44; v. 43, etc.); he
hides himself from men (i. 35; iii. 7; vii. 24). In relation to his
teaching this comes out most acutely in the statement about
parables (iv. 11, 12): the mystery of the Kingdom is deliberately
hidden from those who are 'outside'. It is impossible to deduce
from this that those 'outside' are in any way demonically
possessed. Before they encounter him, the devils already know
the nature of his power and being; the sick in their encounter
become at least partly aware of these; those 'outside' are on the
other hand kept in ignorance; their knowledge is not silenced;
it simply does not exist, and it would appear the effort is made
to keep it from existing. We are not concerned with the question
of the genuineness of this saying about 'parables', nor with its
place in the teaching of the historical Jesus, but only with the
understanding which its present form gives us of Mark's
theology. It is probable that παραβολαῖς is not to be restricted
here to what we normally call 'parables', that is, illustrative
stories or similitudes.

Hence in the evangelist's vocabulary παραβολή was a comprehensive
term. It labelled forms of speech and actions in so far as both kinds
of activity were regarded as media through which the μυστήριον
of the kingdom of God was finding expression, though in such a
manner as to be hidden from οἱ ἔξω.[1]

Mark quotes here from Isa. vi. 9, 10 using a text similar to that
of the Targum. He applies the text to the unbelieving Jews of

[1] G. H. Boobyer, 'The Redaction of Mark iv. 1–34', *N.T.S.* VIII (1961),
59–70, at p. 64.

Jesus' time. These are kept in the dark as to the purpose of Jesus' coming so that they do not understand; matters are however explained privately to the disciples (iv. 33, 34). It is Jesus himself who acts and speaks in such a way that the outsider does not comprehend, and for the Evangelist this means that ultimately God is responsible for the way in which revelation is veiled. Thus it is not to any action of Satan that we should attribute the blindness of the Jews but to God himself.

There is consequently a twofold attitude of Jesus towards his opponents. On the one hand he attempts to enlighten them in argument and on the other he seeks to veil revelation from their sight. Looking at this from another angle we may say that men are both morally responsible and that at the same time they play a role in history determined by God. This appears most vividly in the case of Judas (xiv. 21): the Son of Man must be crucified because it is written, and therefore ordained of God, and yet Judas is fully responsible. This twofold character is probably also present at the back of the conception of 'hardness of heart' when viewed against its Old Testament origin.[1] The double attitude of Jesus in Mark may perhaps also be explained in another way. Where Jesus explains to men the error of their positions he is usually dealing with misunderstandings of already existing revelation of the Old Testament, for example the Sabbath law, or the teaching on purity and uncleanness, but where he veils his true meaning it is in relation to his own purpose and the mystery of the kingdom.

When we examine the discussions Jesus has with his disciples, we find again that he attempts to explain difficulties to them; for example, he endeavours to dissipate their hardness of heart (viii. 14 – 21). To a large extent the twofold veiling and explanation of revelation disappears and the emphasis lies on the explanation. Thus the parables are explained to the disciples (iv. 34). When they do not understand the coming Passion he explains to them three times what is about to happen to himself (viii. 31; ix. 31; x. 33 f.). He even encourages them to say out plainly among themselves who he is, for he asks them that very question (viii. 29). Peter is only rebuked when he refuses to accept the revelation that is given to him (viii. 33), unlike the demons who are rebuked because they announce the revelation

[1] Cf. p. 36, n. 1 and K. L. and M. A. Schmidt, *T.W.N.T.* v, 1024 ff.

that should be kept quiet from men. Thus Jesus is ready to treat his disciples as full human beings who can come to a position in which they can know the truth of God; for their culpable ignorance he holds them responsible and does not blame any hidden demonic influence.

The final encounter of Jesus with evil takes place naturally in the Passion.[1] The whole Gospel builds up to this event. Here again we note the twofold character we observed earlier. On the one hand the Passion proceeds from the evil of men's hearts and on the other its happening is predetermined. The former of these elements begins early in the Gospel with the first sequence of encounters between Jesus and his opponents (ii. 1–iii. 6), which ends with their resolve that he must be put to death (iii. 6). This opposition mounts against him until it bursts in the plot of Judas with the priests and scribes to betray him to death (xiv. 1, 2, 10, 11). From now on at every turn evil appears; the disciples flee (xiv. 50); Peter denies him (xiv. 66–72); false witnesses are brought out against him (xiv. 56–9); he is mocked, spat on, humiliated (xiv. 65; xv. 16–20, 29–32); Pilate clearly designates the envy of the priests which has moved them to kill him (xv. 10). This evil is intensified by the clear indications of his innocence: true witnesses against him cannot be found (xiv. 55); Pilate asks what evil he has done (xv. 14); he is crucified between two obvious wrongdoers (xv. 27); the centurion who watches him die proclaims his innocence in announcing his true nature (xv. 39). What is the reaction of Jesus to this evil in the heart of man? Silence! (xiv. 60 f.; xv. 5). He who had rebuked the demons and told them to keep silence about his true nature now bears silently the evil of men; he who had carefully explained to men their failure to understand the purposes of God now offers no more explanations. The silence is only broken three times. Twice he clearly states who he is (xiv. 62; xv. 2); if previously he has explained men's errors in their interpretation of God's law and kept secret the nature of his person, the process is now reversed: for now he proclaims his own nature and refuses to protest against the injustice of his trial. The third time in which he breaks silence is the cry of dereliction; this however is not addressed to his opponents. Thus the whole attitude of Jesus is one of acceptance

<hr/>

[1] A fuller treatment of the Passion story is given later, pp. 89 ff.

towards the evil that crowds in on him; he does not fight against it but accepts it. This is congruent with that aspect of the Passion in which it is seen to proceed not merely from the evil in the heart of man but also from the inevitableness of the Cross. It has been prophesied by Jesus himself; all happens according to the Scriptures (xiv. 49) now that the hour is come (xiv. 41). Mark makes few direct quotations from the Old Testament, but his whole Passion narrative is full of allusions to it; this very allusiveness shows how deeply determination according to the Scriptures has entered into his view of the Passion. Thus there is no suggestion that behind all this in Mark there is an ever-active Satan leading men on to destroy the Christ so that he may be brought into his (Satan's) power. Men are evil in themselves, but they act in accordance with prophecy.

All this is external evil, coming from outside to assail Jesus, but we have already seen that in the Passion Jesus has to meet evil which begins within himself: xiv. 34–6. The words here are extreme; Jesus is horrified by the prospect of immediate death. His soul is cast down;[1] his will rebels against God's will. It is gratuitous to see at this point a return of the Devil to claim his prey. Jesus is terrified by death, the cup which he must drink, and not by the Devil. But through prayer the incipient weakness within himself is met and he goes to encounter that which he fears. The most terrible evil in the Gospel is not the demonic or sickness but the evil in the heart of man; it comes to its climax in the Passion and lays its hand even on the heart of the Christ himself. It is not diabolical but human.

To summarise, we may say: Evil meets Jesus from different sources in Mark; its origin may lie in demonic forces, in which case it is not moral evil; where Jesus is assailed by sin, this is seen to originate in the human heart; occasionally this is traced back to God's hardening of the heart; Jesus fights sin in men by seeking to lead them to truth and men are held morally responsible for their actions. The nature of the attack by Satan on Jesus is not made clear in the Temptation story; it may well have been temptation to sin. Consequently we may say that for Mark evil may originate with Satan or in the human heart, though not necessarily the heart of the person who is subject to

[1] Cf. Ps. xlii (xli). 6, 12; xliii (xlii). 5; Jonah ii. 8; iv. 9; Ps. xxii (xxi). 15; Ps. cxvi (cxiv). 3.

43

the temptation. The interpretation of the Parable of the Sower is a perfect illustration of the variety of sources from which temptation may come: Satan (iv. 15); persecution, that is, evil originating with other men (iv. 17); covetousness, that is, evil originating within the heart of the person who is tempted (iv. 19).

We must now go on to ask how this fits into the general biblical pattern. Where in the biblical and post-biblical material does sin get its grip on man? Is man continually tempted by a devil who is outside him and waits to lure him astray, or does temptation begin either with himself in his own heart or with others who lead him astray? Since we are primarily concerned with temptation it is unnecessary to widen our inquiry to seek the origin of sickness and physical evil of various kinds.

THE OLD TESTAMENT

Since our question is not, 'How did sin enter into the world?', but rather, 'Where does temptation to a particular sin begin?', we do not need to discuss in detail Gen. iii and its account of the Fall of man;[1] we may note that this has little influence on the Old Testament teaching about sin and temptation and that within the Old Testament period the serpent is not identified with Satan. But the story does show sin as coming to man from outside him; the serpent tempts Eve. We must recognise that within the biblical record this is a historical event, and not, as it is so often interpreted, a typical event showing how temptation and sin enter the life of every man. It cannot thus be taken as representing the beginning of temptation in each man; it is an individual event. But as such it shows that for the Old Testament the onslaught of temptation can be seen as coming from outside; but equally it comes from outside to Adam, who is tempted not by Satan but by Eve. Likewise Jezebel entices Ahab into sin (I Kings xxi. 5 ff.) and Potiphar's wife attempted to seduce Joseph (Gen. xxxix. 6 ff.). Thus temptation comes from

[1] Cf. C. R. Smith, *The Bible Doctrine of Sin*, pp. 37 ff.; W. Eichrodt, *Theologie des Alten Testaments*[4], II/III, pp. 278 ff.; N. P. Williams, *The Ideas of the Fall and of Original Sin*, pp. 12 ff., 39 ff.; F. R. Tennant, *The Fall and Original Sin, passim.*

fellow-humans. But it may also start within a man himself. Jeremiah's statement, 'The heart is deceitful above all things, and desperately corrupt; who can understand it?' (xvii. 9), may go further than much Old Testament teaching, but it is correct in seeing the origin of actual sin in the inner life of man. Thus Esau says in his heart that he will kill his brother Jacob (Gen. xxvii. 41) and God sees that the thoughts of man's heart are evil (Gen. vi. 5). This inwardness of the source of evil comes out more and more as we proceed through the Old Testament. We find it in the Deuteronomist (xv. 7, a hardened heart; viii. 14, an arrogant heart leading to rebellion against God), but more especially in Jeremiah and Ezekiel. For both the heart is the source of sin (Jer. iii. 17; xvi. 12, etc.; Ezek. vi. 9; xiii. 2, etc.) and the new man for the new age will have a new heart (Jer. iv. 14; xxiv. 7; xxxi. 33; Ezek. xi. 19; xviii. 31; xxxvi. 26 – a heart of flesh instead of a heart of stone). The priestly writer testifies to the same (II Chron. xxv. 19; xxvi. 16; xxxii. 25; xxxvi. 13); and the idea is also found in the Psalms (li. 12, 19; xxxvi. 2 – 5; liii. 2) and Job (xiv. 4; xv. 14 – 16; cf. Prov. xii. 20).

There is also another element in the Old Testament which traces sin in men to evil spirits. We have seen that the Fall is not to be taken as in any way showing the general manner in which sin takes place as response to a temptation from the Devil, but there are perhaps other instances of this. There is the evil spirit from the Lord which comes on Saul and leads him to attempt to kill David (I Sam. xvi. 14; xviii. 10–12; xix. 8–10); we may note that this spirit comes from God and that it is regarded as 'possessing' Saul rather than as tempting him (cf. Judges ix. 23). The spirit is sent by God to punish (cf. also Hos. iv. 12; v. 4; Isa. xxix. 10; xix. 14; Num. v. 14).[1] The same idea underlies I Kings xxii. 20 ff. where God wishes to lure Ahab to his destruction and one of the spirits of his council goes to lie to Ahab; this is not temptation. Nor strictly speaking is Job's encounter with Satan; Satan is sent by God to try Job; he never explicitly attempts to make Job sin; it is Job's wife who does this (ii. 9). In Zech. iii. 1, 2 Satan appears in his earlier role of 'accuser'. Perhaps the most interesting case is that of I Chron. xxi. 1 where Satan, through opposition to Israel,

[1] Thus Eichrodt, *op. cit.* p. 30. On 'temptation' in the Old Testament see C. R. Smith, *The Bible Doctrine of Grace*, ch. v.

entices David to number the people; in the earlier account (II Sam. xxiv. 1 ff.) it is God who incites David because he is angry with Israel; probably the later account must be read in the light of the earlier and Satan be regarded as the tool of God as in Job and not as acting independently. Thus we cannot see in the Old Testament any clear place where Satan is depicted as an independent tempter of men to evil, though the support for such a view could be drawn from a passage like I Chron. xxi. 1 once the role of Satan as tempter had been clearly defined. Rather God through his spirit(s) may be viewed as the author of temptation. The origin of sin thus largely lies within man himself in the Old Testament; where he is tempted from without it is not generally the work of Satan but of other humans, or even of God.

THE INTER-TESTAMENTAL LITERATURE

Here we find exactly the same view. Men follow the evil that rises within themselves (I Baruch i. 22; Tobit iv. 13; I Esdras i. 46; Sir. xii. 16; vi. 2; v. 2; Wisd. iv. 12; I Macc. xi. 8; II Macc. xiv. 3). In Sir. xv. 14 it is said that God created man at the first and 'left him in the power of his own inclination', and the context shows that this refers to all men and not to Adam alone.

In Sirach and Wisdom the evidence, taken together, shows that the two Sages believed that in a man's mind there are a number of 'desires' – some a-moral, some moral, some immoral – which all somehow appeal to him to choose them, but *until* he chooses, he is neither moral nor immoral. *When* he commits himself to a good desire (and it becomes his motive), he is good; when he commits himself to a bad desire, he is bad. The *will* is the organ of sin, and in so far as a man *chooses* bad motives he is sinful ... Evil desires are a man's own.[1]

But if men follow the evil within themselves they also may be led to evil by the influence of others (Sir. xi. 29–34; vi. 5–13). Apart from IV Ezra (= II Esdras) the origin of sin in the world is not traced to Satan; in Wisd. ii. 24 death is so traced and in Sir. xxv. 24 Eve is described as the beginning of sin, but there

---

[1] C. R. Smith, *The Bible Doctrine of Sin*, p. 85.

is no real doctrine of original sin. IV Ezra (iii. 21 f.; iv. 30; vii. 116–18) comes much nearer such a doctrine; through the sin of Adam man is given a powerful tendency towards sin, but each man remains free to sin or not to sin; he is accountable for his sin and the tendency within himself to sin is his own. Thus so far we have seen no evidence for the idea that temptation comes from Satan to man, apart from the once-for-all incident of Adam, and even in that case the role of Satan is by no means stressed (cf. especially the passages in IV Ezra). It is only made clear in Wisd. ii. 24; here the serpent may be, though not necessarily is, identified with the Devil;[1] the latter is opposed to God, and is probably no longer his agent. The very omission of reference to the Devil in the day-to-day tempting of men to sin is the more conspicuous.[2] Satan is not then in the Apocrypha the ordinary source of temptation.

Among the rabbis sin is connected above all with the evil impulse in man (יצר הרע).[3] This is probably the same as the *cor malignum* of IV Ezra and the διαβούλιον of Sir. xv. 14. Man has been created with the *yetzer ha-ra'*; it is there from birth having been placed in man by God.

The opportunity or the invitation to sin may come from without, but it is the response of the evil impulse in man to it that converts it into a temptation. It pictures in imagination the pleasures of sin, conceives the plan, seduces the will, incites to the act. It is thus primarily as the subjective origin of temptation, or more correctly as the tempter within, that the *yeṣer ha-ra'* is represented in Jewish literature.[4]

The evil impulse is not connected with the body or flesh in any dualistic fashion but following the general trends of Old Testa-

[1] Cf. Fichtner; Holmes (in Charles, *Apocrypha and Pseudepigrapha*), etc., *ad loc*. The reference may, however, be to the incident of Gen. iv. (cf. Geyer; Gregg, etc., *ad loc*.): Cain's murder of Abel. If that view is taken we have here a case of temptation by the Devil.

[2] Sir. xxi. 27 does not necessitate a reference to Satan; cf. R. S. V. rendering. Tob. iii. 8, 17 refers to an evil demon who has slain men; there is no reference to temptation.

[3] Cf. Moore, I, 474 ff.; Strack-Billerbeck, IV, 466 ff.; W. D. Davies, *Paul and Rabbinic Judaism*, pp. 20 ff.; S. Schechter, *Some Aspects of Rabbinic Theology* (London, 1909), pp. 219–92; Williams, *The Ideas of the Fall and of Original Sin*, pp. 60 ff.; Tennant, *The Fall and Original Sin*, pp. 145 ff.

[4] Moore, I, 481 f.

ment and Jewish anthropology with the heart. We may recall how our examination of the Old Testament has shown how often evil begins within a man in his own heart; the Rabbinic conception of the evil impulse ties in with this. To balance the evil impulse man is given a good impulse (יצר טוב). The evil impulse may be defeated through meditation on the Torah and by the stirring up of the good impulse. Normally the evil impulse is impersonal, but it is frequently personified.[1] It may then be identified with Satan or with the angel of death. However, the Rabbinic references to Satan as the tempter of man are not themselves frequent; for the rabbis Satan is rather man's accuser before God than his tempter, though his activity as tempter is witnessed as early as R. Akiba (†135).[2] The emphasis which the rabbis lay on Satan is very slight compared to that which they lay on the evil impulse; this latter is mentioned again and again in their writings without any reference to Satan. The two ideas must have co-existed; temptation may come from without through Satan who appears, perhaps as a prostitute as in the cases of R. Akiba and R. Meir,[3] but temptation also comes, and more frequently, from within man, from the evil impulse created in him by God, there being no suggestion that this latter is excited by Satan.

In the writings of the Qumran community the Devil occupies a more prominent position than in the earlier Jewish literature; in this the Dead Sea Scrolls are closely linked to the Apocalyptic books, many fragments of which, of course, have been found in the caves. The Devil is normally called Belial; the names Satan and Mastema occur respectively three and four times;[4] the favourite Rabbinic designation, Sammael, does not occur at all. Even where Satan and Mastema are used it is not always clear if these denote the Devil. This is true also of Belial; on each occasion of its use we have to look carefully to see if it is a proper name or a noun.

The noun בליעל, which in the M.T. can mean 'wickedness, worthlessness' (Deut. xv. 9; Nah. i. 11) but also 'worthless,

---

[1] Moore, I, 492 f.
[2] Cf. Strack-Billerbeck, I, 139 ff.; III, 109 f., 372 f.; Foerster, *T.W.N.T.* II, 74 ff.
[3] Cf. Qid 81 *a*, quoted in Strack-Billerbeck, III, 109 f.
[4] Cf. K. G. Kuhn, *Konkordanz zu den Qumrantexten.*

wicked men' in the phrases 'sons of Belial, men of Belial' (Judges xix. 22; xx. 13; I Sam. i. 16; xxx. 22; I Kings xxi. 13; Prov. vi. 12; xvi. 27), now becomes extended to represent a power outside man and attacking him. But it can still occur as an ordinary noun as in the M.T. (cf. I QH iv. 10; ii. 22; vii. 3). The difficulties of interpretation may be seen in the fact that Kuhn[1] lists all the occurrences in I QH as nouns, whereas Mansoor[2] takes many of them as proper names, denoting the Devil. In I QM Belial, who has been created by God (xiii. 11), appears clearly as the leader of the spiritual hosts of wickedness with whom the community is engaged in an apocalyptic war. He is here the enemy of the community rather than of the individual, and is in no way associated with tempting men to do evil, except at xiii. 11, 12 where he is said to seek to destroy men, making them guilty;[3] this latter is also the passage in which he is said to have been created by God, so that there is no absolute dualism (cf. I QS iii. 18 ff.); it is also possible that there is here a reference to his fall, but the text is corrupt.[4] When we turn to the other writings we find that his activities cover a wider range, in large part the same as that of the two senses of the Greek word πειράζειν, namely, 'testing, tempting'. This is the age of Belial (I QS i. 17, 18; ii. 19; cf. I QM xiv. 9) and it is a period of stress and trial for the members of the community (I QS i. 17, 18). Those outside the community are the men of Belial's lot (I QS ii. 4, 5), who oppose the sons of light just as Belial raised up Jamnes and his brother to oppose Moses and Aaron (C.D. v. 18, 19). Belial has been let loose (presumably by God) and uses his three nets of whoredom, wealth and uncleanness to snare Israel (C.D. iv. 13–19), but since God lets Belial loose for this purpose this must be a testing rather than a tempting. Nor is the reference to the sins of Israel during the ascendancy of Belial a necessary allusion to him as tempter (I QS i. 23, 24); the Emperor Domitian would not be described as tempting Christians because during the persecution he instituted some of them apostasised. However, at this stage we

[1] *Ibid.*

[2] *The Thanksgiving Hymns*; cf. especially p. 108, n. 1.

[3] Three words are used שחת (Pi'el; this, however, may denote his own destruction), רשע (Hiphil), אשם (Hiphil).

[4] Cf. J. van der Ploeg, *Le Rouleau de la Guerre, ad loc.*

are not far from the conception of temptation and it is at times difficult to draw a line between testing and temptation. The devices of Belial with which the writer of the hymns is assailed by men of deceit (1 QH ii. 16, cf. iv. 12–14) bring us closer to temptation, though Belial may not here be a proper name. Again the writer is slandered by those on whom Belial has worked (1 QH v. 26). Similarly in two passages from the fourth cave (4 QFl i. 8, 9; 4 QT 23) men of Belial ensnare others and make them stumble. We should notice that in all these references Belial does not attack the members of the community directly but through men who are already in his power; in that sense he is only a tempter at second hand. 1 QH vi. 21 may seem to provide a case of certain temptation, but the text reads quite straightforwardly if we take Belial as a noun; it then says that a wicked counsel is in the heart of men; the same is true of 1 QS x. 21. This shows the difficulty of being precise in an assertion that Belial tempts – or does not tempt; in these two passages, where we come nearest to the conception of Belial as the one who attacks in order to ensnare the soul, we cannot be certain that it is Belial as a personal being who is meant, and not just wickedness. Belial appears also as punishing men (C.D. viii. 2) and as destroying (1 QH iii. 28, 29), and we may assume he acts therein as the agent of God. The case of a man who falls into the power of the spirits of Belial is regarded as possession and contrasted with sin (C.D. xii. 2, 3).

Mastema occurs four times; certainly at 1 QM xiii. 4, 11 it is a noun and not a proper name, unless we are to regard Belial as the angel of Mastema, which is most unlikely. At 1 QS iii. 23 it may be either noun or proper name; it appears in the passage about the two spirits, which we shall shortly see does show temptation as coming from a spirit.[1] At C.D. xvi. 5 Mastema may be a proper name; the angel of Mastema is said to leave a man when he takes seriously the Law of Moses; this appears to imply temptation, and we may note the similarity to the Q narrative of the Temptations of Jesus, in that the words of the Law defeat Satan. The name Satan occurs only in fragmentary portions of the Dead Sea Scrolls (1 QHf iv. 6; xlv. 3; 1 QSb i. 8) and it is not possible to draw any firm deductions from its use.

The passage on the two spirits (1 QS iii. 17 ff.) is very relevant

[1] Cf. P. Wernberg-Møller, *The Manual of Discipline, ad loc.*

to our purpose, though it stands in some isolation from the rest of the Dead Sea Scrolls since the doctrine of the two spirits is not found elsewhere in the Scrolls; it may not then be normative. The Spirit of deceit, made by God, and apparently equated with the angel of darkness, rules the sons of deceit and attempts to make the sons of righteousness err; the latter are generally under the protection of the spirit of truth, or the prince of lights. The reign of the angel of darkness is the cause of all the sins, offences, guilt and iniquitous deeds of the members of the community; the spirits associated with him seek to make the members stumble (1 QS iii. 22–4). At iv. 8–11 a long list is given of the sins caused by the spirit of deceit. We have then here a clear picture of an outside power attacking man in order to lead him to sin, that is, tempting him. There is a certain resemblance to the doctrine of the good and evil impulses in man as found in Rabbinism, in that, were it not for the mention of the angel of darkness, the spirits of truth and deceit could be seen as indwelling the hearts of members of the community like the good and evil impulses; but the angel of darkness implies an outside power. Thus in this passage definitely, and to some extent elsewhere, we find temptation viewed as coming to man from spiritual powers of darkness and not just as emerging from within man himself.

But we also find in the Qumran writings the predominant teaching of the Old Testament, namely, that evil starts within the heart of man. In the Thanksgiving Hymns the psalmist describes himself as 'the foundation of shamefulness, and the source of impurity; the crucible of iniquity, and the edifice of sin'[1] (i. 22, 23; cf. xii. 24, 25). Though this and similar statements are used by the writer of himself it may be assumed that they do not misrepresent the conception of the source of temptation among the community as a whole. So we find the hymn writer referring also to the (evil) devices of his imagination (v. 6), the lusts of the heart (v. 26). In the *Manual of Discipline* those who walk in the stubbornness of their hearts are continually rebuked (i. 6; ii. 14, 26; iii. 3; v. 4, 5; vii. 18, 19, 24; cf. C.D. ii. 18; viii. 19; xx. 9, 10). The eyes and the mind can lead astray (1 QS i. 6; v. 4, 5; xi. 9; C.D. ii. 16). So also a man is led into evil by his spirit, whose desires he chooses (C.D. iii. 7, 11, 12; 1 QS vii. 18, 19, 23; viii. 12). Men may be said to

[1] Mansoor's translation.

pervert themselves (1 QS i. 24). A man may also be said to have a perverted spirit (1 QH iii. 21; i. 22; xi. 12), and the human spirit is meant. The same phrase occurs at 1 QH xiii. 15 where it is said that a perverted spirit has dominion over man; Mansoor[1] takes this to be an external evil spirit, but it might as easily be the man's own perverse spirit which rules him and leads him to evil.

The two conceptions of temptation as coming from outside and as beginning within man himself can sometimes lie close beside one another, as in 1 QH iv. 12–15 (cf. v. 26), where men are said to plot the devices of Belial, but are then described as seeking God with a double heart, as having a root that breeds gall and wormwood in their thoughts and as going astray with stubborn hearts. This anomaly is removed if we take Belial here as a noun, 'worthlessness', rather than as a proper noun; but the co-existence of the two ideas is not impossible in so far as one may be seen to be the original conception of the Old Testament and the other as entering through Iranian influence.

It may also be that the conception of 'flesh'[2] in these writings suggests the origin of sin within man himself. In accordance with the general usage of *basar*, flesh is man in his humanity, often as opposed to God; but there are also references to 'flesh of sin, deceit, guilt' (1 QS xi. 9, 12; 1 QM iv. 3; xii. 12); flesh can be cleansed (1 QS iii. 9; iv. 21). In regard to 1 QS xi. 12 Kuhn says, 'Sin is brought about through "flesh" as that which qualifies human existence as such'.[3] In line with this is Mansoor's translation of 1 QH x. 23, 'carnal intent thou hast not assigned for me'; the impulse (yetzer) of the flesh is sin. Flesh should not of course be equated with the body as if only sexual sins were meant; the wide meaning of flesh as man in his totality is always present. Sin can thus arise within man himself; there is no suggestion that the Devil takes hold of man through his flesh.

As in the Old Testament temptation can of course come from outside a man from other men, as distinct from spiritual powers

[1] *Ad loc.*

[2] Cf. K. G. Kuhn, 'New Light on Temptation, Sin and Flesh in the New Testament', and W. D. Davies, 'Paul and the Dead Sea Scrolls: Flesh and Spirit', both in *The Scrolls and the New Testament*, pp. 94–113, 157–82 (ed. K. Stendahl); Meyer, *T.W.N.T.* VII, 109–13.

[3] Kuhn, *op. cit.* p. 103.

of wickedness. Thus one man may be a snare to another (1 QH ii. 8, 10, 11; 4 Qp Nah. ii. 8). False prophets lead men astray (1 QH iv. 16 f.; cf. C.D. i. 15; 1 Qp Hab. x. 9); the hymn writer encounters opponents who would lead him into evil (1 QH v. 10, 11, 23–36). So certain men are excluded from the community because they may tempt others (1 QS v. 14 ff.).

Turning now to the Apocalyptic writings we find that the spiritual powers of evil occupy an important place and that correspondingly the Devil has become more prominent. In the different writings he appears under various names, for example, Beliar, Mastema, Satan, Sammael; though in some writings he features rarely if at all.[1] He is often seen in the role of tempter in which we are interested; and he appears in this role in almost all the books in which he figures at all largely. Thus we find him enticing men in Jub. i. 20; x. 1; xi. 4, 5; Adam and Eve x. 4; I Enoch viii. 1 ff. (here it is the fallen angels who have the role); xix. 1; lxix. 4–6; T. Dan. i. 7; v. 6; T. Joseph vii. 4; T. Benj. vii. 1, 2; II Enoch xxxi. 6, 7.

Yet at the same time we find that men are tempted by their fellows; this appears particularly in these writings in the way in which women are regarded as enticing men to sexual sin: for example, Jub. xxxix. 5 ff.; T. Reub. v. 3. In Jub. xvii. 4 Sarah becomes jealous when she sees Abraham happy with Ishmael. There is one strange passage in which women are considered to tempt angels, I Enoch vi (cf. lxix. 4), the role of tempter being completely reversed. Concurrently with these trends tracing temptation to Satan and other human beings, we find that evil is also considered as beginning in men's minds. This may not be as prominent here as in certain other parts of the material we have examined; but it needs to be remembered that by the very nature of the case the Apocalyptic writings were not greatly taken up with actual descriptions of the way in which evil actions were conceived and performed but rather with supernatural forces as they appeared at the beginning and end of the world and with their effect on the course of history, individual and national. Yet we do find many statements that suggest that the authors had not abandoned the dominant trend of Old Testament thinking which saw evil as originating within man himself.

[1] In each of *Ass. Moses* and *Sib. Or.* one reference only and none in II Baruch.

In I Enoch xcviii. 4 it is said that sin has come from man himself and *v.* 12 of the same chapter speaks of men who love deeds of unrighteousness. In T. Reub. iii. 12 Reuben says that his mind led him to sin taking in the thought of a woman's nakedness. Many times men are spoken of as 'corrupting themselves' (Jub. v. 10, 19; xxxvi. 8). Men devise evil against others (Jub. xxxvi. 8; xxxvii. 12); a man may be evilly disposed in his heart towards another and so seek to slay him (Jub. xxxvii. 24; cf. *v.* 12; Mart. Isa. i. 12, 13). Men follow their own devices which are regarded as evil (T. Issach. vi. 2). The impulse of youth may blind a man's mind and lead him to sin (T. Judah xi. 1; xiii. 6; cf. xiv. 1 ff.). Sin and evil are attributed to the imagination and desire of men (Jub. vii. 24; v. 2). In the T. Asher i. 3 ff. we meet the two inclinations or impulses which figure so largely in Rabbinic thought on temptation. There are some strange phrases which suggest that Satan takes possession of a man after he has given his heart to evil; in Mart. Isa. ii. 4 Manasseh turns aside his heart to serve Beliar; here Beliar is conceived as a strange god rather than as devil. In T. Simeon v. 3 it is said that fornication brings a man nearer to Beliar, rather than that Beliar incites a man to fornication. In the vast majority of cases where evil is described in these writings (e.g. Jub. xxiii. 14 ff.; xxiv. 6; I Enoch xcv. 1 ff.; xcix. 1 ff.) it is neither attributed to Satan nor is it suggested that it began in man himself; but since the latter was the predominant view within Israel preceding the appearance of Satan on the scene, it must be assumed that where no mention is made of Satan then he is not to be implicitly supposed as active, but that the author held the view of the Old Testament which attributed temptation either to the man himself or to other men. In a number of passages the two ideas that evil begins within man and that it is incited in him by Satan are held in almost adjoining verses (Jub. vii. 24 and 27; T. Dan. i. 4, 7; T. Reub. iii. 1–11), thus showing that in this period no one point of view held sway.

Looking back now over the path which we have traversed from the Old Testament through late Judaism to the New Testament period we see that there are three ways in which a man may be incited to do evil: temptation may start within himself, it may start in the world around him and it may start supernaturally through an assault by the powers of evil (on rare occasions God is viewed as the author);[1] later Christianity crystallised out into the last of these three conceptions so that Satan is seen as the author of all temptation; we must not however read back developed ideas into earlier periods. Historically Satan as the author of temptation arrived late on the scene; it is not necessary to argue whence the idea came; it was presumably from Iranian sources. There is no systematic treatment of Satan in late Judaism which shows him as the author of all temptation; instead our survey of the sources, though brief, has been sufficient to show that the other two conceptions, which are found in the Old Testament, continued into the period of Judaism. Particular instances of sin are traced to Satan and the other supernatural powers of evil, but there is no general statement that in every case he is the tempter. Thus the three ideas exist in parallel, authors sometimes using one and sometimes another. At this stage the issue had not been clearly thought out. The argument that proceeds from the view that because Satan is later regarded as the source of all temptation therefore he must have been also so regarded in the Judaistic period shows a lack of historical sense; we must begin with the earlier period and work to the later and not work back from the later and impose its generalisations on the earlier. Nor can we argue from the conception that Satan tempts, which is perfectly true for this period, to the conclusion that all temptation is due to Satan. As yet in Judaism Satan is not integrated fully into theological thought and he occupies different places in different writings. Thus in the New Testament period we may expect to find varying conceptions of the origin of temptation lying alongside one another. We have already shown this to be so in the case of Mark and for the sake of completeness we proceed to show briefly that it is true also for the rest of the New Testament.

---

[1] 'We are very far from asserting that the beliefs in an interior innate corruption, and in an exterior personified power of evil, are logically irreconcilable or incapable of being simultaneously held by the same person; they were actually held together by the Jews of our Lord's day, with little attempt at harmonisation ...', Williams, *The Ideas of the Fall and of Original Sin*, p. 109.

THE NEW TESTAMENT

In the Pauline and related writings the picture presented is not essentially different from that which we have observed in the preceding. Satan fights against God and seeks to draw men away from God. As tempter he appears most clearly in I Cor. vii. 5 (cf. I Tim. v. 14 f.); Eph. iv. 27; vi. 11; II Cor. iv. 4; II Tim. ii. 26; I Thess. iii. 5.[1] In almost all these passages we find that Satan has his grip on men only because they have first sinned;[2] in II Cor. iv. 4 he blinds the minds of unbelievers, that is, those who refuse to believe (cf. Eph. ii. 2); in I Cor. vii. 5 Satan only has his opportunity because husband and wife have decided to abstain from sexual intercourse and are consequently living under strain; he is not thought of as suggesting that they should stay apart from one another; in Eph. iv. 27 the believer is first angry and thus gives Satan his opportunity to lead him further astray. The idea of deception by Satan is closely related to temptation and is found in II Cor. xi. 14. In Eph. vi. 16 it is by no means sure that the 'fiery darts' of the devil are to be restricted to temptations nor in I Tim. iii. 7 is it certain that there is any reference to the Devil at all. There is no statement whatever that the Devil is responsible for all temptation.

It is consequently not surprising when we find that Paul sees evil as incited in men by other men, including the peril that comes from the tolerance of immoral men in the community (Rom. xiv. 13 ff., 20 f.; I Cor. v. 9; viii. 11; xv. 33; Gal. iii. 1; v. 7–10; Eph. v. 6). The passion of lust may lead a man astray (I Thess. iv. 5; II Tim. ii. 22). Marriage brings anxiety and so the possibility of sin (I Cor. vii. 33 f.). Temptation also begins in men. The beginning of evil against which God's wrath is manifested is in Rom. i. 21 laid at man's own door. To please ourselves (Rom. xv. 1) may be sin, when it makes others stumble. Knowledge puffs up and leads men into evil (I Cor. viii. 1). Men are said to desire evil (I Cor. x. 6). Quite in the manner of the Old Testament the sins of the Gentiles are attributed to their hardness of heart (Eph. iv. 17 – 24), and the Colossian believers (i. 21) are said to have once had minds estranged

---

[1] But Satan is here the one who tests, rather than tempts; the context speaks of the persecutions that assail the Thessalonians.

[2] Cf. Ling, *The Significance of Satan*, pp. 38, 47.

from and hostile to God by which they were led into evil. They run the danger of being puffed up in their sensuous minds (ii. 18). Minds can be corrupt and so lead to sin (II Tim. iii. 8; cf. Tit. i. 15; iii. 11). When Paul begins to write more systematically the source of sin in man is often the 'flesh' (Gal. v. 16, 24; Rom. viii. 4, 5), and the 'flesh' appears as a power to some extent independent of man yet never wholly disassociated from him and certainly never equated with the Devil;[1] in like manner 'sin' becomes a power outside man which makes him go wrong (Rom. vii. 8, 17) and 'law' itself may become the source of evil (Rom. vii. 5, 11), though 'law' is good (Rom. vii. 12, 14). Indeed it is a remarkable fact that if Paul held that Satan was the cause of temptation he succeeded in writing all his major passages about evil (e.g. Rom. vii) without reference to him. It remains only to note that twice God would appear to incite men to evil, namely, when he hardened Pharaoh's heart (Rom. ix. 18; cf. xi. 8 ff.) and when he deluded men in relation to the Parousia (II Thess. ii. 11).

In the Lukan writings Satan appears at the outset as the tempter of our Lord and it is implied in iv. 13 that he returned to tempt Jesus later.[2] At Luke xxii. 3 Satan is said to have entered into Judas so that he went to the chief priests and initiated the process that led to the betrayal of Jesus, and in Acts. v. 3 Satan is said to have filled the heart of Ananias to tell a lie; both these appear rather more like cases of possession in which Satan enters a man than direct temptations in which he remains outside a man and leads him astray; but the idea of temptation certainly cannot be excluded. We encounter also the continuation of the Old Testament strain in which evil appears to begin inside a man himself. Many of the instances in Mark are repeated. In the non-Markan material we may notice the phrase in the story of the rich man who pulled down his barns and built bigger, 'I will say to my soul' (xii. 19) and the very similar phrases at xii. 45; xvi. 3; xviii. 4. The mouth speaks according as the heart is filled with evil or good (Luke

---

[1] If, however, the flesh is not taken as a personified power but as that through which the forces of evil attack man it becomes the channel rather than the source of temptation. But this takes us no further towards an identification of the forces of evil with demonic powers in temptation.

[2] Cf. p. 3, n. 2.

vi. 45). In the Book of Acts jealousy is a continual source of evil, for example, v. 17; xiii. 45; xvii. 5. At Acts xiii. 27 it is said that the Jews killed Christ because they could not understand the Scriptures. Acts vii. 39 repeats an Old Testament way of thinking in a passage retelling the Old Testament, but the same idea is independently present in Luke ix. 47. The Jews incite others to riot and so to sin against the spread of the Gospel (Acts xiii. 50; xiv. 19, etc.); thus the origin of sin lies in others, as we have also found it elsewhere. It is remarkable that although in Acts the Christians are continually seen as guided in all their activities by the Holy Spirit yet Satan does not occupy the corresponding position in respect of deception and temptation.

In the Johannine literature, including the Apocalypse, the spiritual powers of evil appear more consistently as in conflict with men. There is a close relationship between the Devil and the 'world' (I John v. 19; John xii. 31; xiv. 30; xvi. 11); the opponents of Jesus and of the Church are of the Devil (John viii. 44; I John iii. 8; ii. 13, 14). So the Devil is first said to put it into Judas' heart to betray Jesus and then is said to enter him (John xiii. 2, 27). Here Satan appears quite definitely as the tempter. It is doubtful if a reference to the temptations of Jesus should be seen in John xiv. 30 where our Lord says that the ruler of this world has no power over him; rather the general conflict of light and darkness is mirrored here.[1] In Rev. xii. 9; xx. 3 Satan appears as the deceiver of the world. In I John iv. 1 ff. the false prophets who lead men into error are themselves demonically inspired. Here temptation may be regarded as indirectly the work of the Devil. If thus the Devil appears as the tempter and deceiver of men evil is also seen to originate in their hearts. This appears clearly in John ii. 24, 25 where Jesus is said not to trust himself to men because he knew what was in man; this can hardly mean that Jesus knew that man was weak to resist temptation coming from Satan but that he knew men as evil within themselves and that from their own hearts they would plot his death. Nor is the relationship of men

---

[1] The accusation that Jesus has a devil (John vii. 20; cf. viii. 48; x. 20) is an accusation of mental disorder rather than a suggestion that the Devil tempted him to do wrong. Cf. Ling, *The Significance of Satan*, pp. 28 f.; Langton, *Essentials of Demonology*, p. 171.

to the Devil simply one in which he prompts them and so they do wrong; men themselves are ready before he comes to them to do what he wants; they are willing to do his desires (John vii. 44); they love darkness (John iii. 19). The Devil may deceive men, but they can also deceive themselves (I John i. 8). A man may shut up his compassion against a brother (I John iii. 17). Deception and temptation may also come from one man to another; II John 7 speaks of the deceivers who have gone out into the world; Pilate was made to sin through the pressure the Jewish authorities exerted on him (John xix. 12–15).

Matthew does not contain much material different from what we have already examined in Mark and Luke. There are a series of passages (v. 37, 39; vi. 13; xiii. 19, 38) in which πονηρός (-όν) is used and at times it is doubtful whether this is intended as neuter or masculine, and if the latter whether it describes either the Devil or an evil man. It is unnecessary to determine the precise meaning in most cases as the conception of temptation does not enter. The phrase in the Lord's Prayer, 'Lead us not into temptation, but deliver us from evil', may be taken as 'deliver us from the Evil One', but it is very doubtful if πειρασμός means 'temptation' and not rather 'affliction, tribulation, persecution'. In iv. 3 Satan is termed 'the tempter'; this is the nearest we possess to a general statement that temptations come from Satan; yet it does not imply that all temptation comes from him. The only absolutely general statement in the New Testament material is James i. 14 which implies the heart of man as the origin of all temptation. Most of the statements suggesting that the origin of temptation lies either within man himself or comes to him from other men which we have already encountered in Mark and Luke are repeated in Matthew; we need only draw attention to xii. 33–5 (cf. vii. 16–20; Luke vi. 43–5) where men are likened to trees and it is implied that because the tree is bad the fruit will turn out to be bad; the evil deeds of man are the result of the evil disposition within, rather than of the work of the Tempter. At xviii. 7 a woe is called down on the man who brings another into temptation and at xxiii. 16 the Pharisees are termed 'blind guides', since they lead others into sin.

The remainder of the New Testament does not contain much about the Devil. I Pet. v. 8 with its reference to the Devil on the prowl is concerned with persecution rather than temptation, though this may cause temptation. James (iii. 15) refers to the wrong kind of wisdom as devilish, but this again hardly seems to be temptation; probably however the call to resist the Devil at James iv. 7 is a call to resist him as tempter. But these epistles on the other hand contain clear reference to temptation as beginning in man. Noteworthy here is James i. 14, 'Each man is tempted when he is lured and enticed by his own desire'. This is almost a general statement implying that all temptation comes from man himself. James also sees the tongue as the origin of temptation (iii. 1–12) and the strife which exists among church members comes from their passions (iv. 1). The author of Hebrews speaks of the evil unbelieving heart which leads away from God (iii. 12) and goes on in Old Testament quotations and thoughts derived from them to instance the hardened heart which leads into sin (iii. 15; iv. 7; cf. iii. 10). The same author can speak of the deceitfulness of sin (iii. 13). As in James there are references in both the Petrine epistles to the passions as leading men astray (I Pet. ii. 11; i. 14; II Pet. iii. 3; cf. Jude 16, 18). Also in II Peter false teachers are viewed as enticing away the believer (ii. 1 ff.; ii. 14).

We thus find the same pattern appearing throughout the New Testament as we discovered in Judaism; temptation comes either from Satan, or from the man himself, or from other men. There is no statement which suggests that temptation originates with the Devil alone; he is never described as the sole author of temptation. Particularly in the Gospels of Luke and John we find that the activities of Satan centre on the Cross, but this is a development from Mark. We must also recognise that the evil of the Cross while it may be attributed in some way to Satan is much more commonly looked upon as a part of God's predetermined plan.

PART II

THE PASSION

So far we have looked somewhat negatively at the purpose of
the ministry of Jesus. We have argued that he defeated Satan
conclusively at the time of the temptation in the desert and that
thereafter his activities against the demons were in the nature
of mopping-up operations. We have further argued that evil in
Mark is not conceived as basically demonic and that such a
view is not out of step with current Judaism and the remainder
of the New Testament. But if the whole purpose of the ministry
is not the defeat of demonic forces and if these do not dominate
the conception of evil in the Gospel, why then does Mark think
Jesus lived and died? It is therefore necessary now to turn to a
positive assessment of the ministry of Jesus as Mark conceives it.

CHAPTER III

THE MARKAN SEAMS

THE most obvious place to look for Mark's hand is in the words, phrases, sentences which join together the various incidents of the Gospel. The incidents themselves may or may not go back to Jesus himself, but they came to Mark as part of the tradition and he put them together. We turn now to examine these 'seams'. But we do not confine our attention to them alone; we need also to take into account any relevant editing of the material itself – by way of additional phrases or sentences which Mark has added. These are naturally more difficult to detect since statements which may seem out of accord either with the material or a place in the life of Jesus may well have been added before Mark's time and been taken over by him.

The first editorial statement of Mark is obviously his introductory verse (i. 1). The key-word is εὐαγγέλιον. This is defined as the Gospel of Jesus Christ. Is the genitive ’Ιησοῦ Χριστοῦ to be taken as objective or subjective? Perhaps it may be allowed both senses, in that it is the Gospel which the exalted Christ proclaims through Mark to his church and also the Gospel which is about that same Christ.[1] That its content is the Christ appears through its paralleling with him in viii. 35; x. 29 ('for my sake and the Gospel's'). The two are again associated in xiii. 9, 10.[2] The Gospel is something which must be believed, and with this belief repentance is closely linked (i. 15; cf. vi. 12 where the content of preaching is repentance).[3] Repentance is not merely sorrow for sin but also a turning from it to goodness; but it is essentially related to sin as i. 4 shows. It is not then renunciation of the Devil but renunciation of sin. Marxsen[4] has shown that the Markan conception of 'gospel' is

[1] The most recent discussion is that of Marxsen, pp. 77–101. He holds that Mark introduced this word into the Synoptic material.

[2] Cf. Marxsen, pp. 79–83.

[3] E. Schweizer, 'Anmerkungen zur Theologie des Markus', *Neotestamentica et Patristica* (*Suppl. to N. T.* VI), pp. 36 f., shows that the content of 'preaching' (κηρύσσειν) for Mark is repentance.

[4] Pp. 91 f.

closely allied to the Pauline, though not directly dependent thereon. For Paul the Gospel is salvation from sin; it is defined in Rom. i. 16 as the power of God unto salvation and that salvation is set out in Rom. chs. v – viii as a deliverance from sin and its consequences.

Postponing the discussion of the titles 'Christ' and 'Son of God' until later we turn now to i. 14, 15 where Mark summarises the content of the message which Jesus preached. Obviously Mark composed this with an eye to the present condition of his readers and it need not be taken as a summary of the teaching of the historical Jesus. It is strongly coloured by the language of the early Church.[1] We have already looked at εὐαγγέλιον and seen that its content is Christ himself; it is thus related in its usage here to the preaching of the early Church. The same is true of κηρύσσειν.[2] To preach the Gospel is the activity of the Church in the post-Resurrection period. This is obviously so in xiii. 10 and xiv. 9. At i. 45; v. 20; vii. 36 preaching follows directly on exorcism and healing, as it must have done in the early Church; Christ was preached. John's preaching (i. 4, 7) is again for Mark a preaching of Christ; this is his function: to testify to Jesus. He does not occupy an independent position as a preacher of repentance as in Matthew and Luke. In iii. 14; vi. 12 the disciples are described as preaching within the lifetime of Jesus, but these references obviously look forward to and are coloured by the practice of the early Church; the apostles are examples for the activity of the early Church. In i. 38, 39 Jesus is himself described as preaching in the villages of Galilee; probably again Mark thinks of Jesus as preaching about himself. Thus we may conclude that at i. 14, 15 Mark envisaged the preaching of Christ as a preaching not merely by Christ but about Christ.

The phrase 'the Kingdom of God' almost certainly goes back to our Lord, but what content does Mark give to it? Does he regard it as a present reality or as belonging to the imminent future? The former is certainly true of Matthew and Luke who

[1] Lohmeyer, *ad loc.*; Lightfoot, *Gospel*, p. 20; J. Sundwall, *Die Zusammensetzung des Markusevangeliums* (Acta Academiae Aboensis, Humaniora, ix, 2, 1934), p. 8.
[2] See the very long note devoted to the word by Lightfoot, *History*, pp. 106 f.

speak of the exorcism of demons as a manifestation of the Kingdom (Matt. xii. 28 = Luke xi. 20; cf. Matt. iv. 23). That Mark however can regard the Kingdom as future appears in xv. 43 where Joseph of Arimathea is named as one looking for the coming of the Kingdom; here Mark may be indicating the attitude of the believer of his own time. The Kingdom is also viewed as future in Jesus' words that he would not drink of the fruit of the vine again until he did so in the Kingdom (xiv. 25). The strong statement of ix. 1 which says that some shall not die until they see the Kingdom of God come in power may imply that its coming will be soon, but it certainly implies that it is not yet. In three places in ch. iv the Kingdom of God is connected to parables. The first of these is the difficult passage iv. 11, 12. We are not concerned to find the original meaning of this logion and place it correctly either in the life of Jesus or in that of the early Church; there are good grounds to believe that its present position is a Markan creation.[1] We have, however, to interpret it within its place in this chapter. The disciples, and in the Markan context these must be understood to include the believers of his own day, are given (by God) the mystery of the Kingdom, but the parables in which it is unveiled to them serve to conceal its meaning from non-believers.[2] Something of the meaning of the Kingdom of God must therefore be given in the Parable of the Sower, and paticularly in its interpretation, about which Mark will not have had the doubts we may have, and also, since the plural 'parables' is used, in the other parables of this chapter and especially those specifically referring to the Kingdom. Two parables are set out as Kingdom of God parables, namely, the seed growing secretly (iv. 26–9) and the mustard seed (iv. 30–2). In neither case is the Kingdom of God to be taken as like a man who scatters seed nor as the mustard seed; it is the whole action

[1] Cf. Jeremias, *The Parables of Jesus*, pp. 11 f.; Boobyer, 'The Redaction of Mark iv. 1–34', takes iv. 10–13 as a unit.

[2] The line of thought which Mark holds in regard to the parables in iv. 11 f. appears to be carried on by iv. 21–5 (as Markan insertion into the group of parables) and iv. 33 f. (*v.* 33 is certainly Markan; *v.* 34 may be also). It is difficult to accept the implication that ὁ λύχνος is here to be identified with our Lord who 'comes' (ἔρχεται) and is later made manifest. This may have been the meaning in the tradition, but it does not suit the Markan context.

of the parable to which the Kingdom of God is likened.[1] In each of these two parables there is a completed action, a tree in which the birds make nests and a crop being harvested; each of these is future to the first action of the parable – the sowing of the seed – and the emphasis lies on the completion of the action. The Kingdom belongs accordingly to the future though the steps which bring it in have already begun. Turning now to the Parable of the Sower this may have originally been a straightforward parable about the Kingdom in which emphasis lay on a harvest: 'In spite of every failure the Kingdom of God comes at last.'[2] Mark has however transformed this by the addition of the interpretation: the Gospel is preached in the world and some men receive it, that is, to them the mystery of the Kingdom is revealed, and they bring forth fruit; others fail to receive it or receive it and lose it, that is, they lose their understanding of the Kingdom. This itself does not therefore tell us much about the nature of the Kingdom. There remain a number of passages in which men are spoken of as entering or receiving the Kingdom. At ix. 47 entering into the Kingdom must be interpreted in a future manner since it is contrasted with being cast into Gehenna. The phrase recurs in the discussion about the difficulties of the rich in entering the Kingdom of God (x. 23 – 5); this pericope begins with the arrival of the rich man who asks Jesus what he needs to do to inherit eternal life; eternal life is here understood as future (cf. *v.* 30) and not in the Johannine sense as a present possession. It is reasonable then to suppose that references to the rich as entering the Kingdom of God (*vv.* 23 – 5) are to be taken in the future sense; this is confirmed by the final future reference of *v.* 30. It may not be however true that in their original context these passages had a future reference, and Jesus may originally have intended to imply the entering of the Kingdom as a present reality; but in the context they are given by Mark it is difficult to see anything other than a future reference. References to the Kingdom of God occur in the preceding pericope on the receiving of the little children (x. 13 – 16). Since at x. 15 Jesus speaks of receiving the Kingdom as a present possibility the present reference to it cannot be excluded in x. 14. The same is true of the scribe who

[1] Jeremias, *The Parables of Jesus*, pp. 89 f.
[2] Jeremias, *op. cit.* p. 92.

asked concerning the Great Commandment and who was told that he was not far from the Kingdom of God (xii. 34). These latter texts (x. 13–16; xii. 34) may represent the original trend of the teaching of Jesus which emerges despite the editorial work of Mark and the selective action of the early Church. However the main drift of the Markan interpretation of the Kingdom rests on its future nature. We may thus approve of the judgement of V. Taylor, 'in this Gospel (Mark) the main emphasis lies upon the Kingdom as future and, indeed, imminent, and as the community in which God's will is done'.[1]

Returning now to i. 15 we may see that whatever the underlying Aramaic may have meant, when Mark says that the Kingdom of God ἤγγικεν, he does not mean that it has arrived but that it is imminent. In line with this we have found no evidence that Mark connects the Kingdom with the demonic world and its defeat. The Kingdom is considered in terms of men. It is something which men receive or enter; when its accomplishment is considered, as in the Parable of the Mustard Seed, it is the birds of the air, that is, the Gentile nations, that come to it and are part of it.[2] The Parable of the Seed growing secretly up to its reaping in harvest (harvest with its implication of judgement on men) must lead to the same conclusion. And in so far as the Parable of the Sower is connected with the Kingdom it obviously concerns men. Thus the Kingdom of God for Mark is related not to the demonic world and its conquest but to the rule of God over men.

There is no evidence in Mark that Jesus is himself to be regarded as the Kingdom, a view which emerges in the other Synoptics.[3] When Mark says that the Kingdom of God is at hand he does not mean that this should be taken in a spatial sense: 'The kingdom of God has come close to men in the person of Jesus, and in his person it actually confronts them.'[4] This comment of Cranfield cannot be sustained in the light of Mark's general usage of the Kingdom. Mark equates Jesus with the Gospel but not with the Kingdom. The Gospel, that is,

[1] Pp. 114 f.
[2] C. H. Dodd, *The Parables of the Kingdom*, pp. 189–91; T. W. Manson, *The Teaching of Jesus*, p. 133, n. 1.
[3] Cf. K. L. Schmidt, *T.W.N.T.* I, 590 f.
[4] Cranfield, p. 68; cf. pp. 63–8.

Christ, must be believed because the Kingdom is close at hand. Here Mark is speaking to the readers of his own time and is setting before them a decision to be made. It is concerned with repentance and belief, an attitude towards God whose result will be entrance into a future Kingdom which God will bring. Negatively we must observe that Mark makes no reference to the subjection of demons nor to the healing of sickness; in relation to the Kingdom he neither says that Jesus did these things nor does he offer victory in them to the readers of his own time; they, the readers, are instead brought into a relationship towards God and promised a part in the final consummation. The purpose of the ministry of Jesus must then be the bringing of men into this relationship with God. As we proceed we will learn in more detail what this relationship is and how it is brought about by Jesus.

In the incident i. 21–8 it is difficult to determine the extent of the Markan editing. Verse 21a with its reference to Capernaum and v. 28, which is in general terms, may certainly be ascribed to Mark. But can we also put down vv. 21b, 22 to his hand? Verse 27 takes up again what is said in v. 22, and therefore if v. 22 is not part of the traditional material then perhaps we should argue the same for v. 27.[1] But vv. 23–7 read as a whole. Furthermore the reference in v. 22 to the scribes would seem an unlikely addition to a Mark finally compiled in Rome.[2] It is not then easy to conclude that the hand of Mark is to be detected in vv. 21b, 22.[3] Yet v. 23 does read like a fresh beginning; καὶ εὐθύς is a favourite introductory phrase of Mark to a new pericope, and there is the second reference to the synagogue. Perhaps the easiest solution is to assume that vv. 21b, 22 represent a fragment of traditional material which Mark has introduced at this point, observing that they make a suitable preliminary to v. 27.[4] By so doing Mark has emphasised Jesus as teaching men with power prior to his exorcism of

[1] So Bultmann, pp. 209 f.; Bundy, p. 77.

[2] Bussmann, I, 131 f. attributes the whole passage (vv. 21–8) apart from the reference to the scribes to his G; the reference to the scribes he ascribes to his Galilean redactor.

[3] Taylor takes vv. 21–8 as having come to Mark as a unit; Lohmeyer takes vv. 21 f. as Markan.

[4] The reference to the Sabbath in v. 21 is not followed up in vv. 23–7; contrast iii. 1–6.

demons with power: the word of instruction is prior to the word of exorcism and forms the basis for it. It is not then correct to take the first great act of Jesus as an exorcism; it is preceded by teaching, and indeed (*vv.* 16–20) by the powerful word which calls men to him.

i. 39 is another summary statement[1] of Mark describing the activity of Jesus. 'Both the vocabulary and style suggest that this summary statement was added by Mark either in composing the Gospel or at a still earlier stage.'[2] The last phrase of the verse καὶ τὰ δαιμόνια ἐκβάλλων is omitted in the Freer MS (W). Prior to the discovery of this MS, J. Weiss had suggested that it was a redactorial addition to Mark.[3] He argued: (*a*) the words are lacking in the Lukan parallel, and (*b*) in the immediately succeeding pericope describing activity in the sphere of Galilee healings and not exorcisms are described. These reasons do not appear sufficiently cogent to lead us to omit the phrase.[4] In *v.* 38, which would appear to be a part of the tradition received by Mark,[5] Jesus sets out his activity as preaching. Now in *v.* 39 Mark qualifies this by adding to it the phrase 'and casting out demons'. There has already been one exorcism (i. 23–7) and Mark is preparing for his explanation of exorcisms in iii. 22–7.

There seems less ground for taking i. 45 as the work of the evangelist. Without it the section i. 40 ff. lacks a proper climax. It may be however that the words from ὥστε to ἦν are due to Mark since they can be understood in line with his doctrine of a Messianic secret.[6] The close association of κηρύσσειν and λόγος in this verse may have been understood in the sense of the preaching of the Gospel by the early Church, but there is nothing here to help us to determine the content of the Gospel.

ii. 1, 2 certainly bear some signs of Markan editorial work. The anacolouthic εἰσελθών and Mark's favourite πάλιν are an indication of this.[7] But how far does this editorial work

---

[1] C. H. Dodd has argued that many of these summary statements once formed together an outline of the life of Jesus and that Mark has adapted his material to this outline. Cf. p. 112, n. 1.

[2] Taylor, *ad loc.*   [3] P. 151, n. 1.   [4] Cf. Schmidt, pp. 59 f.

[5] Schmidt, pp. 58 f., and the great majority of commentators take *vv.* 35–8 as part of the traditional material. Bussmann puts it in his G source. Bultmann regards all *vv.* 35–9 as a redactional summary.

[6] Thus Schmidt, pp. 66 f.   [7] Cf. Taylor, *ad loc.*

extend? Both Luke and Matthew have entirely different introductory sections to the incident of ii. 3–12; in the incident itself
however they follow Mark very closely. This may suggest
that practically the whole of ii. 1, 2 is Markan. The original
incident may have begun with a simple statement 'He was at
home (in a house, the house)'.[1] We are interested especially in
Mark's statement that Jesus ἐλάλει τὸν λόγον. Qualified by
τοῦ θεοῦ (κυρίου) this phrase was used in the early Church in
the sense of the proclamation of the Gospel (e.g. Acts iv. 29, 31;
viii. 25). Does it carry any of this significance at ii. 2? The
particular phrase recurs at iv. 33 and viii. 32. λόγος by itself
has quite obviously no particular reference to the Gospel in
viii. 38; x. 24; xiii. 31, in all of which it is used in the plural,
nor at v. 36; vii. 29, where it is used of the words of others than
Jesus. At x. 22; xiv. 39 it refers to particular sayings of Jesus;
elsewhere it has a variety of meanings (xi. 29; xii. 13; vii. 13).
In the interpretation of the Parable of the Sower (iv. 14 ff.) it
is used of the sowing of the word in the hearts of men and here
it must have the sense of 'Gospel', if Mark viewed this interpretation as an explanation of the success and failure of the spread
of the Gospel in his own day. This same meaning must appear
at iv. 33 f.; the mystery of the Kingdom (iv. 11), which cannot
be disassociated from the Gospel (i. 15), is made known in the
parables; here in iv. 33 it is said that in the parables the word
is proclaimed. This word must then be the Gospel. i. 45, 'he
spread abroad the word', is less decisive and λόγος may easily
here mean 'an account of what had happened'. At viii. 32
Jesus is himself said to speak the word boldly; this might be
taken as a reference to his preceding prophecy of his passion
and λόγος mean 'saying'; but it is surely difficult to avoid the
meaning 'Gospel' at this point. If the Gospel is linked directly
to the Passion, death and Resurrection of Jesus, of which he has
just spoken, then Jesus proclaimed the Gospel in proclaiming
his death and resurrection; and here moreover he is a pattern
to the early preacher who must also proclaim this very Gospel
'boldly'. We now return to ii. 1. The absolute usage of λόγος[2]
here then leaves it exceedingly probable that Mark had in mind

---

[1] So Schmidt, pp. 78 f.; cf. Lightfoot, *History*, p. 41.

[2] It is natural that when Jesus is the speaker λόγος should not be qualified
with either τοῦ θεοῦ or τοῦ κυρίου.

the proclamation of the Gospel.[1] But what is it that is proclaimed in the succeeding verses? A sick man is brought to Jesus and the first thing he does is to speak a word of forgiveness. The content of the word which is to be spoken is not 'Jesus heals' but 'Jesus offers forgiveness', that is, the essential content of the Gospel is the forgiveness of sin and not victory over sickness (or the Devil). Had Jesus begun by healing the man the Gospel might have been viewed as victory over the demonic forces of the world, but the Gospel is related here to forgiveness. This also is the content of the Gospel that Mark himself would preach.[2]

The section ii. 1 – iii. 6 is generally held to have come to Mark as a unit, a complex of conflict stories.[3] It cannot then include much editorial work apart from its beginning and end. The only verse which merits discussion is ii. 13.[4] This verse is completely omitted in Matthew, drastically shortened in Luke, contains Mark's favourite πάλιν and bears no particular relationship to *vv.* 14 – 17. Mark is creating a background for the incident that is to follow.[5] And in this background we observe how he presents Jesus as teacher, though the quantity of teaching that he gives from Jesus is small compared to that which we find in the other Synoptics. διδάσκαλος is the favourite address of others to Jesus in Mark. It is however when we look at the places where διδάσκειν and διδαχή are used in Mark that the importance of this root for him becomes apparent;[6] for these two words occur largely in the seams between incidents, where we are most likely to see the hand of Mark: thus διδαχή comes in i. 22, 27; iv. 2; xi. 18; xii. 38; but only i. 27 is integral to the incident in which it occurs. διδάσκειν is found in i. 21, 22;

[1] Cf. Lohmeyer; Hauck.
[2] At iv. 33 f. the content of the 'word' would appear to be the eschatological kingdom.
[3] So Dibelius, p. 219; Schmidt, pp. 103 f.; Knox, pp. 8 ff., etc.
[4] Cf. Taylor, *ad loc.*; Schmidt, p. 82. Whether Mark made other additions to this complex it is difficult to determine. ii. 15–17 may have originally lacked the introduction of ii. 14; but ii. 15 requires some explanation concerning whose house Jesus was sitting in and ii. 16 some preceding reference to publicans. Mark may have added ii. 21 f. or ii. 27 f. or they may have been a part of the existing tradition.
[5] Hauck.
[6] Cf. Schweizer, 'Anmerkungen zur Theologie des Markus', pp. 37 ff.

ii. 13; iv. 1, 2; vi. 6; viii. 31; ix. 31; x. 1; xi. 17 (perhaps only a conventional Markan expression[1]); xii. 35, all of which are probably editorial; more doubtful are vi. 2, 34. Only at xii. 14 and xiv. 49 is the word used in a way integral to the pericope; at vii. 7 it is in a LXX quotation; in vi. 30 it is used of the teaching of the disciples. Thus διδάσκειν and its cognates are favourites of Mark. If we examine in this way the 'seams' between the incidents then Mark leaves us with the impression that the main activity of Jesus was teaching; note especially x. 1, where teaching is said to be his custom; this appears much more regularly in the seams than does 'healing' or 'exorcism', and, whereas the incidents recording these gradually disappear towards the end of the book, the teaching of Jesus continues right through to the Passion itself. Probably no distinction is to be made between preaching (κηρύσσειν) and teaching. Preaching seems to be used more often of the activities of others about Jesus (i. 4, 7, 45; iii. 14; v. 20; vi. 12; vii. 36; xiii. 10; xiv. 9) than of the activity of Jesus himself (i. 14, 38). But the connection between the two is seen in the equivalence of such passages as vi. 12 and vi. 30. The content of the teaching of Jesus is not made clear; very often the reference to the teaching of Jesus is general without specific relation to what follows, or in the incident that follows the use of διδάσκειν, etc., no actual teaching of Jesus is given (i. 21, 22; ii. 13; vi. 34; x. 1). His teaching may be connected with the coming of the Kingdom (iv. 1, 2) which is made known through parables; it is directed against the Pharisees (xii. 38) and against the misuse of the temple as market (xi. 17); it sets him forth as greater than David (xii. 35); and most noteworthy, two of the Passion predictions (viii. 31; ix. 31) are introduced as the teaching of Jesus. Thus Mark sets out Jesus as teacher and his teaching is certainly linked with the understanding of his death and resurrection.

While the failure of the disciples to understand Jesus has been a commonplace of Markan criticism since the work of Wrede, Ebeling[2] has shown how this failure is balanced by a corresponding attempt by Jesus to enlighten the disciples. We may note that iv. 13 is balanced at once by the interpretation of the

---

[1] Taylor, *ad loc.*
[2] Ebeling, *Das Messiasgeheimnis*[2], pp. 146–79.

parable which the disciples had failed to understand; likewise their lack of understanding about the miracles of the loaves is followed by teaching (viii. 14–21); in the two incidents on the lake (iv. 35–41; vi. 45–52) the fear of the disciples for themselves, which is closely linked to ignorance of the nature of Jesus, is answered by a revelation of his supernatural nature. Peter's failure to understand his own confession of Jesus as the Christ is followed by teaching on what will happen to the Christ (viii. 27–33); the failure of the disciples to understand the way of service as that along which Jesus goes to the Cross (at ix. 33 ff. and x. 35 ff. following on the second and third prophecies of the Cross they are discussing their own greatness) is balanced with teaching by Jesus on the nature of service. Thus Mark sets out Jesus in his teaching as bringing to men a revelation of himself and of the necessity and nature of his death and resurrection. But we may note that it is not a revelation pure and simple but one linked closely to following Jesus, to discipleship. The way of service along which Jesus goes must also be the way for the disciples (x. 42–4); they have also to take up their crosses and go after him (viii. 34). The understanding only comes to those who go in the way of Jesus. Thus, if Mark sets out Jesus as one who reveals, it is not in the sense of one who admits the curious to see the mysteries of God, but of one who is only understood by his disciples as they enter on the hard path of discipleship.

iii. 7–12 is taken very generally to be a Markan construction. In it Mark sets out the activities of Jesus as twofold, healing and exorcism. We must ask how far this is a clearly Markan construction and how far Mark has used traditional material. If we do not go so far as Knox[1] in attributing this section to the 'Twelve-Source', yet we have to notice certain difficulties in the passage if it is entirely Markan. It is said that the boat is introduced in iii. 9 as preparation for iv. 1, but it seems a quite unnecessary duplication, particularly if iv. 1, 2 is itself a Markan construction; may it not have been a part of the tradition that Jesus taught from a boat at the lake-side, a tradition which Mark has made use of more than once? Further the geographical designations of *vv.* 7, 8 seem unnecessarily detailed for a Roman audience; this again suggests tradition. The early

[1] Pp. 17 ff.

73

Christian preacher must have said something about the life of Jesus and there would have been summary statements about his teaching and activity; cf. Acts x. 38 f. This is true whether or not we accept the view of Dodd that there was a summary outline of the life of Jesus.[1] Mark may have used such traditional material at this point. In particular he allows this material to make reference to exorcism because he is about to introduce the dispute of Jesus with the scribes on this very matter and the one exorcism which he has already related (i. 23–8) is not sufficient to create such a discussion. Noteworthy is the absence of reference to the teaching of Jesus. We have seen that this is a constant Markan theme in the 'seams'; this again suggests we are dealing with traditional material rather than a straightforward Markan construction. Possibly teaching is implied in the reference to the boat; ostensibly the boat is to prevent people jostling Jesus; but once he was in the boat what would he do except teach? This is the purpose of the boat in iv. 1.

There now follow a number of pericopae, the Markan connecting links between which contribute little or nothing to our inquiry. In some cases the seams are of the briefest possible nature, being just sufficient to set the scene, sometimes no more than a mere καί (iii. 13, 19b, 22, 31; iv. 21, 24, 26, 30, 35; v. 1, 21, 25). iii. 19b–34 appears to have been traditional material that came to Mark, perhaps already joined together, though the 'sandwich' (vv. 19b–21, 22–30, 31–5) suggests Mark's hand; in any case there are no seams within it of significance. Mark may have rewritten the material to bring out the meaning he desired; iii. 30 may well be his comment. We have, however, already examined this passage in detail.[2] iv. 1 is certainly Markan, and perhaps the seam also includes iv. 2; in it Jesus is depicted as teacher and the following passages show him as the teller of parables. iv. 11 f., 21–5, 33, 34 are Markan insertions into the parables with the intention of explaining their use; iv. 11 f., 21–5 probably utilise traditional material whose original setting has been lost; iv. 33, 34 would rather appear to be Mark's own conclusion to this passage of parables. There follow (iv. 35–v. 43) four δυνάμεις of Jesus. Then Mark brings him to his own village of Nazareth.

---

[1] Cf. p. 112, n. 1.　　　　[2] Cf. pp. 10 ff.

vi. 1, 2*a* would appear to be Markan. vi. 1 sets the scene for what follows and ἤρξατο διδάσκειν is a Markan phrase (cf. iv. 1; vi. 34; viii. 31) incorporating his favourite use of ἄρχομαι. The following verses (to 6 *a*) clearly contain traditional material emanating from a Galilean source which alone would have interest in the names of Jesus' brothers. Mark may have brought together two separate pieces of material.[1] In the pericope the villagers wonder both at the wisdom of his teaching and at the great works he has done. We are presumably intended by Mark to carry back the allusion to his mighty deeds to iv. 35 – v. 43 in which Mark has recounted in detail four of them – though none of them was performed in Nazareth, Mark's readers still have them in the mind's eye. Since the traditional material also carried reference to his teaching Mark introduces Jesus as teacher in his connecting link (*v. 2a*).

vi. 6*b* is remarkable in that Mark here sends out Jesus on tour round the villages and states his activity as teaching alone; there is no reference to his healing activity or to exorcisms. Matthew corrects this by the introduction of reference to Jesus as healer; Luke has no parallel. The omission by Mark is all the more noteworthy because he proceeds directly to record the sending out of the apostles on a mission in which they heal and exorcise. The original story of the mission here will have probably contained a reference to the sending out of the Twelve followed by the instructions of *vv.* 8 – 11. To this Mark has added in *v.* 7 Jesus' bestowal on them of authority over demons and the whole of *vv.* 12, 13 recounting what the Twelve did.[2] This might appear to give a certain prominence to exorcism as an activity of the apostles since it appears in both *v.* 7 and *v.* 13. This needs to be seen in the light of two facts: (*a*) Jesus is described in *v.* 6*b* by Mark as teaching, and not as exorcising; (*b*) Jesus gives authority to exorcise.[3] Thus Jesus is seen by Mark primarily as a teacher, but also as one who can delegate authority over demons because he already possesses that authority.

In vi. 14 – 16 we may again suspect the hand of Mark.

---

[1] Cf. Schmidt, pp. 152 ff.; *vv.* 2*b*, 4 appear to be linked to Jesus' teaching as mentioned in *vv.* 1, 2*a*, whereas *vv.* 2*c*, 5, 6 may have formed a separate unit relating to his miracles. We note again that the Word (σοφία) precedes the healing (cf. ii. 1–12).

[2] Cf. Taylor.   [3] Cf. below, pp. 187 f. for a fuller discussion.

ἤκουσεν is left without an object; this may have been present in the original context which vi. 14 possessed in the tradition; if so Mark must have torn the passage from there and placed it here. Verses 14–16 are obviously intended as introductory to *vv.* 17–29, the account of the death of John. It is hardly likely, as some commentators suggest, that Mark introduced this merely to indicate the passing of time between the sending out of the disciples (vi. 7–13) and their return (vi. 30). There were presumably many other pericopae Mark could have introduced at this point to serve this purpose: his choice of this one is significant. The death of John foreshadows the death of Jesus; ix. 11–13 closely connects the two deaths.[1] vi. 15, 16 with their three different identifications of Jesus with Elijah, John and one of the prophets recall the scene at Caesarea Philippi (viii. 28); indeed it is possible that the construction of one may have influenced that of the other: '... in describing a new scene, he (Mark) sometimes repeats on an extensive scale words and phrases he has used in an earlier narrative'.[2] If vi. 15, 16 recalls the scene at Caesarea Philippi then let us remember that the identification there is quickly followed by the prediction of the Passion. Thus Mark is indicating to us in vi. 14–29[3] the final end of the forerunner's successor.

vi. 30–4 would appear to be an amalgam brought together by Mark.[4] With most of it we are not concerned since it describes the activity of the disciples rather than that of Jesus; *v.* 34 brings us to the latter. vi. 34 *a* may have lain in the tradition, but 34 *b* is a Markan construction and must be taken as qualifying 34 *a*.[5] σπλαγχνίζεσθαι is also found in the doublet viii. 1–9. Either usage may have inspired the other, but since vi. 34*a* contains a biblical quotation and is not directly connected to the miracle of the feeding it would appear more likely that this has been formed by Mark using the key-word which he met in the other tradition. The sequence of thought in viii. 2 ff. seems

---

[1] Marxsen (pp. 22 f.); Lohmeyer, *ad loc.*, take the absolute use of παραδοθῆναι in i. 14 as a premonition of the Passion.

[2] Taylor, p. 53. Mark may have introduced *vv.* 15, 16 here as a deliberate parallel to viii. 27 f.; cf. Bundy.

[3] It is irrelevant whether we decide vi. 17–29 is bazaar gossip (Rawlinson) or an early Church creation; it came to Mark as part of the tradtion; he uses it as a minor passion pointing to the greater Passion.

[4] So Schmidt, pp. 178–93; Taylor, etc.   [5] Note the use of ἄρχεσθαι.

more natural; Jesus feels compassion for the hungry crowd and so he feeds them. In vi. 34 Jesus sees the crowd as sheep without a shepherd and in his compassion teaches them; then the feeding follows almost as a separate incident.[1] But feeding is much more the task of a shepherd than teaching.[2] How do we explain the intrusion of teaching? The quotation is not a literal reproduction of any particular Old Testament text and may have been inspired by one or more of a number of places, namely, Num. xxvii. 17; III Kgdms xxii. 17; II Chron. xviii. 16; Ezek. xxxiv. 5; Judith xi. 19. Of these III Kgdms xxii. 17 = II Chron. xviii. 16 and Judith xi. 19 are the least likely to have been formative since they do not suggest Jesus as the new Moses, and Ezek. xxxiv. 5 combined with xxxiv. 23 would imply Jesus as the new David, or King of Israel (in the Markan Passion story Jesus is often referred to as the King of the Jews). Num. xxvii. 17 then appears preferable as source because it is possible to make some connection between Moses as lawgiver and teacher and Jesus as the shepherd who teaches (cf. Ps. cxix. 176). Moreover there is a link between Jesus as the new Moses and the Feeding of the Five Thousand; Jesus gives the new manna. Moses fed the people with God's teaching: for man does not live by bread alone but by whatever comes from the mouth of God (Deut. viii. 3, where there is a distinct reference to manna. In John x. 8, 16, 27 the sheep hear and heed the voice of Jesus, which must imply some reference to his teaching).[3] Perhaps then in *v.* 34 we may see a reflection of the view that Jesus feeds men with the word of God just as once he fed them with bread and fishes.[4] Some confirmation of this close relationship of the

---

[1] Lohmeyer alone of commentators appears to observe the strangeness of Mark's reference to the teaching of Jesus. Matthew changes the reference by linking Jesus' compassion to healing; Luke omits the quotation about the shepherd and the reference to the compassion of Jesus, but says that he taught and healed.

[2] On the biblical picture of the shepherd and his activities cf. Jeremias, *T.W.N.T.* VI, 484 ff.

[3] The Shepherd appears as teacher in post-canonical Christian teaching (cf. Jeremias, *op. cit.* p. 496); in Philo the Logos and νοῦς appear as shepherd (*ibid.* pp. 488 f.).

[4] In the Johannine eucharistic discourse Jesus says to the disciples who have found his statements difficult to accept, 'It is the spirit that gives life, the flesh is of no avail; the *words* that I have spoken unto you are spirit and life' (vi. 63).

teaching of Jesus to what he gave to the crowds in the two feeding stories is found in the very difficult passage which terminates his teaching on the understanding of these miracles, namely, viii. 14–21; this again would seem to be a Markan amalgam of traditional sayings.[1] There is continual reference here to the dullness of understanding of the disciples (vv. 17, 18, 21; cf. vi. 52); they had not been able to appreciate his teaching (the leaven of the Pharisees is interpreted in Matthew as their teaching: xvi. 11, 12). To return to vi. 34: Mark sets out Jesus as the shepherd who feeds his people with true teaching; from his supply there is more than enough to feed all their needs[2] (in the feedings there was food over and above what was necessary); but it is not always easy to understand (viii. 14–21); the parables, we may recall, also required their explanation (iv. 11, 12).

vi. 45, 46 do not show much trace of Markan style and are probably part of the tradition which he received; there is good reason to believe that they always adhered closely to vv 35–44.[3] Verses 47, 48 show Mark's hand[4] and perhaps he has made the link at this point between the feeding narrative and the walking on the water, though the fact that the second feeding is also followed by a scene in a boat may imply that this connection lay deep in the tradition. Verse 52 is Markan and again serves to hold together the feeding and the incident on the lake.[5] What concerns us is the reference to Jesus as praying. Mark rarely shows us Jesus in prayer; only elsewhere at i. 35 and xiv. 35 ff. Luke, as is well known, extends these references (iii. 21; xi. 1, etc.). What is the significance of the prayer at this point? Lohmeyer sees a connection between the prayer and epiphany of Jesus to the disciples. May it not however represent the beginning of a new stage in the ministry? The prayer at i. 35 is followed by the decision of Jesus to widen his ministry into the villages around Capernaum, that is, into Galilee; associated with the prayer of Jesus at vi. 46 is the sending of the disciples out of Galilee (Bethsaida) and in the subsequent section (perhaps as far as ix. 30) the incidents largely take place

[1] Cf. Taylor; Klostermann; Dibelius, pp. 228 f.
[2] Cf. G. H. Boobyer, 'The Eucharistic Interpretation of the Miracle of the Loaves in St Mark's Gospel', *J. T. S.* III (1952), 161–71.
[3] Cf. Schmidt, pp. 193 f.
[4] Cf. Hauck, *ad loc.*: use of καί, etc.   [5] Lohmeyer.

outside Galilean, indeed outside Jewish territory. Both prayers are preceded by a great success and followed by movement away from that success.

vi. 53–6 appears to be a Markan summary based on tradition which he has received.[1] The fact of the presence of a place-name (Gennesaret) would emphasise Mark's usage here of tradition. In the passage Jesus is depicted as a popular healer as in iii. 7–13, and as in that pericope no mention is made of him here as teacher. Both these passages we have seen came from the tradition; Mark however continually in his own seams introduces Jesus as teacher. In that he would seem to be correcting the tradition he has received.

In vii. 1–23 Mark gives us a period of sustained teaching by Jesus. There may be Markan seams at vii. 1, 9, 14, 17, and vii. 3, 4 is probably a Markan explanatory addition, but in none of them is there anything which shows us how Mark regarded the activity of Jesus. There follow two miracles to which again there are brief connecting links but nothing of importance for us (vii. 24–30, 31–7). We have already dealt with the second feeding and the subsequent discussion in so far as it concerns us (viii. 1–21). The seam again at viii. 22 (the healing of the blind man of Bethsaida) has nothing to show us.

In the section viii. 27–ix. 1 there are a number of connecting links, namely, viii. 27, 31, 34; v. 30 may also be Markan, relating to the Messianic secret. Presumably the sections viii. 27–9, viii. 31–3, and viii. 34–ix. 1 came to Mark as units; the only doubt would lie in relation to the last of these whether Mark had built it up from separate sayings; since however it concerns discipleship rather than the activities of Jesus we need not enter into its analysis. The introduction of the crowd at viii. 34 suggests that viii. 34–ix. 1 did not originally belong with viii. 27–33; the whole point of the two earlier passages is that Jesus is alone with his disciples in an area where he would not be likely to have a crowd ready to hand. We may suspect that Mark has then added this section. For our purpose the question is much more interesting: has Mark brought together viii. 27–9 and viii. 31–3?[2] The use of καὶ ἤρξατο διδάσκειν, a favourite

---

[1] So Taylor; Schmidt, p. 195; Weiss, pp. 222 f., etc.

[2] Cf. Schmidt, pp. 217 f.; Lagrange; Weiss, p. 237; F. Hahn, *Christologische Hoheitstitel*, pp. 226–30.

editorial phrase, reinforces this suggestion. To make the link Matthew uses ἀπὸ τότε, a stronger phrase than καί; it implies a new stage, and perhaps also a new time, in the teaching about the suffering of Jesus. It must also be noticed that this teaching bears a certain formalised character, being repeated twice more, and Mark may have regarded it as a formula to be inserted at suitable points.[1] On the other hand there is no need in Mark to give ἤρξατο the sense of 'began', as if a new start is intended at this point;[2] similar teaching is introduced with the same word at x. 32. Furthermore the appearance of Peter in both *vv.* 27–9 and 31–3 would have tended to draw these two pericopae together prior to Mark's time even if they were not originally one complete incident in Jesus' life. We must now look a little more closely at Mark's editorial references to the teaching of Jesus. We have seen that though Mark continually draws attention to the teaching of Jesus he gives little content to that teaching. The one place where we have found it strongly linked to actual teaching by Jesus is iv. 1, 2 in relation to the parables. What does the word 'parable' mean? If we trace behind it the Hebrew משל (Aramaic מתלא) with its meaning 'riddle', 'dark saying', and assume that Mark as well as his source understood it in this sense at iv. 11, 12,[3] then it may be possible to argue that where Mark refers editorially to the teaching of Jesus he has in mind teaching which is in riddles, difficult to understand, hard to accept. If we now examine his references to Jesus as teaching, we see that this is true of iv. 1, 2. His teaching in the synagogue of Nazareth causes offence (vi. 2). vi. 34 *b* is followed by the feedings which both crowds and disciples failed to understand (vi. 52; viii. 14–21). viii. 31 and ix. 31 precede predictions of the Passion, which the disciples again found 'hard sayings'. x. 1 is certainly followed by many sayings which it is hard to live out, even if their meaning is clear (x. 9, 21, 24);

---

[1] On the analysis of the Son of Man sayings about the Passion cf. F. Hahn, *op. cit.* pp. 46 ff.

[2] Cf. Howard, *Grammar*, II, 455 f.; Blass-Debrunner, § 392.2; Taylor, pp. 63 f.; Turner, XXVIII (1927), 352 f. ἤρξατο + infinitive is in Mark the equivalent of the imperfect. Cf. J. C. Doudna, *The Greek of the Gospel of Mark*, pp. 111–17.

[3] Cf. Marxsen, 'Redaktionsgeschichtliche Erklärung der Parabeltheorie des Markus', *Z.T.K.* LII (1955), 255–71; Boobyer, 'The Redaction of Mark iv. 1–34'.

observe how the disciples need an explanation of the saying about divorce (*v.* 10); how they find his attitude to the infants difficult (*vv.* 13 f.); and their astonishment at his sayings about riches (*v.* 26). xi. 17 offends the priests and scribes so that they at once plot to kill him (xi. 18). xii. 35 is indeed followed by an enigmatic enough saying. At i. 21, 22 his teaching is with power and provokes great amazement. Further the references to Jesus as speaking the word have equally gnomic character at iv. 33 and viii. 32; at ii. 2 they are followed by Jesus' claim to be able to forgive sins, a claim which causes the scribes to stumble. It may then be that where Mark makes reference to the teaching of Jesus, using either διδάσκειν or λαλεῖν τὸν λόγον, he is drawing our attention to the difficulty of what Jesus says and does for those who are outside the Christian community; those within are given an explanation and understand. These matters are largely taken up with the eschatological nature of the Kingdom (iv. 1 ff.), the nature of the Eucharist (vi. 34 ff.), the meaning and necessity of his death (viii. 31; ix. 31), the claim that sins are forgiven through him (ii. 1 ff.), and certain hard points in Christian ethics (x. 1 ff.). The phrase 'Jesus taught' is to be understood in the sense of the addition 'in parables', which itself is to be understood in the sense of 'riddles, hard sayings, gnomic utterances', obscure to those outside, comprehensible to those within. Whether all this be accepted or not, Mark intends to set out Jesus as active in teaching, and not as an exorcist or as forcing men's minds. Teaching is his custom (x. 1).

The seams (ix. 2, 9, 14, 30) in the immediately succeeding material yield us little of interest; they are mainly geographical and temporal, adding in themselves nothing to our picture of the activity of Jesus other than that he and the disciples were continually on the move.[1] ix. 30–2 is a Markan construction, containing both the secrecy motif and the second prediction of the Passion, introduced by the reference to Jesus as teacher with which we have just dealt. ix. 33–50 is an amalgam of sayings held together by a number of key-words; the editorial connections in the sense of 'seams' hardly exist at all; the sayings themselves deal mainly with the lives of the disciples rather than with the activities of Jesus. Likewise in ch. x, describing Jesus'

[1] Cf. pp. 123 ff. below.

journey to Jerusalem, the seams are brief and mainly topographical (vv. 1, 2, 10, 13, 17, 23, 28 (?), 32, 35, 46). Verse 31 may be an addition of Mark; he also appears to have brought together the sayings of vv. 41–5. We will return to v. 45 later: otherwise there is little here which deals with the activity of Jesus.

With the entrance of Christ into Jerusalem we come to a more closely connected sequence of events in the Markan narrative.[1] Whether they all actually occurred within the short space of a few days as Mark makes out it is not our purpose to inquire; it is very probable that Mark received the account of at least the main events of the last days in Jerusalem as part of the tradition. We need not therefore speculate whether the entrance into Jerusalem took place at the Feast of Tabernacles rather than at Passover-time and what Mark means by changing the festival. If Mark did make this change it was surely to heighten the tension of the crucifixion and the change of itself does not alter the picture which he presents of Jesus.

The topographical elements in the seams at xi. 1, 11 may have been supplied by Mark or derived from the tradition, but in either case they tell us nothing of the activities of Jesus. Taylor suggests that the words ἐφ' ὃν οὐδεὶς οὔπω ἀνθρώπων ἐκάθισεν (xi. 2) may be an embellishment of the original story.[2] Bauer has made out a case to show that the πῶλος was not a young ass but a young horse.[3] It has been further suggested that Jesus in thus riding on an unbroken colt shows his mastery over the demonic.[4] This stretches things too far. Bauer has by no means proved his case,[5] and even if he had there is another possible explanation of the words; in Zech. ix. 9 (LXX) the πῶλος is described as νέος. Animals for sacrifice were not expected to have been used for domestic and farm purposes (Num. xix. 2; Deut. xxi. 3; Horace, *Epodes* ix, 21–2; Virg.

---

[1] On the section xi. 1–xiii. 37 cf. T. A. Burkill, 'Strain on the Secret: An Examination of Mark xi. 1–xiii. 37', *Z.N.T.W.* LI (1960), 31–46.
[2] Pp. 452 f.
[3] W. Bauer, 'The Colt of Palm Sunday', *J.B.L.* LXXII (1953), 220–9.
[4] G. B. Caird, *Principalities and Powers*, p. 71, n. 2.
[5] Cf. O. Michel, 'Eine philologische Frage zur Einzugsgeschichte', *N.T.S.* VI (1959), 81 f.; H. W. Kuhn, 'Das Reittier Jesu in der Einzugsgeschichte des Markusevangeliums', *Z.N.T.W.* L (1959), 82–91.

Georg. IV, 540; Ovid, *Metam*, III, 10–11), and this entry partook of the nature of a sacral event.[1] There is no need then to see in these words a Markan editorial reference to the demonic. Verse 10*a* may also be an addition to the tradition; if so it emphasises the coming of the Kingdom, rather than tells us about the meaning of the activity of Jesus. Jesus enters the city as king, and within the Passion story as told by Mark it is as king of the Jews that he is crucified (xv. 26, etc.). Thus the story here is tied to the Passion by this addition to the shout of the people. But *vv.* 9*b*, 10 also represent the worship of the Church for its exalted Saviour, and in that sense they would be taken by Mark's readers as representing their own worship and faith.[2]

In xi. 12–25 we have one incident sandwiched within another, a favourite Markan editorial trick (cf. iii. 20–35; v. 21–43). We may thus attribute to him the present arrangement. Simple temporal and topographical links at xi. 12, 15, 19, 20, 27 hold it together inwardly and join it to what precedes and what succeeds. The incident of the Cleansing of the Temple may well have been a piece of detached tradition.[3] It is differently placed within the Synoptic and Johannine traditions and taken by itself it was only a prophetic act, insufficient to trigger off the crucifixion.[4] The incident about the fig-tree, whether originally a prophetic and symbolic action or a development of the parable of Luke xiii. 6–9, must also have possessed at one time another place in the tradition; the parenthesis (again typical of Mark),[5] that it was not the time for figs, indicates a certain unhappiness about its present position.[6] It has been presumably placed there in order to imply the judgement of God over the Temple, the city, or Israel – there are many leaves, but no fruit. To this story Mark has appended a number of sayings on faith (xi. 22–5). In the account of the Cleansing of the Temple there

[1] So Taylor; Lohmeyer, etc.   [2] Cf. Lindars, pp. 171 f.
[3] Schmidt, pp. 291 ff. He quotes J. Weiss and Heitmüller writing respectively on Mark and John in *Die Schriften des NTs* (1907/8) and maintaining respectively that the Johannine and Markan datings are correct!
[4] Schniewind. Had Jesus driven out the priests themselves his action would certainly have been much more than prophetic.
[5] Taylor.
[6] This incident and the Entry may have taken place at the festival of Tabernacles; cf. C. W. F. Smith, 'No Time for Figs', *J.B.L.* LXXIX (1960), 315–27.

are a number of traces of Markan editing. Verses 18, 19 are omitted by Matthew and considerably altered by Luke so that the cleansing no longer provides the excuse for the plotting of the Jewish leaders. Quite clearly Mark however does intend us to understand that it did. The key verse is 17 which Mark introduces by a reference to Jesus as teaching. Bultmann conjectures that this replaces something more akin to John ii. 16;[1] a statement such as the latter would not have been enough to invite the Jewish leaders to plot the crucifixion. What, however, does Mark, with his solemn introduction, wish us to see in v. 17? Whose is ὁ οἶκός μου? In Isa. lvi. 7 it is Yahweh's house, but in Mark does it not read more naturally as Christ's own house? Even if the quotation as it stands in Mark represents what Jesus said and if we assume he intended a reference to God's house, that is no reason why the early Church should not have understood the μου of Jesus himself. If Jesus made this claim it does provide sufficient grounds within the Markan story for the plotting of the Jewish leaders (v. 18). Whether this be so or not we do have the close connection between οἶκος and the Church of God (Christ) for the early community (I Pet. iv. 17; Heb. x. 21, etc.). Now it appears that the part of the Temple which Jesus cleansed was the court of the Gentiles.[2] The People of God, the House, the Church, is not for Jews only, but, cleansed by Christ, is for all men. What Jesus accomplishes he accomplishes for all men, Gentiles as well as Jews. Thus Mark also depicts him as healing a Gentile (vii. 24–30) and feeding a Gentile crowd (viii. 1–10).[3]

There now follows a series of incidents (xi. 27–xii. 40) in which the differences between Jesus and the Jewish leaders are sharply defined. These differences are concerned with behaviour, authority and the interpretation of the Law of God. In them the tension between Jesus and his opponents is made quite clear so that the crucifixion becomes reasonable as their reaction

[1] P. 36.

[2] Cf. Lightfoot, *Gospel*, pp. 60–9. It is unlikely that the reference in v. 17 to the Gentiles is a post-Markan addition, though it is omitted by Matthew and Luke. It falls into line with Mark's Gentile interests.

[3] Cf. T. A. Burkill, 'Anti-Semitism in St Mark's Gospel', *N.T.* III (1959), 34–53. The cursing of the fig-tree would indicate the end of the place of the Jewish people in God's redemptive purpose.

to him; it emerges out of their refusal to accept his authority and guidance in the matters under dispute. There are few scholars who would maintain the view that all these incidents occurred on the third day of Jesus' visit to Jerusalem or that they all happened even in Jerusalem. They must have occupied a much longer time, and even if we allow that they took place in Jerusalem it may not have been during the last visit of Jesus to the city. It is difficult to say whether these incidents all formed part of a complex which came to Mark and which he introduced at this point or whether he himself has brought them together. The former has been maintained by Albertz, Taylor and many others. It has been criticised recently by W. L. Knox.[1] The stories do not form any easily recognisable pattern[2] nor do they rise to a climax; for this reason it is perhaps unnecessary to decide who compiled them.

It is possible that xi. 27–33 was always attached to the story of the Cleansing of the Temple.[3] The variation in the introductory formula by Luke, who attaches it to the teaching of Jesus, suggests rather that it may have been a piece of detached tradition that Mark brings in at this point. Bultmann[4] would limit the original tradition (whether coming from Jesus or from the Palestinian community) to *vv.* 28–30; but surely without *v.* 33 these lack a telling conclusion. Verses 31, 32 may well be additions of Mark to bring out the reason for the refusal of the priests and scribes to answer. The authority of Jesus is here linked to the baptism and the prophetic teaching of John the Baptist. Mark has not told us much about John, but what information he has provided concerns John as the forerunner who introduces Jesus and points out his significance. John is the messenger who declares that after him there comes one who is stronger and who will baptise with the Holy Spirit. John's baptism has the authority of heaven and in that baptism Jesus is recognised as the Son of God and the Spirit descends upon

---

[1] Pp. 85 ff.

[2] Daube, *The New Testament and Rabbinic Judaism*, pp. 158 ff.; 'Four Types of Question', *J.T.S.* II (1951), 45–8, indicates that in xii. 13–37 a Rabbinic scheme of questions is followed. If this is so this part of the complex will probably have been compiled prior to Mark during the Palestinian stage of the tradition.

[3] Taylor.   [4] Pp. 19 f.

him. In introducing John again at this point Mark is not merely arguing that Jesus' authority comes from God, as does that of John, but indicating that Jesus' authority is that of the one to whom the heavenly voice said, 'Thou art my beloved Son, with thee I am well pleased'. It is by this authority that Jesus does ταῦτα (v. 28), that is, it is as Son and as Messiah (both ideas seem to lie in the words of the heavenly voice) that he cleansed the Temple – and ultimately it will be because of these claims that he will be crucified.

In the next incident Jesus is clearly set out as the Son of God. The Parable of the Wicked Husbandmen (xii. 1–12) probably had another setting in the life of Jesus,[1] but by the time of Mark it had been adapted to give an interpretation of his death. The process of interpretation was still continuing in the early Church and we find that the allegorisation is given more exact detail in Matthew and Luke (cf. the parallels to Mark xii. 8). It is impossible to say with certainty if Mark was the first to begin this allegorisation, but probably he gave the parable its present position. xi. 27 and xii. 12, both Markan seams, show that it is directed against the leaders of the Jewish people. It sets out briefly the history of that people who are given a vineyard by God; they reject his messengers, the prophets; they reject his Son; so their leaders are rejected and the leadership is given to others. The Son who was rejected is now reverenced by the Church ('this is wonderful in *our* eyes', v. 11). The Church as a building and Christ as its foundations was a commonplace of the ideology of the early Christians (I Pet. ii. 4–8; I Cor. iii. 9–17; Eph. ii. 19–22). It was through the rejection of the Son of God that this new community of the Christian Church (including Gentiles) came into existence. So this passage is used by Mark both as a justification of the New Israel, built on the rejected Messiah, and as providing further grounds for the opposition of the Jewish leaders to Jesus (v. 12). The death of Jesus is given significance in this parable by the resultant creation of the new Israel.

The following three incidents (vv. 13–17, 18–27, 28–34) are juxtaposed with little editorial introductory material. The total

[1] Jeremias, *The Parables of Jesus*, pp. 55 ff.; C. H. Dodd, *The Parables of the Kingdom*, pp. 124 ff.; Wilson, *Studies in the Gospel of Thomas* (London, 1960), pp. 101 f., has pointed out that Logion 65 of Thomas contains the form of the parable thought to be original by Dodd and Jeremias.

effect is to show the discomfiture of those who approach Jesus; the third pericope in which there is some common ground between the scribe and Jesus is concluded with the statement that no one dared to ask him any more questions (xii. 34).

The last of these discussions between Jesus and his opponents (xii. 35–7a) is a question put by Jesus to them in which he confounds them; they give no answer. Whether this incident was originally told either to defend or to deny the Davidic lineage of Jesus does not concern us; Mark quite obviously assumes that lineage;[1] nor need we speculate whether the incident is a community creation[2] or a piece of genuine tradition.[3] In Mark it plays its part in leading to the rejection of Jesus by the Jewish authorities, who certainly could not allow the Christological claim inherent in it.[4] Jesus is here set out not only as Davidic King but as Kyrios. This is the favourite designation of the early community, though not often applied to Jesus by Mark.[5] At the moment of Mark's writing Jesus was sitting at the right hand of God: this was the belief of every strand of thought in the early Church. But are 'his enemies' yet put under his feet? And who are 'his enemies'? There is one line of thought which regards his enemies as powers and principalities and as already subject (I Pet. iii. 22; Eph. i. 20–2); in the other line of thought although he is already sitting at God's right hand he still waits for God to subject his enemies to him (Acts ii. 34 f.; I Cor. xv. 25; Heb. i. 13; x. 12 f.).[6] This latter appears to be the more primitive conception and failing any direct statement to the contrary is the natural conclusion to draw from the Markan passage: there is yet to be an eschato-logical fulfilment of the Lordship of Christ.[7] The Old Testament text recurs at xiv. 62, the confession of Jesus before the High Priest, where combined with Dan. vii. 13 it again possesses eschatological import. Here surely the High Priest must be included among the enemies of Christ who will be made subject to him. This is the only clue which Mark gives concerning whom he regarded as the enemies of the Lord who were to be made subject to him. The placing of the text in

[1] Cf. Lindars, pp. 46 ff. [2] Bultmann, pp. 51, 136 f.
[3] Taylor; Cranfield, in different ways.
[4] Cf. Hauck. [5] Below, pp. 166 f.
[6] Cf. pp. 184–6 below. [7] Cf. Lohmeyer.

xii. 36 where there is controversy between Jesus and the Jewish leaders might again suggest that the enemies are these leaders, that is, men and women. There is no indication that he included powers and principalities among the enemies of Jesus – or that he excluded them. For Mark the moment of subjection is neither cross, resurrection nor ascension. All these things have happened and the enemies are not yet subject. In particular the Cross is not the moment of subjection. If however we take the less probable interpretation of xii. 36, namely that in line with I Pet. iii. 22 and Eph. i. 20–2 it refers to powers and principalities as already subject, then this must be the subjection that took place in the binding of Satan in the Temptation.

xii. 37b–40 continues the conflict between Jesus and the Jewish leaders; the crowd at this stage is not included among the enemies of Jesus as Mark makes clear by his 'seam' (37b). The difference between the common people and the authorities is underlined in xii. 41–4, where the widow's mite is acceptable though the gifts of the rich are not.[1]

With ch. xiii, the Little Apocalypse, we are not concerned in detail. The connecting seams are brief and give no information about the activity of Jesus, other than that he is represented as teaching. But the final verse (37) is important: what Mark says here is for all Christians. Chs. xi, xii have been leading up to the Passion story, yet at this point (ch. xiii) the narrative seems to break off into another theme, the return of Jesus and the consummation of all. Here Mark sets out the subjection of his enemies to him which he has already indicated in xii. 35–7a. This is still future.[2] For the Christian believer there remain

---

[1] This pericope seems at first sight meaningless in relation to the main purpose of Mark. We only understand its importance when we link it closely to xiii. 1–4 (the chapter division at this point is most misleading). xiii. 2 predicts the destruction of the temple to which the woman has given her whole possessions. Jesus commends the woman and prophesies the destruction of that to which she has given her all! Surely this juxtaposition fits the situation of the readers: their world seems to be falling around them in the persecutions they are enduring; need they then give up the ordinary duties of morality and the upkeep of the Christian mission? Like the widow they must continue to give: despite the catastrophic conditions under which they live they must continue the ordinary duties of Christian service.

[2] In regard to what we may learn from ch. xiii about the return of Christ and Mark's editing, cf. Marxsen, pp. 101–40.

many hard days before that consummation. 'Chapter xiii is a great divine prophecy of the ultimate salvation of the elect after and indeed through unprecedented and unspeakable suffering, trouble and disaster.'[1] But is also serves to remind us before we come to the terrible narrative of the crucifixion of the nature of him who is to be crucified; the Jewish authorities did not understand whom they were putting to death; Mark makes sure we do. To reassure us of the ultimate solution Mark might well have put this section after the Resurrection, where it might seem to come logically, but he deliberately puts it earlier so that we see the whole Passion in the light of the ultimate victory of the return of Christ.

The Passion narrative in some form must always have been a part of the Christian tradition. It is difficult to see how the death of Jesus could have been referred to at all in preaching without some account being given of how it had taken place and an attempt made to show that Jesus was not guilty but innocent; moreover it is likely that from the beginning his death was shown as in accord with the will of God and also that men were held responsible for it.[2] If the Passion narrative was so used in the early community it is obvious that there are certain parts of it, for example the account of the Last Supper, which are not germane to this purpose and must have been added later. This additional material consists of two kinds: some of it, for example the account of the Last Supper, could be inserted at no other point in the total Gospel story than in the Passion narrative; some of it could have been inserted earlier in the Gospel but has been adapted to the Passion narrative, for example the Anointing (xiv. 3–9). We are not here making a judgement on the historicity of the material Mark used; even if it were argued that Jesus never kept the Last Supper with his disciples yet very early in the course of the tradition an account of this took its place closely tied to the death of Christ; from its first telling it can never have had any other place but in the

[1] Lightfoot, *Gospel*, p. 48. Cf. pp. 48–59 for a discussion of the detailed links which join ch. xiii to chs. xiv, xv.
[2] It is unnecessary to argue these points in detail: cf. Taylor, pp. 653 ff.; Dibelius, pp. 178 ff.; Schmidt, pp. 303 ff.; Knox, I, 115 ff.; Lightfoot, *History*, pp. 126 ff.; T. A. Burkill, 'St Mark's Philosophy of the Pa⸻' *N.T.* II (1958), 245–71.

context of the death of Jesus. Mark then had no control over the placing of this incident. We cannot however go on to argue that under no circumstances could Mark omit it from his account of the Passion; John succeeded in doing exactly that. Mark may be suspected of including it for at least two reasons: (*a*) as an account of the origin of the Eucharist; (*b*) for the light it throws on an understanding of the Passion. From these general considerations we must now turn to the narrative itself. It will be seen that the seams connecting incidents are of much less importance in the Passion narrative than elsewhere – by reason of the very fact that it was a connected narrative before Mark began work on it.

It is generally accepted that xiv. 1, 2, 10, 11 must have been the original beginning to the Passion narrative into which Mark has set the pericope of the Anointing.[1] This sandwiching of one event by another is a common Markan editorial device (cf. iii. 20 – 35; v. 21 – 43; xi. 12 – 25). The story exists in variant form in Luke vii. 36 – 50 and John xii. 1 – 8. It cannot thus have been firmly attached to the Passion. It may have been told earlier to set out the duties of almsgiving and worship over against one another,[2] but in Mark it is given a definite relation to the death of Jesus by *v.* 8*b*. In the light of the plots of the Jewish authorities it shows that Jesus was well aware of the closeness of his death, and since he accepts the anointing it implies that he accepts the death. He is anointed on the head (contrast Luke and John where the anointing is on the feet): such an anointing implies appointment to an office; it is thus as Messiah, the Anointed, that Jesus willingly goes to his death.[3]

If the account of the Last Supper is an interpolation in the Passion story as used in preaching, it is almost certain that *vv.* 12 – 16 which relate to the preparation for the meal are also

[1] Cf. Taylor; Dibelius, p. 180; Burkill, 'St Mark's Philosophy of the Passion', p. 246, etc.

[2] Burkill, 'St Mark's Philosophy of the Passion', p. 253.

[3] It is unnecessary for us to enter into the discussion of the meaning of εἰς μνημόσυνον αὐτῆς. Jeremias has held that this originally meant that God would remember the woman in the Last Judgemenet ('The Gentile World in the Thought of Jesus', *Bull. S.N.T.S.* III (1952), 21 f.; *Jesus' Promise to the Nations*, pp. 22 f.), but he admits that Mark (and Matthew) must have understood the saying as presupposing a world-wide mission which would remember the woman's action.

a Markan insertion at this point. There is however no editorial significance in its placement here; there is no other possible position for it in the whole Gospel. However it does make clear to us that Mark regarded the Last Supper as a Passover meal. There are indications in xiv. 2, where the Jewish authorities plot the arrest of Jesus before the Feast, that the original narrative adhered to the Johannine dating of the Crucifixion. It is unlikely that Mark made the change; there must have been a second stream of tradition from before his day from which he drew *vv*. 12–16 and in which it was maintained that the Last Supper was a Passover meal. It is sufficient for our purpose to realise that Mark's use of *vv*. 12–16 implies that he did not regard Jesus as the Passover lamb. This is a negative conclusion in regard to Mark's understanding of Jesus and yet not to be ignored for that reason. His more positive understanding of the death of Jesus in relationship to the Last Supper is obviously contained within that account itself (especially *v*. 24), and to this we shall have to return later.[1] However we may say here that just as the Jewish Passover in addition to commemorating a past event looks forward to a future deliverance, so the Christian Eucharist points forward, within the narrative to the death that is to follow and beyond the narrative to the consummation at the end of time.[2]

The account of the preparation for the Lord's Supper is not followed directly by the Supper account itself but there is interpolated the prophecy of the Betrayal. Here again we have Mark's sandwiching effect. The Betrayer is mentioned in *vv*. 10, 11; then comes the preparation for the Last Supper, *vv*. 12–16; then Jesus shows his awareness of the Betrayer's actions, *vv*. 17–21; and this is again followed by the account of the Last Supper *vv*. 22–5. (A kind of double sandwich). If *vv*. 10, 11 with their announcement of the existence of the Betrayer were part of the original narrative then it is likely that *vv*. 17–21 were also. The story of the Betrayer answers the question how the enemies of Jesus came to be able to seize him; *vv*. 17–21 make us realise that Jesus was aware of what was happening and yet did nothing to prevent it. The double reference to eating in *v*. 18 and *v*. 22 reinforces the suggestion that in *vv*. 17–21 and *vv*. 22–5 we have two sources or traditions which Mark has

[1] Below, pp. 144 ff.   [2] Cf. Lightfoot, *History*, pp. 140 f.

brought together.[1] Within *vv.* 17–21 we may note the strong element of predetermination in regard to the death of Jesus (*v.* 21, 'just as it is written' and *v.* 18, if ὁ ἐσθίων is the correct text, is a quotation of Ps. xli (xl). 10).

Taylor suggests that *vv.* 26–31 are a Markan construction and this appears reasonable. It is noticeable that Mark sets the prophecy of the denial of Peter and of the scattering of the disciples on the way to Gethsemane, whereas Luke and John set it in the Upper Room. Mark's positioning brings sharply into contrast the disloyalty of the disciples to Jesus and his own loyalty to his Father. It serves thus to emphasise the evil in men over against which the drama of the Cross is played out. Verse 28 is exceptionally difficult. It can be omitted from the pericope without hindering the flow of thought in relation to the denial of Peter; we may thus assume its introduction by Mark. Set directly after a prophecy of the scattering of the disciples it must refer to their gathering again, and so to a new relationship of Shepherd and sheep which follows on the Resurrection. Whether this new relationship is to take place through the resurrection appearances themselves or through the Parousia has been disputed; the answer is closely linked to the understanding of the use of 'Galilee' in Mark.[2] Whichever of these two points of view be accepted[3] the verse is presumably inserted here, first, to set the Passion in the light of the eventual triumph of the Resurrection and/or Parousia and, secondly, to show that our Lord himself expected the continuance of the fellowship of the disciples both with himself and with one another. Out of the Cross there comes a Christ who will draw together again those who have failed him.

The incident in Gethsemane, *vv.* 32–42, reads like an amalgam of two separate accounts,[4] probably two separate narratives of the same incident. It begins by telling how Jesus

[1] Bultmann, pp. 265 f., 276.

[2] Lightfoot, *Locality*, pp. 111–26; Lohmeyer, *Galiläa und Jerusalem*, pp. 10–14, 26–36; Marxsen, pp. 36 ff.; M. Karnetzki, 'Die Galiläische Redaktion im Markusevangelium', *Z. N. T. W.* LII (1961), 238–72.

[3] We believe that the reference is to the resurrection appearances; cf. below, pp. 173 ff.

[4] Cf. Bultmann, pp. 267 f.; Bussmann, I, 193 ff.; Knox, pp. 125 ff.; R. Thiel, *Drei Markus-Evangelien*, pp. 23, 65–8; though these reach different conclusions as to the division of the material.

leaves his disciples and says that he is going to pray (*v*. 32). But he is then said to take the inner three, Peter, James and John, and he talks to them (*vv*. 33, 34*a*); these again he leaves telling them to wait for him (*v*. 34*b*). If we follow the narrative strictly only Peter, James and John will have been with him at the time of the arrest (*vv*. 42 – 3), yet in *v*. 50 'all' are said to flee, which suggests the whole company of the disciples rather than the three. There is again the paralleling of the passing of the hour (*v*. 35) and the taking away of the cup (*v*. 36). By the very fact that Mark feels compelled to bring together these accounts so that nothing is omitted he emphasises the importance of the incident. Certainly for the early Church a large part of this importance lay in the references to the correct attitude to trial – cf. *v*. 38, and the praying attitude of our Lord – but we may also discern both the incomprehension of the disciples even at this late hour concerning what is about to happen to their master and the attitude of Christ himself towards the fate that lay ahead of him. Whereas in the Temptation and the Baptism, where we might have expected Mark if he was at all biographically inclined to have said something about the struggle in the soul of Jesus, we do not find such, here we are given a glimpse. Mark, who at the time of writing will have known of the death of many martyrs, must have been very much aware of the difference in the attitude of Jesus and of those who like Stephen went most joyfully to their death. Despite the manner in which Mark has shown Jesus to be conscious of the necessity of his death he now shows him afraid before it.[1] This may appear an inconsistency; if so it is an inconsistency which must have been forced on Mark by the material itself. But it may not be an inconsistency. On the one hand Mark shows the death of Jesus as predetermined and on the other he shows sinful men engineering it. We see their sin not only in the plotting of the Jewish authorities but also in the incomprehension of the disciples; already we are aware that one of them will betray him and another deny him. These two lines of thought now come together in Gethsemane; Spirit[2] and flesh are opposed;

---

[1] We may note that Luke omits *v*. 33 and thereby reduces the fear shown by Jesus. We find it difficult to minimise this element in Mark as Ebeling does (*Das Messiasgeheimnis und die Botschaft des Marcus-Evangelisten*, pp. 174 – 8).

[2] We take τὸ πνεῦμα in *v*. 38 to refer to the Spirit of God; cf. above, p. 30.

God and man are opposed; evil now comes as close to Jesus as it possibly can; it attacks from within. At the conclusion of the incident the element of predetermination reappears, 'the hour is come' (*v.* 41) and Jesus hands himself over to 'sinners'. His destiny lies in their hands; their plots will now have their issue.

The next pericope, *vv.* 43–52, the arrest of Jesus, probably contains an original core, *vv.* 43–6, recounting the actual arrest, to which Mark has added various sayings and peripheral incidents. We observe that he describes Jesus again as teaching (*v.* 49). That there were many around the temple who needed healing is shown by the story of the crippled beggar at the gate (Acts iii), but there is no reference to Jesus as healing. His main activity is teaching.

Verses 53–72 are again a sandwich of which the central portion is the trial before the High Priest and the first and third parts concern the failure of Peter when put to the test of loyalty; this again suggests a Markan arrangement.[1] It is unlikely that the denial of Peter formed a part of the original Passion narrative, but some form of the trial must have appeared in order to show the innocence of Jesus and to make clear the grounds of his condemnation. This the present account certainly does. Jesus affirms that he is the Son of the Blessed, the Christ.[2] The impressiveness of this statement is driven home by the silence of Jesus before false accusations.[3] He however clearly attests his true being and this is followed directly by the statement that all held him worthy of death (*v.* 64). Whether Jesus

---

[1] It has been analysed in different ways; cf. Taylor; Bultmann, pp. 269–71; Knox, pp. 131 ff.; Bussmann, pp. 198 ff.; etc.; the trial may be a doublet of xv. 1. Dibelius (pp. 192 f., 213) rightly views the trial before the High Priest as the central action in the Markan account.

[2] The Markan text may have originally read σὺ εἶπας ὅτι ἐγώ εἰμι. Such a supposition accounts more easily for the Matthean and Lukan text and also takes account of the variation in the Markan textual tradition; cf. Taylor, *ad loc.* If so, the reply is not a direct affirmation; it implies that the statement is true with a different interpretation. Mark's readers would, of course, take it as an affirmation of Sonship and Messiahship. We do not need to inquire what the High Priest meant by his question (if he asked it in that form); Mark takes it in its full sense of 'sonship'. Cf. J. Blinzler, *Der Prozess Jesu*[2] (Regensburg, 1955), p. 76.

[3] Verse 58 is difficult. It may rest on a genuine statement of Jesus (so most commentators), but Mark clearly indicates it is a false accusation. It thus serves to highlight the true grounds of condemnation.

really maintained a secrecy about his own being or not, Mark draws out in unmistakable terms the nature of that being and the resultant necessity of death. Jesus is both Christ and Son of the Blessed, that is Son of God. Here come together two titles which have been chasing one another through the Gospel. From the beginning (even if the reading υἱοῦ θεοῦ is false in i. 1), Jesus has been set out as Son of God in the voice at the Baptism, at the Transfiguration and in the cries of the demons. He has been hailed as Messiah by Peter in the confession at Caesarea Philippi, in the entry into Jerusalem and in the Anointing (xiv. 3 – 9). Now Mark brings these two titles together. We tend to separate them in our discussions of their origin and probable meaning. It may well be that Mark did not see the distinction between them that we do but regarded them almost as interchangeable.[1] In any case it is because of the central picture of Jesus exemplified in these two terms that Mark has given us in his Gospel that he is put to death. Jesus continues after the affirmation of his nature and status to say that the High Priest will see his power. But when Mark writes the High Priest of that time is already dead. Mark must have also then seen meaning in this statement for his own readers. They will see the Christ in his glory. We are recalled here to the Little Apocalypse. The ultimate victory is as certain as the imminent death; and since the death has already happened Mark's readers may be assured that they will see the victory.[2]

xv. 1 gives in summary form the trial of Jesus before the Jewish authorities. They then hand him over to Pilate. Verse 2 reads as an addition to the original account; in vv. 3 – 5 Jesus is said to have answered nothing, yet in v. 2 he has spoken to Pilate even if it was only very ambiguously. Though xv. 2 is an addition to the account it is very unlikely that Mark of his own accord introduces Jesus at this point as the King of the Jews. The kingship motif sounds all through this stage of the Passion; cf. vv. 9, 12, 17 f., 26, 32. Though Mark has brought this title of

---

[1] Cf. Wrede, *Das Messiasgeheimnis in den Evangelien*, pp. 75–7; but see below, pp. 107 f., 165–73.

[2] Even if we accept the interpretation of J. A. T. Robinson, *Jesus and His Coming*, pp. 43 ff. (cf. Taylor), that the original reference in ἐρχόμενον (xiv. 62) related to the Son of Man's going to God, Mark will still have viewed it as a victory which his readers are to behold; the High Priest never saw it fulfilled; Mark's readers may.

Jesus into extreme prominence yet it will have lain in the tradition and may indeed go back to the inscription on the Cross: Pilate must have had some grounds for condemning Jesus. 'King of the Jews' is the political side of the Messianic title; that this is so appears in *v.* 32 where we have the variant, 'The Christ, the King of Israel'; here Jews speak; on the other occasions it was Gentiles who used the title, 'King of the Jews'. It is clear that Mark wishes us to see Jesus condemned and crucified as the Jewish Messiah. It is also clear that he does not wish this to be taken in a political sense. The political leader is Jesus Barabbas[1] who is set in contrast to Jesus the Christ. The ambiguous answer of Jesus to Pilate (xv. 2) implies that while Jesus accepts the title of King he queries the meaning Pilate reads into it. 'It is an affirmation which implies that the speaker would put things differently.'[2] Pilate quite obviously does not see Jesus as a dangerous political offender. Indeed the encounter with Pilate serves to underline the hostility of the Jews to Jesus in that it shows Pilate making some attempt to save him. Not only are the Jewish leaders now involved in this hostility but so also is the crowd (xv. 11 ff.). In contrast the innocence of Jesus is again shown clearly (xv. 14).

There follows the account of the mocking by the soldiers, xv. 16–20*a*, the theme of which repeats that of xiv. 65 and appears again in xv. 29–32. The humiliation of Jesus is heavily underlined in this threefold repetition. The evil in men is again displayed in the presence of the Messianic Son of God. It is probable that Mark has added each of these accounts of the mocking to the original Passion narrative.[3] In the first account certain anonymous people in the house of the High Priest mock him,[4] in the second, Roman soldiers, in the third, passers-by (i.e. presumably the 'crowd'),[5] the High Priests and scribes

---

[1] We assume, with most modern commentators, that the original reading in Matt. xxvii. 16 was Ἰησοῦν Βαραββᾶν and that Matthew copied this from an original Ἰησοῦς Βαραββᾶς in Mark xv. 7. στασιαστής, στάσις (xv. 7) suggest revolution. As against this view, cf. R. Dunkerley, 'Was Barabbas also called Jesus?', *E. T.* LXXIV (1963), 126 f.   [2] Taylor, *ad loc.*

[3] So Taylor; Bultmann, pp. 271, 284; etc.; cf. P. Winter, *On the Trial of Jesus* (Berlin, 1961), pp. 21 f.

[4] It almost reads as if Mark intended us to view the High Priests as themselves carrying out the mockery; cf. Knox, p. 132.

[5] In Luke the crowd watches but does not mock.

and the crucified thieves. Thus no section of humanity stands apart from the general hostility. On each occasion the mocking attacks a claim that might be made for Jesus: the first, that he was a prophet; the second, that he was King of the Jews; the third, that he could save and that he was the Messiah. In the third we may note how the word σῴζειν is used; this cannot be detached from its soteriological reference; Jesus as Messiah is the one who saves men; this is why he dies. Here Mark is implicitly setting out the purpose of the life and death of Jesus and it is connected to his relationship to men, not his relationship to the demonic world.

The section xv. 20b–32 describes the actual carrying out of the crucifixion. Probable Markan additions within it are the reference to Simon of Cyrene (v. 21), the notice of time (v. 25) and, as we have already mentioned, the mocking (vv. 31, 32). Apart from their role in the mocking Mark makes no explicit use of his mention of the two thieves, though the later textual tradition makes clear reference to Isa. liii. 12. So many of Mark's Old Testament references are indirect that it is possible, though not likely, that he intended such a reference here.

xv. 33–41 describes the incidents attending the death of Jesus. In particular we may notice the darkness (v. 33), his great cries (vv. 34, 37), the rending of the temple veil (v. 38) and the confession of the centurion (v. 39). All these are in some sense signs of the tremendous event that is taking place. Which part of this material was original to the Passion narrative and which has been added by Mark is not easy to determine. It is easy to say that the references to the darkness and the temple veil are legendary, but that does not mean that they had not been added to the account prior to Mark. It is possible also to argue that the two references to a great cry by Jesus (vv. 34 and 37) are doublets (Luke gives the great cry in another form xxiii. 46), but again we cannot be sure that Mark has added one or other.[1] We may assume that the original Passion account has under-

[1] For an analysis of xv. 33–41 see the various commentators, Bultmann, pp. 273 f.; Knox, pp. 142 ff.; F. C. Grant, *The Earliest Gospel*, pp. 175 ff. Taylor, pp. 649–51, 653–64 is particularly valuable. Schreiber, p. 157, n. 5, gives an analysis different from that usually found, holding that Mark added vv. 34b–36, 39–41. Details of his analysis are lacking, but are apparently to appear in a future work.

gone modification and that Mark agrees with the form of it which he produces. There is then first the strange natural portent of darkness; this cannot be taken other than as a cosmic event. There are many references to natural portents accompanying the death of great men[1] and this may well be the present intention of the reference. But the darkening of the sun is also a sign that judgement is taking place (Amos viii. 9; Jer. xv. 9; Mark xiii. 24).[2] This judgement is not however a judgement on nature or the powers of evil but on men, the darkness signifying the moment of enactment. We may observe that Matthew increases the cosmic emphasis in the sense that he records further unusual events, namely the earthquake, the split rocks, opened tombs and the reappearance of dead saints (xxvii. 51–4). This by no means implies that Matthew takes a more 'cosmic' view of the death of Jesus, in the sense that it has to do with the defeat of cosmic powers, than Mark does. The recording of unusual events, as the darkness, is not then necessarily a sign that the powers of evil are being judged. In Matthew and in Mark it is men who are being judged and the darkness is a sign of this. If this is the interpretation it coheres with the rending of the veil in that both denote judgement on Israel[3] (in both Amos viii. 9 and Jer. xv. 9 it is the chosen people or Jerusalem that is judged) and Mark has prepared us for this judgement on Israel by the way he has shown the continued

---

[1] Virg. *Georgics* I, 466 ff.; Diog. Laert. IV, 64; Plut. *Pelop.* 295 A (31, 2); cf. Strack-Billerbeck, I, 1040–2.   [2] Cf. Iren. *Adv. Haer.* IV, 33, 12.

[3] While it is probably true that for apologetic reasons Mark with the other evangelists attempted to lay the blame for the death of Jesus as far as possible on the Jews (Winter, *On the Trial of Jesus*, stresses this much more than Blinzler, *Der Prozess Jesu*[2]), it must not be overlooked that this was also a theological tendency within his work; Jesus is at issue with the Pharisees from the beginning (iii. 6); the Cross is judgement on Judaism (the rending of the veil, the darkness, the destruction of the temple and its rebuilding in three days). Judaism must therefore be shown to be fully involved in the crucifixion.

This does not imply that Judaism alone came under judgement. We must remember: (*a*) Pilate is in part responsible for Jesus' death and therefore under judgement; (*b*) many Jews, for instance the disciples, are not under judgement but through the Cross have become members of the new community which replaced Judaism; (*c*) the Jews come under judgement principally because they have been God's People; judgement must begin at the House of God, but it does not end there.

opposition of the Jews to Jesus. The veil may be either that separating the Holy of Holies from the Holy Place or that separating the Holy Place from the outer courtyard. If it was the outer veil its rending must indicate a judgement on Judaism;[1] if it was the inner this element of judgement will still remain but there will be added to it the sense of open access to God (cf. Heb. vi. 19 f.; ix. 8; x. 19 f.).[2] Into this same complex of ideas it would seem we must also fit the mocking of the passers-by who repeated the false accusation that Jesus would destroy the Temple and build it again in three days (xv. 29; xiv. 58). The rending of the veil is in effect the destruction of the Temple. It will be rebuilt in three days – with the Resurrection the new community will be formed (xvi. 7). The conception of the Christian community as the temple was a commonplace of early Christianity, a temple not made with hands but spiritual.[3] Whatever the original intention of this accusation this reference to the destruction of Israel and the creation of the new community through the death and Resurrection of Jesus would appear to be Mark's aim in recording the words as part of the mocking at this point.[4] If the rending of the veil indicates judgement on Israel's exclusive way to God and the removal of a barrier preventing access to him it is also appropriate that it is immediately followed by the confession of the Gentile centurion that Jesus is the Son of God.[5] This title has played too big a part in the Gospel for it to be taken at this point as the testimony of an eye-witness to the courageous death of a martyr; such may be the Lukan interpretation (xxiii. 47), but

[1] Jesus' judgement on the Law is earlier emphasised by Mark (ii. 23 – iii. 5; vii. 1–23, especially vii. 19b). This element in Mark is played down by Matthew; cf. Bornkamm in Bornkamm, Barth and Held, *Tradition and Interpretation in Matthew*, p. 31, n. 2. The rending of the veil is also found in Gnosticism; cf. R. McL. Wilson, *The Gospel of Philip* (London, 1962), pp. 139 ff., 189 ff. The theme connected to it is not usually 'judgement'.

[2] Cf. Test. Levi x. 3 f.; Test. Benj. ix. 3 f. On the variant tradition in the Gosp. Heb., cf. Klostermann, *ad loc.* It seems too fanciful to connect the rending of the veil with the rending of the heavens at the Baptism as Lightfoot, *Gospel*, pp. 55 f.; Yates, *The Spirit and the Kingdom*, pp. 232–7.

[3] Cf. Best, *One Body in Christ*, pp. 160 ff. and the references given there.

[4] Cf. Lindars, pp. 66 ff.

[5] Cf. Lohmeyer. It would be to go too far to take the rending of the veil as the removal of a covering which permits the true Son of God to be seen in the crucified Jesus; the veil rent, the centurion sees and believes.

in Mark it is clearly a confession of faith. In Matthew (xxvii. 54) the centurion utters his confession on seeing the earthquake and darkness; in Mark he makes it on hearing the final cry of Jesus and observing his death.[1]

It has been suggested that the strong cry, which is mentioned twice (*vv.* 34, 37), is surprising in a crucified man, who would normally die slowly from exhaustion,[2] and must therefore be given special significance as a cry of triumph. But Jesus died unexpectedly early for a victim of crucifixion who usually lingered many days in his agony; this is recognised in Mark in Pilate's amazement at Jesus' early death (xv. 44). It is possible that the great cry was the immediate cause of his death in using up his available reserves of strength. Obviously we are concerned only with the second great cry (*v.* 37) – the first (*v.* 34) is the cry of dereliction and cannot contain the thought of triumph. The two cries were probably originally doublets, though Mark will not necessarily have regarded them as such. Yet if the second great cry is to be taken as different in content from the first we might expect some clear indication of its meaning. Schreiber[3] suggests that we should see it as the cry of victory in exaltation since it is immediately followed by the confession of the centurion, who uses the words that apply to the exalted one, namely, the Son of God (cf. Ps. ii. 7). But it is difficult to see in Mark sufficient grounds for identifying the moment of death with that of exaltation.[4] Moreover alternative explanations of the great cry are possible. Luke (xxiii. 46) and John (xix. 30) both give interpretations of it in which they take it as a cry of triumph in the sense that the task set to Jesus by God has been completed; what has been predetermined throughout the whole Gospel, his death, has now been brought to its end in obedience. Such an explanation may be traced in Mark's view of the centurion's words as his recognition of Jesus as Son of God. If, as we believe, there is a close connection

[1] The text of Mark is difficult at this point, but probably originally contained a reference here to the 'cry' of Jesus; thus Taylor; Cranfield; Lohmeyer; etc., reading κράξας (or ἔκραξεν καί) before ἐξέπνευσεν.

[2] Cf. Klostermann; Lagrange; Wellhausen; *ad v.* 39.

[3] P. 163. Cf. H. W. Bartsch, 'Historische Erwägungen zur Leidensgeschichte', *Evangelische Theologie*, XXII (1962), 449–59.

[4] Cf. below. pp. 130 ff.

between this title and the sacrifice by Abraham of Isaac then the centurion's confession of him as Son may be linked to the great cry in that it is the cry of triumphant obedience to the sacrifice required and signifies willing acceptance of it. No ram is forthcoming to replace the Son on the Cross and he now accepts that there is no deliverance for him.[1] We are not then required to see in the great cry a shout of victory over opposing spiritual powers. The very fact that it is a man, the centurion, who confesses Jesus in the moment of death, and not a cosmic power which bends the knee to him, shows that Mark is setting the death of Jesus firmly in relationship to men: it is an event whose significance exists for man, rather than for nature or the spiritual powers.

Lastly we must look at the content of the earlier cry, the cry of dereliction (*v.* 34). Mark underlines its importance, first by quoting the Aramaic, the actual words of Jesus,[2] and then giving a translation, and secondly by recounting how the group around the Cross misunderstood it. It comes at the end of the period of darkness and yet within that period; if that darkness signifies judgement then Mark is indicating that Jesus is, as we might say, at the wrong end of judgement. If Israel is judged and forsaken by God (the veil of the Temple is rent) then in Jesus that judgement is seen executed; there are places within the Gospel, the Temptation, the Baptism, where Mark appears to look on Jesus as Israel; this may be another such passage. It is probably also to be linked to Gethsemane: Jesus encounters the evil within and outside the soul of man; only evil could drive God away from man.

The second piece of mockery in this passage, when Jesus' words on the Cross are misunderstood and he is offered a drink to prolong his life so that the spectators may see if Elijah will come to his aid (xv. 35 f.), must underline the sacrifice of Jesus.[3]

[1] Perhaps the first great cry (*v.* 34) might then refer to his disappointment that God had not produced the necessary ram. God had not forsaken Isaac but provided the substitute. Here there is no substitute provided; the Son must be the sacrifice.

[2] We need not delay to argue whether Jesus spoke Hebrew or Aramaic; obviously Mark understood him to speak Aramaic, witness to which are the other Aramaic phrases preserved in the Gospel.

[3] It may represent the combination of two traditions, 35, 36*b* and 36*a*; cf. Taylor.

Elijah, = John the Baptist, has already come and suffered a Passion. Though popular Jewish belief looked on Elijah as one who would come in the hour of need,[1] he has already come, been rejected and cannot come again. Perhaps there is deeper irony: Elijah's coming was to be associated with judgement (Mal. iii. 1 ff.); judgement is now being suffered by the one whom Elijah would have expected to execute it.

In the last two verses xv. 40 f. of the section on the death of Jesus Mark mentions the women who watched the crucifixion. He names women again in the next section concerning the burial (xv. 42–7) and again in the story of the empty tomb (xvi. 1–8).[2] It may be that he wishes to emphasise them as eye-witnesses, but the threefold repetition of the names suggests rather that he is putting together three sections which were once separate. Whether this is so or not there is nothing in xv. 42–7 which concerns us. xvi. 1–8 is the necessary completion to the story of the Cross: necessary because in the Markan predictions of the Cross the Resurrection has always been mentioned; it is a part of that which is determined beforehand. Whatever the significance of *v.* 7 it meant that Jesus is raised for the benefit of his followers: they are to see him again in Galilee.[3] Thus the meaning of the Cross and Resurrection is again tied down to its relationship to the believer rather than given a cosmic setting in relation to the subjection of evil powers. Out of the event of death and resurrection the new community emerges.

[1] Cf. Strack-Billerbeck, IV, 769 ff.

[2] The Western text omits the women at xvi. 1 and may be original.

[3] On Galilee cf. below, pp. 173 ff. xvi. 7 is probably a Markan addition, cf. Bultmann, p. 287; Johnson (*ad* xiv. 28); Burkill, 'St Mark's Philosophy of the Passion', p. 271, etc.

CHAPTER IV

THE SELECTION OF THE MATERIAL

WHEN we ask why Mark has chosen the particular pericopae which we find in this Gospel we meet an initial difficulty: we do not know what material was available to him out of which he could select. If we knew that Mark had a great amount of material about the teaching of Jesus, say a 'copy' of Q and only three exorcism accounts, and chose to omit most of the teaching and put in all three exorcisms, this would obviously lead us to conclude that for him exorcisms were most important. Equally had he at his disposal only the teaching of Jesus which he has inserted and a hundred exorcism stories from which he selected the present three then we would come to quite a different conclusion about the importance of the exorcisms for Mark. Unfortunately we are not in a position to draw either conclusion. We may note that most of the expansion of Matthew and Luke is in the direction of giving fuller teaching by Jesus; in proportion there are not added as many new pronouncement stories and miracles as direct teaching. This would suggest that Mark used most of the available material about the activities of Jesus, other than about his teaching. We must not therefore assume that Mark had unlimited material at his disposal (cf. John xxi. 25) from which he made a judicious or injudicious selection. The early Church may already have trimmed down the amount of available material and left Mark with little from which to select. That Matthew and Luke give more teaching of Jesus does not mean that Mark deliberately eliminated most of this material as if suggesting that Jesus was a man of action rather than of speech; it may not have been available to him; in any case we have seen how in his editorial seams Mark has stressed the fact that Jesus taught.

But even if Mark was fairly well confined to certain material and did not have an unlimited choice we may still ask why he has included the material that he has. There was naturally no radical cleavage between Mark and the early Church in which he found the material and he will have included it for very similar reasons to that which led to its preservation, or creation, within the Christian community. He may also have had additional private reasons of his own, as we might say, but he will hardly have greatly disagreed with the reasons of the early Church. To look at the material itself may give some indication of the reasons for its inclusion. To ask why a particular incident has been included might be answered formally by saying that the evangelists included it because it happened. But many things happened which they have not included. Jesus must have eaten every day of his ministry, but they do not record these meals; yet certain meals are recorded: a meal with Levi, because of the sayings about the purpose of the ministry to which it leads (ii. 13 – 17); a final meal with his disciples, because in it the early Church (including Mark) saw the basis for its own celebration of the Eucharist (xiv. 12 – 25); and two mass feedings (vi. 30 – 44; viii. 1 – 9). These are all recorded because they have greater significance than other meals which were eaten only with the intention of nourishing the body.

We may begin by looking at what we may term the 'mighty works' of Jesus, the miracles and healings.[1] And since we have already mentioned the two mass feedings we commence with them. They are obviously linked through their wording with the Eucharist; they are also connected with the Old Testament manna feedings in the wilderness and seemingly thereby with the expected eschatological meal. But we must not forget that they show us Jesus as the wonder-worker who is able to supply the needs of men; he has compassion upon them (viii. 2). Men should open their eyes to behold in the giver of food for the thousands the one who can supply all their needs.[2] We have already seen[3] that by his linking of the feeding incidents to vi. 34 *b* and viii. 14 – 21 Mark indicates that one of the needs of

[1] G. H. Boobyer, 'The Redaction of Mark iv. 1–34', has argued that in iv. 12 τὰ πάντα includes not only the strictly so-called parables but also the δυνάμεις and διδαχή of Jesus. We have ourselves seen (pp. 80 f.) the connection between Jesus as teacher and mysterious sayings, i.e. παραβολαί. If the δυνάμεις, as seems likely, are also to be included among the παραβολαί then they must be carefully examined for the meaning they reveal to the eye of faith.

[2] Hunger need not necessarily be for material food but can be given a spiritual turn, e.g. Amos viii. 11; Isa. lv. 1; Ps. xlii (xli). 2 – 4; Matt. v. 6.

[3] Pp. 76 f.

the soul which Jesus meets is that of true teaching. Jesus may then, in the Markan interpretation, be seen as the one who brings spiritual understanding to men; if they will but look at what he, the wonder-worker, has done, they will understand (viii. 17, 18, 21). This would represent the Markan interpretation as distinct from, and over and above, that of the early Church.

Closely allied to the two feedings are the two accounts of storms on the Sea of Galilee (iv. 35–41; vi. 45–52);[1] indeed Mark has deliberately linked the second to the first feeding (vi. 52).[2] In both instances the astonishment of the disciples serves to underline the greatness of their master; there is no situation in which he is not supreme. There seems no reason to doubt that the traditional interpretation of the second of these passages is basically correct, namely that in moments of testing the Christ will come to the ship of the Church and bring calm. This may be conceived both as a present coming of the risen Lord in every emergency[3] and also as his once-for-all coming in the Parousia to bring final deliverance. The same thought of deliverance from times of testing lies in the first account (iv. 35–41),[4] but here the storm that has come on the Church is regarded as of demonic origin: it is rebuked in very similar words to those in which demons are rebuked (i. 25).[5] Accord-

---

[1] Whether they are parallel accounts of one incident and what measure of historical kernel they contain it is not necessary for us to determine.

[2] Verse 52 is a Markan comment; it is omitted by Matthew.

[3] This story may either have received colouring from the resurrection narratives or itself been originally a resurrection narrative transferred to the pre-resurrection period; cf. C. H. Dodd, 'The Appearances of the Risen Christ: An Essay in Form-Criticism of the Gospels', in *Studies in the Gospels* (ed. D. E. Nineham), pp. 9–35. Loisy views it as a symbolic representation of the Resurrection itself.

[4] P. J. Achtemeier, 'Person and Deed. Jesus and the Storm-Tossed Sea', *Interpretation*, XVI (1962), 169–76 considers that the stilling of the storm depicts Jesus as the one who turns chaos into order. The sea represents the power of chaos; but in the Old Testament (Ps. lxxiv; Isa. li. 9 f.; etc.) 'God's work of creation and his work of redemption are … closely linked'. Thus the stilling of the storm is an act of redemption. Similarly, we might add, to walk on the sea (vi. 45–52) is a sign of his power over demonic chaos (cf. Job ix. 8; Ps. lxxvii (lxxvi). 20).

[5] Hoskyns and Davey, *The Riddle of the New Testament*, pp. 69–71 have shown the inner Old Testament links which connect iv. 35–41 and v. 1–20.

ingly Jesus is depicted as the deliverer of men from evil, including that which may be directly traced to the activity of evil
supernatural powers. Jesus is present in the Church, the ship;
so believers need not be afraid in the midst of persecution. This
takes us on to the exorcisms in which again we see Jesus as the
deliverer of men from demonic forces. The early Church continued to practise exorcism (Acts xvi. 16–18; cf. xix. 13), and
certainly one factor in the preservation of these stories will have
been that of example: this is how to carry out an exorcism (cf.
ix. 29, a verse omitted in Matthew and Luke; indeed in this
whole pericope the method of Jesus is contrasted with the
method, or the lack of it, of the disciples; there is on this occasion no confession of Jesus by the demon and no instruction
to silence by Jesus). Two peculiarly Markan factors enter into
the exorcism accounts: the confession by the demons of the
Divine Sonship of Jesus (i. 24, 34; iii. 11; v. 7) and the testimony
that a successful exorcism gives to the fact that Jesus has already
conquered Satan (iii. 27). Possibly the command to silence laid
by Jesus on the demons should also be listed here as a Markan
factor, but it is part of a more general command to silence about
his healing activity. The exorcism stories therefore both bear
witness directly to the being of Jesus and to his activity in his
already accomplished victory over Satan and his continued
ability to deliver men from Satan's underlings.

In all the remaining healing stories Jesus is again set forth
as the one who performs mighty works.[1] They are recounted
because they show us Jesus as the mighty deliverer of men, this
time from sickness, and because they are examples to the early
Church of how to carry on healing activity. Various types of
healing are signs of the eschatological age – though this appears
more clearly in Matthew (xi. 5) and Luke (vii. 22). We have
already seen that Mark makes in ii. 1–12 a strong connection
between the forgiveness of sin and the healing of sickness.[2] The
same is true of the preceding miracle (i. 40–5), where a leper is

---

[1] But the miracle stories are not told merely to show Jesus as wonder-
worker (iv. 41). The ancient world knew too many such wonder-workers to
be easily convinced by the wonders of another that he was the Son of God.
Cf. A. Richardson, *The Miracle Stories of the Gospels*, pp. 20 ff. Mark makes this
clear at viii. 11 f.

[2] Pp. 69 ff.

cleansed;[1] leprosy was sometimes a punishment for sin (Miriam, Num. xii. 10; Gehazi, II Kings v. 27; Uzziah, II Kings xv. 5);[2] the leper is excluded from the worship of God and when he is accepted as clean it is on the presentation of a sin offering and guilt offering (Lev. xiv. 10 ff.).[3] The same word καθαρίζειν is used of the removal of sin (Acts xv. 9; II Cor. vii. 1; Eph. v. 26; I John i. 7, 9, etc.) and of cleansing from leprosy (i. 40, 41, 42).[4] Leprosy is then a type of sin. But more generally sin and sickness are related. This may be seen in the LXX translation of Isa. liii. 4 where חֳלִי is rendered by ἁμαρτία – a fact of which Matthew makes use (viii. 17). In the LXX rendering of Isa. liii. 3, 4 the servant is said to bear both μαλακία and ἁμαρτία, implying their equivalence; μαλακία may mean 'moral weakness', but in Hellenistic Greek certainly means 'sickness' (cf. Matt. iv. 23; ix. 35; x. 1). A similar connection to that between leprosy and sin may exist also in the case of the woman with the unclean issue of blood (v. 25–34), for those so afflicted were also excluded from Jewish worship (Num. v. 2 ff.).[5] Into the valediction of Jesus, 'Go in Peace', may be read a deeper meaning; peace is not merely health but peace with God, through the reconciliation that has taken place with him in healing and therefore in the restoration to the congregation of Israel.[6]

The healings testify not only to the power of Jesus to forgive sin but also to certain other closely related activities. He gives sight to the blind (viii. 22–6; x. 46–52). Blindness in Mark is not mere pardonable ignorance but culpable rejection of the truth; so the power of Jesus to give sight to the blind lies close

[1] Cf. Lightfoot, *Gospel*, pp. 25 f.

[2] The rabbis also looked on leprosy as a punishment for sin; cf. Moore, II, 149, 248; Strack-Billerbeck, IV, 747 ff.

[3] Richardson (*The Miracle Stories of the Gospels*, p. 61) goes beyond the evidence when he argues that Jesus in touching the leper takes on himself the burden of defilement and is revealed thereby as the sin-bearer. This may be true, but there is no indication in Mark that he wishes us to make this deduction. Jesus often touched the sick in healing.

[4] F. Hauck and R. Meyer, *T.W.N.T.* III, 416 ff. To connect 'cleansing' the leper with sin seems as valid as to connect it to 'unclean' spirit, and so make it 'demonic' as Ling does (*The Significance of Satan*, pp. 14 ff.).

[5] Cf. Richardson, *The Miracle Stories of the Gospels*, p. 61.

[6] Cf. Schniewind, *ad loc.*

to his power to forgive sin. The first of these accounts, the restoration of sight to the blind man of Bethsaida, is closely linked to the blindness of the disciples; in viii. 18 they have been accused of having eyes but not seeing; in the immediately succeeding pericope (viii. 27 – 30) Peter 'sees' Jesus as the Christ. Lightfoot[1] has drawn attention to the close parallels between viii. 22 – 6 and viii. 27 – 30, implying that Mark has deliberately placed this healing story in order to underline the confession of Peter. But the blind man receives his sight in two stages; Peter in viii. 27 – 30 does not yet 'see' fully; he sees Jesus as Messiah, the first stage, but is unwilling to accept what the Messianic ministry involves for Jesus, the second stage. It will require the Resurrection before he is completely restored; hence Peter's confession is followed by the story of the Transfiguration (ix. 2 – 8).[2] At x. 52 the second blind man who is healed immediately becomes a disciple and follows Jesus on the way to Jerusalem and thus on the way to the Cross:[3] receiving his full sight all at once, he takes up his cross (viii. 34) and follows Jesus in the manner which Peter was bidden but rejected; Peter had had his sight only partly restored. The giving of sight to the blind was an eschatological sign (Isa. xxxv. 5 f.; xxix. 18 f., etc.) as was also the making of the dumb to speak and the deaf to hear; this is explicitly brought out in the story of the healing of the deaf man with the impediment in his speech (vii. 32 – 7, see especi-

[1] *History*, pp. 90 f.

[2] Johnson, *ad loc.* A. Kuby, 'Zur Konzeption des Markus-Evangeliums', *Z.N.T.W.* XLIX (1958), 52 – 64, holds somewhat similarly that in the first part of the Gospel (up to viii. 21) the disciples do not understand Jesus, from viii. 27 onwards they understand he is great but misunderstand the nature of his greatness, i.e. they receive their true knowledge of Jesus in stages. viii. 22 – 6 is thus a transition section; cf. x. 46 – 52; xiv. 3 – 9. A. M. Farrar, *A Study in St Mark*, pp. 105 ff. sees similar significance in the two stages of recovery of sight in viii. 22 – 6.

[3] Note the use of the title 'Son of David' in x. 46 – 52 and in the succeeding sections (xi. 9 f.; xii. 35 – 7), and of the almost equivalent 'King of the Jews' in the Passion story. Cf. Kuby, 'Zur Konzeption des Markus-Evangeliums'. J. B. Tyson, 'The Blindness of the Disciples in Mark', *J.B.L.* LXXX (1961), 261 – 8 holds that the original disciples never did come to understand correctly the meaning of Jesus' death and that Mark is writing in conscious opposition to them. Under the influence of Paul he has come to see both its necessity and redemptive significance, to which the Church in Jerusalem still remained blind.

ally *v.* 37). In the raising of Jairus' daughter[1] (v. 21–5, 35–43) the claim is quite obviously made that Jesus has power over death; those believers who have lost loved ones should remember that they are but asleep and that Jesus, who is himself the risen Lord, will raise them.[2]

There are two key-words which run through almost all the healings of Jesus and are closely related to the theme of redemption, namely σῴζειν and πίστις. The first of these possesses the double meaning, 'heal', 'save'. As alternatives ἰᾶσθαι or θεραπεύειν could have been used. The former of these is indeed used once by Mark (v. 29); it is more frequent in the other New Testament writers, and in Jewish Greek and the Apostolic Fathers does attain the same double sense of 'heal' and 'save'.[3] It also possesses this double sense at times in the New Testament (e.g. Matt. xiii. 15). θεραπεύειν does not anywhere have the double sense; it is used by Mark at i. 34; iii. 2, 10; vi. 5, 13. It is significant that every one of these instances except iii. 2 occurs in summary statements of the healing activity of Jesus. In the stories which tell the great deeds of Jesus Mark uses σῴζειν. iii. 2 occurs in what is a Pronouncement Story rather than a healing account. The summaries may emphasise only the great healing activity of Jesus, but the accounts of particular healings take us into the second meaning of σῴζειν; this confirms our analysis that in them we are to see indications of the redemptive power of Jesus. We must now look more closely at those passages in which σῴζειν has the meaning 'save' so that we may learn from another angle what is the inner meaning of the healing miracles. It is interesting to observe that the word is featured in two of the healing stories (v. 25–34; x. 46–52) in which the redemptive significance is otherwise less obvious. That Mark is aware of the redemptive meaning given by the early Church to σῴζειν appears clearly at viii. 35; x. 26; xiii. 13, 20. Most interesting

---

[1] Whether this was originally a story of restoration of life or not need not concern us; for Mark it was such.

[2] Certain other miracles of Jesus are told with emphasis solely on the lesson to be drawn from them and not on the element of great power in Jesus; e.g. the man with the withered hand in the synagogue (iii. 1–5) and the Syro-Phoenician woman's daughter (vii. 24–30).

[3] Cf. Bauer, *Wörterbuch*.

is xv. 30, 31. This has obviously undergone Christian redaction. In *v.* 30 σῶσον will be taken in the sense of 'preserve the life' and can represent an original comment of a mocker, but in *v.* 31, 'He saved others; himself he is not able to save', we may discern the modification or creation of the early Church. If we take the sense of 'preserve life', the second clause could be a true comment, but it is unlikely that the High Priests said that Jesus preserved the lives of others; for taken in relationship to the accounts we have this must refer to saving from death and only Jairus' daughter was so saved. If, however, 'save' means 'heal' in the first clause, which the priests might admit, it cannot mean such in the second. It is easier then to see this as a Christian comment on the crucifixion put into the mouths of the scorners.[1] Jesus is able to save men, but the divine necessity requires that he does not save himself. The reader will connect the 'save' of the first clause both to its occurrences within the Gospel in relation to healing and to his own experience of salvation; he will thus see the first as a pattern for the second.

The second key-word which sounds throughout the healing accounts is πίστις (ii. 5; v. 34; x. 52; cf. iv. 40; πιστεύειν in v. 36; ix. 23, 24; ἀπιστία in vi. 6). But this word, just as much as σῴζειν, is a part of the Christian redemptive vocabulary. The healing stories with the stress they lay on the necessity of faith in God's power working through Jesus are examples to the Christian of the need for faith if he is to be redeemed.

Thus we may conclude that Mark in no way intends us to see the mighty works of Jesus as merely mighty works so that we are only impressed by the miraculous. He uses them to teach about redemption. The element of greatness is not to be ignored: they do set forth the mighty Son of God, but they set him forth as the Redeemer.

When we turn to the other types of material which Mark uses the reason for their inclusion is normally much more obvious. The teaching of Jesus contains within its own content the reason for its selection. It may deal with problems of Christian conduct (xii. 13–17; ii. 18–20; ii. 23–iii. 5, etc.); with difficulties raised for the Christian believer by outsiders (xii. 18–27); with the beginning and nature of discipleship (i. 16–20; ii. 13 f.; x. 17–22; viii. 34–ix. 1; ix. 33–7, etc.); with the nature of

[1] So similarly *vv.* 29 *b* and 36 reflect Christian views.

Christian belief (e.g. the parables of the Kingdom; the Parousia, ch. xiii); with the nature of Christian worship (the Last Supper, and possibly x. 13 – 16 in relationship to the admission of infants to the Church). But in using this material Mark has also given it particular slants of his own; for example, in using the parables he has taken up and emphasised, or created, a theory of the blindness of the crowds and of the disciples. The teaching of Jesus is given with authority (Mark i. 21 – 8); Mark wishes us to see it as a mighty work; in it we see Jesus' glory just as much as in the miracles; for all who come to him he has the answer which cannot be gainsaid (ii. 1 – iii. 6; xi. 27 – xii. 37). Moreover the teaching, as the mighty works, is redemptive because in it men's minds are opened to see the truth. Within the teaching there are statements by Jesus about the purpose of his ministry: these we shall treat later.[1] The remainder of the material largely consists of narrative portions telling us who Jesus is (Baptism, Transfiguration, etc.) and the connected story of the Passion which we have already considered in some detail.

[1] Ch. VI.

CHAPTER V

THE ORDER OF THE MATERIAL

WE turn now to the order in which Mark has put together the
material he has selected. It must be realised that Mark was not
completely master of the situation. The story of the Passion
could not be put at any other point than at the end of his book;
likewise the account of John's preaching and baptism of Jesus
must come at the beginning. Between these two fixed points it
is a matter of conjecture how far genuine biographical considerations ordered the material.[1] Mark's plan of the ministry
in which Jesus does not appear in Jerusalem until the last few
days would not appear to be borne out by the evidence from the
other Gospels. But if Mark has decided that there is only one
short period of ministry in Jerusalem then all the material
concerned with Jerusalem must appear at that point. There is
another way in which Mark may not have been fully master of
the order of his material. Whereas some of it may have come to
him as individual pericopae which he was free to insert where
he wished, some of it also came to him as complexes (i. 16 – 39
or ii. 1 – iii. 5) either in, or aprt from, written sources and he
appears to have kept together at least some of the material that
came to him in this way; at any rate, if he did not, then it would
be impossible today to detect the pre-Markan complexes.

The most striking feature of the Markan arrangement is the
disproportionate amount of space given to the death of Jesus.
This dominates the whole Gospel, being indeed a case of the
tail wagging the dog.[2] Whether or not the thought of the

[1] It will be seen that we side with Professor Nineham rather than with
Professor Dodd on the nature of the order of events in the Gospel of Mark.
Cf. C. H. Dodd, 'The Framework of the Gospel Narratives', *New Testament
Studies*, pp. 1–11, and D. E. Nineham, 'The Order of Events in St Mark's
Gospel – an Examination of Dr Dodd's Hypothesis', in *Studies in the Gospels*
(ed. Nineham), pp. 223–39. Cf. also H. Sawyerr, 'The Marcan Framework',
S.J. Th. XIV (1961), 279–94; H. A. Guy, *The Origin of the Gospel of Mark*,
pp. 20 ff., 48 ff.
[2] M. Kähler's often-quoted dictum is apposite: 'Passionsgeschichte mit
ausführlicher Einleitung.' Cf. Dehn (p. 15), 'Es (the Gospel) ist der weitere
Rahmen zu Tod und Auferstehung Jesu'.

Suffering Servant is contained in the words of the Heavenly Voice at the Baptism, the element of opposition to Jesus has certainly entered the Gospel by ii. 1–12 and is explicitly seeking his death by iii. 6. From then on it never disappears. The death and Resurrection of Jesus are thus Mark's main subject. In the Passion then we must seek the meaning of Jesus for Mark. In his scheme the Cross is no chance happening. The subtle allusions to the fulfilment of the Old Testament in the Passion story[1] (ix. 12; xii. 1–12, etc.), the sense of divine necessity (viii. 31, 33; xii. 11; xiv. 36), Jesus' own deliberate purpose to go to his death (x. 32–4; xiv. 36) combine to illuminate the Cross as predetermined plan. Yet, as we have already seen, men are not excused their share of guilt,[2] and Mark draws out how they conspired to put him to death led on by their own obstinate rejection of the truth (iii. 1–6; xiv. 10, 11, 17–21, 55; xv. 15). At the same time the innocence of Jesus is maintained (xiv. 55–6; xv. 14); the accounts of the great deeds of Jesus earlier in the Gospel serve this same end in that they have depicted him going about and doing good. In part then this detailed account of the Passion and the underlying currents that led up to it answers the question which must have been often asked in the early Church, Why did Jesus die?[3] From the beginning the Cross was a stumbling-block to the Jews and an offence to the Greeks, and part of the emphasis on the Passion in the Gospel is an attempt to meet this criticism. But the Cross had not merely to be explained as fact, it had also to be given meaning; if it was part of the divine plan, for what purpose had God designed it? Or, to put it another way, what did Jesus achieve for men, for the world, when he died and rose again? What theological interpretation does Mark put on his death?

We may now begin to trace, somewhat hastily, the course of events as narrated by Mark. Obviously much of what Mark records will not throw direct light on our central problem of the soteriology of the Gospel and we shall only pause where we feel that light is thrown on this by the order of the material.

Mark begins (i. 2, 3) by linking his Gospel firmly to the Old

---

[1] Cf. Burkill, 'St Mark's Philosophy of the Passion', *passim*.

[2] Cf. above, pp. 36 ff.

[3] Cf. J. H. Ropes, *The Synoptic Gospels*, pp. 10 ff.; F. C. Grant, *The Interpreter's Bible*, VII, 633.

Testament.[1] This is the only place in the Gospel where he quotes by name from the Old Testament. Elsewhere his Old Testament references either occur in the teaching of Jesus or they are not explicitly introduced as from the Old Testament. This first quotation must then be seen as the conscious linking of what follows to the Old Testament. Though *v.* 1 has spoken of a beginning, the sequel is to be read in the light of Old Testament categories. The bridge between the old and the new is John the Baptiser, who is Elijah (cf. the description of *v.* 6 and the explicit identification of ix. 11–13). John's function is to testify to Jesus; this he does, saying not only that Jesus is the greater (*v.* 7), but also that he will perform a greater ministry, baptising with the Spirit, whereas he John himself baptises only with water. Thus at the outset we are faced with a prophecy that Jesus has come to act on behalf of men. To its meaning we shall return later.[2] The 'Coming One' is now identified, first as the man Jesus from Nazareth and then in his baptism as the Son of God.[3] We postpone until later a fuller consideration of the content of the Heavenly Voice, in particular whether it intends the equation of Jesus with the Suffering Servant.[4] Identified as Son he is given the Spirit; he who is to impart it must first receive it. This spirit then leads him into conflict with the Devil. The latter comes to tempt him, seeking to intervene and prevent the ministry which is beginning. He suffers, however, a crushing defeat (cf. iii. 27). The Devil now disposed of, Jesus begins to preach.

Up to this point Mark had probably not much choice in the ordering of his material. The Old Testament must come before

[1] It is doubtful if the quotation from Malachi in *v.* 2*b* should be read. The original reading in *v.* 2*a* refers to Isaiah alone; Matthew and Luke use only the quotation from Isaiah, omitting the remainder. This might be the correction of an obvious mistake on Mark's part, but it is more likely that the quotation from Malachi is an early gloss. Contrast Schreiber, p. 160. Because Mark ties his Gospel thus firmly to the Old Testament at the beginning and continues to reinforce the tie with Old Testament allusions we must contest Bundy's statement (p. 42) that what Mark narrates 'does not emerge from the stream of history'.

[2] Below, pp. 134 f.

[3] Whatever the primitive Church may have believed, the words of the Heavenly Voice are not for Mark an adoption formula but an announcement or revelation of who Jesus is. Cf. Mauser, p. 96, n. 3.

[4] Below, pp. 148 f., 167 ff.

the New Testament. John must precede Jesus and testify to him; the Baptism must precede the ministry. The temptations alone might have been delayed or spread throughout the ministry. Since the Devil tempts other men continually it would have appeared *a priori* probable that Mark would have regarded Jesus as continuously tempted. This we have found he did not do. Mark deliberately places the Temptation before Jesus moves out to meet men, confirming the earlier analysis we had made of its meaning for him.

From now on he is freer to place his material in the order he chooses. i. 16–38 (39) was probably in existence in its present form prior to Mark. Sometimes it is said that Mark sets it where he does as illustrating a typical day in the activity of Jesus. This may have been the original reason for its compilation, though it is difficult to see how Jesus would have called disciples every day. It is much more likely that he follows the statement of the preaching activity (i. 14, 15) of Jesus with a verification of its effectiveness (i. 16–20) and then the remainder of this complex perforce follows. We have seen that i. 14, 15 reflects the terminology of the early Church and that Mark thinks of the preaching of the Gospel which is Jesus Christ rather than of preaching by Jesus.[1] The proclamation of the Gospel is immediately followed by the response of men – as it was in the early Church.[2] The Gospel, to Mark, includes the whole activity of Jesus, in particular his Passion, which occupies so much of his book, and his Resurrection. The preaching of the Gospel by the early Church thus leads to the formation and growth of the Church itself. The result of the Cross is the existence of the Church. One of the things which Jesus does for men is to create the Christian community. And this community must be self-perpetuating. Those who are called are themselves to be fishers of men. Jesus has preached and has netted men; they in their turn must now go and fish. This theme is repeated in ii. 13–17. Jesus calls Levi (v. 14) after he has taught (*v.* 13) and Levi begins the process of catching men by inviting publicans and sinners to his house to meet Jesus (*v.* 15),[3] and this leads on to a statement by Jesus of the purpose of his ministry,

---

[1] Above, pp. 64 ff.
[2] The disciples are here typical believers rather than Apostles; cf. Bundy, pp. 71 f.   [3] We assume that Levi gave the feast.

namely, to call sinners (*v.* 17). We shall have to return to the nature of the Christian community which Mark views as created through the ministry of Jesus;[1] it is sufficient now to see how Mark by the ordering of his material views its creation as a result of the preaching of the Gospel, the Gospel which is Jesus Christ himself in his life, death and Resurrection.

Within the complex i. 16–38 the next event is the first account of an exorcism by Jesus. This follows appropriately near to the Temptation. Because Jesus has won his victory in the conflict with Satan he now conquers Satan's subordinates, who in the process acknowledge the person of Jesus (i. 21–8). Matthew destroys this sequence and Luke delays considerably the account of the exorcism; this they may do because for them there is not the same close association of it with the Temptation. There follow the healing of Peter's mother-in-law as in the original complex (i. 29–31) and a summary statement of healings and exorcisms which obviously depends on the fact that a sample exorcism and healing have just been recounted (i. 32–4).

At the conclusion of this complex Mark adds on another healing account, that of the leper (i. 40–5), before taking up and following through the next complex (ii. 1–iii. 6). As we have seen leprosy is a type of sin,[2] and in the first story of the next complex (ii. 1–12) the theme of sickness and sin is continued.[3] Thus at the first available point[4] Mark indicates that the healing activities of Jesus are a type of his work in saving men from sin, and in this light we have to read the remainder of the healing accounts. After this Mark continues with the complex ii. 1–iii. 6 with its mounting tension and its conclusion that Jesus must be put to death. We may note that before Mark indicates the determination of the Jewish leaders to eliminate Jesus he has already shown Jesus' awareness of the need for his own death (ii. 19, 20), and he sets out the nature of the

---

[1] Ch. VIII.   [2] Pp. 106 f. above.

[3] J. Sundwall, *Die Zusammensetzung des Markusevangeliums*, pp. 11 f., shows that certain verbal links exist between i. 40–5 and ii. 1–12 and concludes that Mark intended them to be taken together.

[4] He would have had to break the complex i. 16–38 (it is tightly sewn together with temporal notes) if he had inserted the account of the cleansing of the leper earlier; or else he would have had to rewrite i. 29–31 entirely, a course also probably not open to him.

salvation which Jesus achieves in his death, that is, redemption from sin, both by explicit statement (ii. 17) and under the type of healing (i. 40 – ii. 12). The complex thus contains the story of the Gospel in miniature, ending with the Passion (iii. 6).

iii. 6 almost demands that the account of the Passion should follow directly. But there is a sudden change of theme: the popularity of Jesus. This theme had already been present in i. 16 – 39; now it reappears contrasting strongly with the hostility of the Jewish leaders. And with it occurs a second theme which also had appeared in i. 16 – 39 – the new community. There we had seen the call of the first disciples (i. 16 – 20); now we see further steps taken in the creation of the new community, namely, the appointment of the Twelve (iii. 13 – 19). Even though death comes there will be a continuing community,[1] and the community will not be a disorganised body but one in which there will be those appointed to special positions. Though Mark may not give to 'apostle' a technical sense we cannot deny that in the appointment of the Twelve there are the rudiments of organisation. This organisation would seem to be linked also to the twelve tribes of Israel, so that the new community is the new Israel. In between these two items about the crowd and the appointment of the Twelve there is another reference to exorcism and the confession of Jesus by the devils (iii. 11, 12). Thus over against the threatening Cross we see the goodness of Jesus to men testified by his popularity with the crowd, a supernatural confession of his true being by the demons, and his own preparation for the period after his death.

With iii. 20 – 35 the theme of conflict returns. His own family[2] and the scribes now together join in criticism and their criticism is concerned with 'possession', a theme which arises naturally out of the preceding accounts of exorcism (i. 21 – 8; iii. 11, 12). Jesus answers with 'parables' (iii. 23 – 7) which

---

[1] Cf. Dehn, p. 74. However, Dehn's suggestion that the crowd of iii. 7 – 12 represents the true Israel is unlikely. In Mark the crowd is an amorphous and anonymous background generally expressing wonder or amazement at the actions of Jesus; cf. B. Citron, 'The Multitude in the Synoptic Gospels', *S.J. Th.* VII (1954), 408 – 18.

[2] In the opposition of Jesus' own family we see in microcosm the rejection by the nation.

those who have eyes to see (iv. 11, 12) can understand; he is 'possessed', if he is 'possessed', by the Holy Spirit alone, in whose power he defeated Satan and now expels demons. We are made aware again of the believing community which is present and does see – the true family of Jesus (iii. 33–5). We also learn something more of the nature of the new community called into existence by the Gospel, namely, its members do the will of God. But also they have eyes to see the inner nature of all the activities of Jesus, and so we pass naturally to the Markan account of the parables in iv. 1–34.[1] Already in his Gospel Mark has drawn attention to the 'secrecy' motif: the demons are silenced (i. 24, 25; iii. 11, 12); the cleansed leper is forbidden to speak about his healing (i. 44). But those who are 'with Jesus' (iii. 14) are given understanding (iv. 11, 12); to them not only his acts but also his mysterious words testify to his true nature. Within the first parable itself, that of the Sower, two attitudes to Jesus are set out, that of believing acceptance (the new community) and that of temporary and partial acceptance (the crowds, if not also the Jewish authorities). These parables have also their place in asserting the ultimate victory of the Gospel; despite opposition the Kingdom will come and the stand of the community for Jesus will be justified.

iv. 35–v. 43 consists of four mighty works each recounted in detail.[2] Thus Jesus is again set out as the mighty Son of God, who can save (v. 23, 28, 34). Leaving apart what inner meaning these stories possess we can say they depict Jesus as mighty over against both the opposition of men and demonic powers and as over against the humiliation of the Cross which has been already indicated and is shortly to be formally announced (viii. 31).

From this manifestation of his saving power we are transferred at once by Mark to another reminder of the opposition:

---

[1] On the connection here see Boobyer, 'The Redaction of Mark iv. 1–34'.

[2] It has often been held that iv. 35–v. 43 was a complex taken over by Mark: thus Taylor, pp. 94 f.; Schmidt p. 135. Against this may be argued: (a) The Greek of v. 25–34 is different from that of v. 21–4, 35–43 (cf. the participles of vv. 25–7), indicating different sources (cf. Lohmeyer, ad loc.). (b) The insertion of one incident inside another is a favourite Markan editorial device. Cf. Sundwall, *Die Zusammensetzung des Markusevangeliums*, pp. 32–5.

Jesus is rejected by his own village (vi. 1−6*a*).[1] There is a certain vagueness in the way in which Mark introduces this incident: Jesus comes εἰς τὴν πατρίδα. It is only as the incident progresses that we realise Nazareth (cf. i. 9) is intended. This vagueness suggests the possibility that here we have a minor 'rejection'. Jesus' own πατρίς is also Jerusalem; when he goes there he will again be rejected by his own people (cf. John i. 11). Already we have learnt that his true family are those who do his will (iii. 35). The Jews reject him and the new family of the Church takes their place (cf. xii. 9). Returning to vi. 1−6*a* and Nazareth we find that to its people he is but the son of Mary; envy corrupts their hearts so that they stumble. Thus we can see Mark setting fairly and squarely on the shoulders of men their rejection of Jesus. Where there is this unbelief Jesus is powerless. Then once again we swing from rejection to hope for the future: the Twelve are sent out to their mission (vi. 6*b*−13), and they return from it filled with success (vi. 13, 30).

At this point a new stage opens in the Gospel in which Jesus is continually on the move (vi. 14−x. 52). It begins with a miniature passion − that of John the Baptist (vi. 14−29).[2] At first sight it is peculiar that such a story is told in detail; all that is needed for the subsequent narrative (viii. 28) is a mere reference to the death of John; instead we are given a full account. John and Jesus suffer comparable fates (ix. 11−13). The account of the death of John ends almost precisely as that of the death of Jesus − disciples come, obtain the corpse and bury it (vi. 29; cf. xv. 42−7). For Jesus there is a sequel − the Resurrection (xvi. 1−8); but resurrection is not omitted in the case of John; it is only one who has risen from the dead who could work the mighty works of Jesus (vi. 14). Now these works are still found in the early Church; the account of what the

---

[1] Lightfoot, *History*, pp. 184 ff., sees in this account a parallel and contrast to i. 21−8. We have two synagogue scenes, one at the beginning and the other at the end of his Galilean ministry, implying his rejection in Galilee.

[2] It may be that Elijah is mentioned before Moses in Mark's account of the Transfiguration, ix. 2−8 (contrast Matthew and Luke), because it is Elijah = John the Baptist who suffers and dies, and is therefore for Mark a more important figure than Moses. Cf. A. Feuillet, 'Les perspectives propres à chaque évangéliste dans les récits de la transfiguration', *Biblica*, XXXIX (1958), 281−301.

Twelve do encases this story of John the Baptist (vi. 6*b* –13 and vi. 30); in the mighty works of the early Church is to be seen the presence of the risen Christ. Thus though the passion of John has no resurrection we are made aware that the Passion of Jesus will have such a Resurrection. And again as in the conflict with the Jewish authorities (ii. 1–iii. 6) and in Nazareth (vi. 1–6*a*) we see evil arising in the heart of man and bringing opposition and death, for doubtless Mark sees the court of Herod as wicked and Herod himself as skilfully manoeuvred by an evil woman.[1]

We now come to two sections which have long been recognised as to some extent parallel (vi. 30–vii. 37 and viii. 1–26). Each section begins with a feeding, contains the account of a voyage, has statements about the lack of understanding of the disciples, speaks of controversy with the Jewish leaders and ends with a miracle in which a dead faculty (hearing, eyesight) is restored. Mark may either have composed these two sections from separate pericopae or he may have found them in existence (in part or in whole). The latter is more probable; he will then have modified them to suit his purpose by additions, and possibly subtractions. Thus he may well have added a considerable part of the discussion with the Pharisees in vii. 1–23 and the whole incident with the Syro-Phoenician woman (vii. 24–30). This latter, following directly on the controversy with the Pharisees about uncleanness, may be Mark's way of saying that Jesus finding opposition among the Jews turned to the Gentiles – a common pattern in Acts (xiii. 46; xviii. 6). The Cross does not hang as obviously over these two sections as over some of the earlier, but its presence is perhaps felt in the two accounts of feeding the multitudes which the early Christians saw as prefigurations of the Eucharist, and this is strongly tied to the Death of Christ. The compassion of Jesus towards men is emphasised (vi. 34; viii. 2), and his power in the miracles he works. To his goodness and greatness are opposed the scheming of the Jews and the obstinate stupidity of the disciples. But the removal of their lack of understanding is signified in the two miracles of the restoration of men's senses (vii. 32–7; viii. 22–6).

[1] The difficult references to the Herodians at iii. 6 and xii. 13 may bear some relation to the place of Herod in this minor Passion, since Herod plays no part in the Markan story of Jesus' own Passion.

On the placing of the latter we have already commented:[1] it is a suitable introduction to the confession of Peter, and its use in this way may have led to the placing of the whole complex. The entire passage vi. 14 – viii. 26 deals largely with a journey in Gentile territory and therefore instances Jesus' relationship to the Gentiles, indicating that the Gospel is also for them.[2]

With viii. 27 we appear to enter a new atmosphere in which the Cross is no longer a remote threat but looms a terrifyingly short distance ahead. Whether the confession of Peter was a turning point in the life of Jesus himself we need not stop to examine; certainly it represents a turning point in the narrative of Mark. The Cross is now explicit; the crowd largely disappears; the disciples are prominent; the mighty works, with the exception of teaching, recede. We are instructed in the nature of the ministry of Jesus and in the meaning of discipleship. The section lasts until x. 52, where Jesus reaches Jerusalem and the events of the last week begin. It is conceived as a journey towards Jerusalem and death, and the instruction is given to the disciples on the journey.[3] Discipleship is a pilgrimage. Here we have an approximation to the theme of the Epistle to the Hebrews; there, however, the emphasis is laid on a pilgrimage towards the heavenly city and rest; here the pilgrimage is towards suffering, persecution and a Cross. Discipleship is not static but dynamic. This appears not only from the layout of the whole passage (viii. 27 – x. 52) but in the individual pericopae where it is regarded as 'following' Jesus (viii. 34).

We commence with the confession of Peter, who begins to see (cf. viii. 22 – 6). Mark shows that Peter does not see clearly; Jesus announces his Passion and Peter refuses to believe it (viii. 31 – 3). We have reason to believe that Mark may have brought together these two incidents,[4] and if he has not done so he has certainly emphasised their connection by his use of διδάσκειν. In v. 31 it is the Son of Man who it is said must suffer; in v. 29 Peter has confessed Jesus as the Christ. The abrupt transition from one term to another suggests that for Mark the two mean the same person. It may be noted that in

[1] Pp. 107 ff. above.   [2] Cf. Schmidt, pp. 208ff.
[3] The sense of movement is continually present: viii. 27; ix. 2, 9, 14, 30, 33; x. 1, 17, 32, 46.   [4] Pp. 79 f. above.

the other predictions of the Passion Mark also uses the term 'Son of Man'. T. W. Manson has argued that 'in Mark it is possible to trace a gradual narrowing of the denotation until at the last the term has become a name for Jesus alone. The point in the Markan narrative at which this takes place is significant: it is at the Last Supper.'[1] It is not clear from this whether Manson means that it is only at the Last Supper that Mark identifies Jesus with the Son of Man or whether it is only at that point that we can discern in the Markan narrative that Jesus identified himself with the Son of Man. The former would hardly appear to be true. We have already pointed to the quick change of term from Christ to Son of Man (*vv.* 29, 31). Peter's rebuke and Jesus' reply in the Markan narrative would again suggest that Mark understood Jesus as referring only to himself in *v.* 31. There is also the unique position that Jesus gives to himself in *vv.* 34 – 8; the disciples may have to suffer, but if so it is for the sake of Jesus and it is Jesus whom they follow. ix. 9 would also appear in Mark to be a reference to the personal Resurrection of Jesus and not to that of a corporate Son of Man, whatever the original reference may have been. In x. 33 f., the third prediction of the Passion, the details are so approximated to the actual Passion story as told by Mark that there is no room for doubt that here Mark took the Son of Man to be Jesus himself. At ii. 10 the Son of Man is said to be able to forgive sins; at ii. 5 Jesus has just done this very thing. At xiv. 21 it is the Son of Man who is to be betrayed into the hands of sinners, but a few verses earlier (xiv. 18) Jesus had spoken of himself as about to be betrayed. At xiv. 24 and x. 38 we have two sayings about the suffering of Jesus which are cast in the first person; Mark only envisages in God's plan the suffering of one man; this again implies the identification by Mark of the Son of Man with Jesus. There is indeed no point in the Markan account where difficulty is caused by assuming that Mark identified the Son of Man with Jesus, and there is much that causes difficulty if we suppose that Mark held that the Son of Man was someone other than Jesus or that he was a corporate person. To say this is not, of course, to make a decision on the use by Jesus of the

[1] 'Realized Eschatology and the Messianic Secret', in *Studies in the Gospels* (ed. D. E. Nineham), p. 215. Cf. his *The Teaching of Jesus*, pp. 211 – 34, for a fuller discussion of his doctrine of the corporate Son of Man.

term; there are indications in Mark that Jesus' usage was not as simple and direct as Mark implies.

To return to the Markan narrative. In viii. 27–30 Peter has said that Jesus is the Christ; in viii. 31–3 Jesus goes on to say that to be the Christ means to suffer; in viii. 34 – ix. 1 he adds further that to be a Christian means to suffer. From the prediction of the Passion we move directly to the nature of discipleship. And we find that the same is true of each of the other predictions. After the second (ix. 31) Jesus teaches that discipleship means service (ix. 33 ff.) and the same theme reappears after the third prediction (x. 33 f. and x. 35–45). The nature of discipleship is thus set in the light of the Cross; the understanding of discipleship proceeds from an understanding of the Cross. Thus we see again how closely Mark links the death of Jesus to men; its primary importance lies not in a conquest of demons but in the creation of true disciples. The nature of discipleship and the distinction between it and the ministry of Jesus concern the details of the pericopae rather than their order and we shall return to it later.[1]

The first prediction of the Passion and the teaching to which it leads on discipleship is followed by the account of the Transfiguration. The latter is closely linked to the preceding by a stated time interval[2] – a most unusual procedure for Mark outside the closely woven Passion narrative: the Cross is to be succeeded by glory. We are thus again sharply reminded of the nature of him who suffers. He is God's Son, superior to all that belongs to the Old Testament dispensation. Perhaps it is also an indication to disciples that if they take the Cross they also will attain to glory (cf. Rom. viii. 17). Though for a moment Mark lifts us to glory, we do not long escape the Cross, and the disciples coming down from the mountain are reminded of its proximity (ix. 9–13). John the Baptist, that is Elijah, did not restore all things; he was killed. What else may they expect for the Messiah? Then again we move back sharply to the might of Jesus: he heals the epileptic boy whom the disciples had failed to restore: the goodness of Jesus is set against the Cross and his power to save against the weakness of death.

The pattern continues in ix. 30 – x. 31 and in x. 32–52, namely, a prediction of the Passion with a following discussion

---

[1] Pp. 154 ff. below.   [2] Cf. Mauser, pp. 111 f.

of discipleship in its light. There are of course variations. In x. 2–12 a discussion with the Pharisees and disciples about divorce is introduced. This may be either because as Jesus nears Jerusalem the pattern of conflict begins to reappear, the conflict that will eventually lead to his death, or it may be that in this teaching Mark sees Jesus as performing here a mighty work, teaching with authority (i. 22). There follow two apparently very different passages on discipleship: the first (x. 13–16) suggests that discipleship is a matter of reception: the second (x. 17–22) suggests the need for effort. As Wellhausen[1] has pointed out this is the antinomy of discipleship that finds classical expression in Phil. ii. 12, 13. The third section on the Passion and discipleship ends with a mighty work, the healing of blind Bartimaeus (x. 46–52); but perhaps more important than its significance in showing the greatness of Jesus is the fact that Bartimaeus becomes the disciple of Jesus; he follows him into the city (xi. 1 ff.); he thus, as it were, takes up his cross in the wake of that of the Lord.[2] As the three sections on the Passion and discipleship were preceded by the healing of a blind man who received his sight in two stages, here a blind man is healed all at once and becomes the true disciple who follows Jesus towards the Cross; unlike Peter he sees fully.[3]

The remainder of the Gospel we have already examined in

[1] *Ad loc.*

[2] Indeed he is the only person whom Jesus cures who follows him as his disciple; cf. Bundy, p. 410.

[3] Wellhausen, p. 66, has argued that in this section (viii. 27 – x. 52) the idea of repentance which was prominent earlier in the Gospel in relation to discipleship is now abandoned and that of 'following' Jesus substituted. 'Following' is not the only conception of discipleship in this section: there is also ministry, self-denial (which is closely related to repentance) and being as a little child. Alongside 'repentance' in the earlier part is also set 'belief in the Gospel' (i. 15); the Gospel is Christ himself, and in the context of the whole book this must be the Christ of the Cross. Discipleship in viii. 27 – x. 52 is, as we have seen, also set in the light of the Cross; it is not mere imitation of Christ; this is excluded by viii. 35, 38 where Christ is given a unique position. The two conceptions of 'following' and 'repentance' are held together by the Cross. We meet repentance first in the Gospel because repentance is necessarily prior to following. Repentance implies following since repentance is never merely sorrow for sin but also a turning from it to good: following is based on repentance since we cannot go on the new way until we have turned from the old.

more detail[1] and it is only necessary here to redraw the main lines. Mark has apparently decided to have only one Jerusalem ministry and so material appears here which may have belonged to other periods in the life of Jesus. The conflict stories of xii. 13–40 are no more acute than those of ii. 1–iii. 6, but Mark must have needed some conflict stories at this point to bring out the opposition between Jesus and the Jewish leaders, and so he now uses these. The sequence begins with the setting out of the authority of Jesus in the royal entry into Jerusalem, the cleansing of his own house, the Temple, and the proclamation of judgement in the cursing of the fig-tree. It is not then surprising that in xi. 27–33 the question of the authority of Jesus is directly taken up. And the nature of Jesus as the Son of God is clearly set out in the parable of the vineyard (xii. 1–12). Mark will leave us in no doubt as to the being and authority of him who is to suffer. At the same time he underlines the guilt of those who bring about the Cross (xi. 18; xii. 12). There follows the sequence of conflict stories (xii. 13–40), in which again he emerges as mighty in word and as the master in speech of all who come to him. On this there follows the Little Apocalypse and again we are reminded who is the one who will die on the Cross. The Passion narrative itself (chs. xiv, xv) has already been discussed in some detail. Mark had here least control over the ordering of his material. The lines were already set and he had to follow.

This would seem the point to examine the view of Schreiber who finds an overall pattern in the Gospel in that Mark proclaims the Hellenistic kerugma in terms of the tradition about Jesus. He finds this Hellenistic kerugma principally in Phil. ii. 6–11, to which he allies I Cor. ii. 8; these with the kerugma have come under the influence of the conception of the θεῖος ἀνήρ and the Gnostic Saviour myth. The hidden Saviour is crucified by the powers that do not recognise him, but in so dying he conquers them and saves men (cf. I Cor. ii. 8).

Mark's Gospel is a Passion history with a detailed introduction because the Cross was the decisive event for the Hellenistic kerugma.[2] The journey to Jerusalem (viii. 27–x. 52) shows Jesus as the hidden servant who humbles himself in obedience

---

[1] Pp. 82 ff. above.   [2] Pp. 156–9.

to death but is exalted in his death (Phil. ii. 8 f.).[1] Mark has set out Jesus in i. 2 as the messenger of God who comes to the Temple (Mal. iii. 1) and in the Gospel he spends almost all the time of his visit to Jerusalem in the Temple.[2] xi. 1–11, the triumphal entry into the city, would be seen by the Hellenistic Christian as the heavenly greeting to the already exalted Saviour.[3] This Saviour has already been seen in the Transfiguration (ix. 2–8) which took place six days after Peter's confession – a similar period to that which Jesus spent in Jerusalem beginning with the confession of the crowds and ending with his death; the death must then also be the exaltation.[4] The title Son of God is the most important for Mark, and after Jesus' death he is so addressed, indicating that the crucified is the exalted and enthroned Son of God (cf. Ps. ii. 7 where the king is enthroned).[5] In the title Son of Man the ideas of humiliation and exaltation are united; it is noticeable that in viii. 38; xiii. 26; xiv. 62 there is no mention of judgement though Christ's return is indicated; judgement has already taken place through the Cross.[6] In conformity with the Hellenistic kerugma and the Gnostic Saviour myth Mark sets out the pre-existence of the Son of God in the Parable of the Vineyard (xii. 1–12), where God sends his only Son.[7] Closely allied to the Saviour are the saved, the Christian community which Mark views as knowing the Messiah hidden from the world and which has been created by the exalted Lord, in conformity with the Gnostic myth of the Saviour and the saved.[8] This theory of exaltation on the Cross fits in with his account of Jesus as journeying only once to Jerusalem: as the divine Saviour can only once ascend to the heavenly Jerusalem so Jesus can only once go up to the earthly Jerusalem.[9] But if the Cross is the moment of exaltation then what of the Resurrection? Mark gives no account of resurrection appearances.[10] In ix. 2–13 he binds closely together the Ascension (ix. 2–8 speaks of the exalted Christ), the death (ix. 12, 13) and the Resurrection (ix. 9, 10); what happened secretly on the Cross is seen openly by the believer at Easter.[11] An analysis of xvi. 1–8 confirms this view. The women alone

---

[1] Pp. 160 f.　　　　　[2] P. 160.　　　　　[3] P. 161.
[4] Pp. 161 f.; cf. H.-W. Bartsch, 'Historische Erwägungen zur Leidensgeschichte'.　　[5] P. 163.　　[6] Pp. 164–6.　　[7] Pp. 166 f.
[8] Pp. 167–70.　　[9] Pp. 170 f.　　[10] P. 173.　　[11] Pp. 173–5.

are given the message of the Resurrection because they alone followed Jesus to the Cross; this is in conformity with Mark's general view that only he shares in salvation who takes up his cross.[1] xvi. 7 is a Markan insertion, but refers neither to the Parousia nor to the Resurrection but to the exaltation; in Galilee of the Gentiles, that is on the Gentile mission, the Church will see its exalted Lord.[2] Here Mark carries further his campaign against Peter and the Jewish-Christian kerugma which has no place for the Gentile mission. The leaders of the Jewish-Christian Church (Peter, James, John) did not obey the Lord (ix. 6) but were blind and did not go to Galilee.[3] In his as yet unprinted dissertation, *Der Kreuzigungsbericht des Markusevangeliums. Eine traditionsgeschichtliche Untersuchung von Mk. xv. 20b – 41*,[4] Schreiber has analysed in detail the account of Jesus' death and claims to have found there evidence that the moment of death was the moment of ascension. Mark has combined two ancient traditions, one of which sets out the Cross as world judgement (in *vv* 33, 37, 38). In so weaving them together he has modified them to show the death of Jesus as both judgement and salvation, the former to unbelievers, the latter to believers.

In this view of Mark there are many valuable insights, but we cannot accept its central thesis that the moment of death is also that of exaltation and victory over the demonic powers. However, before we examine this, we may take leave to doubt if Schreiber has correctly stated the Hellenistic kerugma and if the Gnostic Saviour myth and the θεῖος ἀνήρ conception have affected this kerugma and Mark as much as he argues.

Schreiber bases his account of the Hellenistic kerugma principally on Phil. ii. 6 – 11. We may allow that this is a pre-Pauline passage, but there are also pre-Pauline passages in the Apostle's letters which stress other aspects of the death of Jesus, for example I Cor xv. 3 f.;[5] Rom. x. 9;[6] Rom. iv. 24b, 25;[7]

---

[1] Pp. 175 f.   [2] Pp. 176 f.   [3] Pp. 177 f.

[4] A reference to this is given on p. 157, n. 5. I have no knowledge of the dissertation itself.

[5] Cf. Bultmann, *Theologie des Neuen Testaments*, p. 82; A. M. Hunter, *Paul and his Predecessors*, pp. 15 ff.

[6] Bultmann, *Theologie des Neuen Testaments*, p. 81; Hunter, *Paul and his Predecessors*, pp. 28 ff.

[7] Hunter, *Paul and his Predecessors*, pp. 30 ff.

Rom. iii. 24–6;[1] I Thess. i. 9, 10.[2] Now if it is objected that some if not all of these passages are to be traced back to the Palestinian community, it may be answered that the distinction between the Palestinian kerugma and the Hellenistic may not be as great as Schreiber makes out, but that the latter is a continuation and development of the former.[3] More particularly it may be answered to Schreiber that if the Palestinian kerugma is to be found in Q as he alleges[4] then Q takes no account of the death of Jesus and gives no interpretation of it, and these passages cannot then belong to the kerugma of that community. Thus we may conclude that these passages bear witness to the kerugma of the Hellenistic Church, and that they set out the death of Jesus as a death for the sin of men. This conception of the death of Jesus as an offering for sin was present in the early Hellenistic community, as Bultmann has shown in detail.[5] The Hellenistic kerugma contained therefore a much wider conception of the death of Jesus than is revealed in Phil. ii. 6–11.[6] It is not our purpose to argue that the two conceptions (e.g. Phil. ii. 6–11 and I Cor. xv. 3 f.) are reconcilable (we may observe that Paul apparently found he could use both), but to determine how far Mark is governed by either, by both, or by some other conception. Before leaving this we may note that in the passages to which we have drawn attention the Resurrection of Jesus is either set out in parallel to his death (I Cor. xv. 3 f.; Rom. iv. 25) or occupies the central position (Rom. x. 9). For the Hellenistic community belief in the Resurrection, which may have been identified with the

---

[1] Bultmann, *Theologie des Neuen Testaments*, p. 47; Hunter, *Paul and his Predecessors*, pp. 120 ff.

[2] Cf. Neil, *Thessalonians* (Moffatt Commentary), *ad loc.* Contrast J. Munck, 'I Thess. i. 9–10 and the Missionary Preaching of Paul', *N.T.S.* IX (1963), 95–110.

[3] Thus e.g. Hunter traces I Cor. xv. 3 ff., *Paul and His Predecessors*, p. 17.

[4] Pp. 172 f.   [5] *Theologie*, pp. 84–6.

[6] There may have been two formulations of the Hellenistic kerugma: I Cor. xv. 3–5 would be the example of one type and Phil. ii. 6–11 (cf. I Tim. iii. 16) the example of the other: cf. E. Schweizer, 'Two New Testament Creeds Compared', *Current Issues in New Testament Interpretation* (ed. W. Klassen and G. F. Snyder), pp. 166–77. The first creed almost certainly originated in Palestinian Christianity but was carried over into Hellenistic Christianity; the second originated in the Hellenistic atmosphere. Cf. Leivestad, *Christ the Conqueror*, pp. 288 ff.

Ascension, had as central a place as belief in the Cross and was distinct from it.[1] In the Hellenistic kerugma the moment of exaltation cannot then have been the moment of death; the latter could only be accepted if Phil. ii. 6–11 by itself was regarded as defining the kerugma, an argument which we cannot allow.

When we turn to the Gnostic Saviour myth it is at least open to doubt if this has affected primitive Christianity to the extent which Schreiber assumes. 'The myth of the Urmensch-Redeemer has been adequately examined by others, and the view that such a myth, if it ever existed, exercised a formative influence on the early Church is now generally rejected.'[2] Only if we find overwhelming evidence within the Gospel itself of influence from the myth may we assume that Mark has shaped his Christology and soteriology in its light. Some of the evidence which Schreiber produces for this is most slender. The derivation of the pre-existence of the Son from the Parable of the Vineyard (xii. 1–12) may serve as an example; such pre-existence was of course an essential item in the myth. According to Schreiber[3] the Son of the parable is sent by the Father, and this can only be a sending from heaven in view of the general usage of ἀποστέλλειν. But (a) The servants are also sent; the same verb is used. Must pre-existence then be assumed for the prophets? (b) The sending of both servants and Son is an essential item in the story of the parable; it could not be told without this element; but the emphasis does not lie on this detail of the narrative; it is wrong therefore to over-emphasise it unless Mark gives us the hint to do so, and this he does not do. Schreiber further argues that as the Redeemer of the myth associates the saved with himself, so in Mark there is a community associated with the Saviour.[4] Undoubtedly there is a community associated with the Saviour in Mark, but many great men have left behind them a community of disciples dedicated to carry on their work; that does not imply they were influenced by the

---

[1] Bultmann, *Theologie des Neuen Testaments*, pp. 80–2.

[2] Wilson, *The Gnostic Problem*, p. 220; for substantiation of this judgement see pp. 218 ff. and the references given in the notes. Cf. G. Quispel, 'The Jung Codex and its Significance', in *The Jung Codex* (ed. F. L. Cross), pp. 76–8; C. Colpe, *Die religionsgeschichtliche Schule* (Göttingen, 1961), p. 191.

[3] Pp. 166 f.   [4] Pp. 167–70.

myth. Moreover the distinctive traits that we find in the Gnostic saved community are lacking in Mark; in the myth the association of the saved with the Saviour is described in fundamentally non-personal terms; they are drawn to him because they have souls that respond as sparks of the divine; they are worn by him as a garment.[1] In Mark the relationship of the community to its Lord remains couched in purely personal terms, in terms of following and obedience. The terms of Pauline theology, 'the Body of Christ', 'in Christ', etc., which with somewhat more justification have been viewed by some scholars as reflecting the myth, are wholly absent in Mark. Lastly when Schreiber argues that Mark portrays Jesus as successful in exorcism and miracle and in the routing of those come to dispute with him and that this shows the influence of the θεῖος ἀνήρ idea,[2] we may rejoin that many ancient biographers, and some modern also, glorify their heroes in the same way and are not therefore necessarily suspected of being under the influence of the myth. Schreiber does not reckon with the possibility that Jesus may in fact have exorcised demons, healed the sick and out-argued his opponents! Mark would not thus seem to adhere to the myth as closely as Schreiber suggests, and when he does adhere he is only following the general tendency of all writers, and therefore ideas similar to some of those adhering to the myth need not be traced to the myth.

In a sense, hoever, these are minor points; our major concern is with Schreiber's view that the Cross is Christ's exaltation; though, if we have shown that the influence of the myth on Mark cannot be stated as dogmatically as he assumes, we have removed a possible reason why we should support Schreiber in the peculiar position he has adopted in regard to the death of Christ. Schreiber's main arguments lie in his understanding of the crucifixion scene as told by Mark and in his playing down of the significance of the Resurrection for Mark, to which he adds certain confirmatory evidence from earlier parts of the Gospel.

When we turn to Schreiber's view of Mark's account of the crucifixion scene (xv. 20 – 41) we are at a great disadvantage since his work on this has not been published. But reading

[1] Cf. Best, *One Body in Christ*, pp. 85–7, 224 f.
[2] Pp. 158, 163, 173.

between the lines we may suppose that he has drawn attention to certain 'cosmic' elements in the account which suggest a cosmic victory, for example the great cry, the rending of the Temple veil, the darkness. These appear in the apocalyptic source which he separates out in the account. We have already discussed these in detail and have seen that they can be interpreted satisfactorily without reference to Christ's Ascension. They fit the pattern of a death which is both a judgement on the sin of men and a deliverance for them from sin.[1]

A further point at which it might be argued that a cosmic dimension should be seen in the Passion would lie in the linking of it to I Cor. ii. 8. If the high priests and those who crucified Jesus are taken as representatives of the demonic powers, then their failure in that he rose from the dead may be an indication of his victory over them. It was a common belief of the time[2] that behind governing authorities were 'supernatural powers' (cf. Rom. xiii. 1–7) and that the actions of the two were closely related. Amongst the Jews the nations were regarded as under the control of folk-angels. There is, however, no trace of such a view in Mark. The priests and leaders of the Jews whom Mark largely holds to be responsible for the death of Christ hardly occupy the same role as the civil authorities of the nations. Moreover if Mark viewed them as demonically inspired in their behaviour we should expect that as in many of the other demonic incidents they would have displayed supernatural knowledge of the true nature of Jesus, and Jesus' self-testimony of xiv. 62 would have been unnecessary. In I Cor. ii. 8 there is obviously a different theory of demonic knowledge from Mark's. The supernatural authorities behind civil rulers were not necessarily regarded as evil; if Mark accepted the common position in this matter then xii. 13–17 would probably imply that he regarded rulers and their 'angels' at least as neutral. When Mark tells the story of the Passion he seems however to treat the high priests, etc., as individuals, as men, and not as front-pieces for spiritual powers.

[1] Pp. 97 ff. above.
[2] This has been clearly demonstrated by C. D. Morrison, *The Powers that Be* (London, 1960), though he himself would not connect the Lordship of Christ over them with his Cross but would rather see it as a fact of creation; cf. Morrison, *ibid.* pp. 116 ff.

We must now examine how Mark deals with the Resurrection. It must be admitted with Schreiber that, if xvi. 8 is the conclusion of the Gospel, then Mark contains no account of any Resurrection appearances. But this is not necessarily evidence for the belief that Mark makes the moment of death the moment of exaltation. It is equally evidence for the equation of the exaltation and the Resurrection. There are good grounds for holding that in the primitive kerugma Ascension and Resurrection were not clearly distinguished; the risen Jesus is the exalted Jesus. This is probably found reflected in Phil. ii. 6 – 11, where the death might be the moment of exaltation but need not necessarily be taken so. We may also allow to Schreiber that the Christ of the Transfiguration is the exalted Christ, but this is no proof that the exaltation took place on the Cross.[1] If the exaltation and the death are identified then no place is left for the Resurrection as a distinct event; such a place may remain however even if the Resurrection and the exaltation are identified. Mark moreover does appear to give the Resurrection a distinct place. It is always μετὰ τρεῖς ἡμέρας (viii. 31; ix. 31; x. 34).[2] The distinctness of the Resurrection as an event is also implied in the empty tomb; the crucified Christ is left there; by the third day he is risen; the Resurrection is thus subsequent to the burial and the death (xvi. 6). These passages may have come to Mark in the tradition, but surely he must have accepted what he received when it was set down so clearly; he could easily have modified the predictions of the Passion and Resurrection by the omission of μετὰ τρεῖς ἡμέρας and so have created the possibility that the exaltation might be contemporaneous with the death.[3] Lacking convincing evidence that Mark desired such a modification of the primitive kerugma we must reject the idea that the moment of death was the moment of exaltation, and therefore we cannot use this theory

[1] Though admittedly there is no easy explanation, Schreiber's interpretation of the six days (ix. 2) is too fanciful (pp. 161 f.); for other suggestions cf. Mauser, pp. 111 f.; C. E. Carlston, 'Transfiguration and Resurrection', *J.B.L.* LXXX (1961), 233–40.

[2] The three days of xiv. 58; xv. 29 are almost certainly also implicit references to the Resurrection of Jesus; viii. 2 may be also.

[3] If the addition of the reference to the Resurrection in the Passion predictions was made by the early Church, it would have been all the easier for Mark to omit it.

to substantiate the view that the Cross is the victory over the forces of spiritual evil.

At the same time we must conclude that Mark is not dominated by the kerugma of Phil. ii. 6 – 11. Mark in the course of his narrative does not depict Jesus as the humble servant.[1] There are passages in which this idea is found, for example x. 35 – 45, but the general impression that Mark leaves is of a strong Son of God who has authority. Whatever Jesus may have been in reality, to the readers of Mark's Gospel he is the Son of God with power, so announced at the beginning (i. 11, if not i. 1) and so depicted throughout in his mighty works.

[1] Cf. below, pp. 140 ff.

CHAPTER VI

THE WITNESS OF JESUS AND OTHERS TO HIMSELF

WE now consider those verses within the material in which statements are made either by Jesus or others concerning his function and activity and the purpose of his work. We do not now look at the seams or the order of the material but into the material itself. This may have undergone some editing at the hands of Mark; if we can show such in any of the statements to be considered it will of course be primary evidence for the Markan view. Most of the statements however came to Mark in the material and his inclusion of them is at least secondary evidence for his own point of view; if they had definitely cut across it he would either not have included them or would have modified them. It could be argued that he might have permitted an occasional statement which was at variance with his own main theology through loyalty to the material transmitted to him or because he did not himself realise its divergence from his main position. We shall find however that there are a considerable number of statements all conveying more or less the same view, one not out of harmony with what we have already learnt; so this possibility is excluded.

We begin with the statements of John the Baptist about Jesus, i. 7 f. Mark appears to have used traditional material without modification here.[1] There are two significant phrases: Jesus is described as ὁ ἰσχυρότερος, and he is said to baptise with Holy Spirit.

In the use of ἰσχυρός Grundmann[2] claims to detect a very primitive Christology in which Jesus is set out as the 'stronger' conqueror of Satan, who is the 'strong one', and his hosts (cf. Luke xi. 20–2). It is not our purpose to dispute this claim but only to indicate our doubt that it formed part of the Markan Christology. Mark makes no use of the 'stronger' conception

[1] Schmidt, pp. 18–22; Bultmann, pp. 245–7; cf. Taylor; Lohmeyer; Klostermann, *ad loc.*
[2] *T.W.N.T.* III, 402–5.

in his discussion of the defeat of Satan (Mark iii. 27: his parallel to Luke xi. 20–2). Moreover, Mark does not depict Jesus in i. 7 as stronger than Satan but as stronger than the Baptist. Thus this suggested primitive Christology is not present here in the mind of Mark. But what does he mean by saying that Jesus is stronger than the Baptist? Lohmeyer[1] suggests that ὀπίσω should be understood spatially rather than temporally; we would expect the one who follows John to be his servant or disciple, but in fact he is the greater; John would loose his shoes: in this lies the paradox. ὀπίσω is also used by Mark to indicate the place of the disciple in respect of Jesus (i. 17, 20; viii. 34). John precedes Jesus to death, and as we have already seen John's Passion is an indication of the Passion of Jesus;[2] Jesus precedes his disciples to death (viii. 34); the contrast lies in this – the disciples are less than Jesus but Jesus is greater than John. None of these explanations makes it entirely clear why Jesus is 'stronger' than John, and perhaps the original allusion is lost. Mark certainly indicates by the word the superiority of Jesus to John; the remainder of the Gospel makes clear in what this superiority lies.

The Baptist also contrasts himself with Jesus in respect of baptism: Jesus will baptise with Holy Spirit. It is impossible to enter here into a full discussion of the origin of this logion and of the difference between it and the Q form. Elsewhere I have attempted to show that both the Markan and the Q sayings are variants of an original word of the Baptist that Jesus would baptise with wind and fire, and that the reference in the Markan form is to Pentecost (cf. Acts i. 5).[3] If this is so then the reference is here to the gift of the Spirit by the exalted Christ to the Church. Part of the achievement of Jesus is to have given to his Church the Spirit. Unfortunately, Mark includes very little material which tells us in detail what the Church of the Spirit is like, though we do learn that through the Spirit the members of the Christian community are able to stand firm in persecution and to witness therein (xiv. 38; xiii. 11).

i. 16–20 has already been considered in relation to the

---

[1] *Ad loc.*   [2] Pp. 119 f. above.

[3] Best, 'Spirit-baptism', *N. T.* IV (1960), 236–43. For the reasons advanced there the contentions of Yates, *The Spirit and the Kingdom*, pp. 22 ff., are to be rejected.

arrangement of material in the Gospel;[1] it however also contains a statement in which by implication Jesus sets out his own purpose: He calls disciples to send them out as fishers of men. If their purpose is to fish for men at his command, then his purpose must also be to fish for men – both directly and through them. That is to say, his objective is men; it is not the defeat of Satan, though this may be involved, but the creation of a community of men who are his disciples. It is towards men that his activity is directed.

In i. 24 there is a statement about the purpose of Jesus made by one of his enemies, the demon who is being exorcised, and who alleges that Jesus is come to destroy demons.[2] This certainly describes the activity of Jesus in relationship to the evil powers, but it would be wrong to extend it so as to take it as a statement of the whole purpose of Jesus.[3] It must be held within its context, that of an exorcism, and it must be remembered that it is the statement of an enemy who looks at things from his own limited point of view. We may not then take this as a statement of the full activity of Jesus or even as a part of the central activity unless there is corroborative evidence elsewhere.

i. 38 forms the conclusion to the passage i. 35–8 which we have accepted as part of the tradition received by Mark.[4] Our concern is with the final clause εἰς τοῦτο γὰρ ἐξῆλθον. Is this merely a reference to Jesus' departure from Capernaum or is deeper meaning to be seen in it? The preceding narrative seems to imply that Jesus went out to avoid the crowds of sick who were pressing him and to pray in quietness to his Father. Yet v. 38 implies that he came out in order to go and preach in other towns; and at ii. 1, 2 he is back preaching in Capernaum. It is these slight discrepancies that have made many commentators[5] assume that Mark intends us to see here a deeper

[1] Cf. pp. 115 f. above. i. 16–20 is again a passage which came to Mark in the tradition.

[2] The phrase may be read either as a question (so most of the English Versions) or as a statement; for our purpose it is unnecessary to decide between these alternatives.

[3] Cf. Kallas, *The Significance of the Synoptic Miracles*, p. 78.

[4] Cf. above, p. 69.

[5] E.g. Lohmeyer; Lagrange; Klostermann; Rawlinson; Schniewind; Swete; Hauck (?); Schmidt, p. 58; Lightfoot, *Gospel*, p. 24; Bundy, pp. 85 f.; etc. Contrast Taylor; Dehn; etc.

Christological meaning: a coming out from God into the world to preach. Certainly this was the view of Luke, the earliest commentator (cf. Luke iv. 43). In the praying of Jesus we are deliberately brought back to the God from whom he came forth. Perhaps there is a deliberate correction of the assertion of the demons (i. 25) that Jesus is come to destroy them: [1] preaching is rather his true activity. And 'preaching' in the eyes of Mark's readers will obviously mean the whole content of the Gospel: Jesus Christ crucified and risen, together with the meaning that they put on his death, which is, as we are seeing, that Jesus died for men who are sinners.

In ii. 10 the activity of Jesus is described, and therefore indirectly his purpose. We have already seen how in this passage forgiveness of sins precedes healing and dominates it. [2] At ii. 10 the Son of Man, who for Mark is Jesus himself, says that he has power on earth to forgive sins. [3] Probably Mark's readers when they read of Jesus forgiving sins would think of him as continuing to possess this power in his exalted state and as forgiving their sins. It is not, however, directly indicated in this passage how he is able to forgive, but the use of the title 'Son of Man' in relationship to the forgiveness of sins may imply a link with the Passion. It is this title that is used frequently in the predictions of the Passion (viii. 31; ix. 12, 31; x. 33 f., 45; xiv. 21, 41). There may thus, then, be an implicit reference at this point to the Passion. This in itself may throw light on another problem: to those who view Mark as a strictly historical book in which the story of Jesus is told there is the difficulty that Jesus forgives sins here by word and prior to his death; the early Church, however, appears to have accepted the view that forgiveness came through the death of Jesus (I Cor. xv. 3). If, however, Mark was thinking primarily of the activity of the exalted Christ, [4] who has passed through the Passion, and if he

---

[1] Cf. Lohmeyer.　　　　　　　　[2] Pp. 35 f., 69 ff.

[3] The exact significance of ἐπὶ τῆς γῆς is difficult. Textually its position is uncertain. It may mean that the Son of Man while on earth had power to forgive sins (and the early Church would add, 'as he now has in Heaven'), or it may mean that the Son of Man has power to forgive sins on earth, i.e. before the final judgement, while the sinner is still alive on earth.

[4] 'Son of Man' is also used of the risen and exalted Christ (ix. 9; xiv. 62); Mark possibly uses this term here because it suggests both the crucified and the exalted Lord.

shows the connection of forgiveness to the Passion by means of the title 'Son of Man', this will have been no problem for him. The problem may have existed for the underlying tradition, but it did not arise for Mark.[1] Before passing from this verse we may note finally that there is no exclusive activity of Jesus set down here, nor is the forgiveness of sin said to be his main purpose.

The connection of his coming with men's sin does however appear to be his main purpose in the next verse at which we must look, ii. 17, 'I am not come to call righteous but sinners'. The whole passage ii. 15–17 bristles with difficulties: has ii. 15–17 been added to ii. 14 in the tradition or was it originally connected to it? In whose house did the meal take place, Levi's or Jesus'? Does καλέσαι mean 'call' or 'invite'? Is ii. 17b an interpretative addition to ii. 15–17a? We do not need to answer all these questions. It is probable that the material as it came to Mark in the complex of conflict stories (ii. 1 – iii. 6) already joined together ii. 14 and ii. 15–17a and contained ii. 17b. The introduction of the proper name Ἰησοῦς in v. 15b probably indicates that Mark took the earlier αὐτοῦ as referring to the house of Levi. Luke by his addition of εἰς μετάνοιαν at the end of v. 17 certainly took καλέσαι to mean 'call' rather than 'invite'; the application to table fellowship within the Christian community, an issue of which Acts shows that Luke was very much aware, cannot therefore have appeared to him as prominent in the Markan account; we may thus doubt if it was important for Mark himself, though we may not deny that overtones are present. The addition of Luke thus probably represents the Markan point of view.[2] Within the saying δικαίους occasions difficulty, whether the saying be taken as originating with Jesus or not. Neither he nor the early Church would have allowed that there were righteous who did not need to be summoned to repentance. Presumably then a certain amount of irony must underlie its use here.[3] Lastly, who are

[1] The original incident may never have contained the words ἵνα ... γῆς (v. 10); this clause may either be a comment of the early Church or of Mark himself (so Cranfield, ad loc.).

[2] It may, however, have been the interest in table fellowship which led to the preservation (Taylor) or creation (Bultmann, pp. 92, 105) of this pericope in the early Church. [3] So Taylor; Rawlinson; etc.

the ἁμαρτωλοί who are summoned? In ii. 15, 16 they are set in parallel with the τελῶναι; these latter were despised not only by good Jews but throughout the ancient world.[1] The ἁμαρτωλοί are either those of immoral life or the '*am ha aretz* who were defiled by association with Gentiles; since the '*am ha aretz* would probably have included the τελῶναι, ἁμαρτωλοί should be given the sense of 'immoral people'. However, in ii. 17*b* we find ἁμαρτωλοί alone; no longer are tax-collectors and sinners set in parallel. Does it then continue to have the same meaning? It seems very probable that it has now slid into the Pauline sense (Rom. v. 8, 19; Gal. ii. 17) and means 'sinners': all men are sinners and Jesus calls all. For Mark's Roman readers there would have been little interest in the '*am ha aretz*; and, if ἁμαρτωλοί means 'immoral people', why should the parallel τελῶναι be dropped, since these were despised in the Gentile world as much as in Judaism and would have been considered as equally in need of the call of Jesus? Thus we take ἁμαρτωλούς in *v.* 17*b* to mean 'sinners' in the religious sense for Mark and his readers.[2] Since in *v.* 17*b* ἦλθον must definitely be given the sense of 'purpose', that is, Jesus has come into the world in order to call, we see the saying as a statement of the purpose of Jesus – to call sinners. Here is a quite simple statement of the object of his activity. There is, of course, no relationship made between this call of Jesus to sinners and his death, though the whole complex ii. 1 – iii. 6 bears a Passion reference implicitly in its recital of 'conflict' stories and explicitly at ii. 20 and iii. 6.[3]

The predictions of the Passion do not tell us anything about what was achieved in the Passion. They make clear its importance: it was a divine necessity (δεῖ viii. 31, cf. ix. 12). This divine necessity did not lie in the other events in the life of Jesus; he might have healed other sick people than those he did

---

[1] Cf. Cicero, *De Off.* 1, 150; Aristophanes, *Eq.* 247 f.; etc.

[2] Our analysis might be used to suggest that ἁμαρτωλοί in *v.* 17*b*, standing by itself, originally meant the '*am ha aretz*, whereas in *vv.* 15, 16 it meant 'immoral people' in parallel with τελῶναι. Verse 17*b* thus might have been a saying of Jesus, or certainly have originated on Palestinian soil, independent of *vv.* 15–17*a*, and later have been attached thereto. This might account for the difficulties of associating *v.* 17*b* with *vv.* 15–17*a* as indicated by Dodd, *The Parables of the Kingdom*, pp. 117 f.

[3] Cf. pp. 116 f. above.

heal, or called another twelve than the Twelve he called; but it was necessary that he should die and rise again. He might well have said 'I am come to suffer, die and rise again'. The statements do not themselves reveal the meaning of the 'coming'; for this we must look to other statements of Jesus and to the other evidence of his activity that we have been considering.

We encounter another text about the coming of the Son of Man in the celebrated 'ransom' saying of x. 45. Its context is service. The sons of Zebedee have sought a reward for their discipleship; the other disciples complain about the ambitious Zebedees; Jesus tells them that true greatness does not lie in superior position but in service; from this he goes on to say, 'the Son of man did not come to be served but to serve, and to give his life a ransom for many'. Mark again undoubtedly equates Jesus with the Son of Man. What Jesus teaches in the first part of this logion is both for himself and his followers: both his mission and theirs is to serve and not be served. But the second part of the logion is peculiar to Jesus alone; it particularises the nature of his service – to give his life a ransom for many. Much has been written concerning the authenticity of this saying. Three positions are possible: (*a*) it is a genuine logion of Jesus; (*b*) it was created in the early Church and came to Mark as part of the tradition; (*c*) we owe it to Mark or the particular community in which he wrote. If this last was true then it would be especially valuable in fixing the Markan doctrine of the purpose of Jesus. But the evidence suggests that one or other of the first two views is more likely, and for our purpose it is unnecessary to determine which; for in either case the saying will have come to Mark in the material he received.

The claim for the Markan authorship of the saying is usually based on two grounds: (*a*) its omission in Luke; (*b*) resemblance to Pauline theology.[1] As against these we may argue: (*a*) The Lukan passage, xxii. 24–7, shows the influence of the Hellenistic Church organisation of the later part of the first century (cf. νεώτερος, ἡγούμενος) and is thus not in its present form original; the Markan saying has been modified to suit the Lukan context of Church discipline; to this Mark x. 45*b* was

[1] Rashdall, *The Idea of the Atonement*, pp. 29 ff., 49 ff. Bultmann, p. 144; Klostermann; Branscomb, *ad loc.*

irrelevant, and it was therefore dropped.[1] (b) Paul does not make use of the concept of λύτρον but rather of ἀπολύτρωσις which has its roots in the Exodus experience.[2] If Mark x. 45b reflects a servant Christology which is found also in Paul, then it may be argued that the servant Christology found in Paul already lay in the tradition which he accepted,[3] and since it lay in already existing material, therefore its presence in Mark is not necessarily a sign of Pauline influence. It is also sometimes argued that x. 45b does not follow directly from x. 45a but takes us into a new world of thought;[4] this does not appear an insuperable objection to its existence prior to Mark; if Mark could make the jump, then someone earlier could have made it; the new step only particularises what the διακονία of Jesus was. Finally, it may be said that positive explanations of the saying, basing it either on a servant Christology or on the Maccabean martyrs, set it firmly in a Palestinian context and therefore as pre-Markan. We are thus left with two possibilities: either the saying is an authentic word of Jesus or it came into existence in the Jewish Christian Church as the comment of a preacher on x. 45a. Between these we do not need to decide. It is probable that x. 41-5 is a Markan composition in which he has put together traditional sayings of Jesus.[5] We may note the use of καί at the beginning of each of vv. 41, 42, 44, 45. Some of the sayings of the passage appear in variant form and differently arranged in Luke xxii. 24-7. If Mark in any way put together vv. 41-5 then he added v. 45, or at least there was the real possibility open to him of omitting it, as Luke did. Hence **we may argue with confidence that it is important ·for his** understanding of the death of Jesus.

From this we must turn to consideration of the meaning of the logion. Whether accepted as genuine or not, the vast

---

[1] Cf. R. H. Fuller, *The Mission and Achievement of Jesus*, p. 57; Büchsel, *T.W.N.T.* IV, 343.

[2] Cf. Fuller, *The Mission and Achievement of Jesus*, p. 57; Feine, *Theologie des NTs*[8], p. 109; Taylor, pp. 445 f.; Taylor, *Jesus and His Sacrifice*, pp. 99-105.

[3] Jeremias, in W. Zimmerli and J. Jeremias, *The Servant of God*, pp. 88 f., 93 (= *T.W.N.T.* v, 703 f., 706); A. M. Hunter, *Paul and his Predecessors*, pp. 31 f., 141 f.

[4] Wellhausen, *ad loc.*

[5] Cf. Taylor; Lohmeyer; Hauck.

majority of commentators have found the background to the saying in the concept of the Suffering Servant. This has now been severely challenged by Professor Barrett[1] and Miss Hooker.[2] We feel that their points are well taken. Briefly they are: (a) In the Isaianic passages which describe the Servant he is set forth as the Servant of *God*, that is, basically he serves God; but in Mark x. 44 f. the service is that of *men*; Jesus who might technically claim to be the ruler of the disciples as their master sets himself out as their servant. (b) Linguistically Mark x. 45 uses διακονεῖν, a word which with its cognates is very common in the New Testament, but which is rarely used in the LXX and never used in reference to the Servant of God (παῖς and the word-group δοῦλος are found).[3] (c) Mark's phrase ψυχὴν διδόναι is too common in Jewish and secular Greek to be necessarily traced back to παρεδόθη εἰς θάνατον ἡ ψυχὴ αὐτοῦ (Isa. liii. 12). (d) אשם (Isa. liii. 10) and λύτρον are not linguistic equivalents; the former is never rendered in the LXX by the latter or any of its cognates; the latter never renders the former nor any of its cognates. (e) אשם and λύτρον do not carry the same connotation. The former is the sacrifice offered at the same time as restitution is made for a wrong done (Lev. v. 14–19); it is not itself restitution, nor is there any idea of compensation or equivalence involved in it. The latter contains the idea of equivalence, but the word-group associated with it is often used of God's redemption of Israel without any suggestion that he makes a payment. (f) The main verbal link between Isa. liii and our logion is the use of πολλοί; this occurs three times in Isa. liii. 11 f.; but the word is too common for a serious argument to be based on it. (g) The first part of our logion provides a strong contrast in the opposite ideas of serving and being served. If the saying is conceived in terms of the Suffering Servant it is a 'little precious'[4] to suggest that the Servant did not come to be served, but it fits in admirably

---

[1] 'The Background of Mark x. 45', in *New Testament Essays*, ed. A. J. B. Higgins, pp. 1–18.

[2] *Jesus and the Servant*, pp. 74–9 Hahn, *Christologische Hoheitstitel*, pp. 54 ff., defends Isa. liii as the background of x. 45b and xiv. 24.

[3] Cf. J. A. Emerton, 'Some New Testament Notes', *J.T.S.* XI (1960), 334 f.

[4] Barrett, 'The Background of Mark x. 45', p. 8.

with the contemporary apocalyptic conception of the son of Man who came to rule.[1]

If then we reject the explanation of Mark x. 45 in terms of the Suffering Servant, how are we to understand it? Here Dr Hooker and Professor Barrett part company. She, following the connection of the word-group associated with λύτρον, takes it in the general sense of redemption. The death of Jesus is the redemption of men. Sin is thus not emphasised but is certainly implied since it render redemption necessary. Professor Barrett, however, points out that λύτρον is followed by ἀντί and that this suggests some idea of equivalence.[2] He finds this conception of the equivalence of one man's death to the life of others in the contemporary Jewish idea of the death of the martyr (II Macc. vii. 37 f.; IV Macc. vi. 27 ff.; xvii. 22; xviii. 4),[3] where the self-sacrifice of the martyrs means deliverance and purification for Israel. In itself this is but an example of the more widespread conception in the Old Testament and Judaism of the One and the Many; the One takes the place of the Many, as their representative. But the idea of the Suffering Servant is itself a part of the conception of the One and the Many and the Maccabean martyrs may themselves have been influenced by it. We cannot therefore ignore the indirect influence of the Isaianic Servant passages on Mark x. 45 even if their direct impact is denied. Barrett's derivation seems preferable to Miss Hooker's and yields a closer connection between the death of Jesus and sin.

If however these arguments are not thought sufficiently

[1] This argument is to some extent nullified if 'Son of Man' did not retain for Mark its full apocalyptic significance but was becoming one among a number of interchangeable titles used of Jesus.

[2] Cf. L. Morris, *The Apostolic Preaching of the Cross*, pp. 26–35.

[3] λύτρον does not occur in these passages, but the idea which it represents is present, being expressed by ἀντίψυχον (IV Macc. vi. 29). On the place of expiatory suffering in Rabbinic thought cf. Moore, I, 546 ff.; J. Downing, 'Jesus and Martyrdom', *J. T.S.* XIV (1963), 279–93. F. C. Grant, 'Biblical Theology and the Synoptic Problem', in *Current Issues in New Testament Interpretation* (ed. W. Klassen and G. F. Snyder), pp. 79–90, taking a similar point of view to Barrett, lists also Pal. Sanhedrin, II.30c, 28, 'The drops of blood which fell from those righteous men (I Kings xx. 35–7) made atonement for all Israel'. C. Maurer, 'Knecht Gottes und Sohn Gottes im Passionsbericht des Markusevangeliums', *Z. T.K.* L (1953), 1–38, rejects the reference to the Maccabean martyrs.

strong to lead to the rejection of the Suffering Servant idea as basic to Mark x. 45, then we still move in somewhat the same territory in that in Isa. liii the death of the Servant is definitely a death for the sin of his fellows.[1] The meaning is well expressed in the words of Rawlinson: 'The phrase sums up the general thought of Isa. liii, and expresses the idea of a vicarious and voluntary giving of life, with the thought also implied that the sacrifice was in some way mysteriously necessitated by sin.'[2]

Finally we may observe that there is no suggestion in the saying that the λύτρον is paid to the Devil: nor is it stated in so many words from what the Many[3] are freed. Neither are these matters made precise in the Maccabean passages to which we have drawn attention; since in Mark the death of Jesus is a divine necessity it is probable that if he were pushed to the point of saying to whom the ransom was paid, he would say 'to God'.[4] If the Suffering Servant conception lies behind the logion then the guilt offering was definitely paid to God. There is thus no reason to find a reference to the Devil here.

The Markan passage (xiv. 22–5) about the Last Supper is relevant to our inquiry. It is obviously not our concern to decide whether the Markan account is prior to the Pauline nor to determine which of them more accurately represents the original words of Jesus. It is highly unlikely that Mark interfered with the words of institution as they came to him in the tradition.[5] Liturgical texts are normally treated with great reverence. It seems very likely that the references to the

[1] It may be that either through the Maccabean martyrs or through the Suffering Servant we should see here a connection with the sacrifice of Isaac; cf. below, pp. 169 ff.

[2] *Ad loc.*

[3] That πολλῶν is used in place of, and means, πάντων accords with a common Semitic idiom; cf. Jeremias, *T.W.N.T.* VI, 536 ff.

[4] Cf. Büchsel, *T.W.N.T.* IV, 345 f.

[5] Jeremias, *The Eucharistic Words of Jesus*, pp. 118 ff., has drawn attention to the many Semitisms in the Markan account. He considers that the position of μου in the saying about the cup would have been impossible in Aramaic. J. A. Emerton, 'τὸ αἷμά μου τῆς διαθήκης: The evidence of the Syrian versions', *J.T.S.* XIII (1962), 111–17, rightly disputes the conclusion of Jeremias; cf. Dalman, *Jesus-Jeshua*, pp. 160 f. If Jeremias is correct then, τῆς διαθήκης must have been added on Hellenistic soil; however, the connection of διαθήκη with the Supper is found also in Paul and may therefore be assumed to be primitive and have belonged during the Palestinian period.

covenant and to the pouring out of blood in the saying attached to the cup are interpretative additions to the original words of Jesus, but they will have been in the text before Mark received it. If of course they were Markan additions then they would emphasise strongly the view that Mark was putting out on his own a doctrine of the death of Jesus which connected it to the sin of men rather than the defeat of the Devil. We, however, assume that Mark did not add them; but in using them in the account he presumably agreed with their interpretation of the death of Jesus. It is important for the understanding of the Markan account that we realise that it was a Paschal meal at which the Eucharist was instituted (xiv. 12, 14, etc.). Mark may or may not have known of the alternative tradition which made Jesus die at the time of the slaughtering of the Passover lamb and thereby made the Last Supper take place prior to the Passover, but he clearly excludes it by his careful description of the preparation for the meal. The account is also firmly held within the Passion story; there may be allusions to the Eucharist in the feeding accounts, but the institution is tied to the night before the death of Jesus, and accordingly must be interpreted in the light of that death.

The saying about the bread is left without interpretative addition and whatever meaning we give to it must be read out of the total context, or out of the meaning of σῶμα itself, or out of its parallelism with the saying about the cup. It is almost certainly erroneous to derive the meaning of the bread logion from the fact of its fraction, that is, that as the bread is broken, so Christ's body is broken in death. The breaking of bread was a normal part of the action of asking a blessing on a meal,[1] and the actual words, 'This is my body', are connected in the account to the distribution and eating of the bread and not to its breaking.[2] Equally the saying about the cup is not to be connected to its pouring out but to the participation in it; the saying actually follows the participation. If the bread logion is taken by itself, and we shall see that this is more probable, then σῶμα probably has the meaning of 'self' – the body is the outward expression of the self and cannot be detached from the

---

[1] Cf. C. F. D. Moule, *Worship in the New Testament*, p. 19; A. J. B. Higgins, *The Lord's Supper in the New Testament*, pp. 51 f.

[2] Cf. Jeremias, *The Eucharistic Words of Jesus*, p. 142.

self.[1] To eat the bread which is Christ himself is then to participate in Christ, and the saying will be interpreted along the lines of I Cor. x. 16 f.[2] Naturally the Christ in whom the Christian participates is the crucified Christ, but this of itself does not tell us anything about the meaning of the death of Christ. For an interpretation of this we must turn to the saying associated with the cup.

When we now consider this we are forced, as in the case of x. 45, to accept the argument that there is not sufficient evidence to show formative influence from the Servant concept.[3] It is possible to link the usage of covenant with the Servant concept through Isa. xlii. 6; xlix. 8,[4] but the theme of the covenant is so general in the Old Testament that it is impossible to tie it down to these two texts, especially since it is here connected to the shedding of blood, of which there is no mention in the Servant passages; moreover in the Isaianic passages the Servant is himself the covenant. It is much more natural then to see in the cup-logion when it speaks of the covenant a reference to Exod. xxiv. 8 or Zech. ix. 11 under the influence of Jer. xxxi. 31 ff.; or to circumcision. The use of πολλοί is again as in x. 45 too widespread a Semitic idiom to ensure a connection to Isa. liii. 11, 12; and ἐκχύννειν has no place in the Servant imagery. The most difficult phrase in the saying is τὸ αἷμά μου τῆς διαθήκης. As it stands this would normally refer in Judaism to the blood of circumcision.[5] This hardly seems possible in the present context. Blood and the institution of a covenant are also associated in Exod. xxiv. 8; if this connection is accepted, then Jesus would be understood as instituting a new covenant, διαθήκη, carrying within itself the concept 'new',[6] and this saying would be brought into line with the

[1] Cf. Pedersen, *Israel*, 1–11, p. 171, cf. pp. 171–81; Best, *One Body in Christ*, pp. 215 ff.

[2] Cf. F.-J. Leenhardt in Cullmann and Leenhardt, *Essays on the Lord's Supper*, pp. 41–3.

[3] The majority of commentators appear to accept the influence of the Servant concept. It is rejected by Hooker, *Jesus and the Servant*, pp. 80–3, and doubted by Behm, *T.W.N.T.* 11, 136.

[4] Fuller, *The Mission and Achievement of Jesus*, pp. 72–5.

[5] Jeremias, *The Eucharistic Words of Jesus*, p. 134.

[6] In the Qumran writings there are many references to the 'covenant'; normally 'the new covenant' is intended though the adjective 'new' is

similar Pauline cup-logion. If the connection is made to Zech. ix. 11 then it is unlikely that we deal here with the institution of the covenant; rather we are concerned with its maintenance through the daily sacrifice.[1] The association with Exod. xxiv. 8 appears preferable. The presence of this phrase about the covenant renders difficult any attempt to create a parallelism between the cup and bread sayings and to interpret them together. Most of those who take them as closely associated, for example Jeremias,[2] draw their conclusions from the form of the sayings which they regard as primitive and prior to the Markan. Thus we cannot argue that Mark would have taken the two sayings together as referring to a sacrificed animal in the moment of its death when flesh and blood are separated.[3] It is interesting that Mark places the saying about the cup after it has been drunk, and not at the moment of distribution, as in the case of the bread. This would again indicate that he did not see the two as closely associated in meaning; the bread refers to the fellowship of believers with Christ and the cup to the sacrifice of Christ for them. Within the early Christian Church the two ideas were inevitably linked together – Christ in us and Christ for us. The reference to the death of Jesus is present in the pouring out of the blood; ἐκχυννόμενον may probably be taken as having a future meaning and as passive, God being the subject;[4] this underlines the frequent idea of the Gospel that the death of Jesus is divinely determined. It is a death ὑπὲρ πολλῶν, that is, as we have seen, for all. Jesus does not die for himself; he does not die merely as a martyr, he dies for men. Moreover we are forced to see here a sacrificial significance; as the old covenant was instituted through the death of an animal, so the new is instituted through the death of the Son of God for the benefit of men. The fact that men drink the wine and do not merely watch it poured out suggests that the blessings of the death are for them to participate in.

added only on four occasions, and the cognate verb is used only four times (cf. Kuhn, *Konkordanz*). Equally the concept of the 'covenant' was widespread in early Christianity and need not always have required the addition of 'new' to imply that the 'new covenant' was intended.

[1] So most commentators.
[2] *The Eucharistic Words of Jesus*, pp. 139 ff.
[3] So Jeremias, *op. cit.* pp. 143 ff.   [4] So Jeremias, *op. cit.* pp. 122 f.

At this point we must diverge from our study of individual texts to inquire whether Mark makes use of the Servant Christology, and if so in what way. We have dismissed a direct relationship to the Servant in x. 45 and xiv. 24; the literary links are not sufficiently clear. Yet we do move in a realm of ideas which is not far distant from that of Isa. liii: the death of Jesus is for men and benefits them. Moreover the Servant Christology cannot be eliminated from the early Church.[1] How far has Mark come under its influence? The presence of this conception has been seen in a series of texts in Mark beginning with the divine voice of baptism.[2] At no point can it be said that identification with the Servant of Deutero-Isaiah is certain, and indeed in many of the suggested passages the identification has been disputed. Typical in this respect is i. 11 (cf. ix. 7). It is generally accepted that the Markan report of the words of the heavenly voice represents the tradition more faithfully than the western form of the Lukan text (iii. 22). In the Markan text the identification with the Servant supposes the existence of an Old Testament translation of Isa. xlii. 1 in which ὁ ἀγαπητός replaced the ἐκλεκτός of the LXX; Matt. xii. 18–21 implies this possibility. Yet many commentators are convinced that 'sonship' rather than 'servanthood' is the predominating theme in Mark i. 11.[3] There are three possibilities. (a) In the logion as it reached Mark there was no reference to servant-hood; Mark then introduced the reference. If so, he did it very poorly. This possibility is most unlikely.[4] (b) The logion is in the form in which it reached Mark and he has preserved it unchanged.

---

[1] We believe that Jeremias in Zimmerli and Jeremias, *The Servant of God*, pp. 79 ff. (= *T.W.N.T.* v, 698 ff.), has made out a much better case for its presence in the very early tradition used in Acts and by Paul than Miss Hooker (*Jesus and the Servant*) allows. For further criticism of Jeremias, etc., cf. Iersel, '*Der Sohn*' *in den synoptischen Jesusworten*, pp. 20–3, 52–65.

[2] Miss Hooker (*Jesus and the Servant, passim*) has gathered together the various passages in which a Servant Christology is suspected, and we use this as the basis of our discussion. She gives full references both to those who have upheld and those who have disputed the reference to the Servant in these passages.

[3] E.g. Taylor, *ad loc.*; Fuller, *The Mission and Achievement of Jesus*, pp. 87 f. Moreover the use of ἀγαπητός can be explained in terms of Gen. xxii. 1–18; cf. below, pp. 169 ff.

[4] Cf. Hahn, *Christologische Hoheitstitel*, pp. 338, 340, who considers that an original עַבְדִּי was replaced by ὁ υἱός μου in i. 11; ix. 7.

In that case we must again say that, since the reference to the Servant in the saying is not certain, Mark has not made it clearer and therefore cannot be said to have thought the conception important at this point. (c) Mark has modified the logion as he received it in order to emphasise the conception of sonship, and thereby has pushed servanthood into the background.[1] A decision between (b) and (c) is hardly possible on the evidence at our disposal. We can certainly say that Mark does not stress servanthood here, but rather shows his interest is in Jesus as Son of God.

The remainder of the material in Mark in which the Servant influence is suspected may be divided into two classes – material which he received in the tradition and passed on more or less unchanged, and material which he himself created or, receiving it, considerably modified.

Let us take first the former category: (a) i. 9, 10, the descent of the Spirit on Jesus at baptism: Mark has certainly not introduced this and he has done nothing to ensure an obvious connection with the Servant. In the reference to the opening of the heavens Luke and Matthew modify Mark's use of σχίζειν to ἀνοίγειν which is found at Isa. lxiii. 19. (b) i. 11; ix. 7, the voice at Baptism and Transfiguration; we have already discussed this. (c) x. 45, see above (pp. 140 ff.). (d) xiv. 18, 21, the use of παραδίδωμι. The fact of the betrayal must have come to Mark in the tradition and this is the natural word to describe it (cf. Isa. liii. 6, 12).[2] (e) xiv. 24, see above (pp. 144 ff.). (f) xiv. 65; xv. 16–20, the mocking of Jesus. Mark will hardly have introduced this event into the account; the references to the Servant are not sufficiently certain. (g) xv. 27, the crucifixion between two thieves: as the Markan gloss shows this was early interpreted as a reference to Isa. liii. 12. Mark is unlikely to have invented the detail about the thieves; if it was created by the early Church it would imply that it viewed Jesus as the Servant, but the point is not made clear in Mark; if it is an historical event then it can hardly be closely linked to the

---

[1] Maurer, 'Knecht Gottes und Sohn Gottes im Passionsbericht des Markusevangeliums', indicates that the Servant Christology lay in the material prior to Mark and gradually received less emphasis.

[2] Iersel, 'Der Sohn' in den synoptischen Jesusworten, pp. 57 f., argues that it is a general word by no means restricted to the Servant imagery.

Isaianic passage. To sum up, we may say that some of the material which Mark received may have contained the idea of Jesus as the Servant, but in the places we have discussed he has done nothing to sharpen the conception.

But what of the second category, the material he has modified or created; (a) i. 1-3, the use of εὐαγγέλιον and the Old Testament quotations. Whether we retain the quotation from Mal. iii. 1 as an original part of the Gospel or not, the use of Isa. xl. 3 is certainly Markan. The combination of this and εὐαγγέλιον shows Mark's indebtedness to Deutero-Isaiah at this point. But it is difficult to trace a precise reference to the Servant; Deutero-Isaiah is concerned with a great deal more than the Servant alone. If Mark intended us to see such a connection he has not done much to ensure we do. He has made clear that the salvation of which Deutero-Isaiah spoke is present in Jesus Christ. (b) iii. 27. We take this verse here because it may have been partly formed by Mark under the influence of his view of the Temptation. Isa. xlix. 24 f. probably lies behind it; but in Isa. xlix. 24 f. it is God, and not the Servant, who spoils his enemies. (c) viii. 31; ix. 12; ix. 31; x. 33 f., the passages in which Jesus predicts his death. These may have been modified by Mark; but if so it has not been to bring them into line with Isa. liii, but to make them closer predictions of the actual Passion. Many details and words from Isa. liii. could easily have been incorporated; the fact that this has not been done suggests that the Servant theology does not dominate them. (d) xiii. 27, 31, in the Little Apocalypse, cannot be excluded from Markan editorship, but they do not make a clear connection to the Servant. (e) xiv. 21, the statement that Jesus goes to his death 'as it is written about him'. The predetermination of the death of Jesus is a Markan theme. But what Scripture has he in mind here?[1] It is natural to think of Isa. liii. and difficult to think of any other suitable passage.[2] But though the divine predetermination of the death of Jesus is strongly emphasised by Mark, it would seem probable that Mark would not have left the reference to Scripture so vague if

---

[1] Possibly Gen. xxii. 1-18; cf. below, pp. 169 ff.

[2] On the predictions, and the use of παραδίδωμι in them, cf. H. E. Tödt, *Der Menschensohn in der synoptischen Überlieferung* (1959), pp. 142 f., 144-50, 155 f.

the reference was due to him; rather he has received it in the tradition (the use of the term 'Son of Man' is traditional rather than Markan), and left it vague because he himself did not know the precise reference. This passage should then be classified rather with the material that Mark has transmitted than with that which he has modified. (*f*) xiv. 61; xv. 5, the silence of Jesus. This has been traced to Isa. liii. 7. This may be its origin, but in Mark the silence of Jesus appears to play a definite role independent of a hidden reference to the Servant; in each case it is strongly contrasted with an immediately preceding or following statement of Jesus himself about his own position. Isa. liii. 7 would demand a total silence. The silence in Mark is dramatically rather than biblically determined.

To sum up, we may say that Mark has transmitted some material in which the concept of the Servant may be present, but that he has not modified material to introduce the conception or to clarify it where it already appeared only dimly. Moreover if Mark has set out Jesus as the strong Son of God – victor in every circumstance, clothed with authority from heaven, in control of his own destiny – this clashes with the conception of the Servant who meekly suffers (cf. Isa. xlii. 2, 3). 'The very terms (meekness and gentleness) are unknown to Mark. But they are typical of the Servant.'[1] The conception has consequently not been absorbed into a dominant place in the Christology of Mark. Certainly there are explicit Old Testament referencs within the Passion narrative, but a glance at the margin of a Nestle text will show that these are to the Psalms rather than to Isaiah. We must thus conclude that Mark does not emphasise Jesus as the Isaianic Servant.[2]

Before we return to the discussion of the passages in which the activity of Jesus is set out we will look for a brief moment at those Old Testament passages which are found in Mark's Passion narrative. With the exception of Zech. xiii. 7, which we discuss later,[3] they are all taken from the Psalms. There is a sense in which their quotation may be regarded as 'superficial'. They are not deeply wrought into the traditional material but have been imposed on it to show its correspondence with the

---

[1] Bacon, *The Gospel of Mark, p.* 223.
[2] *Ibid.* pp. 227 f.　　　[3] Below, pp. 157 f.

Old Testament.[1] (The quotation of Ps. xxii. 2 would appear to lie more deeply in the tradition.) We cannot be sure that they were added by Mark, but, since they lie on the surface and are more than allusions, he must have been aware of them and consciously accepted their use. The other evangelists added many more similar quotations and modified those used by Mark. All are intended to show that what happened to Jesus was in accordance with the Old Testament, and a part of the divine necessity. Thus the quotation of Ps. xli. 10 at xiv. 18 demonstrates that the part played by Judas was within the purpose of God. Most interesting is the use of Ps. xxii. Whether the word of Jesus from the Cross (Ps. xxii. 2 = xv. 34) is genuine or not we must hold it to have been in the tradition from a very early stage. This drew attention to the Psalm from which the other verses were quoted as confirmatory of events in the Passion (Ps. xxii. 8 = Mark xv. 29; Ps. xxii. 19 = Mark xv. 24). This is a Psalm in which the sufferings of the righteous Psalmist are described. So also are Pss. xli, xlii, xliii, lxix from which quotations are drawn (Ps. xli. 10 = Mark xiv. 18; Ps. xlii. 6, 12; xliii. 5 = Mark xiv. 34; Ps. lxix. 22 = Mark xv. 36). Nothing is said in these Psalms suggestive of any interpretation of the meaning of the Passion as redemptive, but it is worthy of note that each of them concludes in such a way as to suggest that God has delivered the Psalmist from his trials, just as God delivered Jesus in the Resurrection (cf. Ps. xxii. 23 ff.; xli. 12 ff.; xlii. 6*b*, 12*b*; xliii. 5*b*; lxix. 31 ff.).[2]

Returning now to those passages in which Jesus testifies to the purpose of his own ministry we examine Mark x. 38 f. In it two images are combined, Baptism and the drinking of a cup. Matthew omits the former, which is undoubtedly the more difficult; Luke has the saying about Baptism in another form, drawn from his special material, and he does not record the saying about the cup. The metaphors refer in the first instance to the whole mission of Jesus; we note the present tenses

---

[1] Cf. Lindars, pp. 90 f. On Mark's use of the Psalms in the Passion narrative cf. A. Rose, 'L'influence des psaumes sur les annonces et les récits de la Passion et de la Résurrection dans les Évangiles', *Le Psautier* (ed. R. de Langhe), pp. 297–356.

[2] Lindars, pp. 89 ff., 106 f.; cf. Iersel, *'Der Sohn' in den synoptischen Jesus-worten*, pp. 55–7.

πίνω, βαπτίζομαι, but for Mark the whole mission of Jesus is summed up in his death, and these images ocur in a passage which has explicit reference to that death (v. 45). We are not then incorrect in taking the principal reference in the sayings as we find them in Mark as being to the Passion of Jesus.

The saying about the cup has occasioned less divergence among commentators than that about the Baptism. Paralleled in xiv. 36, it would appear to be solidly based on Old Testament imagery. Thus viewed it is neither a metaphor for destiny or fate in general, nor for suffering and death in particular. It denotes the judgement of God (Jer. xxv. 15–38; xlix. 12; li. 7; Ezek. xxiii. 31–4; Isa. li. 17, 22, etc.).[1] That God reaches out the cup of wrath to men (Ezek. xxiii. 31; Hab. ii. 16; Jer. xxv. 15, 17) accords with Mark's view that the Passion of Jesus is determined by God. At xiv. 36 Jesus shrinks from taking this cup; this can hardly mean only that he feared physical death but implies something more terrible; he is himself the object of the wrath of God. This interpretation accords with the cry of dereliction (xv. 34).

The meaning of the image of Baptism is by no means so easily determined. It is extremely unlikely that the saying should be taken in the later sense of martyrdom as a Baptism of blood; evidence for this is lacking earlier than Irenaeus.[2] The real question is, Does the word contain an explicit reference to Baptism or is it used purely metaphorically of overwhelming floods bringing disaster? Cullmann,[3] contending for the first alternative, argues that Jesus himself, unlike John, did not baptise men, but in his death underwent a general baptism on their behalf, and it is to this that reference is made in x. 38 f. Here we would then find the origin of the Pauline connection of baptism into the death of Christ.[4] On the other hand, Delling has argued cogently that 'baptism' did not have its

---

[1] Cf. Goppelt, T.W.N.T. VI, 149 ff.; G. Delling, 'βάπτισμα βαπτισθῆναι', N.T. II (1957), 92–115. In Rabbinic Judaism the image may denote 'destiny, fate', but that the Old Testament understanding of it continued through to the New Testament period is testified by its use in such passages as I QpH xi. 10–15; Ps. Sol. viii. 14.

[2] Cf. Oepke, T.W.N.T. I, 536, n. 44; J. H. Bernard, 'A Study of St Mark x. 38, 39', J.T.S. xxviii (1927), 262–70.

[3] Baptism in the New Testament, pp. 19 f.

[4] Flemington, The New Testament Doctrine of Baptism, pp. 31 ff.; cf. Fuller, The Mission and Achievement of Jesus, pp. 59 ff.

fixed theological sense in the time of Jesus but attained this after his death.[1] Therefore the saying contained originally the idea of disaster in water; this disaster did not necessarily imply the death of the one on whom it fell, but was rather symbolic of his judgement (Ps. lxix. 2, 3, 15, 16; Ps. xlii. 8; cxxiv. 3–5; xviii. 17, 18; xxxii. 6; Job xxii. 11).[2] Delling further argued that in the parallel passage in Luke (xii. 49 f.) the baptismal metaphor is associated with that of judgement by fire (i.e. the same theme of judgement), and that similarly his interpretation accords with the parallel of the 'cup' in Mark x. 38 f. However, even if we allow that originally the usage of the baptismal image by Jesus was a reference to the judgement he was about to suffer in death, it is unlikely that by the time Mark wrote, when Baptism was most definitely a technical word in the Christian vocabulary, the word could carry no reference to Baptism. Already the connection of the Baptism of the believer with the death of Christ was widespread; note that Paul in writing to the Romans regards it as something known to them, although he himself has not previously been instructing them about it (Rom. vi. 3).[3] The conception of judgement will have remained attached to the saying, but there will have been added to it the idea that the death of Jesus was a Baptism: as Mark's Gospel begins with a Baptism, that by John, so it ends with another, that of the crucifixion,[4] and if we take seriously the present tenses in *v.* 38 then it is also a Baptism which continued throughout his ministry. Closely related to the Baptism of Jesus is that of his disciples, James and John; their Baptism is yet to take place, that is, future in terms of the Baptism of Jesus. James and John must surely be taken here as typical believers; for Mark all believers must pass through this future Baptism and drink this future cup.[5] Mark is not interested in the historical fate of two disciples, but in the way all disciples should live.

We must examine how the disciples are brought into this

---

[1] *N.T.* 11 (1957), 92–115.

[2] *Ibid.* p. 97. Cf. Lagrange, *ad loc.*; Moulton-Milligan, Stählin, *T.W.N.T.* V, 437 f. Although βαπτίζειν was not usually used in the LXX translation its use is found in Aq. (Job ix. 31; Ps. lxix. (lxviii). 3); Al. (Ps. ix. 16).

[3] Fuller, *The Mission and Achievement of Jesus*, p. 60.

[4] Cf. Wellhausen, *ad loc.*

[5] The evidence for the martyrdom of John the Apostle is not satisfying.

saying. On the surface it might appear that they are to suffer exactly the same fate as Jesus, and that therefore their fate would achieve the same result as his. This cannot be the meaning of Mark. He sets out the person and ministry of Jesus as unique. Throughout the Gospel strong contrasts are drawn between the faithfulness of Jesus and the unfaithfulness of the disciples (e.g. ix. 14 – 29; xiv. 32 – 42); between his sight and their blindness (e.g. viii. 14 – 21; viii. 31 – 3); between his humility and their self-importance (e.g. ix. 33 – 7; x. 32 – 45). The testimony of the divine voice at his Baptism and Transfiguration strongly reinforces this uniqueness. Furthermore, as we have seen, his death is given a special significance (x. 45; xiv. 24), even though others are commanded to take up their cross and follow him (viii. 34). In the very passage we are discussing (x. 35 – 45) we must note that, while x. 45 is linked to x. 44 through the idea of service, it goes much beyond it; both Jesus and disciples serve, but only Jesus gives his life a ransom for many. It would therefore be wholly wrong to imagine that Mark saw in the statement about the Baptism which the disciples would have to undergo any suggestion that their deaths would be comparable to the death of Jesus. If the original reference in the baptismal statement of x. 38 was to the overwhelming tragedy which would engulf like flood-water, then probably this was taken in the early Church to refer in the case of the disciples to the persecution and death that lay ahead for believers. These sufferings, necessarily entailed in a faithful following of Jesus, were not just in imitation of his, but to some extent part of the Messianic woes which had to be fulfilled before the Messiah would come, or, in Christian terms, before he would return (cf. Col. i. 24; I Pet. iv. 13).[1] But if as Mark uses the saying we cannot restrict the reference to overwhelming floods in the case of Jesus, neither can we in the case of the disciples. It must therefore in their case also carry a reference to Baptism. This can only be their own Baptism. The Baptism of the believer according to the Pauline pattern, which was also that of the Primitive Church,[2] is not simply a re-enactment of the dying of Jesus; in Baptism the believer is carried back to the

---

[1] So Delling, *N. T.* II (1957), 92 – 115; Schniewind, etc. On the Messianic woes cf. Schlier, *T. W. N. T.* III, 144 ff.; Strack-Billerbeck, IV, 977 – 86.
[2] Cullmann, *Baptism in the New Testament*, p. 15.

y death of Jesus and participates in it.[1] But the death of us was the principal incident of his ministry and therefore of the Baptism which he himself underwent. In this sense the believer is carried back to the Baptism with which Jesus was baptised and is baptised with the same Baptism and therefore committed to take up his cross and follow after Jesus. The once-for-all death with Jesus is followed by a daily dying.[2] In this way we approach a position similar to that of Dr J. A. T. Robinson, who speaks of the Baptism of Jesus as all-inclusive.[3] All men participate in his Baptism, which is of course more than the literal Baptism of Jordan, but includes also his ministry and Passion. Thus again we come back to the position that the ministry and death of Jesus are on behalf of men. Within the Primitive Church, in so far as the New Testament bears witness, Baptism is in no way connected to the conquest of Satan but is related to forgiveness of sin.

Before we turn to examine the saying about the cup in relation to discipleship we must look at the second occasion on which Jesus refers to his own drinking of the cup, xiv. 36. Here it refers quite obviously to his death, something which lying in the just immediate future he prays he may escape. He shrinks from it, ἤρξατο ἐκθαμβεῖσθαι καὶ ἀδημονεῖν. This cannot be a shrinking only from physical pain and death; his own followers, as Mark knew, faced death for his sake more courageously than that. The cup must be given its full significance: it is the cup of the wrath of God. God can take the cup from him, so God must be the one who gives it; this is fully in line with the Old Testament references to the cup as given by God to men to drink. But why should he be the object of the wrath of God and what will his drinking of the cup achieve for men? This is certainly not made clear on the surface. We must remember that the cup is mentioned a third time in Mark, xiv. 24 – and it is remarkable that Jesus talks about bread and cup and not bread and wine which are the natural equivalents. The cup carries here again a reference to his death in that it is ὑπὲρ πολλῶν. The cup of wrath will then also be drunk ὑπὲρ πολλῶν. But may we link x. 38 and xiv. 36 with xiv. 24? Are

---

[1] Cf. Best, *One Body in Christ*, pp. 44 ff. [2] *Ibid.* pp. 49 f.
[3] *Twelve New Testament Studies*, 'The One Baptism', pp. 158–75 = *S.J. Th.* VI (1953), 257–74.

not the cups entirely different? Here we must remember that in the Old Testament there is a cup of salvation (Ps. cxvi. 13, cf. xxiii. 5) as well as a cup of wrath,[1] there is the peculiar usage of ποτήριον instead of οἶνος in Mark xiv. 24 and there is the association of the cup of salvation in Ps. cxvi with the death of God's saints, an association which is made all the closer because the LXX omits *v*. 14 of the Psalm. We are thus entitled to see in the cup of wrath which Jesus drinks a cup which is partaken for others. Now quite obviously Mark no more means to imply by the reference to James and John in x. 38 f. that they will share in the drinking of the cup of wrath (at xiv. 36 Jesus stands starkly alone in relation to the cup), which is also the cup of salvation 'for many', than that they must undergo the same Baptism for all as Jesus endured. May we not conclude that as in x. 38 f. the application of Baptism to the disciples means their own Baptism, so the cup which they drink is the cup of the Eucharist?[2] It is the cup which renews their participation in the death of Christ and their obligation to take up their own crosses and follow after him.

Expressing a somewhat similar thought to the drinking of the cup of judgement is the picture of the striking of the shepherd (xiv. 27). This is derived from Zech. xiii. 7*b*. Mark follows the A text of the LXX rather than the B; the A is itself closer to the Hebrew. The B text speaks of shepherds in the plural from whom the ἄνδρα πολίτην μου (*v*. 7*a*) must necessarily be distinct. The A text, as the Hebrew, permits the identification of this person with the shepherd himself. There is thus one person who is smitten. In Zech. xiii. 7 God speaks to his sword to smite; in Mark xiv. 27 the first person singular is used: it is presumably God himself who smites,[3] for it would be difficult to believe that Mark saw Jesus as striking his shepherd Peter, which the first singular of *v*. 28 might lead us to suppose.[4] The

---

[1] The cup of Ps. cxvi. 13 as a cup of thanksgiving may be related to the 'cup of blessing' of I Cor. x. 16; cf. H.-J. Kraus on Ps. cxvi.

[2] Cf. Lohmeyer, *ad. loc.*

[3] xiv. 27*b*, 28 appear to break the flow of the narrative from *v*. 27*a* to *v*. 29 and are probably a Markan insertion, cf. pp. 90, 173 ff.; this would make them all the more important for the determination of his view of the death of Jesus. Mark would appear to have an especial fondness for Zech. ix–xiv; cf. Smith, 'No Time for Figs', pp. 321 f.

[4] Cf. Lindars, pp. 127–32.

one who is struck by God is described in the LXX (A text) as ποιμήν μου καὶ ἀνὴρ πολίτης μου (v. 7a).[1] The shepherd is then probably one who is acceptable to God. But the whole theme of the passage in Zechariah is judgement and salvation.[2] Judgement is meted out on this shepherd and on the flock, two-thirds of which perish, but one-third of which are saved as a remnant. In Mark, however, the shepherd bears the whole judgement meted out by God, just as he had to drink the cup of God's judgement. Thus Mark sets forth Jesus as smitten by God in God's judgement over his people Israel. But just as the passage in Zechariah is not without its message of salvation as well as judgement – one-third of the people are saved – so here the quotation from Zechariah is followed by the promise that Jesus goes ahead of the community into Galilee; whatever this may mean, it means at least the recreation of the community, the remnant saved because the Shepherd has been struck by God. Thus again the Cross means judgement borne by Jesus for men. And if, as is probable,[3] xiv. 27b, 28 is a Markan editorial insertion, then this represents the Markan view of the death of Jesus; it is a view which we have found to be echoed in the meaning of the cry of dereliction (xv. 34), in the Baptism endured for men (x. 38) and in the cup drunk on their behalf (x. 38; xiv. 36). We may observe that we have suspected Markan editorial work also in xiv. 36, where there would appear to be the combination of two accounts of the incident at Gethsemane.[4] In this view of the death Mark is not then merely reflecting the ideas of the material he had received but is positively putting his own interpretation on the death of Jesus by introducing, or creating, material in which a particular view was expressed.

It is possible that a similar line of thought is to be detected in the Temptation story, that is, that in the wilderness Jesus

---

[1] M.T. reads גֶּבֶר עֲמִיתִי: an unusual phrase meaning someone standing near.

[2] Cf. C. F. Evans, 'I will go before you into Galilee', *J. T.S.* V (1954), 3–18. He also argues, 'The sequence of events in the Marcan account of the last week in Jerusalem – triumphal entry, cleansing of the temple, cursing of the fig tree, the saying about "this mountain", the blood of the covenant, the prophecy of the smiting of the shepherd and of the scattering of the flock, all preceded by the discourse on the last things – reflects a similar presence, if not combination, of ideas in Zechariah' (p. 8).

[3] Cf. p. 157, n. 3.   [4] Cf. pp. 92 ff.

bore the judgement of God. This would be so if Jesus' expulsion by the Spirit to the desert was conceived as similar to that of the scapegoat bearing the sins of the people and driven out to Azazel (Lev. xvi. 7–10, 20–2).[1] Azazel was regarded in Judaism as an evil spiritual being[2] and therefore Mark might have taken him to be Satan. We cannot accept this suggestion because its assumptions have not been proved, namely, that for Mark Jesus was the scapegoat and Azazel the supreme evil being.

[1] Mauser, p. 98, n. 2.
[2] Langton, *Essentials of Demonology*, pp. 43 f., 108, 130–2.

CHAPTER VII

THE TITLES OF JESUS[1]

JUST as place-names and personal names become liable to alteration, subtraction and addition in the handing on of the tradition in the primitive community, so it is reasonable to assume that the titles used of Jesus might also have been changed. If the same person is known by a number of titles it is *a priori* probable that the title used in a particular speech or account could be varied, provided the particular title is not relevant to the content of what is being said. Preachers, speaking from memory, constantly misquote texts through the substitution of one title of Jesus for another. Young people repeating answers to catechism questions frequently make the same mistake. Paul had a number of variants for the phrase 'in Christ', for example 'in the Lord', and there does not appear to have been much alteration in the total meaning of the phrase when he varied the title.[2] Different schools of theological thought have favourite titles for Jesus; for example, the liberal school popularised the title 'Master', and this because it represented a strong strain in their thinking about Jesus. It may thus be that an author's choice of titles for Jesus may reveal something of his theology. We therefore examine the titles used by Mark to see what we can learn from them about his theology in relation to the mission of Jesus.

If we consider the manner in which Luke and Matthew have varied the titles used by Mark of Jesus, it will be seen that they cannot have regarded Mark's choice as sacrosanct. On certain occasions they were not free to make changes unless they were prepared to alter drastically the content of the passage; for example, to eliminate the use of 'son' in the words of the Divine Voice at the Baptism and the Transfiguration and replace by another of the titles, say King, would have completely altered the fact that the Divine Voice by its particular choice of title

[1] V. Taylor, *The Names of Jesus*, is valuable for its accumulation of material. Cf. also Hahn, *Christologische Hoheitstitel*.

[2] Cf. Best, *One Body in Christ*, pp. 30-2.

on those occasions set up a relationship between God and Jesus, whereas the other title 'King' would have set up a relationship between him and men. Neither Matthew nor Luke is keen on Mark's title 'King of the Jews (Israel)' used in the Passion narrative (xv. 2, 9, 12, 18, 26, 32), so they succeed in altering or omitting it; Luke does so by completely rewriting some of the passages where it occurs, or by using another source; both can change it to 'Christ' (Matt. xxvii. 17, 22; Luke xxiii. 35). Luke eliminates the term 'Son of God (of the Blessed)' from Mark xiv. 61 and xv. 39. Matthew adds references to Jesus as Son of God at xiv. 33; xxvii. 40 (cf. xxvii. 43). Luke adds a reference to Jesus as King of the Jews at xxiii. 37 where Mark has no title and Matthew has independently added 'Son of God'. On a number of occasions when Mark has 'teacher' Matthew has changed this to κύριος (viii. 25; xvii. 4, 15; xx. 31–3),[1] and where Mark has either no address or the personal pronoun he has introduced it (Matt. viii. 2; xvi. 22; xxvi. 22); Luke has also brought in this title at v. 12; xviii. 41; xxii. 61. To Peter's confession that Jesus was the Christ (Mark viii. 29) Matthew adds 'the son of the living God' (xvi. 16). At Mark xv. 32 where Mark uses the double title 'Christ' and 'King' Matthew omits the title 'Christ' but retains 'King'. On a number of occasions Matthew adds the title 'Christ' (xvi. 20, 21; xxiv. 5; xxvi. 68). Matthew replaces the title 'Son of Man' at Mark viii. 31 with the personal pronoun (cf. Mark viii. 38 with Matt. x. 33 and Luke xii. 9). Matthew introduces this same title at xvi. 13 (cf. xvi. 28). These variations may have been made either because Matthew or Luke thought the choice of title was a matter of indifference, or because they had favourite titles they wished to use, or because the change expressed more adequately their thought at that particular point. It is unnecessary for us to enter a discussion of their reasons for change. The fact that they did change renders it *a priori* probable that Mark will have altered the titles in the material as it came to him. We have no adequate means of checking if he did so, but because change was a possibility it is natural to assume that the titles which he wrote in his manuscript meant something to him. If he retained them from the

---

[1] For Matthew's use of κύριος cf. Bornkamm in Bornkamm, Barth and Held, *Tradition and Interpretation in Matthew*, pp. 41–3.

tradition it was not out of mere respect for it but because they expressed what he wished to say; if he varied them it was because the variation expressed his meaning more fully.

SON OF MAN[1]

This most enigmatic of titles is varied very little by Matthew and Luke in their adoption of the passages in which it occurs in Mark. This would suggest a particular reverence for it. It was continued because its use lay deep in the tradition; this view is reinforced by the fact that it is to be found in all the strata of the tradition, Mark, Q, Special Matthew and Special Luke; most scholars therefore assume that its usage goes back to Jesus himself. We do not need to argue whether this is so or not, nor do we need to argue whether when Jesus used it he intended himself or someone other, or whether he regarded the Son of Man as a corporate being; for Mark the Son of Man is Jesus.[2]

It is generally recognised that the Son of Man title is used in the Gospels in three different ways: in relationship to (a) the incarnate activity of Christ, (b) his sufferings, (c) his appearance in glory. All these three usages appear in Mark. Our only question is whether Mark, having received one type of saying, may have applied the title to other types; for example, if the eschatological type of saying came to Mark in the tradition did he derive the title from that type and then take it and apply it to sayings about suffering? We have seen that x. 45, a saying of type (b), probably came to Mark in the tradition.[3] It also seems reasonable to assume that at least one of the three Passion predictions came as traditional material to Mark; he may have manufactured the others on the basis of one but would

---

[1] A valuable summary of views on the Son of Man and full references to recent literature will be found in A. J. B. Higgins, 'Son of Man', in *New Testament Essays* (ed. Higgins), pp. 119–35. To this we may add E. Schweizer, 'Der Menschensohn', *Z.N.T.W.* L (1959), 185–210, 'The Son of Man Again', *N.T.S.* IX (1963), 256–61; Hahn, *Christologische Hoheitstitel*, pp. 13 ff.; M. Black, 'The Son of Man Problem in Recent Research and Debate', *Bull. J. Rylands Lib.* XLV (1963), 305–18; Tödt, *Der Menschensohn in der synoptischen Überlieferung*. Most of the discussion of the title is taken up with the way in which Jesus himself used the phrase and does not relate directly to Mark's usage.

[2] Above, pp. 121 ff.   [3] See pp. 140 f. above.

hardly have invented *ab initio* the idea of prediction. viii. 31 has a typically Markan editorial introduction,[1] but the remainder of the verse is not particularly Markan. Furthermore, sayings of type (*b*) are found, possibly independently, in Special Luke (xxii. 22; xxiv. 7). The two sayings of type (*a*) which occur in Mark (ii. 10, 28) may originally have been sayings in which 'Son of Man' was not a title but meant 'man'; it is possible that Mark may have sharpened them to apply only to Jesus, but it seems more probable that they came to him already with this application. On the face of it it seems much more likely that possessing sayings of type (*b*) Mark should have added sayings of type (*c*), for here he would have biblical material (Daniel vii. 13) to guide him; but this is such an obvious addition that it would almost certainly have taken place in the tradition earlier than Mark and not be due to him; xiv. 62 is too closely interwoven into its incident for it to have been added by him. We may therefore conclude that in the material as Mark received it the title occurred, certainly in forms (*b*) and (*c*), and probably also in form (*a*). If Mark moulded one or more of the Passion predictions on the model of one that he had received which itself used the title Son of Man, then the use of the same title in the others can hardly be termed editorial in the full sense. But it is not certain that Mark did form any of the Passion predictions. We cannot then speak of Mark's use of the title Son of Man as editorial. He received it in the tradition and preserved it. He may have preserved it either because it had meaning for him or because its meaning had been lost and it had become almost magical in its use; not knowing its meaning he would not know to what other title he might change it.

The majority of sayings in Mark about the suffering and death of Jesus are cast in terms of the Son of Man. There are certainly some that are not, but in most of these the metaphor which is used forbids reference to the Son of Man; for example, the reference to the death of Jesus at ii. 19 f. is so expressed in terms of marriage that it would be unthinkable to change 'bridegroom' to 'Son of Man', cf. xii. 6–8, 10 f.; xiv. 27. To say at xiv. 8 that the woman had anointed the body of the Son of Man would be clumsy. xiv. 24 and x. 38 are cast in terms of

[1] See pp. 79 f.

the first person and this almost seems a necessity of their context. The suffering sayings are not connected with any of the other major titles, for example Son of God. Certain of the Son of Man sayings are concerned with the divine necessity (viii. 31) which may be explained as pre-ordained in Scripture (ix. 12; xiv. 21). It is natural to include within the Scriptural reference the term 'Son of Man'. A suffering Son of Man is found in Scripture in at least two places: Dan. vii. 13, 21, 25, 27 and Ps. lxxx. 18.[1] In each case there is a period of suffering followed by restoration at God's hand, which would correspond to the Resurrection. And since Mark (xiv. 62; xiii. 26) does connect Jesus to the Son of Man of Dan. vii. 13 these may well be the passages he had in mind. We may note the use of παραδίδωμι in both Mark xiv. 21 and Dan. vii. 25 (LXX). Whether this is the ultimate origin of the use of the term Son of Man in the suffering sayings is another matter altogether. The fact that Mark preserves the term Son of Man in reference to one whom he can also describe as yet to come in clouds with power and glory (xiii. 26; xiv. 62) brings out the paradox of the nature of the one who suffers. From the beginning of his Gospel Mark has made it clear to us that it is the Gospel of the Son of God whom men killed. The double use of the term Son of Man to describe both suffering and glory underlines this. It achieves the same effect as Mark's insertion of the Little Apocalypse directly before the Passion.

Mark first introduces us to the Son of Man as one who forgives sin (ii. 10) and immediately afterwards he sets him out as superior to the law which defines what sin is (ii. 28).[2] So also the final references to the Son of Man coming in glory carry similar implications in that they set him out with judicial functions; the High Priest who has judged him will himself be judged, and the elect, the faithful, will be gathered from all parts. The Son of Man is thus set in a definite relationship to sin: he as Lord of the Sabbath can define the Law and therefore

[1] Cf. W. D. Davies, *Paul and Rabbinic Judaism*, p. 280, n. 1; C. H. Dodd, *According to the Scriptures*, p. 117, n. 2.

[2] It is perhaps incorrect in the case of Mark to speak of ii. 10 and ii. 28 as sayings of the incarnate Christ, i.e. of type (a). In them Mark sees the exalted Lord as speaking through the incarnate Christ with authority in relation to sin and the Law.

define what sin is; he can forgive it and he can judge men in respect of it. It is only natural then that the suffering sayings should bear the same positive relationship to sin; this comes to the surface explicitly at x. 45, where as we have seen the death of the Son of Man is for the sin of men. As Son of Man, a title which Mark receives in the tradition and retains, Jesus is set out as the one who deals with sin either through forgiveness or punishment; he is not set in relationship to the cosmic powers.

THE CHRIST

This title does not appear to have great significance for Mark, despite the fact that it forms the substance of Peter's confession at Caesarea Philippi. A brief review of the evidence will confirm this conclusion. In the very instance of Peter's confession, Jesus when he speaks of himself varies the title to that of Son of Man (viii. 31). Likewise at xiv. 61 when the High Priest asks Jesus if he is the Christ, the Son of the Blessed, Jesus while admitting this makes a positive statement in terms of the Son of Man (xiv. 62).[1] The same is apparently also true of xiii. 21, where the presence of false Christs is contrasted with the coming of the true Son of Man (xii. 26). At xv. 32 the title is used by the enemies of Jesus who mock him on the Cross and its use is in no sense a confession of faith. At xii. 35, which has been regarded both as a defence of the Davidic descent of the Messiah and as an attack upon it, 'Christ' is the natural title to use. The usage at ix. 41 is not textually certain; it implies the existence of a community centred on Christ. All these instances would appear to have come to Mark in the tradition.[2] The one usage of Christ which is certainly Markan is found in i. 1; it is significant that it is not here a title but a personal name.[3] Matthew and Luke use the title more frequently than Mark, Luke adding it to Markan material at iv. 41 and Matthew at xvi. 20 (in *v.* 21 it is not a title); xxiv. 5; xxvi. 68; xxvii. 17, 22.

[1] If we do not accept the reading ἐγώ εἰμι at xiv. 62 then Jesus does not necessarily agree even with the High Priest's use of the title 'Christ'.

[2] The reading ὅτι Χριστοῦ ἐστε, ix. 41, even if part of the genuine text of Mark, can certainly not be traced back beyond the early Church to Jesus himself.

[3] We have not considered i. 34 where the appearance of 'Christ' in some texts is very probably due to assimilation to Luke iv. 41.

Mark leaves the title, so far as we know, in the material as it comes to him; he does not deny that Jesus is the Christ, nor does he stress it. In itself the title tells us nothing about the achievement of Jesus; it may even suggest a false conception of the central figure of Mark's Gospel.

THE KING OF THE JEWS[1]

This title is used five times by Mark in one chapter (xv. 2, 9, 12, 18, 26), always on the lips of Gentile enemies of Jesus; once we have 'King of Israel', spoken by the Jews in mockery at the Cross. Both Matthew and Luke freely change it; Luke adds it on one occasion (xxiii. 37). Apart from the Johannine writings it is scarcely used elsewhere in the New Testament. It may be that in the early Church it was partly equivalent to κύριος, denoting the Lordship of Christ over the Church;[2] but if so, nothing of this appears in Mark's usage. It is a variant of the Messianic title (cf. Matt. xxvii. 17, 22 and Luke xxiii. 35 with Mark xv. 9, 12, 32), and the fact that Jesus is crucified as the Jewish king emphasises the guilt of the Jews. It fails to disclose anything more of the Markan conception of the achievement of Jesus.

SON OF DAVID

This is closely related to the Messianic title. It occurs four times in Mark (x. 47, 48; xii. 35, 37). It would appear to have come to Mark in the tradition of the two incidents in which it appears. It adds nothing to our knowledge of the Markan soteriology.

LORD

This title is rarely used by Mark of Jesus;[3] Matthew and Luke insert it frequently and its use was widespread in early Christianity. When Mark uses the word we have to determine whether he refers it to Jesus, and, if so, whether he intends it in the full sense which it attained in the early Church, or whether it is only used as a title of respect like Rabbi. The one certain place where

---

[1] Cf. above. pp. 95 f.

[2] Cf. Cullmann, *The Christology of the New Testament*, pp. 220 ff.

[3] If, as Schreiber maintains, Mark reflects the Hellenistic kerugma we should expect the title to be prominent.

it is used of Jesus in its full sense by Mark is xii. 36, 37; here the reference is eschatological: at some future point the enemies of Jesus are to be under his feet. At v. 19 the original reference was probably to God; the healed demoniac is told to go and preach what God had done to him; but the fact that in v. 20 he is said to tell what Jesus had done (ποιεῖν is used in both cases) makes it likely that Mark and his readers would have understood that 'the Lord' was Jesus: here then Jesus as Lord is seen in his present saving activity; he is Lord over the demonic world. The use of the vocative κύριε by the Syro-Phoenician woman (vii. 28) may well be original; she intended it as a title of honour without any special significance; it would be the equivalent of 'teacher' as used by Jews of Jesus; again it may have been taken in a fuller sense by Mark and his readers, but if so this passage throws little light on what it meant for them. At xi. 3 the natural meaning is to take it of Jesus;[1] as a designation of Jesus, at whose disposal are all things, it would be here an appropriate title. As Jesus is Lord of all that has been created, so he is also Lord of the Law (ii. 28). The title thus expresses the Lordship of Jesus over all things and therefore his saving power in this present age and the eschatological fulfilment of his Lordship in the age to come.

SON OF GOD

It is generally recognised that this is the most important of the titles of Jesus in Mark – yet it is used sparingly and, with the possible exception of i. 1, there is no point at which we can be certain Mark introduced this title into the material; it is possible that on various occasions (for example xv. 39) Mark altered some other title to it, but we cannot prove this. Like the other titles it lays emphasis on the being of Jesus rather than on his activity. An initial problem concerns the reading in i. 1; there are good grounds for accepting υἱοῦ θεοῦ as original,[2] but we cannot be certain; whether we accept it or not, its actual usage here has no light to shed on its meaning.

[1] Taylor, *ad loc.*, takes it for the unidentified actual owner of the colt; again this may have been the original meaning, but it hardly retains it in the Markan context.
[2] Cranfield makes a strong defence.

It is pre-eminently the title of confession. If the reading is correct at i. 1 then Mark confesses Jesus as Son of God at the very beginning. But even if this reading is not allowed then at i. 11 God himself confesses Jesus as his Son. The Gospel is not a mystery story in which the identity of the main character has to be guessed; from the outset it is made clear who this is – the Son of God. This divine confession is repeated at the Transfiguration (ix. 7); if at the Baptism it is made to Jesus alone, on the second occasion it is made to the inner ring of disciples; but in the Gospel it is made on each occasion to all its readers. Between these two divine testimonies there lie the two demonic (iii. 11; v. 7). Thus the opposite sides of the spiritual world, as we might say, agree in their witness. It is also his own testimony to himself at the solemn moment of his trial before the High Priest. Finally it is the confession of the centurion after his death. Whether the centurion used the title in a Hellenistic way as denoting someone with exceptional powers or not, Mark clearly understands it as a unique designation of Jesus. Thus the Gospel beginning with the divine testimony to the sonship of Jesus ends with the same human testimony; Jesus is the Son of God, and he is this, not despite, but because of his death. Closely allied to the conception of confession is that of obedience. The demons who confess him are subject to him; at iii. 11 the demons have already fallen down before him when they acknowledge his sonship; at v. 7, as *v.* 8 shows, he has already demanded their obedience; *v.* 8 may indeed be an editorial comment of Mark justifying *vv.* 6, 7.[1] When in the Transfiguration the divine voice has described Jesus as Son it goes on at once to tell the disciples to 'hear' him; 'hear' must be given its full sense of 'obedience'; the only true hearing known to the Bible is obedient hearing. In so far as the title 'Son of God' implies obedience it is used somewhat similarly to κύριος in other parts of the New Testament.

But how is the title used in relationship to the activities of Jesus? It is as Son of God that he overcomes the demons. Just as he had been proclaimed Son of God at the Baptism and then went into the wilderness and defeated Satan,[2] so as Son he

---

[1] So Taylor, *ad loc.*

[2] In the Q account of the Temptations Jesus is expressly tempted as Son of God.

deprives Satan's minions of their power. As Son of God he has a certain status and evil must be subject to one of that status. And yet though possessing that status he dies. In the Parable of the Vineyard (xii. 1–9) it is because he is the Son that he is put to death. And it is in his dying that he is recognised as Son by the centurion.[1] Perhaps also the nearness of the Transfiguration, in which he is announced as Son, to the first prophecy of the Cross is meant also to indicate the role of suffering in the destiny of the Son of God.[2] In xiv. 36 Jesus in the Garden of Gethsemane and face to face with death calls on God as his Father; elsewhere he speaks little in this Gospel of God as Father, either as his own Father (viii. 38; xiii. 32) or as the Father of the disciples (xi. 25). The invocation of God as Father is emphasised moreover in xiv. 36 by the double use of the address, ἀββὰ ὁ πατήρ. Thus the title of Son is linked closely to the death of Jesus. This is unexpected since in the early Church it would appear to have been linked rather to his Resurrection; cf. Rom. i. 4; I Thess. i. 10; Acts xiii. 33.[3] This latter connection is of course found in Mark in the use of the title in the Transfiguration. It is the natural connection, made through Ps. ii. 7; the relationship of sonship to death is by no means so obvious.

What is there in 'sonship' which relates it to the death of Jesus? It may be that in i. 11 we should associate the 'Servant' conception with that of 'sonship' and hence arrive at a 'dying' sonship; we have already given reasons for supposing that the 'Servant' Christology did not occupy a large place in the Markan theology.[4] It cannot then have profoundly modified the sonship theme. Moreover this would only connect sonship to death indirectly, whereas the evidence seems to require a more direct link.

Another approach is possible. We may link ἀγαπητός in i. 11 and ix. 7 with Isaac. As Isaac was almost a sacrifice so Jesus is a sacrifice. ἀγαπητός is used in Gen. xxii. 2, 12, 16 of Isaac. C. H. Turner has demonstrated that the probable

---

[1] In Matthew (xxvii. 54) Jesus is recognised as Son of God by the centurion because of the accompanying miracles.

[2] In viii. 38 the Son of Man and the Son of God are identified by means of the reference to the Father.

[3] Cf. Iersel, '*Der Sohn*' in den synoptischen Jesusworten, pp. 174 f.

[4] Cf. pp. 148 ff.

meaning of the word is 'only' rather than 'beloved'.[1] He supplies evidence to show that it was taken in this way in pre- and post-biblical literature. He also points out that in taking it with this meaning both Irenaeus (*Adv. Haer.* IV, 5, 4) and Athanasius (*Oratio IV contra Arianos*, 24) relate it to the story of Isaac. Further confirmation that the Abraham-Isaac imagery might be seen in the baptismal account (i. 9–11) is given by Test. Levi xviii. 6, 7.

The heavens shall be opened,
And from the temple of glory shall come upon him sanctification,
With the Father's voice as from Abraham to Isaac.
And the glory of the Most High shall be uttered over him,
And the spirit of understanding and sanctification shall rest upon
    him in the water.[2]

Charles brackets the last three words as a Christian editorial addition. If the remainder is pre-Christian then it shows that the Isaac imagery was already attached to the figure of the new priest whom God would raise up and whom Christians would naturally identify with Christ; the addition of the words 'in the water' shows that in fact the early Christians did make this identification of Jesus with Isaac. If, however, the whole passage should be taken as a Christian construction then again we see that Christ was seen as the new Isaac at an early period.[3] We can also see evidence within the New Testament that Jesus was taken as the new Isaac.[4] It is found in Heb. xi. 17–19 where the sparing of Isaac at the last moment is a type of the Resurrection.[5] The same idea is also probably present in Rom.

[1] *J. T. S.* XXVII (1926), 113–29; XXVIII (1927), 152; A. Souter, 'ΑΓΑΠΗΤΟΣ', *J. T. S.* XXVIII (1927), 59f.

[2] Translation as in Charles, *Apocrypha and Pseudepigrapha*, II. Cf. M. Black, 'The Messiah in the Testament of Levi xviii', *E. T.* LX (1949), 321 f.; LXI (1950), 157 f.; and J. R. Porter, *E. T.* LXI (1949), 90f.

[3] Cf. Richardson, *An Introduction to the Theology of the New Testament*, pp. 180, 228.

[4] From Barnabas vii. 3 onwards Isaac becomes a type of Christ in Patristic literature; cf. J. Daniélou, 'La typologie d'Isaac dans le christianisme primitif', *Biblica*, XXVIII (1947), 363–93; *Sacramentum Futuri* (Paris, 1950), pp. 97 ff. Cf. A. M. Smith, 'The Iconography of the Sacrifice of Isaac in Early Christian Art', *Amer. J. Archaeology*, XXVI (1922), 159–69.

[5] Even in Judaism it could be taken as a symbol of Resurrection; e.g. Pirqe de Rabbi Eliezer 31 (16 b), quoted in Strack-Billerbeck, III, 746. Cf. E. R. Goodenough, *Jewish Symbols in the Greco-Roman Period*, IV, 172–94.

iv. 24;[1] Jesus was not spared as Isaac was but he did, like Isaac, come back from the dead. At Rom. viii. 32 Paul will have had Isaac in mind;[2] knowing that ἀγαπητός means 'only' he uses in its place ἴδιος; he repeats φείδεσθαι from Gen. xxii. 12; God did not spare his Son as Abraham was permitted to spare his. We may also suspect its presence in Acts iii. 25 f.; the quotation here of Gen. xxii. 18, which was closely related in the Targumic tradition to the redemptive sacrifice of Isaac (the *Akedah* or binding of Isaac), seems to imply the equation of Jesus with the seed of Abraham.[3] The *Akedah* may again be the background to the very difficult reference to the lamb in John i. 29; Jesus is Isaac, the lamb, by whom the sins of men are taken away.[4]

Knowledge of the *Akedah* must have been widespread in Judaism of the first century: Josephus, *Ant.* I, 225 – 36 (especially 227, 232); IV Macc. xiii. 12; xvi. 20; Ps.-Philo, *Liber Antiquitatum Biblicarum*, XVIII, 8; XXXII, 2 – 4; XL, 2; it is also found in the various Targums, in particular the *Fragmentary* and *Neofiti*.[5] In these passages Isaac appears as the willing victim who requests that he be bound for the sacrifice.[6] In Rabbinic teaching the sacrifice of Isaac, though no blood was shed, came to be accepted as the one perfect sacrifice by which the sins of the people of Israel were forgiven.[7]

In short, the Binding of Isaac was thought to have played a unique role in the whole economy of the salvation of Israel, and to have a permanent redemptive effect on behalf of its people. The merits of his sacrifice were experienced by the Chosen People in the past, invoked in the present, and hoped for at the end of time.[8]

[1] Cf. Barrett, *Romans, ad loc.* He considers that the Isaac imagery is also present at Rom. viii. 32. Cf. H. J. Schoeps, *Aus frühchristlicher Zeit*, pp. 229 – 38, and *Paul*, pp. 141 – 9; G. Vermes, *Scripture and Tradition in Judaism*, p. 220.

[2] Turner, *J.T.S.* XXVII (1926), 119 f.

[3] Vermes, *Scripture and Tradition in Judaism*, pp. 221 f.

[4] *Ibid.* pp. 224 f. Cf. Richardson, *An Introduction to the Theology of the New Testament*, p. 228.

[5] All the relevant passages are quoted in Vermes, *Scripture and Tradition in Judaism*, pp. 194 ff.; cf. Schoeps, *Aus frühchristlicher Zeit*; Moore, I, 536 ff., 549. C. K. Barrett, *From First Adam to Last*, pp. 26 – 30, is more sceptical about the prevalence of the developed Jewish ideas on Isaac in the New Testament period.   [6] Cf. Sifrè Deut. § 32 on Deut. vi. 5.

[7] Vermes, *Scripture and Tradition in Judaism*, pp. 204 – 8.

[8] *Ibid.* p. 208.

The Rabbis also taught that Jerusalem was Mount Moriah[1] and that the sacrifices offered in the Temple had their foundation in the once-for-all sacrifice of Isaac.[2]

According to ancient Jewish theology, the atoning efficacy of the *Tamid* offering, of all the sacrifices in which a lamb was immolated, and perhaps, basically, of all expiatory sacrifice irrespective of the nature of the victim, depended upon the virtue of the Akedah, the self-offering of that Lamb whom God had recognised as the perfect victim of the perfect burnt offering.[3]

Whereas later tradition associated the *Akedah* with the New Year Festival, Vermes has shown that it was earlier related to the Passover.[4] It may also be that Jewish tradition in the first century A.D., or earlier, had already connected the *Akedah* with the Suffering Servant,[5] though the evidence for this is not so certain. It may also be noted that in IV Macc. (xiii. 12; xvi. 20) Isaac is the sacrificed Martyr; elsewhere in this book we find allusion to the blood of the martyrs (vi. 27 ff.; xvii. 22; xviii. 4). Either the connection of Isaac with the Suffering Servant or with the idea of the meritorious blood of the martyrs may have inspired the doctrine of his atoning sacrifice; or it may have emerged from the general Jewish doctrine of the merits of the Fathers.

Returning now to the death of Jesus, we may view him in Mark's picture as an only (i. 11; ix. 7) and an obedient (xiv. 32 ff.) son who goes willingly to his death like Isaac, and whose death is a sacrifice for the sins of men. If this interpretation is accepted, sonship is fulfilled in willing sacrifice, which is for others, and sonship is recognised in the moment of death (cf. xv. 39). Thus taking Jesus to be the new Isaac we find that

---

[1] In II Chron. iii. 1 Mount Moriah is the temple hill; in Gen. xxii. 14 the same idea is suggested by the reference to the 'Mount of the Lord' (cf. Isa. ii. 3; xxx. 29; Ps. xxiv. 3); it is made more explicit in T. Onk. and in Gen. R. lvi. 10 on Gen. xxii. 14. Cf. Schoeps, *Aus frühchristlicher Zeit*; Vermes, *Scripture and Tradition in Judaism*, pp. 208 f.

[2] Vermes, *Scripture and Tradition in Judaism*, pp. 209–11. The *Akedah* is depicted on the right of the Torah Shrine panel in the synagogue of Dura-Europos, thus showing redemptive significance, cf. C. H. Kraeling, *The Synagogue* (Part 1 of *The Excavations at Dura-Europos Final Report VIII*), pp. 54–62 and plate XVI.

[3] *Ibid.* p. 211.　　　　　[4] *Ibid.* pp. 214–18.

[5] *Ibid.* pp. 202 f.

THE TITLES OF JESUS

the theme of sonship is linked to the sacrifice of the Cross, with the underlying conception, as in Judaism, of a sacrifice for others (cf. Rom. viii. 32). (See Addendum on p. 177).

TEACHER

Unlike the preceding title this is not one which describes the status of Jesus but one which rather contains within itself a designation of his activity. Mark uses διδάσκαλος twelve times[1] and Rabbi, an equivalent, three times.[2] Matthew and Luke often vary the usage. In almost every case the words appear in the vocative case as parts of the material which will have come to Mark in the tradition. We have already seen that in his editorial seams Mark has set out Jesus as 'teacher'.[3] His retention of the word in the material, whereas Matthew and Luke vary it, is in accordance with this trait in his own presentation of Jesus.

SHEPHERD

In two places Mark depicts Jesus as the shepherd (vi. 34; xiv. 27). The former of these two we have seen to be an editorial insertion of Mark in which he showed the shepherd Jesus feeding his people with the Word.[4] xiv. 26 – 31 is probably also a Markan construction.[5] In particular it would appear that *v.* 28 here interrupts the flow of thought from *v.* 27*a* to *v.* 29; cast in the first person its grammatical subject is Jesus, but its actual subject must be God.[6] Probably therefore it and *v.* 27*b* were inserted at this point by Mark. It is future in form and therefore preparatory for xvi. 7, but this does not explain the reason for its insertion precisely at this point. Rather it may be regarded as explanatory of *v.* 27: the shepherd is killed; the sheep are scattered; the shepherd rises again and gathers together his scattered flock in Galilee. προάγειν has two possible meanings; it can either refer to going on ahead in time or going on ahead in space, that is leading. C. F. Evans[7] has argued that the

---

[1] iv. 38; v. 35; ix. 17, 38; x. 17, 20, 35; xii. 14, 19, 32; xiii. 1; xiv. 14.
[2] ix. 5; xi. 21; xiv. 45.
[3] Pp. 71 f.   [4] Pp. 76 f.   [5] Pp. 92, 157 f.
[6] Cf. Lohmeyer, *ad loc.*; Marxsen, pp. 47 f.; Lindars, p. 129.
[7] 'I will go before you into Galilee.'

173

latter is the more usual meaning of the word. As we have seen it fits the conception of the shepherd leading his flock; moreover it corresponds to x. 32: Jesus leads his people in suffering and in salvation. But does not xvi. 7, which is parallel to xiv. 28, conflict with this interpretation? Jesus according to xvi. 7 is already in Galilee where he awaits his disciples to show himself to them in the Resurrection.[1] This assumes that Galilee is used here as an actual place, but as we shall shortly see Galilee is a theological term in Mark and denotes the place where the Gospel is preached; therefore it does not denote a place where the disciples will find Jesus but an activity to which Jesus leads them. In 'Galilee' the flock is reconstituted, and this is the work of the Shepherd who has willingly been smitten (cf. Zech. xiii. 9b).

Before we leave this we must examine the view that the reconstitution of the flock does not take place until the Parousia. Lohmeyer, followed by Marxsen, has maintained that xiv. 28 and xvi. 7[2] refer to the Parousia as about to happen in Galilee. Lohmeyer alleged that ὄψεσθε must refer to the Parousia rather than the Resurrection for which the technical term is ὤφθη.[3] Furthermore, Galilee was the land of eschatological fulfilment; Jerusalem according to the other Gospels the place of Resurrection appearances. Thus xvi. 7, and consequently xiv. 28, refer to the Parousia. Marxsen elaborates this thesis by his stress on the theological meaning of Galilee for Mark. Galilee is introduced at appropriate places into the Gospel narrative by Mark because it is geographically important to his readers who expect the conclusion of all things to come shortly in that land.[4] That Mark does not use Galilee in a simple geographical sense has been recognised since Lightfoot's fundamental work.[5] We may observe that Galilee is mostly

---

[1] As Evans, *ibid.*, points out the idea of Resurrection appearances in Galilee arises out of this verse; the natural place for their occurrence was Jerusalem, where Luke places them. If Galilee is taken as a theological term, then this divergence of statement in regard to their locality is removed.

[2] Neither xiv. 28 nor xvi. 7 can be a gloss but either, probably both, were insertions made by Mark into existing material.

[3] *Ad* xvi. 7; cf. Lohmeyer, *Galiläa und Jerusalem*, pp. 10 ff.

[4] Marxsen, pp. 33–77.

[5] Cf. p. 92, n. 2.

mentioned in verses which are Markan, either summaries
(i. 14, 39; iii. 7?) or seams (i. 16, 28; iii. 7?; vii. 31; ix. 30).[1]
Mark's Gospel divides into two sections: the first recounts the
activity of Jesus in Galilee and Gentile environs, the second his
Passion in Jerusalem. 'Galilee is the sphere of revelation,
Jerusalem the scene only of rejection.'[2] Despite this rigid
division of the Gospel in regard to locality there are indications
within the material received from the tradition and incorporated
in Mark that Jesus had been in Jerusalem before his final entry
and was known there (xi. 2 f.; xiv. 3; xiv. 13–16; xiv. 49;
xv. 43).[3] If then Mark used Galilee editorially why did he
introduce it and what did he intend to teach us by his introduction of it? We see at once how often it is connected with the
proclamation of the Gospel by Jesus (i. 14, 39, iii. 7); it is the
place of the call of disciples (i. 16), of the spread of reports
about him (i. 28) and of the instruction of disciples about his
coming Passion (ix. 30). The Gospel is not written as an
historical outline of the life of Jesus but to instruct its readers in
their Christian faith and duties; they have to proclaim the
Gospel, which is Jesus; we have seen that his proclamation is
meant to be typical of theirs (e.g. i. 14 f., which is expressed in
the theology of the early Church). The readers of Mark's
Gospel are thus in the stage of 'Galilee' – that is, that of the
preaching of the Gospel.[4]

So far we can go, but Marxsen takes this a stage further,
arguing that Galilee is also the place of the completion of the

[1] Apart from these instances Galilee is used at i. 9, where it is in a Markan
passage describing the origin of Jesus, but this must have been a fixed fact
of the tradition; vi. 21, Herod's feast, does not describe the activity of Jesus;
xv. 41, referring to the days of Jesus' activity in Galilee; xiv. 28 and xvi. 7,
with which we are at present concerned.

[2] Lightfoot, *Locality*, p. 125.

[3] Cf. Schmidt, pp. 301–3.

[4] It is probably also the stage of preaching to the Gentiles; Galilee is
Galilee of the Gentiles; cf. Evans, 'I will go before you into Galilee', p. 13;
Karnetzki, 'Die Galiläische Redaktion im Markusevangelium', pp. 249 ff.;
G. H. Boobyer, 'Galilee and Galileans in St Mark's Gospel', *Bull. J.
Rylands Lib.* XXXV (1952/3), 334–48. Boobyer would appear to go too far in
practically restricting the preaching of the Gospel to Gentiles alone; Jesus'
disciples were Jews; so were most of those who were healed. Mark provides
justification for the Gentile mission, but this does not mean he would have
excluded Jews.

Gospel: here it began with the preaching of Jesus and here it ends with his Parousia. We cannot follow him at this point. If, as he himself shows, Galilee is a theological term and denotes the place of preaching it cannot then revert in xiv. 28 and xvi. 7 to the status of a geographical term. Apart from these two texts, and they are the texts in dispute, there is not sufficient evidence that Galilee is connected with the Parousia. Further it is exceedingly doubtful if we read Mark aright when we argue that he expects an imminent Parousia. Mark incorporates the growth parables in ch. iv and must be surely credited with realising their import, namely, that there is a period of growth before the Kingdom comes, and that that period of growth is still in progress.[1] An uncertainty about the time of the coming of the Parousia is seen in xiii. 32–7; xiii. 10 would suggest a certain measure of delay. xvi. 7 is in the present tense and, if addressed not only to the women at the tomb but also to the Church of Mark's day, this requires a present and continuous fulfilment. Unless then there is some definite reason for regarding xvi. 7 as referring to the Parousia it is easier to refer it to the Resurrection/Exaltation and to a present fulfilment. Lohmeyer considered he had found such a reason in the use of ὄψεσθε. It must be granted that ὤφθη is the normal word used in describing Resurrection appearances. However we do find ὁρᾶν used of them in Matt. xxviii. 10, 17; John xx. 18, 25, 29; I Cor. ix. 1. Mark refers so little to the Resurrection that it is impossible to say which term he would have used for seeing the risen and exalted Jesus. We find therefore no difficulty in taking the natural meaning of xiv. 28 and xvi. 7 which makes them refer to the Resurrection.[2] The early Church is now in Galilee, but there, as a Shepherd, it has its Lord with it and can see him as it carries on the work of proclamation to which he has called

[1] Cf. Karnetzki, 'Die Galiläische Redaktion im Markusevangelium', pp. 249–51. He also criticises Marxsen, holding that Bussmann's B redaction emerged from a Hellenistic Jewish community situated in Gentile territory, ibid. pp. 241 ff.

[2] Cf. W. G. Kümmel, Promise and Fulfilment, pp. 77–9; Taylor, ad loc.; Marxsen, pp. 53 f. There would appear to be no reason for insisting on a risen Christ as distinct from an exalted Christ; the Resurrection and the Exaltation were probably not conceived as distinct events by Mark (see above, pp. 132 ff.). The Christ who leads his Church in Galilee, and therefore in all its mission, is the exalted Christ.

it, and for which he has gathered together its scattered members, and to which he leads it.[1] Here is the Markan equivalent of the 'Great Commission' of Matt. xxviii. 16–20.[2]

ADDENDUM

R. le Déaut, *La Nuit Pascale* (*Analecta biblica*, 22), only came into my hands after this chapter was finished and had gone to the Press. Chapter III of his book covers much the same ground as Vermes, *Scripture and Tradition in Judaism*, with whom he agrees at almost all points. Le Déaut stresses more especially the Paschal association of the *Akedah*. Although in Mark's chronology Jesus was not killed at the same time as the Passover Lamb, yet his death has certainly Paschal associations (xiv. 24). In any case Isaac's death was associated with the Paschal night rather than the time of the slaughter of the Paschal Lamb in the afternoon. It may be that the darkness of which Mark speaks (xv. 33) is meant to correspond to that of the Paschal night.

[1] Cf. G. Herbert, 'The Resurrection Narrative in St Mark's Gospel', *S.J.Th.* XV (1962), 66–73. The same thought of the recreation of the community through the Resurrection is probably present in xiv. 58 and xv. 29; cf. p. 99.

[2] Cf. Evans, 'I will go before you into Galilee'.

CHAPTER VIII

THE CHRISTIAN COMMUNITY

WE are not concerned here to discover the nature of the fellowship of the disciples with Jesus in Galilee, but to determine the kind of community which Mark envisages as arising from the preaching of the Gospel he records.

The place of the apostles in the Gospel might appear somewhat ambiguous: are they to be regarded as typical believers of the new community? As typical of its leaders? Or as the foundation on which the new community is built? Mark uses the word 'apostle' of the Twelve only once (vi. 30), though he does use the cognate verb of their activity on two occasions (iii. 14; vi. 7); on each of these two occasions it was the natural word to use. We cannot then say that Mark stresses the position of the Twelve as apostles. In Luke and Matthew they occupy a much more official position.[1] Mark cannot but have known the discussion about the authority of the apostles as evidenced in the Pauline letters, yet he lays no emphasis on that authority. The only reference to their leadership in the Christian community is negative: in x. 42–4 they are instructed in the nature of true rule over others as service. The activities to which the Twelve are called are those of any Christian (iii. 14, 15; vi. 7); the mission charge of vi. 8–11 is in quite general terms and cannot be restricted to the Twelve alone. ix. 38–40 would seem to contradict deliberately any attempt to reserve special functions to them alone; the work of any man who casts out demons in the name of Jesus must be accepted. We may then conclude that in Mark's eyes the Twelve are typical believers rather than officials of the Church.

We have no need to examine all that Mark envisages about the community called into being by the Gospel but only what sheds light on our central problem: what did Jesus accomplish by his ministry? If we view this primarily as the defeat of Satan, then we should expect to meet a community living in the light of that victory; if we view this primarily as the redemption

[1] Cf. Matt. xix. 28 and Luke's frequent use of the term 'apostle'. Cf. C. H. Turner, *J. T. S.* XXVI (1925), 232f.

of men from sin, then we shall expect to meet a community whose members enjoy the forgiveness of sin and overcome its power in their own lives.

Much of what we should say has already been considered in detail and therefore need only be mentioned. If Christ by his death ransoms the many, then we must assume that the community has been ransomed (x. 45); if the community is called into existence by the preaching of the word, and that word is the forgiveness of sin (ii. 2, 5),[1] then we may assume that the sins of the community are forgiven. Thus those statements which we examined in chapter VI about the activity of Jesus in relation to men must be considered as fulfilled, at least in part, in the members of the community. We have already seen that in those statements the main emphasis lay on Jesus as bearing the judgement and wrath of God and on his ability to save from sin; the community must then be one which has been saved from sin and is no longer under God's judgement. We do not need then to recapitulate the passages discussed there and the conclusions drawn therefrom.

The community has been called into existence by Christ (i. 17, 20; ii. 14; x. 21); its members are the elect, those who have been chosen (xiii. 20, 22, 27). This called community is also the 'calling' community: those who have responded to the call become themselves those who issue it as fishers of men (i. 17). The community is thus extending itself, widening the circle of those who enjoy the privileges and duties which belong to membership. The aim of members of the community is to bring others into the position in which they themselves are. And this means bringing in Gentiles, as well as Jews;[2] in the summary statement of iii. 7 f. the crowds come to Jesus from Gentile as well as Jewish areas. In vii. 24 – viii. 26 Mark depicts Jesus on a journey which takes him into Gentile territory. In particular we note that the Syro-Phoenician woman was a Gentile (vii. 24 – 30) and Jesus healed her daughter.[3] It would

---

[1] Cf. pp. 69 ff.

[2] We are not concerned to argue whether Jesus himself envisaged a Gentile mission (cf. J. Jeremias, *Jesus' Promise to the Nations*), but only what Mark had in mind.

[3] Ἑλληνίς means a 'pagan' or 'Gentile' and not a Greek speaker; cf. Turner, *J.T.S.* XXVI (1925), 150. To a Greek it might more properly

appear that the second feeding (viii. 1–9) was a feeding of Gentiles;[1] the Gadarene demoniac may well have been a Gentile. At xii. 9 the 'others' to whom the vineyard is given at least include the Gentiles.[2] These indications are reinforced if we accept the suggestion that Galilee signifies for Mark the Gentile mission.[3] But if then membership of the community does not depend on birth or race, on what does it depend?

The answer is surely faith. J. M. Robinson has shown that the fundamental attitude of the disciple is not numinous awe but faith.[4] Indeed the member of the community may be defined simply as 'the believer' (ix. 42). The fundamental call of Jesus (i. 15) is to repentance and belief; we have seen that this is formulated in the theological terms of Mark's own time and is addressed to his contemporaries.[5] Faith is also the continuing attitude of the disciple; by faith he is saved from evil of one kind and another: this appears in the healing miracles of Jairus' daughter (v. 36), of the woman with the issue of blood (v. 34), of the man with the epileptic son (ix. 19, 23, 24), and of blind Bartimaeus (x. 52), and in the deliverance from the storm at sea (iv. 40). While in the last incident we are to see a parallel to the delivery from demonic powers, the healing miracles represent delivery from sin.[6] Faith is explicitly connected with the forgiveness of sin in ii. 5, where the man carried by four others is forgiven his sin because of their faith. Through their faith the disciples are able to carry out the tasks laid on them by the Gospel: lack of faith prevented them healing the epileptic boy (ix. 19); faith enables them to remove mountains (xi. 22–4). Mark does not make clear towards whom or what this faith is directed. At xi. 22 it is connected with God; in other places it seems related to the healing and saving activity of Jesus; even though at times it appears to be expressed

designate the opposite to 'barbarian'; cf. e.g. M. Hadas, *Hellenistic Culture* (New York and London, 1959), pp. 11 f.; but this would hardly be the meaning to a Jew or a Christian, cf. Rom. i. 16.

[1] G. H. Boobyer, 'The Miracles of the Loaves and the Gentiles in St Mark's Gospel ', *S.J.Th.* VI (1953), 77–87, holds that in both feedings the crowds were composed of Gentiles.

[2] Cf. p. 86.   [3] Cf. pp. 174 ff.

[4] Pp. 68–78. Cf. J. C. Fenton, 'Paul and Mark', *Studies in the Gospels* (ed. Nineham), pp. 107 ff.

[5] Cf. pp. 64 ff.   [6] Cf. pp. 106 ff.

absolutely (x. 52; v. 34), as if faith itself saved, this faith can never be dissociated from the active presence of Jesus. Thus the disciple is someone who has been saved through faith both from demonic evil arising outside himself and from sin arising within his own nature, saved through the power of God active in Jesus Christ.

Closely linked to the conception of faith is that of understanding. The disciples are given an understanding of the Kingdom of God through the parables (iv. 11 f.); this, as we have seen in our discussion of the Kingdom of God in Mark,[1] is an insight into the coming of the Kingdom, which is still future for Mark. Likewise in the Little Apocalypse (ch. xiii) they are given some understanding of the consummation of all things. Those outside cannot understand many of the matters in which Jesus instructs the disciples (iv. 11, 34; vii. 17; x. 10). Some things the disciples themselves fail to understand, for example the two feedings (vi. 52; viii. 17), and are reproved for their failure. In these feeding accounts we see Jesus as supplying the needs of men with spiritual food and with spiritual understanding; the disciples must understand that in the Eucharist Jesus is continually ministering to their requirements, and that his ministry is connected with his death (xiv. 24). But the major points at which the disciples fail to understand are in relation to the nature of Jesus himself and to the divine necessity of his death (viii. 32 f.; ix. 32). The Christian reader of the Gospel is in no doubt about these things. From the very beginning Mark makes clear who Jesus is by the testimony of God, the demons and the centurion, and Jesus himself continually proclaims the necessity of his death and its meaning. At no place is there emphasised an understanding of the demonic world or of its defeat by Jesus. The very fact that the understanding of the disciple is stressed and that there is no suggestion that the demons prevent understanding shows how little Mark is concerned to show the member of the Christian community over against the demonic world.

Closely related also to faith, but on the other side from understanding, as if to preserve against intellectualism, is the conception of 'following'. It us the duty of the disciple to come after Jesus (i. 17, 20; ii. 14), to take his cross like Jesus (viii. 34)

[1] Cf. pp. 64 ff.

and to serve like Jesus (x. 42 – 5). But any idea that this is only imitation of Jesus is removed by the central place that is given to Jesus' own death.[1]

The community lives in tension in the world. This is shown first in the interpretations of the Parable of the Sower (iv. 14 – 20). The community is a mixed bag containing those who bear good fruit and those who promise for a while but then fail. Three different reasons are given why failure may come – and these reasons represent some of the tensions under which the community lived. There is first the Devil who comes and takes away the word that has been sown (iv. 15); it is not specified how the Devil does this. Secondly the tension comes from those who persecute the Church (iv. 17); there is no reason to see the Devil as behind this persecution and thus as troubling the Church in another way;[2] we have seen that evil affects men quite independently of the Devil.[3] There is no reason to suppose that in *vv.* 17, 19 Mark is explaining *v.* 15; these are three different ways of failure, not one followed by two interpretations of it. Indeed the failure of those mentioned in *v.* 17 would appear to be due to a fault within themselves – οὐκ ἔχουσιν ῥίζαν ἐν ἑαυτοῖς;[4] tribulation plays on this inner weakness and works their downfall. The third cause of failure is a combination of worry, wealth and lust (iv. 19); wealth similarly caused tension in the case of the rich man who asked Jesus about eternal life (x. 17 – 31). The three causes of failure given in this parable are not the only tensions which exist, but they summarise them and indicate that the Devil is only one cause of tension alongside others.

If we are correct in interpreting the two stories about storm at sea as indicating the lot of the community, a ship in the storm of life,[5] then here again we find the tension in which the community lives. In the earlier of these two stories (iv. 35 – 41) the storm is addressed like a demon, indicating that tension does

---

[1] Cf. pp. 154 f.   [2] So Robinson, p. 77.
[3] Cf. chap. II.
[4] So Swete; Lagrange; Wohlenberg. It is interesting to observe that we have to go back to commentators of a generation or two ago for comments on the interpretation of the parable. Modern commentators having decided that it is an early Church creation have apparently written it out of Scripture and see no need to deal with it in detail.
[5] Cf. pp. 105 f.

come from demonic forces; probably this interpretation should be applied also to the second storm (vi. 45 – 51). It is interesting that in neither of these stories can we see clearly where the Devil applies his pressure to the Church; this is left open as in iv. 15. The source of tension is made quite clear however in the case of the weakness of the disciples at the time of the arrest of Jesus; the context is that of possible persecution, but the weakness lies in 'the flesh', that is, in the disciples themselves.[1] The combination of outward attack by hostile men and inner weakness is strikingly similar to what we have just seen in the second group in the interpretation of the Parable of the Sower (iv. 17). The tension arising from the opposition of men appears again in the Little Apocalypse. Authorities persecute and the Christian is to take care how he bears witness in the moment of such persecution (xiii. 9 – 13). Tension may come from the mere fact that war exists (xiii. 7). The tension becomes professedly future from the standpoint of Mark's readers in the reference to τὸ βδέλυγμα τῆς ἐρημώσεως (xiii. 14). If we assume that Mark wrote prior to A.D. 70 the reference is probably to Anti-Christ; Luke, writing later, makes the reference purely historical. The historical is not necessarily excluded in Mark; the μετὰ τὴν θλῖψιν ἐκείνην (xiii. 24) suggests that the sacrilege of v. 14 takes place within the time sequence, but II Thess. ii. 3 – 10 combined with the masculine ἑστηκότα supports the idea of Anti-Christ. The two conceptions may well be combined in that the appearance of Anti-Christ may be a historical event. With the reference to Anti-Christ we pass from trials inflicted by men on the Church to those arising from the demonic world. Thus this future tension is demonic, but now wholly so; for in xiii. 21 f. the saints are deceived by false preachers. This is true also of an earlier stage in the eschatological events, where (xiii. 5 f.) false preachers are again said to lead astray members of the community. Lastly the tension is seen more remotely in the call to disciples to take up their crosses and follow after Jesus; in so far as the opposition to Jesus at the time of the Passion was human rather than demonic so the tension will come to the community from human rather than demonic agents.

To sum up, the tension under which the comunity lived arose from a number of different sources of which the demonic

---

[1] Cf. p. 30.

was one. It is not the underlying source from which the others derive their power but one source alongside the others. Thus while it is true 'that the struggle between the Spirit and Satan continues in the history of the Church'[1] this is only part of the truth. The opposition does not come from Satan alone but also from the persecution of men, from the enticements of the world, and from the inner weakness of the members of the community.

At this juncture we must return to a point which we raised in our first chapter:[2] If Satan has been already bound how is it that the early Christians were very much aware of his power? In particular, how is it that Mark can refer to Satan as assailing members of the community (iv. 15)? We have already seen that in the Apocalyptic literature the binding of Satan is often temporary.[3] In the majority of cases Satan is restrained thereby until his final judgement and condemnation (I Enoch x. 4–6; x. 11 f.; xviii. 12–xix. 2; Jub. v. 10). But in Jub. xlviii. 15 f. Mastema is said to be bound for five days until Israel is able to make its escape from Egypt, and is then set free again to assail it; in Rev. xx. 2 f. Satan is bound for a thousand years and then set free for a short period to make a final assault on the Church (xx. 7 f.). It may be that Mark regarded Satan as bound during the time of Jesus on earth, the time of the new Exodus, and then as again set free to attack the community.

It may, however, be that Mark is inconsistent at this point. It is only at iv. 15 that there is a direct reference to the assault of Satan on the early Church. Elsewhere the Church is seen in conflict with demons, Satan's underlings, not Satan himself (iii. 15; vi. 7; ix. 29; iv. 35–41; vi. 45–51). The material which Mark received will have included the interpretation of the Parable of the Sower and Mark may have incorporated it without realising that his main line of argument in relationship to Satan was not in harmony with this allusion to him. We may note that while for Mark there is a final cataclysm (ch. xiii) there is no account in it of the defeat of Satan.[4]

There is a third possibility. Mark does not always use 'Satan' of a personal devil, but sometimes in a corporate manner of the community of unclean spirits. This is his usage in iii. 23–6,

---

[1] Robinson, p. 63.   [2] P. 15.   [3] Cf. pp. 12 f.
[4] τὸ βδέλυγμα τῆς ἐρημώσεως (xiii. 14) may be an historical figure, and even if not, it is not necessary to equate him with Satan.

where Satan is imagined as divided against himself and the unclean spirits which are cast out are described as Satan. Yet in iii. 27 the personal aspect reappears. It may then be that in iv. 15 Mark has in mind this corporate aspect of Satan, and we may observe that in the part of the parable corresponding to iv. 15 it is 'birds' (plural) who take away the seed (iv. 4). Just as after the defeat of Satan in the Temptation there still remain demons whom Christians have the power to exorcise, so there remain demons, corporately described as Satan, who are able to afflict them in the moral sphere.

This is all part of a more general question which arises, whether we place Christ's victory over Satan and the powers of evil at the Temptation or at the Cross and Resurrection. iv. 15 does not really apply to the time of Jesus between the Temptation and the Cross but to the time of the early Church; it was presumably composed after the death of Jesus.[1] If we suppose that Christ won his victory over the Devil in the Cross and Resurrection how can Satan still be regarded as assailing members of the community? By moving the victory to that period we do not remove the problem. Robinson writes,

The history which Mark selects to record is presented in its unity as the eschatological action of God, prepared by John the Baptist, inaugurated at the baptism and temptation, carried on through the struggles with various forms of evil, until in his death Jesus has experienced the ultimate of historical involvement and of diabolic antagonism. In the resurrection the force of evil is conclusively broken and the power of God's reign is established in history.[2]

But if the force of evil, which Robinson would hold to be Satan in Mark's Gospel, is conclusively broken how can it still afflict man either morally (iv. 15) or through possession, and require to be exorcised?

This problem might be evaded if we were to hold that the victory of Christ in the Cross and Resurrection or in the Temptation were purely a personal victory, for example that in the Resurrection he escaped the clutches of the Devil and was enabled to live on. This would hardly seem a possible solution, for the whole New Testament lays too much stress on the

[1] Cf. Jeremias, *The Parables of Jesus*, pp. 61 ff.
[2] P. 53; cf. p. 51.

Resurrection as a triumph for mankind as well as for Christ; it would mean that the Resurrection of Christ was no longer 'for us' but only a display of the might of God. We cannot then escape the question in this way.

It is easy to see that the problem is not one that occurs in the exegesis of Mark alone. It arises in every writing which speaks both of a conclusive victory over Satan and also sees man as still under assault by evil spiritual forces. On the one hand, evil powers are viewed as still able to operate against man, I Cor. v. 5; II Cor. ii. 11; Gal. iv. 9; II Thess. ii. 3–10; Eph. vi. 10 ff.; I Pet. v. 8 f.; I John iv. 3; v. 19; Rev. xii. 12. On the other hand they are regarded as already vanquished, Rom. viii. 38 f.; Col. ii. 15; Eph. i. 20 ff.; I Pet. iii. 22; John xii. 31 f.; xvi. 11, 33; I John iii. 8[1] We note that often the same writers contain both ideas. If the spiritual powers are defeated, how can they still be regarded as rampant? The apparent inconsistency that we have found in Mark[2] would thus seem to be written into the texture of the whole New Testament, but to pursue this problem further would take us far beyond our present purpose. Mark has been caught in a difficulty which exists for the whole New Testament and which exists whether we put the defeat of Satan in the Temptation or in the Passion, and we cannot claim that he has wholly resolved it.

Returning to the tensions under which we have seen the Christian lives and which come from the spiritual forces of evil,

---

[1] Col. i. 20 stands apart in that it speaks of the reconciliation of the spiritual powers to God. I am unable to accept the argument of C. D. Morrison, *The Powers that Be*, pp. 116 ff., that the Lordship of Christ over the powers belongs to the sphere of creation rather than of redemption, and that the Cross made the Church to be the place in which that Lordship is effective. The texts we have quoted do seem to imply that in the event of Jesus Christ something happened to the powers themselves, and not merely that the Lordship was given to believers over them. Christ's own relationship to the powers would appear to be different now that he has returned to Heaven and sits at God's right hand from what it was prior to his incarnation. Paul and some of the other New Testament writers would place the moment of this victory in the Cross–Resurrection–Ascension event. Mark (and perhaps John xii. 31 f.) places it in the Temptation. Even if the thesis of Morrison was to be accepted we would have to argue that for Mark the moment in which the Lordship of Christ over the powers became effective for his followers was the Temptation rather than the Cross.

[2] Cf. Mark xii. 36 and pp. 87 f. above.

the persecution of men, the enticements of the world, and the inner weakness of members of the community, we must go on briefly to indicate the forces which sustain the Christian in this tension. (*a*) The community has been baptised with the Holy Spirit (i. 8), and he is present to support it in moments of strain (xiii. 11; xiv. 38). We may note that the Holy Spirit is not set over against Satan or any spiritual force of evil in these references. (*b*) There is Jesus' own presence; he delivers his followers from the storms (iv. 35–41; vi. 45–51); when men are shepherdless he feeds them (vi. 34, 35–44; viii. 1–9; xiv. 22–5). His disciples are chosen to be 'with him' (iii. 14); he regards them as his brothers and sisters, with all this implies in the way of help within the family (iii. 33–5). (*c*) Man needs the grace of God to enter the Kingdom (x. 26 f.), and doubtless this is supplied. Likewise through prayer he is enabled to heal (ix. 29). (*d*) In the losses he has sustained through entry into the Christian community he is upborne by the fellowship that he finds within its membership (x. 29, 30).

Jesus has given the community a task in and to the world. Given representatively to the apostles, it is, in fact, laid on the whole Church. It is found first in i. 16–20, where Peter and Andrew, called by Jesus, are to fish for men. When the Twelve are appointed they are sent to preach and to have authority to exorcise demons (iii. 14 f.). At the moment when they are sent out two by two Jesus is only said to have given them authority over unclean spirits (vi. 7), but once they are on the mission their activities are described as preaching repentance, exorcising demons and healing the sick by anointing (vi. 12 f.). When they return to Jesus they tell him what they have done and taught (vi. 30). Of these passages i. 16–20 came to Mark in the traditional material; vi. 7, 12 f., 30 are his creations;[1] it is difficult to determine whether iii. 15 came in the tradition or not. We can thus conclude that Mark sees the activity of the community as threefold: to preach repentance, to exorcise demons and to heal the sick.

The phrase ἵνα ἀποστέλλῃ ... ἔχειν ἐξουσίαν ἐκβάλλειν τὰ δαιμόνια (iii. 15) is very awkward.[2] We find it modified by DW to ἔδωκεν αὐτοῖς ἐξουσίαν. At vi. 7 Mark uses the much

---

[1] We find an accumulation of Markan terms; cf. Tayor, *ad loc.*

[2] Cf. Lagrange; Wohlenberg.

simpler phrase ἐδίδου αὐτοῖς ἐξουσίαν, whence DW probably derived their correction of iii. 15. It may be that the original tradition as received by Mark read ἵνα ἀποστέλλῃ αὐτοὺς κηρύσσειν καὶ ἐκβάλλειν τὰ δαιμόνια; Mark, however, did not wish to say that they were sent to cast out demons (cf. vi. 7), but rather wished to stress the element of authority which came from Jesus' original victory over Satan; he could not say, 'they were sent to give authority', so he inserted the awkward ἔχειν. If this explanation is not correct and Mark is held to have composed the sentence (it surely could not have come to him in the tradition in this form!), then he has done his best to avoid saying that the disciples were sent to exorcise and has rather emphasised their authority. This, of course, is what we find in vi. 7. We must then conclude that Mark does not envisage the community as sent to exorcise. This is important. It agrees with the way in which Mark depicts the activity of Jesus. With one exception he never describes Jesus as going to a conflict with demons or with Satan. Where he encounters demon-possessed men, he heals them; he is not depicted as going to search for them. He speaks of himself as sent to preach (i. 38), but never as sent to exorcise. The one exception to this is the Temptation. Here, driven out by the Spirit, he seeks Satan and defeats him; thereafter he exercises the victory he won in the desert whenever he encounters demons, but he does not go to seek them. Similarly the community is sent to preach the Gospel and given authority over demons; it is not sent to exorcise, but where demons are encountered it may exercise the authority Jesus has won and given to it. Thus the community is not sent out to a conflict with Satan; it is sent out to preach repentance – to deal with sin of men. In passing we may note that a similar attitude exists in Jesus in relation to sickness. In every story of healing except one Mark shows the sick or their friends as coming to Jesus and appealing to him to heal; in his summary statements he shows the sick being brought to Jesus in crowds and then he heals them; at i. 35 Jesus even seeks to avoid the crowds of sick. There is no occasion on which Jesus calls the sick to come to him to be healed, nor is he depicted as going to look out the sick. The sole exception is iii. 1–5; here Jesus does pick out the man with the withered hand; but this pericope is told, not to demonstrate the healing power of Jesus, but for the sake of the final pronouncement of Jesus on the Sabbath; thus the form-critics do not classify it among the miracle stories but among the pronouncement stories. If Jesus does not go to heal the sick, likewise in Mark he does not send the disciples to this task. Their primary task is to preach, they are to fish for men; if they encounter evil as sickness or demon-possession they have authority to deal with it. Their task is not to defeat Satan nor wage a continual war with him, but to call sinners to repentance, to proclaim the death of Jesus, with which the whole of Mark's Gospel is taken up, and to show its meaning as the fulfilment of the judgement of God and as a ransom for men, to show his blood as poured out for them. This reflects the primary concern of the Markan Gospel, a concern with the redemption of men from sin rather than with the cosmic defeat of Satan, and the greater achievement of Jesus is the former, not the latter.

CHAPTER IX

CONCLUSION

FOR Mark the Devil is defeated so far as the life of Jesus is concerned at the Temptation; in this conclusive contest Satan is bound and Jesus is thereafter able to reduce to obedience evil-spiritual powers, the demons which possess men and evil-cosmic forces met in sea storms. This encounter with the Devil in the Temptation is the decisive meeting of the forces of light and darkness, of order and chaos, of good and evil; this struggle which lay behind so much of the Old Testament and of the religion of the Near East of the period has now had its issue. But all the evil in the world is not seen by Mark as due to the Devil. In particular sin may arise from the tempting power of the Devil, but also from the seductive power of wealth, from the fear of persecution, from the enticements of other men and women, and from a man's own inner weakness in that he is flesh and not Spirit. Undoubtedly later Christian thought regarded the Devil as responsible for all temptation, but we are no more correct in reading such a view back into Mark than we are in reading it back into the Old Testament. How then is this other sin in men dealt with?

In the first place Mark views Jesus as the authoritative teacher who brings men to an understanding of the truth. This truth is known in the Church but is veiled from the eyes of those outside. Yet Jesus is not just a Gnostic revealer who gives insight to the initiated. The main purpose of his teaching is to bring his followers to an understanding of his own Cross, not only as redemptive, but also as a way of life for themselves; they must take up their crosses as he did and serve as he served. Thus it is not that he only enlightens their minds but that he calls for them to go on the way of discipleship, which is the way of love and service. In teaching he is, however, meeting the evil of ignorance and leading men away from it.

But ignorance and sin are not the same, and if in Mark the teaching of Jesus is ultimately directed towards the Cross he teaches not only about its necessity but also about its meaning.

The Cross is judgement; this is seen in the rending of the veil and the darkness that came over the world at the time. The judgement is borne by Jesus, in that he drinks the cup of God's wrath, is the shepherd smitten, and is the one who is overwhelmed by the floods of baptism for men. His blood is shed for others as his life is given for them. And all this is not to turn from men the wrath of Satan nor to conquer him, but to bring them into the new community which is formed out of the Cross and Resurrection from those who are saved, enjoy the forgiveness of their sin and themselves go to seek others as fishers of men.

What Mark thereby preaches is not the kerugma of Phil. ii. 5–11; it lies nearer that of I Cor. xv. 3, 4. Yet the kerugma of Phil. ii. 5–11 is fulfilled in intention because the Devil and the evil-spiritual powers were overcome – in the Temptation but not in the Cross and Resurrection. The fact of the appearances of Jesus is not stressed; instead he is felt throughout the Gospel as the risen and exalted Lord who is still speaking to his disciples and who leads them in 'Galilee' on the mission of preaching himself. Unlike I Cor. xv. 3, 4 the empty tomb is brought into the picture; this is necessary since if the risen Lord is to be seen in the stories of the Gospel then he must be recognised as having left the realm of death. No stories of resurrection appearances are told since to have recounted them would have marred the conception of risen Lord in the whole of the Gospel.

BIBLIOGRAPHY

Achtemeier, P. J. 'Person and Deed. Jesus and the Storm-Tossed Sea', *Interpretation*, XVI (1962), 169–76.
Albertz, M. *Die synoptischen Streitgespräche* (Berlin, 1921).
Bacon, B. W. *The Gospel of Mark: Its Composition and Date* (New Haven, 1925).
Barrett, C. K. *The Epistle to the Romans (London, 1957)*.
—— 'The Background of Mark x. 45', in *New Testament Essays*, ed. A. J. B. Higgins, pp. 1–18 (Manchester, 1959).
—— *From First Adam to Last* (London, 1962).
Bartsch, H. W. 'Historische Erwägungen zur Leidensgeschichte', *Evangelische Theologie*, XXII (1962), 449–59.
Bauer, W. 'The Colt of Palm Sunday', *J.B.L.* LXXII (1953), 220–9.
Bauernfeind, O. *Die Worte der Dämonen im Markusevangelium* (Stuttgart, 1927).
Behm, J. διαθήκη, *T.W.N.T.* II, 127–37.
Bernard, J. H. 'A Study of St Mark x. 38, 39', *J.T.S.* XXVIII (1927), 262–70.
Best, E. 'Mark ii. 1–12', *Biblical Theology*, III (1953), 41–6.
—— *One Body in Christ* (London, 1955).
—— 'Spirit-Baptism', *N.T.* IV (1961), 236–43.
Beyer, H. W. διακονέω, κτλ., *T.W.N.T.* II, 81–93.
Billerbeck, P. *See* Strack, H. L.
Black, M. 'The Messiah in the Testament of Levi xviii', *E.T.* LX (1949), 321 f.; LXI (1950), 157 f.
—— *An Aramaic Approach to the Gospels and Acts*, 2nd edn. (Oxford, 1954).
—— 'The Son of Man Problem in Recent Research and Debate', *Bull. J. Rylands Lib.* XLV (1963), 305–18.
Blinzler, J. *Der Prozess Jesu*[2] (Regensburg, 1955).
Boobyer, G. H. 'The Eucharistic Interpretation of the Miracle of the Loaves in St Mark's Gospel', *J.T.S.* III (1952), 161–71.
—— 'Galilee and Galileans in St Mark's Gospel', *Bull J. Rylands Lib.* XXXV (1952/3), 334–48.
—— 'The Miracles of the Loaves and the Gentiles in St Mark's Gospel', *S.J.Th.* VI (1953), 77–87.
—— 'The Redaction of Mark iv. 1–34', *N.T.S.* VIII (1961), 59–70.
Bornkamm, G. in Bornkamm, G., Barth, G. and Held, H. J. *Tradition and Interpretation in Matthew* (London, 1963).
Bousset, W. *Die Religion des Judentums in späthellenistichen Zeitalter*[3], ed. H. Gressmann (Tübingen, 1926).

Branscomb, B. H. *The Gospel of Mark* (Moffatt Commentaries; London, 1937).
Büchsel, F. *Der Geist Gottes im Neuen Testament* (Gütersloh, 1926).
—— γενεά, κτλ. *T.W.N.T.* I, 660–3.
—— λύτρον, *T.W.N.T.* IV, 341–51.
Bultmann, R. *Theologie des Neuen Testaments* (Tübingen, 1953).
—— *The History of the Synoptic Tradition*, Eng. trans. J. Marsh (Oxford, 1963).
Bundy, W. E. *Jesus and the First Three Gospels* (Cambridge, Mass., 1955).
Burkill, T. A. 'St Mark's Philosophy of the Passion', *N.T.* II (1958), 245–71.
—— 'Anti-Semitism in St Mark's Gospel', *N.T.* III (1959), 34–53.
—— 'Strain on the Secret: An Examination of Mark xi. 1–xiii. 37', *Z.N.T.W.* LI (1960), 31–46.
—— *Mysterious Revelation* (Ithaca, New York, 1963).
Bussmann, W. *Synoptische Studien*, I–III (Halle, 1925–31).
Caird, G. B. *Principalities and Powers* (Oxford, 1956).
Carlston, C. E. 'Transfiguration and Resurrection', *J.B.L.* LXXX (1961), 233–40.
Charles, R. H. (ed.). *The Apocrypha and Pseudepigrapha of the Old Testament*, 2 vols. (Oxford, 1913).
—— *Revelation* (*I.C.C.*), 2 vols. (London, 1920).
Citron, B. 'The Multitude in the Synoptic Gospels', *S.J.Th.* VII (1954), 408–18.
Colpe, C. *Die religionsgeschichtliche Schule* (Göttingen, 1961).
Conzelmann, H. *The Theology of Saint Luke*, Eng. trans. G. Buswell (London, 1960).
Cranfield, C. E. B. *St Mark* (Cambridge, 1959).
Cross, F. L. (ed.). *The Jung Codex* (London, 1955).
Cross, F. M. *The Ancient Library of Qumran* (London, 1958).
Cullmann, O. *Baptism in the New Testament*, Eng. trans. J. K. S. Reid (London, 1950).
—— *Peter: Disciple, Apostle, Martyr*, Eng. trans. F. V. Filson (London, 1953).
—— *The Christology of the New Testament*, Eng. trans. S. C. Guthrie, Jr., and C. A. M. Hall (London, 1959).
Dalman, G. *Jesus-Jeshua*, Eng. trans. P. P. Levertoff (London, 1929).
Daniélou, J. 'La typologie d'Isaac dans le christianisme primitif', *Biblica*, XXVIII (1947), 363–93.
—— *Sacramentum Futuri* (Paris, 1950).
Daube, D. 'Four Types of Question', *J.T.S.* II (1951), 45–8.

BIBLIOGRAPHY

Daube, D. *The New Testament and Rabbinic Judaism* (London, 1956).
Davey, F. N. *See* Hoskyns, E.
Davies, W. D. *Paul and Rabbinic Judaism* (London, 1948).
—— 'Paul and the Dead Sea Scrolls: Flesh and Spirit', in *The Scrolls and the New Testament*, ed. K. Stendahl (London, 1958).
Déaut, R. le *La Nuit Pascale* (*Analecta Biblica*, 22; Rome, 1963).
Dehn, G. *Der Gottessohn*[6] (Hamburg, 1953).
Delling, G. 'βάπτισμα βαπτισθῆναι', *N.T.* II (1957), 92–115.
Dibelius, M. *From Tradition to Gospel*, Eng. trans. B. E. Woolf (London, 1934)[7].
Dodd, C. H. *The Parables of the Kingdom* (London, 1943).
—— *According to the Scriptures* (London, 1952).
—— 'The Framework of the Gospel Narratives', in *New Testament Studies*, pp. 1–11 (Manchester, 1953).
—— 'The Appearances of the Risen Christ: An Essay in Form-Criticism of the Gospels', in *Studies in the Gospels*, ed. D. E. Nineham (Oxford, 1955).
Doudna, J. C. *The Greek of the Gospel of Mark* (J.B.L. Monograph Series, XII; Philadelphia, 1961).
Dunkerley, R. 'Was Barabbas also called Jesus?', *E.T.* LXXIV (1963), 126 f.
Ebeling, H. J. *Das Messiasgeheimnis und die Botschaft des Marcus-Evangelisten* (Berlin, 1939).
Eichrodt, W. *Theologie des Alten Testaments*, II/III, 4the edn. (Stuttgart and Göttingen, 1961).
Emerton, J. A. 'Some New Testament Notes', *J.T.S.* XI (1960), 334 f.
—— 'τὸ αἷμά μου τῆς διαθήκης: The evidence of the Syrian versions', *J.T.S.* XIII (1962), 111–17.
Evans, C. F. 'I will go before you into Galilee', *J.T.S.* V (1954), 3–18.
Farrar, A. M. *A Study in Mark* (*Westminster,* 1951).
Feine, P. *Theologie des Neuen Testaments.* 8th edn. (Berlin, 1953).
Fenton, J. C. 'Paul and Mark', *Studies in the Gospels*, ed. D. E. Nineham (Oxford, 1955).
Feuillet, A. 'Les perspectives propres à chaque évangéliste dans les récits de la transfiguration', *Biblica*, XXXIX (1958), 281–301.
Fichtner, J. *Weisheit Salomos* (*Handbuch zum Alten Testament*, Zweite Reihe, 6; Tübingen, 1938).
Flemington, W. F. *The New Testament Doctrine of Baptism* (London, 1948).
Foerster, W. Βεεζεβούλ, *T.W.N.T.* I, 605 f.
—— δαίμων, κτλ, *T.W.N.T.* II, 1–21.

Foerster, W. διαβάλλω, διάβολος, T.W.N.T. II, 69–80.

—— σατανᾶς, T.W.N.T. VII, 151–64.

Fuller, R. H. *The Mission and Achievement of Jesus* (London, 1954).

Geyer, J. *The Wisdom of Solomon* (London, 1963).

Goodenough, E. R. *Jewish Symbols in the Graeco-Roman Period*, IV (New York, 1954).

Goppelt, L. ποτήριον, T.W.N.T. VI, 148–59.

Grant, F. C. *The Earliest Gospel* (New York and Nashville, 1943).

—— 'The Gospel according to St Mark' (*Interpreters' Bible*, VII; New York and Nashville, 1951).

Gregg, J. A. F. *The Wisdom of Solomon* (Cambridge, 1922).

Grundmann, W. ἄγγελος, κτλ. T.W.N.T. I, 72–5.

—— ἰσχύω, κτλ. T.W.N.T. III, 400–5.

Guy, H. A. *The Origin of the Gospel of Mark* (London, 1954).

Hadas, M. *Hellenistic Culture* (New York and London, 1959).

Hahn F. *Christologische Hoheitstitel* (Göttingen, 1963).

Hauck, F. *Das Evangelium des Markus* (Theologischer Handkommentar zum N.T.; Leipzig, 1931).

—— καθαρός, κτλ. T.W.N.T. III, 416–21, 427–34.

Hebert, G. *The Christ of Faith and the Jesus of History* (London, 1962).

—— 'The Resurrection Narrative in St Mark's Gospel', *S.J.Th.* XV (1962), 66–73.

Higgins, A. J. B. *The Lord's Supper in the New Testament* (London, 1952).

—— 'Son of Man', in *New Testament Essays*, ed. A. J. B. Higgins (Manchester, 1959).

Holmes, S. 'Wisdom of Solomon', in *The Apocrypha and Pseudepigrapha of the Old Testament*, vol. 1, ed. R. H. Charles (Oxford, 1913).

Hooker, M. D. *Jesus and the Servant* (London, 1959).

Hoskyns, E. and Davey, F. N. *The Riddle of the New Testament*, London, 1947.

—— *The Fourth Gospel*, 2nd edn. (London, 1947).

Hunter, A. M. *Paul and his Predecessors*, 2nd edn. (London, 1961).

Iersel, B. M. F. van. *'Der Sohn' in den synoptischen Jesusworten* (*Supplements to N.T.* vol. III; Leiden, 1961).

Jeremias, J. 'The Gentile World in the Thought of Jesus', *Bull. S.N.T.S.* III (1952), 21 f.

—— *The Parables of Jesus*, Eng. trans. S. H. Hooke (London, 1954).

—— *The Eucharistic Words of Jesus*, Eng. trans. A. Ehrhardt (Oxford, 1955).

—— *Jesus' Promise to the Nations*, Eng. trans. S. H. Hooke (London, 1958).

BIBLIOGRAPHY

Jeremias, J. 'Αδάμ, *T.W.N.T.* I, 141-3.
—— ποιμλην, κτλ. *T.W.N.T.* VI, 484-501.
—— πολλοί, *T.W.N.T.* VI, 536-45.
—— 'Nachwort zum Artikel von H.-G. Leder', *Z.N.T.W.* LIV (1963), 278 f.
Jeremias, J. and Zimmerli, W. *The Servant of God*, Eng. trans. H. Knight *et al.* (London, 1957), = παῖς θεοῦ, *T.W.N.T.* V, 653-713.
Johnson, S. E. *The Gospel According to St Mark* (London, 1960).
Kähler, M. *Der sogenannte historische Jesus und der geschichtliche, biblische Christus* (Leipzig, 1896). New edition (Munich, 1956).
Kallas, J. *The Significance of the Synoptic Miracles* (London, 1961).
Karnetzki, M. 'Die Galiläische Redaktion im Markusevangelium', *Z.N.T.W.* LII (1961), 238-72.
Kittel, G. ἄγγελος, κτλ. *T.W.N.T.* I, pp. 79-87.
Klostermann, E. *Das Markusevangelium*[2] (Tübingen, 1926).
Knox, W. L. *The Sources of the Synoptic Gospels*, vol. I (Cambridge, 1953).
Kraeling, C. H. *The Synagogue* (Part I of *The Excavations at Dura-Europos Final Report*, VIII; New Haven and London, 1956).
Kraus, H.-J. *Psalmen*, 2 vols. (*Biblischer Kommentar: Altes Testament*, xv) (Neukirchen, 1960).
Kuby, A. 'Zur Konzeption des Markus-Evangeliums', *Z.N.T.W.* XLIX (1958), 52-64.
Kuhn, H. W. 'Das Reittier Jesu in der Einzugsgeschichte des Markusevangeliums', *Z.N.T.W.* L (1959), 82-91.
Kuhn, K. G. 'New Light on Temptation, Sin and Flesh in the New Testament', in *The Scrolls and the New Testament*, ed. K. Stendahl (London, 1958).
—— *Konkordanz zu den Qumrantexten* (Göttingen, 1960).
Kümmel, W. G. *Promise and Fulfilment*, Eng. trans. by Dorothea M. Barton (London, 1957).
Lagrange, M.-J. *Évangile selon Saint Marc* (Paris, 1947).
Langton, E. *Essentials of Demonology* (London, 1949).
Leder, H.-G. 'Sündenfallerzählung und Versuchungsgeschichte; zur Interpretation von Mc i. 12f.', *Z.N.T.W.* LIV (1963), 188-216.
Leenhardt, F.-J. (with O. Cullmann). *Essays on the Lord's Supper*, Eng. trans. J. G. Davies, (London, 1958).
Leivestad, R. *Christ the Conqueror* (London, 1954).
Lightfoot, R. H. *History and Interpretation in the Gospels* (London, 1935).
—— *Locality and Doctrine in the Gospels* (London, 1938).

BIBLIOGRAPHY

Lightfoot, R. H. *The Gospel Message of St. Mark* (Oxford, 1950).

Lindars, B. *New Testament Apologetic* (London, 1961).

Ling, T. *The Significance of Satan* (London, 1961).

Lohmeyer, E. *Galiläa und Jerusalem* (Göttingen, 1936).

—— *Das Evangelium des Markus*[11] (Göttingen, 1951).

Loisy, A. *L'Évangile selon Marc* (Paris, 1912).

Manson, T. W. *The Teaching of Jesus*, 2nd edn. (Cambridge, 1943).

—— 'Realised Eschatology and the Messianic Secret', in *Studies in the Gospels*, ed. D. E. Nineham (Oxford, 1955).

Mansoor, M. *The Thanksgiving Hymns* (Leiden, 1961).

Marxsen, W. *Der Evangelist Markus*[2] (Göttingen, 1959).

Maurer, C. 'Knecht Gottes und Sohn Gottes im Passionsbericht des Markusevangeliums', *Z.T.K.* L (1953), 1–38.

Mauser, U. W. *Christ in the Wilderness* (Studies in Biblical Theology, 39; London, 1963).

Mead, R. T. 'The Healing of the Paralytic – A Unit', *J.B.L.* LXXX (1961), 348–54.

Menzies, A. *The Earliest Gospel* (London, 1901).

Meyer, R. καθαρός, κτλ. *T.W.N.T.* III, 421–7.

—— σάρξ, κτλ. *T.W.N.T.* VII, 109–18.

Michel, O. 'Eine Philologische Frage zur Einzugsgeschichte', *N.T.S.* VI (1959), 81 f.

Milik, J. T. *Ten Years of Discovery in the Wilderness of Judaea*, Eng. trans. J. Strugnell (London, 1959).

Moore, G. F. *Judaism*, 3 vols. (Cambridge, Mass., 1927–30).

Morris, L. *The Apostolic Preaching of the Cross* (London, 1955).

Morrison, C. D. *The Powers that Be* (London, 1960).

Moule, C. F. D. *Worship in the New Testament* (London, 1961).

Munck, J. 'I Thess. i. 9–10 and the Missionary Preaching of Paul', *N.T.S.* IX (1963), 95–110.

Neil, W. *Thessalonians* (London, 1950).

Nineham, D. E. 'The Order of Events in St Mark's Gospel – an Examination of Dr Dodd's Hypothesis', in *Studies in the Gospels*, ed. Nineham (Oxford, 1955).

—— *Saint Mark*, The Pelican Gospel Commentaries (London, 1963).

Opeke, A. βάπτω, κτλ. *T.W.N.T.* I, pp. 527–44.

Pedersen, J. *Israel*, I–II (Oxford, 1926).

Ploeg, J. van der. *Le Rouleau de la Guerre* (Leiden, 1959).

Porter, J. R. 'The Messiah in the Testament of Levi xviii', *E.T.* LXI (1949), 90 f.

Procksch, O. ἅγιος, κτλ. *T.W.N.T.* I, 101–16.

BIBLIOGRAPHY

Quispel, G. 'The Jung Codex and its Significance', in *The Jung Codex*, ed. F. L. Cross (London, 1955).
Rad, G. von. ἄγγελος, κτλ. *T.W.N.T.* I, 75–9.
—— διαβάλλω, διάβολος, *T.W.N.T.* II, 69–80.
Rashdall, H. *The Idea of the Atonement* (London, 1920).
Rawlinson, A. E. J. *The Gospel According to St Mark*, Westminster Commentaries (London, 1925).
Richardson, A. *The Miracle Stories of the Gospels* (London, 1941).
—— *An Introduction to the Theology of the New Testament* (London, 1948).
Robinson, J. A. St. *Paul's Epistle to the Ephesians*, 2nd edn. (London, 1909).
Robinson, J. A. T. *Jesus and His Coming* (London, 1957).
—— *Twelve New Testament Studies* (London, 1962).
Robinson, J. M. *The Problem of History in Mark* (Studies in Biblical Theology, 21; London, 1957).
Ropes, J. H. *The Synoptic Gospels* (Oxford, 1960).
Rose, A. 'L'influence des psaumes sur les annonces et les récits de la Passion et de la Résurrection dans les Évangiles', *Le Psautier* (ed. R. de Langhe), pp. 297–356.
Sawyerr, H. 'The Marcan Framework', *S.J.Th.* XIV (1961), 279–94.
Schechter, S. *Some Aspects of Rabbinic Theology* (London, 1909).
Schlatter, A. *Der Evangelist Matthäus*[3] (Stuttgart, 1948).
Schlier, H. θλίβω, θλῖψις, *T.W.N.T.* III, 139–48.
Schmidt, K. L. *Die Rahmen der Geschichte Jesu* (Berlin, 1919).
—— βασιλεία, *T.W.N.T.* I, 579–92.
Schmidt, K. L. and M. A. παχύνω, κτλ, *T.W.N.T.* V, 1024–32.
Schniewind, J. *Das Evangelium nach Markus*[6] (Göttingen, 1952).
Schoeps, H. J. *Aus frühchristlicher Zeit* (Tübingen, 1950).
—— *Paul*, Eng. trans. H. Knight (London, 1961).
Schreiber, J. 'Die Christologie des Markusevangeliums', *Z.T.K.* LVIII (1961), 154–83.
Schulze, W. A. 'Der Heilige und die wilden Tiere', *Z.N.T.W.* XLVI (1955), 280–3.
Schweizer, E. 'Der Menschensohn', *Z.N.T.W.* L (1959), 185–210.
—— 'Anmerkungen zur Theologie des Markus', in *Neotestamentica et Patristica* (*Suppl. to N.T.* vol. VI) (Leiden, 1962).
—— 'Two New Testament Creeds Compared', in *Current Issues in New Testament Interpretation*, ed. W. Klassen and G. F. Snyder (London, 1962).
Schweizer, E., Baumgärtel, F. and Sjöberg, F. *Spirit of God*, Eng. trans. A. E. Harvey (London, 1960), = πνεῦμα, κτλ. *T.W.N.T.* VI, 330–453.

Seesemann, H. πεῖρα, κτλ. *T.W.N.T.* VI, 23–37.

Smith, A. M. 'The Iconography of the Sacrifice of Isaac in Early Christian Art', *Amer. J. Archaelogy*, XXVI (1922), 159–69.

Smith, C. R. *The Bible Doctrine of Sin* (London, 1953).

—— *The Bible Doctrine of Grace* (London, 1956).

Smith, C. W. F. 'No Time for Figs', *J.B.L.* LXXIX (1960), 315–27.

Souter, A. 'ΑΓΑΠΗΤΟΣ', *J.T.S.* XXVIII (1927), 59 f.

Stählin, G. ὀργή, *T.W.N.T.* V, 419–48.

Strack, H. L. and Billerbeck, P. *Kommentar zum Neuen Testament aus Talmud und Midrash*, 5 vols. (Munich, 1922–8).

Sundwall, J. *Die Zusammensetzung des Markusevangeliums*, Acta Academiae Aboensis, Humaniora, IX, 2 (Åbo, 1934).

Swete, H. B. *The Gospel According to St Mark* (London, 1908).

Sykes, M. H. 'And do not bring us to the test', *E.T.* LXXIII (1961/2), 189 f.

Taylor, V. *Jesus and His Sacrifice* (London, 1943).

—— *The Gospel According to St Mark* (London, 1952).

—— *The Names of Jesus* (London, 1953).

Tennant, F. R. *The Fall and Original Sin* (Cambridge, 1903).

Thiel, R. *Drei Markus-Evangelien* (Berlin, 1938).

Tödt, H. E. *Der Menschensohn in her synoptischen Überlieferung* (Gütersloh, 1959).

Turner, C. H. 'Marcan Usage: Notes, Critical and Exegetical, on the Second Gospel', *J.T.S.* XXV (1924), 377–86; XXVI (1925), 12–20, 145–56, 225–40, 337–46; XXVII (1926), 58–62; XXVIII (1927), 9–30, 349–62; XXIX (1928), 275–89, 346–61.

—— 'Ο ΥΙΟΣ ΜΟΥ Ο ΑΓΑΠΗΤΟΣ', *J.T.S.* XXVII (1926), 113–29.

—— 'A Textual Commentary on Mark i', *J.T.S.* XXVIII (1927), 145–58.

—— 'Western Readings in the Second Half of St Mark's Gospel', *J.T.S.* XXIX (1928), 1–16.

Tyson, J. B. 'The Blindness of the Disciples in Mark', *J.B.L.* LXXX (1961), 261–8.

Vermes, G. *Scripture and Tradition in Judaism* (Leiden, 1961).

Volz, P. *Der Geist Gottes* (Tübingen, 1910).

Weiss, J. *Das Älteste Evangelium* (Göttingen, 1903).

Wellhausen, J. *Das Evangelium Marci* (Berlin, 1903).

Wernberg-Møller, P. *The Manual of Discipline* (Leiden, 1957).

Williams, N. P. *The Ideas of the Fall and of Original Sin* (London, 1929).

Wilson, R. McL. *The Gnostic Problem* (London, 1958).

—— *Studies in the Gospel of Thomas* (London, 1960).

Wilson, R. McL. *The Gospel of Philip* (London, 1962).

Winter, P. *On the Trial of Jesus* (Berlin, 1961).

Wohlenberg, G. *Das Evangelium des Markus* (Leipzig, 1910).

Wrede, W. *Das Messiasgeheimnis in den Evangelien*[2] (Göttingen, 1913).

Yates, J. E. *The Spirit and the Kingdom* (London, 1963).

Zimmerli, W. *See* Jeremias, J.

INDEX OF AUTHORS

Thiel, R., 92
Tödt, H. E., 150, 162
Turner, C. H., 29, 80, 169f., 171, 178, 179
Tyson, J. B., 108

Vermes, G., 171, 172
Volz, P., 3, 4

Weiss, J., 69, 79, 83
Wellhausen, J., 100, 124, 141, 154

Wernberg-Møller, P., 50
Williams, N. P., 44, 47, 55
Wilson, R. McL., 86, 99, 129
Winter, P., 96, 98
Wohlenberg, G., 182, 187
Wrede, W., 16, 17, 95

Yates, J. E., 14, 99, 135

Zimmerli, W., 141, 148

INDEX OF SUBJECTS

INDEX OF SUBJECTS

Evil (*cont.*)
in apocalyptic literature, 53f.
in the New Testament, 56–60
Evil impulse, 47f., 51, 52, 54
Exalted Lord, *see* Ascension
Exodus, 5, 184
Exorcisms
by Jesus, 11–27, 33–6, 65, 68f., 73f.,
81, 103, 105, 116, 117f., 136f., 167,
180f., 188f.
by disciples and early Church, 75,
106, 180f., 187–9
by others, 17, 178

Faith, 30, 109f., 118, 180f.
Flesh, 30, 47, 52, 57, 77, 93f.
Forgiveness, 35f., 71, 81, 106f., 137f.,
156, 164f., 171–3, 179, 180f.
Forty days, 5f., 27

Galilee, 78f., 92, 102, 127, 174–7, 191
Gentiles, 84, 86, 113, 120, 127, 179f.
Gethsemane, 27, 30, 43, 92–4, 101,
156f., 169
Gnosticism, 126–33, 190
Gospel, 63f., 66, 67f., 69–71, 115,
125–33, 178, 188, 190f.
see also Kerugma; Preaching

Isaac, 101, 144, 169–73, 177
Israel, 32, 83, 99, 101
Jesus as, 5, 10, 101
New Israel, 86, 99
see also Jews

Jerusalem, 82f., 85, 112, 121, 125, 126,
158
Jesus
as Conqueror of demonic evil, 1–44,
82f., 102, 105f., 118, 127, 131,
132f., 167, 181, 184–6, 190f.; *see
also* Exorcisms by Jesus
as Israel, 5, 10, 101
as Second Adam, 6f., 8, 10
as Holy One of God, 16f.
as healer, 35f., 69–71, 73, 75, 79, 104,
106–11
as Shepherd, *see* Shepherd
as praying, 78f., 93, 136f.
as Suffering Servant, *see* Servant
as prophet, 97
as exorcist, *see* Exorcisms
as teacher, *see* Teaching of Jesus

as King, *see* King
as Son of David, 108, 166
as Son of God, *see* Son of God
as Son of Man, *see* Son of Man
as Lord, *see* Lord
as saving, 97, 109f., 116, 118, 123,
125–33; *see also* Salvation
mocking of, 96f., 99, 101f., 109f.,
149, 165
death of, *see* Death of Jesus
Jews, 84, 96, 98–100, 101, 113, 120, 121,
179f.
John the Baptist, 6, 19, 76, 85f.,
101f., 114, 115, 119f., 123, 134f.,
185
Judas, 41, 57, 58, 91f.
Judgement, 67, 83f., 98–100, 101, 102,
125, 126, 131, 153–9, 179, 191

Kerugma, x, xi, 125–33, 190f.; *see
also* Gospel; Preaching
King (of the Jews), 77, 87f., 95f., 97,
108, 160f., 166
Kingdom (of God), 35, 40, 64–8, 70,
71, 72, 81, 83, 187

Last Supper, 89–92, 122, 144–7
Leprosy, 20, 34f., 116–18
Lord, 87f., 127, 161, 166f., 168
Luke's use of Mark, ixf., 3, 5, 72f., 59,
69, 71, 77, 84, 85, 86, 90, 92, 97,
103, 106, 116, 119, 137, 138,
141, 149, 152, 160, 165–7, 173,
183

Mastema, 7, 48, 50, 53
Matthew's use of Mark, x, 3, 29, 39,
59, 71, 77, 80, 84, 86, 98, 100, 103,
106, 116, 119, 149, 152, 160,
165–7, 173
Messiah, 8, 9, 86, 90, 95f., 97
see also Christ
Messianic secret, 15f., 40–2, 65, 69,
72f., 79–81, 107–9, 118
Miracles of Jesus, 22, 23f., 34, 74f., 78–
80, 104–11, 120f.
healing miracles, 20, 23f., 34–6, 38,
69–71, 79, 104, 106–11, 139f.,
180f., 187, 188f.
feeding miracles, 76–8, 79, 104f.,
179f., 181
Mocking, *see* Jesus, mocking of
Moses, 5f., 77

205

INDEX OF PASSAGES QUOTED

INDEX OF PASSAGES QUOTED

217

218

INDEX OF PASSAGES QUOTED

INDEX OF GREEK WORDS